A Family Affair

A Family Affair
cinema calls home

EDITED BY MURRAY POMERANCE

WALLFLOWER
LONDON & NEW YORK

First published in Great Britain in 2008 by
Wallflower Press
6 Market Place, London W1W 8AF
www.wallflowerpress.co.uk

A catalogue record for this book is available from the British Library.

ISBN
978-1-905674-55-8 (pbk)
978-1-905674-56-5 (hbk)

Book design by Elsa Mathern

Printed and bound in Poland; produced by Polskabook

Contents

Troubles, Dreams, Family

Acknowledgements

No collection of this diversity and range can be assembled without the staunch collaboration of the contributors, each of whom deserves a very special thanks for their exceptional work here. Some editors are playful, some are demanding: I am both. I hope the experience of working with me has had its pleasures, but the pleasures in working with these writers have certainly been mine. In addition, I wish to thank Frances Gateward (Urbana), Nathan Holmes (Chicago), E. Ann Kaplan (New York), David Kerr (Toronto), Nay Laywine (Toronto), Mia Mask (Brooklyn), Peter Murphy (Toronto), Jay Wolofsky (Toronto) and Carla Cassidy, Dean of Arts, Ryerson University (Toronto) for their kind support. I am also indebted to Ron and Howard Mandelbaum and their engaging staff at PhotoFest (New York).

This book was born in a conversation I had with Yoram Allon, editorial director at Wallflower Press, over six years ago. He has since become what all great editorial directors truly are, a writer's sweet friend; his inspiration and contribution were complex and spontaneous, but involved more than anything offering me a licence to be free in the construction of a book that would be dear to my heart. For the opportunity, and the continual good-natured assistance along the way, my sincere thanks.

My own family, Nellie Perret and Ariel Pomerance, could not have been more important or more generous in their contributions to this volume. Those who remain at a distance from the act of editing anthologies have little idea of the value for an editor of his family mates' patience and continual encouragement, and Nellie and Ariel have been unstinting, and also witty, which has made it a delight to work on this. Family is memory, of course. I remember with love my parents, Michael and Sadie (Shub) Pomerance, and the world they gave me to learn in, which included, always excitingly, the movies.

Finally, my gratitude to colleagues at Wallflower Press who have put their love and attention into fashioning *A Family Affair*: Gavin Bradshaw, Jacqueline Downs and Elsa Mathern.

Toronto
May 2008

List of Illustrations

Chapter 1

Gino Monetti (Edward G. Robinson, left) tyrannises his entire family, save Max (Richard Conte), who is Gino's clear favourite. Max tries to save his father from imprisonment, but his brother foils him and he is soon the favourite son no more. *House of Strangers* (Joseph L. Mankiewicz, Twentieth Century Fox, 1949). Courtesy Jerry Ohlinger's Movie Materials Store.

Chapter 2

Banks family harmony: 'Let's go fly a kite!' Glynis Johns and David Tomlinson (rear) with Karen Dotrice and Matthew Garber in *Mary Poppins* (Robert Stevenson, Walt Disney Productions, 1964). Digital frame enlargement.

Chapter 3

Love isn't so funny ...or is it? 'I've not been lucky', says Loretta Castorini (Cher, left) and Ronny Cammareri (Nicolas Cage) replies, 'I don't care about luck', in *Moonstruck* (Norman Jewison, MGM, 1987). Digital frame enlargement.

Chapter 4

Family is defined through land use in the classical American western. Charley Waite (Kevin Costner, left) and Boss Spearman (Robert Duvall) surveying the free land in *Open Range* (Kevin Costner, Touchstone, 2003). Digital frame enlargement.

Chapter 5

In *An Unseen Enemy* (D. W. Griffith, Biograph, 1912), the orphaned sisters' confinement in an enclosed 'space' is rearticulated by the repetitious use of a confining frame, a medium-close shot view of the girls' physical immobility and expressions of terror; this recurs fifteen times in the cutting sequence that relays their brother's race back home to the rescue. Lillian Gish is at left, her sister Dorothy at right. Digital frame enlargement.

Chapter 6

Within the bosom of the 'typical American family'. Uncle Charlie (Joseph Cotten, centre) and Young Charlie (Teresa Wright) with Henry Travers (left), Edna May Wonacott, and Charles Bates (far right) in *Shadow of a Doubt* (Alfred Hitchcock, Skirball/Universal, 1943). Digital frame enlargement.

Chapter 7

The Prodigal Mother (Barbara Stanwyck, left) at table with her husband (Richard Carlson), two daughters (Lori Nelson and Marcia Henderson), and housekeeper (Lotte Stein) in *All I Desire* (Douglas Sirk, Universal International, 1953). Courtesy Photo-Fest New York.

Chapter 8

The Free Spirit and the Feminine Old World: Yancey Cravat (Richard Dix, standing), Sabra Cravat (Irene Dunne, left), and Felice Venable (Nance O'Neil, right) in *Cimarron* (Wesley Ruggles, RKO, 1931). Digital frame enlargement.

Chapter 9

From top left, reading across: Conformist individualism – Britney Spears doffs her Pepsi uniform, revealing an individualist wardrobe that better conforms to the dictates of gendered expectations; in the double-bind of female looking, female desire is limited to a poor counterfeit emulation of Spears' performance, with Spears inviting viewers to laugh along and look away from the sham version of her performance; a low-angle camera shot mimics intercourse amid the visual logic of Pepsi ejaculate and the horny abstinence of Dole, who as presidential candidate once railed against the mainstreaming of deviancy, and then became spokesperson for Viagra; edited sequences visually putting African Americans in their place, either as a step-dancing janitor, or at the margins of the frame where they can be easily cropped out in subsequent shots.

Chapter 10

As Betsy (Frances Dee) looks on from her bed in the middle of the night, Carrefour (Darby Jones) heads off to bring Jessica Holland back to the voodoo camp in *I Walked with a Zombie* (Jacques Tourneur, RKO, 1943). Courtesy Jerry Ohlinger's Movie Materials Store.

Chapter 11

Mrs Croft (Eileen Atkins, left) and Mrs Wilson (Helen Mirren) in a rare Altman moment of emotional openness and catharsis that results in sibling reconciliation in the midst of family tragedy, separation and revenge. *Gosford Park* (Robert Altman, Capitol Films, 2001). Digital frame enlargement.

Chapter 12
In *Daddy Day Care* (Steve Carr, Revolution, 2003), Charlie (Eddie Murphy) initially has no interest in caring for his son (Khamani Griffin, left), seeming to regard parenting as a demeaning task. Here, his wife Kim (Regina King) demands the keys to their Mercedes, signalling her appropriation of the public signs of masculine success that Charlie mourns. Digital frame enlargement.

Chapter 13
A new conception of the middle-class home as privatised fortress. *Firewall* (Richard Loncraine, Warner Bros., 2006). Digital frame enlargement.

Chapter 14
Under pressure at work, Frank Whitaker (Dennis Quaid, right) has been told to take some time off, and his wife Cathy (Julianne Moore) thinks it might be the best thing for the both of them. Frank's real 'problem', that threatens to destroy his family, is something else altogether. The darkness reveals underlying and increasingly erupting tensions, in *Far from Heaven* (Todd Haynes, Alliance Atlantis, 2003). Digital frame enlargement.

Chapter 15
In *Brokeback Mountain* (Ang Lee, Paramount, 2005), stark visual design and almost chiaroscuro lighting are used to delineate the cold emptiness of Jack's boyhood home as his parents (Roberta Maxwell, Peter McRobbie) refuse to let Ennis (Heath Ledger, centre) fulfil Jack's last wishes: to have his ashes spread on Brokeback Mountain. Digital frame enlargement.

Chapter 16
In James M. Cain's novel, when Mildred Pierce walks in on Veda and Monte, Veda is naked in Monte's bed. In the film (Michael Curtiz, Warner Bros., 1945), Mildred is treated to a different surprise (Zachary Scott and Ann Blyth). Digital frame enlargement.

Chapter 17
Home is reduced to real estate when we confront the physical presence of the past. Marty McFly (Michael J. Fox) after his travel through time to the suburbs in *Back to the Future* (Robert Zemeckis, Amblin/Universal, 1985). Digital frame enlargement.

Chapter 18
The end of an era: dying southern patriarch Big Daddy Pollitt (Burl Ives) towers over his sycophantic son Gooper (Jack Carson) in Richard Brooks's film adaptation of *Cat on a Hot Tin Roof* (MGM, 1958). Collection Jerry Mosher.

Chapter 19

Two-page spread from *Movie Secrets* magazine, August 1956, of an article purportedly written by Charlton Heston in the form of a letter to his son. The image on the left is labelled 'Chuck as Moses', and on the right the caption informs us that Fraser Heston ('Fray') 'surprised Lydia and Chuck by arriving after eleven years of their very happy married life, making them happier'. In the letter, Chuck explains that 'Every man wants to have a son – not that he doesn't welcome daughters when they come along. But a son is his chance at immortality.' Copyright 1956 by Sterling Group, Inc.

Chapter 20

Bonnie Grape (Darlene Cates) protecting her spratty baby Arnie (Leonardo DiCaprio), an eighteen-year-old with the mind and impulse control of a child of ten, who drools and likes to climb the town radio tower. Amy Grape (Laura Harrington) looks on. *What's Eating Gilbert Grape* (Lasse Hallström, Paramount, 1993). Digital frame enlargement.

Notes on Contributors

JENNIFER M. BEAN is Director of Cinema Studies and Associate Professor of Cinema Studies and Comparative Literature at the University of Washington-Seattle. She is co-editor of *A Feminist Reader in Early Cinema* (2002) and author of the forthcoming *The Play in the Machine: Gender, Genre and the Cinema of Modernity*. She is currently editing a collection on the origins of American film stardom.

HARRY M. BENSHOFF is Associate Professor of Radio, TV, and Film at the University of North Texas. He is the author of *Monsters in the Closet: Homosexuality and the Horror Film* (1997) and co-author of *America on Film: Representing Race, Class, Gender and Sexuality at the Movies* (2004). Most recently he co-edited *Queer Cinema: The Film Reader* (2004) and co-authored *Queer Images: A History of Gay and Lesbian Film in America* (2006).

JAMES BUHLER is Associate Professor at the University of Texas at Austin. He is co-editor of *Music and Cinema* (2000). Besides his work on music and sound in film, he has published on the music of Gustav Mahler and the musical writings of Theodor W. Adorno. He is currently working on a monograph covering auditory culture of early American cinema.

STEVEN ALAN CARR is Associate Professor of Communication at Indiana University-Purdue University Fort Wayne. He is the author of *Hollywood and Anti-Semitism: A Cultural History up to World War Two* (2001). His present project, which explores the response of the American film industry to the growing public awareness of the Holocaust, received an award from the National Endowment for the Humanities in 2002.

WHEELER WINSTON DIXON is the James Ryan Endowed Professor of Film Studies, Professor of English at the University of Nebraska, Lincoln, Series Editor for the State University of New York Press's 'Cultural Studies in Cinema/Video', and, with Gwendolyn Audrey Foster, Editor-in-Chief of the *Quarterly Review of Film and Video*. His recent books include *Experimental Cinema: The Film Reader*, co-edited with Gwendolyn Audrey Foster (2002), *Visions of the Apocalypse: Spectacles of Destruction in American Cinema* (2003), *Straight: Constructions of Heterosexuality in the Cinema* (2003), *Lost in the Fifties: Recovering Phantom Hollywood* (2005), *Visions of Paradise: Images of Eden in the Cinema* (2006), *Film Talk: Directors at Work* (2007) and *A Short History of Film*, written with Gwendolyn Audrey Foster, (2008). He is editor of *Film and Television After 9/11* (2004) and *American Cinema of the 1940s: Themes and Variations* (2006). On April 11–12, 2003, Dixon was honoured with a retrospective of his films at The Museum of Modern Art in New York, and his films were acquired for the permanent collection of the Museum, in both print and original format.

LUCY FISCHER is Distinguished Professor of Film Studies and English at the University of Pittsburgh where she serves as Director of the Film Studies Programme. She is the author of *Jacques Tati* (1983), *Shot/Countershot: Film Tradition and Women's Cinema* (1989), *Imitation of Life* (1991), *Cinematernity: Film, Motherhood, Genre* (1996), *Sunrise* (1998) and *Designing Women: Art Deco, Cinema and the Female Form* (2003), and the co-editor (with Marcia Landy) of *Stars: The Film Reader* (2004). Forthcoming is her edited volume, *American Cinema of the 1920s: Themes and Variations*. She has published extensively on issues of film history, theory and criticism in such journals as *Screen, Sight and Sound, Camera Obscura, Wide Angle, Cinema Journal* and *Journal of Film and Video*, among others, and has held curatorial positions at the Museum of Modern Art and the Carnegie Museum of Art. She has been the recipient of a National Endowment for the Arts Art Critics Fellowship as well as a National Endowment for the Humanities Fellowship for University Professors. She is a former President of the Society for Cinema and Media Studies.

GWENDOLYN AUDREY FOSTER teaches film studies, women's studies and cultural studies in the Department of English at the University of Nebraska, Lincoln. Her most recent books are *Class Passing: Performing Social Mobility in Film and Popular Culture* (2005) and *A Short History of Film*, written with Wheeler Winston Dixon (2008). Her monograph *Performing Whiteness: Postmodern Re/Constructions in Moving Images* (2003) was named as an Outstanding Title in the Humanities for 2004 by *Choice*. Her other published works include *Captive Bodies: Postcolonial Subjectivity in Cinema* (1999), *Troping the Body: Gender, Etiquette and Performance* (2000), *Experimental Cinema: The Film Reader* (2002; co-edited with Wheeler Winston Dixon) and *Identity and Memory: The Films of Chantal Akerman* (2003). She is also Co-Editor-in-Chief of *Quarterly Review of Film and Video*, with Wheeler Winston Dixon.

MARY BETH HARALOVICH is Professor in the School of Media Arts at the University of Arizona in Tucson where she teaches film and television history and directs the Media Arts Internship Programme. Her recent film history essays include: '1950: Movies and Landscapes' in *American Cinema of the 1950s: Themes and Variations* (2005), 'Marlene Dietrich is Blonde Venus: Advertising Dietrich in Seven Markets', in *Dietrich Icon* (2006), the reprint of 'All that Heaven Allows: Color, Narrative Space, and Melodrama' in *Color: The Film Reader* (2006) and the forthcoming 'Flirting with Hetero Diversity: Film Promotion of *A Free Soul* (1931)', in *Hetero*. She is co-editor (with Lauren Rabinovitz) of *Television, History, and American Culture: Feminist Critical Essays* (1999).

NATHAN HOLMES is a student in the Cinema and Media Studies doctoral programme at the University of Chicago. He has written on heist films and has published in *CineAction* on the pleasures of *The Big Sleep*.

ANDREW HORTON is the Jeanne H. Smith Professor of Film and Video Studies at the University of Oklahoma, an award-winning screenwriter, and the author of eighteen books on film, screenwriting and cultural studies including *Writing the Character-Centered Screenplay* (1994, 1999), *The Films of Theo Angelopoulos* (1997), *Laughing Out Loud: Writing the Comedy-Centered Screenplay* (2000), *Henry Bumstead and the World of Hollywood Art Direction* (2003) and *Screenwriting for a Global Market* (2004). His films include *Something In Between* (1983) and *The Dark Side of the Sun* (1989); in pre-production is *Route 66*.

MARCIA LANDY is Distinguished Professor of English/Film Studies with a secondary appointment in the Department of French and Italian Languages and Literatures at the University of Pittsburgh. Her publications include *Fascism in Film: The Italian Commercial Cinema, 1929–1943* (1986), *Imitations of Life: A Reader on Film and Television Melodrama* (1991), *British Genres: Cinema and Society, 1930–1960* (1991), *Film, Politics, and Gramsci* (1996; with Amy Villarejo), *Cinematic Uses of the Past* (1996), *The Folklore of Consensus: Theatricality and Spectacle in Italian Cinema 1929–1943* (1998), Stardom Italian Style (1998), *Italian Film* (2000), *The Historical Film: History and Memory in Cinema* (2001), *Stars: The Film Reader* (2004, co-edited with Lucy Fischer) and *Monty Python's Flying Circus* (2005).

GLENN MAN is Professor of English at the University of Hawaii at Manoa. He is the author of *Radical Visions: American Film Renaissance, 1967–1976* (1994) and his publications include articles on Hollywood and its genres – *The Godfather* films, *Thelma & Louise*, the South Seas film, the bio-pic, American films of the 1970s – and on film adaptations of *David Copperfield*, *The Third Man* and *The French Lieutenant's Woman*.

ADRIENNE L. McLEAN is Professor of Film Studies at the University of Texas at Dallas. She is the author of *Being Rita Hayworth: Labour, Identity, and Hollywood*

Stardom (2004) and *Dying Swans and Madmen: Ballet, the Body, and Narrative Cinema* (2008), and co-editor (with David Cook) of *Headline Hollywood: A Century of Film Scandal* (2001). She is co-editor of the 'Star Decades' series at Rutgers University Press.

WALTER METZ is interim department head and Associate Professor in the Department of Media and Theatre Arts at Montana State University-Bozeman, where he teaches the history, theory and criticism of film, theatre and television. In 2003–04, he was a Fulbright lecturer at the John F. Kennedy Institute for North American Studies at the Free University in Berlin, Germany. He is the author of *Engaging Film Criticism: Film History and Contemporary American Cinema* (2004) and *Bewitched* (2007).

JAMES MORRISON is the author of a memoir, *Broken Fever* (2001), a novel, *The Lost Girl* (2007), and several books on film, most recently *Roman Polanski* (2007), and, as editor, *All That Heaven Allows: The Cinema of Todd Haynes* (2007). He teaches film, literature and creative writing at Claremont McKenna College.

JERRY MOSHER is Assistant Professor in the Department of Film and Electronic Arts at California State University, Long Beach. He has published essays in the anthologies *Bodies Out of Bounds: Fatness and Transgression* (2001), *The End of Cinema As We Know It: American Film in the Nineties* (2001), *Where the Boys Are: Cinemas of Masculinity and Youth* (2005) and *From Hobbits to Hollywood: Essays on Peter Jackson's Lord of the Rings* (2006).

MURRAY POMERANCE is Professor of Sociology at Ryerson University. He is the author of *Magia d'Amore* (1999), *An Eye for Hitchcock* (2004), *Johnny Depp Starts Here* (2005), *Savage Time* (2005) and *The Horse Who Drank the Sky: Film Experience Beyond Narrative and Theory* (2008), the editor of *Enfant Terrible!: Jerry Lewis in American Film* (2002), *American Cinema of the 1950s: Themes and Variations* (2005), *Cinema and Modernity* (2006) and *City That Never Sleeps: New York and the Filmic Imagination* (2007), and the co-editor of *Where the Boys Are: Cinemas of Masculinity and Youth* (2005; with Frances Gateward) and *From Hobbits to Hollywood: Essays on Peter Jackson's Lord of the Rings* (2006; with Ernest Mathijs), among other volumes. He has contributed to *Film Quarterly*, *Quarterly Review of Film and Video*, *The Paris Review*, *New Directions*, *The Kenyon Review*, *Chelsea*, *The New Review of Literature* and *Descant*.

WILLIAM ROTHMAN is Professor of Motion Pictures at the University of Miami School of Communication. His books include *Hitchcock – The Murderous Gaze* (1982), *The 'I' of the Camera* (1988, 2004), *Documentary Film Classics* (1997) and *Reading Cavell's The World Viewed* (2000). He is the editor of *Cavell on Film* (2005) and *Three Documentary Filmmakers: Errol Morris, Ross McElwee, Jean Rouch* (2008).

CHRISTOPHER SHARRETT is Professor of Communication and Film Studies at Seton Hall University. He is the author of *The Rifleman* (2005), and editor of *Crisis Cinema: The Apocalyptic Idea in Postmodern Narrative Film* (1993) and *Mythologies of Violence in Postmodern Media* (1999), and co-editor (with Barry Keith Grant) of *Planks of Reason: Essays on the Horror Film* (2004). His work has appeared in *Cinema Journal, Cineaste, Film International, Senses of Cinema, Postscript, Cineaction, Kino Eye, Framework, Journal of Popular Film and Television,* and numerous anthologies, including *The Dread of Difference: Gender and the Horror Film* (1996), *The New American Cinema* (1998), *Sam Peckinpah's The Wild Bunch* (1998), *Car Crash Culture* (2002), *Fifty Contemporary Filmmakers* (2002), *BAD: Infamy, Darkness, Evil, and Slime on Screen* (2004) and *Cinema and Modernity* (2006). He is currently writing a book on the politics of the neoconservative Hollywood cinema.

YVONNE TASKER is Professor of Film and Television Studies at the University of East Anglia. She has published widely on questions of gender, sexuality and popular culture. Most recently she has co-edited (with Diane Negra) *Interrogating Postfeminism: Gender and the Politics of Popular Culture* (2007).

A family affair was not subject to investigation ...
it concerned nobody; anyone might conduct a family
affair in broad daylight while all the world looked on.

Alexandre Dumas, *The Three Musketeers*

Introduction: Family Affairs

MURRAY POMERANCE

In *The 5,000 Fingers of Dr T* (1953), a film that is nothing if not strange from start to finish, dictatorial and comically malevolent Dr Terwilliker (Hans Conreid) has assembled five hundred cowed little boys to play in unison on his gargantuan signiform piano. 'What a lovely family we will be!' he coos, marching around in a fuchsia tuxedo while the kids scramble to find their seats. That this film was written by Dr Seuss is perhaps a clue to invocation of the familial bond: his productions, onscreen and in print, had to address conventional socialisation in politically acceptable, if creative and bizarre, ways. But in this film the family is smashed and tortured. Our little protagonist Bartholomew Collins' (Tommy Rettig) mother (Mary Healy) enters his protracted dream – which is the main body of the film – as a stentorian monster who will neither help nor love him; he adopts as a 'father' the happy-go-lucky and relatively unimaginative plumber who is his mother's (rather eccentric) friend (Peter Lind Hayes), and the omnipresent and always demanding (if not utterly demented) Dr Terwilliker has nothing on his mind but causing little boys to give their fingers over to him. Bartholomew bounces around with a five-finger beanie perched on his head, trying to make everything right in this Seussian world where the ladders all climb to nowhere, the rooms all cant off in lime green and magenta at angles reminiscent of *The Cabinet of Dr Caligari* (1920), and nothing will assuage Dr T but obedience and correct fingerwork. Why, indeed, in such an utterly fascinating and self-sufficient world, invoke family at all?

The family is a cultural dream obsession to which we return and return. The felt home of our music and our torture, birthplace of pleasure and wonder, it is at once a mechanism and a phantasmagoria, just as *The 5,000 Fingers of Dr T* shows. Family is our womb, and also, as R. D. Laing pointed out acerbically, our *reality*:

> We, our family, and our family's families, our school, our church, our town, our state and our country, our television and cups and saucers and display cabinet, and our Aunt Jessie, are real: and true; we can trust each other: and we have a full life. The world comes to our town; and if we sometimes do wrong: we do our best. We don't wish any evil on anyone. We *are*. And those to whom *we* do not exist, do not exist, and, if we can help it, shall not exist.

... what are we defending ourselves against? Nothing? Oh no! The danger, the menace, the enemy, Them, are very real ... we must destroy them before they destroy us before we destroy them before they destroy us ... which is where we are at the moment ... We need not worry that the kill ratio between Them and Us will get too high. There are always more where *they* came from. From *inside Us*. (1970: 25–6)

Thus, the family is our rationale, our licence. The family is our logic, our repository, our sacred fire and source of light; and also, of course, the origin of a darkness we project outside of it.

In the conservative America of the 1950s and 1960s, a culture mirrored – and represented with unthinking faithfulness – by conservative Hollywood, family represents the first bulwark against the entropic forces of anarchy and revolution that might threaten the newly secured hegemony of the postwar state. The family, after all, is a tiny factory in which ideological commitment, unquestioning devotion to both capitalism and the wage economy, and attachment to ideals of identity patterning, belief, attitude and existential purpose are systematically reproduced in the name of those principles – individualism, freedom, progress, Divine architecture – on the basis of which the ruling class secures its position; and this, generation after generation after generation. As Niños, the old man in Barcelona's Parque Comunal, says in Michelangelo Antonioni's *The Passenger* (1975):

I've seen so many of them grow up. Other people look at the children and they all imagine a new world, but me, when I watch them, I just see the same old tragedy begin all over again. They can't get away from us. It's boring.

If in the family we learn to imagine and shape the world, there we also learn to obey our elders and those in authority – a lesson far more important than the mere acceptance of our vulnerability to power; since although power dominates it dominates brutally, and obedience to authority is achieved only by a voluntary act of acquiescence. Thus it is that our obedience is extended over a territory even power cannot reach. It is in the family that we learn which propositions to take seriously as truth, which to chuckle at as deviant or lighthearted. And it is in the family that we learn an overriding lesson that outreaches all others: to eagerly make families. What better panacea, then, to heal us from the wounds of arrogance and weakness that are inflicted in Dr Terwilliker's bitter domain than a family that can keep us 'together', bring 'nurture', provide 'warmth' and, more generally, offer salvation and see us through?

Just as the family is paramount as a social institution in our world, so in cinema it is today, and has always been, a central feature of screen depiction (and of screen narration, either implied or expressly stated). To consider some of the very earliest films: the Lumières' *Le Repas de bébé* (c. 1895) – not even quite a 'film' yet – is, above all, a 'charming family scene', with mother and father gently protecting the adorable infant, whose ingestion – its rhythm, its choreography, its materiel – is being supervised, shaped, formed as a regularity; *The Great Train Robbery* (1903) depends for its emotional thrust upon the loving and dutiful bond between a girl and her father, as does *The Lonedale Operator* (1911); *The Cabinet of Dr Caligari* revolves around the disruption of an affiancement; *The Arab* (1915) and the sheik films of the 1920s do likewise; in *The Last Laugh* (1924), a man's employment relations come into conflict with his family relations, first, to his agony, then, to his great relief; in *Stella Dallas* (1937), a woman selflessly disappears from her daughter's life in order that the daughter may have an opportunity to shed the heavy baggage of the mother's class identity and perhaps make a decent way for herself; the self-sacrificing mother returns in the woe-filled *Mildred Pierce* (1945); in *It's a Wonderful Life* (1946), God intervenes to keep a decent smalltown family intact when economic forces threaten to dissolve it; in *Rebel Without a Cause* (1955), the middle-class family is a site of disease and corruption; the twin protagonists of *Easy Rider* (1969) reconstitute a kind of primal, global family by bonding in powerfully intimate but transitory moments with strangers as they travel across the country, nicely anticipating a definition of 'family' that would surface in a 1998 episode of the television programme, *South Park*: 'Family isn't about whose blood you have. It's about who you care about'; *Bob and Carol and Ted and Alice* (1969) also reflects this sentiment, suggesting bluntly that monogamous sexual relations need not be seen as the only structural foundation of family; *Kramer vs. Kramer* (1979) explores the thesis that the maternal bond is not the only imaginable structural foundation of adult/child relations in the family; *My Own Private Idaho* (1991) explicitly treats the homosexual family in relation to conventional bourgeois heterosexist relations; in the recent Harry Potter films, youngsters are shaped and tutored by a mix of good and bad 'parents', their education a kind of cultural banquet the consumption of which leads to adulthood, and their emotional bonds to these elders, especially Harry's to Prof. Dumbledore (and young Daniel Radcliffe's to old Richard Harris in the early films) can be read as a form of familiarisation, a substitute parenting that brings love, trust, fidelity, courage, even moments of ebullient joy; through a similar process of 'adoption', Johnny Depp took Vincent Price as 'father' while shooting *Edward Scissorhands* (1990), Jerry Lewis for *Arizona Dream* (1993), Marlon Brando on *Don Juan DeMarco* (1995) and *The Brave* (1997), Al Pacino as 'brother' on *Donnie Brasco* (1995), Hunter S. Thompson as some sort of 'uncle' for *Fear and Loathing in Las Vegas* (1998), Keith Richards first as a model for, then as the literal progenitor of, Cap'n Jack Sparrow (2005; 2007) (see Pomerance 2005a).

This listing barely scratches the surface of films in which the constitution or disruption of family is structurally central. In every genre, signal films revolve around family as a problem. For a taste of family in comedy, consider the fraternal bond underpinning the Marx Brothers films; or the merry-go-round of engagement and incipient marriage that spins in Vincente Minnelli's *The Long, Long Trailer* (1954); or the familial casting of a grotesque joke, the multivariate repetition of which forms the content of *The Aristocrats* (2005); or the pitfalls that await the meeting of in-laws in *Meet the Parents* (2000) and its sequel *Meet the Fockers* (2004); or the incongruity of brotherhood between Danny De Vito and Arnold Schwarzenegger in *Twins* (1988). In crime films, we can examine the warm, sometimes too warm, families of *The Godfather* (1972, 1974, 1990), *Goodfellas* (1990), *Mickey Blue Eyes* (1999), *Donnie Brasco*, and a legion of other possibilities. We can look to the centrality of family in historical epics – the circus troupe as 'family' in *The Greatest Show on Earth* (1952), the orphaning and adoption of Moses in *The Ten Commandments* (1956), Judah Ben-Hur's relation to his mother and sister in *Ben-Hur* (1959). Disaster films always implicate some tortured family bonds: the recent *Poseidon* (2006) involves Kurt Russell's concerns about his daughter's love life; in *Volcano* (1997), Tommy Lee Jones has similar concerns about his daughter. Ersatz but intensified 'family' relations are instantaneously formed in closed-space disaster or horror scenarios, from *Airplane!* (1980) through *A Nightmare on Elm Street* (1984) to *Scream 3* (2000). In horror, further, it is specifically the deep-seated emotional bonds of family that are tortured: *Psycho* (1960) about a mother and a son; *Bunny Lake is Missing* (1965) and *The Ring* (2002) about a mother and a daughter, and so on and on into the darkest of darknesses. Film noir, westerns and melodramas are simply unthinkable except in terms of family relationships and their vulnerabilities – imagine trying to discuss *Double Indemnity* (1944) or *Detour* (1945) without referring to family damage, or *Red River* (1948), *Shane* (1953) and *The Searchers* (1956) without referring to family destruction, or *All That Heaven Allows* (1955) without referring to family secrets. Science fiction very frequently plays with monstrous transformations of family or with alien threats to it: *The War of the Worlds* (1953) and *War of the Worlds* (2005) both notably spin out this format, along with *Things to Come* (1936), *Invaders from Mars* (1953), *Lost in Space* (1998), and many other films. In *Men in Black* (1997), the alien family is a recurring motif. In the *Star Wars* films (1977–2005), family relations are at the origin of the principal characters' lines of motivation. In the *Star Trek* films (1979–2002) and television series (1966 onward), the various crews of the Enterprise and other dominant spacecraft/locales constitute de facto families, with parental captains, sibling bonds and rivalries among the featured subordinates, and continual confrontations with the generally indiscernible world 'outside'. We can find families in war films – either explicit, as in *Since You Went Away* (1944) or implied through the platoon: *Bataan* (1943), *Pork Chop Hill* (1959), *The Great Escape* (1963). And family relations always gird the masculine violence in boxing movies: *Body and Soul* (1947), with John Garfield's bond to his mother; *The Set-Up* (1949), in which Robert Ryan's need to fight jeopardises his marriage to Audrey Totter; *Requiem for a Heavyweight* (1962), with Anthony Quinn's hopeless love for Julie Harris; *Cinderella Man* (2005), where Russell Crowe's fighting puts his entire family on the line. The heist film often focuses on family: Peter O'Toole invading Audrey Hepburn's relationship with her father, Hugh

Griffith, in *How to Steal a Million* (1966), or the family complications of Richard Conte as a centrepiece of Lewis Milestone's *Ocean's 11* (1960); and the spy film often goes to pains to negate it (Richard Burton's tender and raw affection for Claire Bloom, but refusal of bonding, in *The Spy Who Came In from the Cold* (1964)).

On the timeline of American cinema between 1903 and the early twenty-first century run a numberless pack of films involving love (*Gone With the Wind* (1939), *Casablanca* (1942), *Now, Voyager* (1942), *The Clock* (1944)) and marriage (*Sunrise* (1927), *Notorious* (1946), *Father of the Bride* (1950)), parenting (*The Courtship of Eddie's Father* (1963)), the prolongation of family bonds into old age (*On Golden Pond* (1981), *Until the End of the World* (1991)), the rebellion involved as children break away from parents (*Wall Street* (1987)), sibling rivalries (*Gosford Park* (2005)), extended families (*The Wizard of Oz* (1939)), the discovery of hitherto undisclosed family relations (or 'family relations') among characters who had taken themselves to be strangers to one another (*Great Expectations* (1946)), perversions of 'normal' love bonds among family members or of forms of 'normal' family love (*Candy* (1968), *Chinatown* (1974)), inter-racial and inter-ethnic families (*Guess Who's Coming to Dinner* (1967)), as well as ersatz families of all kinds, including the Dead End Kids of the 1930s, Fagin and his family of pickpockets in the several versions of *Oliver Twist* (1916, 1922, 1933, 1948...), the familial girl band of *Some Like It Hot* (1959), and the family of Israeli assassins killing and dining together in Steven Spielberg's *Munich* (2005). Families have been framed as derivative of culture and its dictates (*Moonstruck* (1987), *Le Grand voyage* (2004]), *Goodfellas*), and as the product of the most arbitrary mechanical operations (*A.I. Artificial Intelligence* (2001)). As is implicit in these pages, families in film appear centrally not only in all genres but in both indep productions and studio-controlled productions, seriously and for fun, seen critically and taken utterly for granted. Because in virtually every film family makes some sort of appearance, marginal or central, stated or implied, it is unthinkable to treat the subject adequately here or in any single volume, but we can sketch some of the more interesting lines of approach and suggest some fascinating films and filmic moments to watch.

However, in at least three significant ways the family is important to Hollywood film quite beyond its presence as a narrative construct, although it is principally the family as narrative construct that will interest the contributors to this volume. First, as Danae Clark elucidates, part of the problem solved by the studio system in general was regulating labour, both in terms of minimising demands (for compensation, perquisites and working conditions) made by employees (onscreen and off-) and for producing what Talcott Parsons once called 'latent pattern maintenance' – that structured and enduring set of forces members of a social system yield to in remaining attached and committed to organisational projects. For example, while the seven-year contract did legally bind actors to studio films, after the DeHavilland decision of 1943 it was no longer the case that suspensions meted out to actors who refused parts could be added to their contract time. Some structural process was necessary to keep people from loosing their bonds, when the contract was insufficient. The family, Clark notes, was a central myth invoked by the studio as a way of 'binding' employees together, this in the face of the egregious and extremely discernable differences between stars, character players, extras, carpenters, publicity agents, directors, writers, and so on. To be recalcitrant, to be resistant, to be demanding, to be petulant, to have memory problems on set, to neglect moral self-regulation in one's private life (in an arena where reporters were everywhere looking for stories that would pay their rent) – all of this was to fail in one's 'family' obligation. The studio, after all, was enveloping, embracing, protective, 'nourishing', encouraging and, it must be stressed, *reliably* all of these, in an era of, first, economic uncertainty and class division (the 1930s), then, world war (the 1940s), then, military-industrial build-up in the face of pervading and invisible threat (the 1950s and beyond). The studio was a family that would cherish its employees and do everything to make their lives amenable and pleasant – or at least keep them busy – if they would but commit themselves to it heart and soul.

Secondly, in the age of the classical cinema, Hollywood motion pictures often involved in their production the labour of actual families, sometimes dynasties, and this arrangement has continued. Filmmaking, after all, depends on personnel who possess complex (and historical) knowledge and who can therefore communicate with one another in a terse intensivity: if you have grown up with film, in a filmmaking family, you have advantages, even just linguistic ones. One need but think of the Fairbankses (Douglas, Mary Pickford and Douglas Jr), Carradines (John, David, Keith and Robert), Bridgeses (Lloyd, Jeff and Beau), Fondas (Henry, Peter and Jane), Baldwins (Alec, Adam, Billy, Daniel), or Culkins (Macauley, Kieran, Rory and their aunt Bonnie Bedelia), the Beerys (Wallace and Noah), the Keaches (Stacy and James), the Barrymores (Lionel, John, Ethel, Drew), the Beattys (Warren and Shirley MacLaine), the Hickmans (Darryl and Dwayne), Olivia DeHavilland and Joan Fontaine, the Redgraves (Michael, Rachel [Kempson], Vanessa, Lynn, Corin, and Natasha and Joely Richardson), the Alberts (Edward, Eddie and Edward Jr.), Catherine Deneuve and Françoise Dorleac, or the Howards (Trevor and Leslie) onscreen; the Westmores in the studio make-up rooms; the Selznicks (David and Myron) and the Mayers (Louis B. and Irene) upstairs; the Scotts (Ridley and Tony), the Wachowskis (Andy and Larry), the Hugheses (Albert and Allen), the Gershwins (George and Ira) behind the camera; the omnipresent Coppolas (Carmine composing, Francis and Sofia directing, Talia Shire and Nic Cage acting), and so on. In many cases the power to green light a production resided around a family dinner table, this entirely neglecting the countless circumstances in which a film or film career resulted from a chance encounter between members of the same family: Wes Craven's teenage daughter saw Johnny Depp acting on *21 Jump Street* and demanded that her father cast him in *A Nightmare on Elm Street*; the rest is history.

But there is a third, less mechanical, sense in which family plays a role in Hollywood, and that is the far more nebulous, yet powerful, 'family feeling' that can develop on a set between people working together for long hours day after day on the same intricate project. The cast and crew of a film become something of a 'family' during production at least in the sense that emotions flow freely within the bounded space members share and in the sense that sacrifice and continual adaptation are required of everyone in order that the vital compromises can be achieved that the project requires. Executive Producer Herbert Coleman and Director Alfred Hitchcock had an avuncular relationship with Christopher Olsen on *The Man Who Knew Too Much* (1956); Olsen slid into the routine of clipping their cigars. The sense of family taking over an entire set is beautifully evoked in François Truffaut's *Day for Night* (1973), a film about exactly such a production where the cast, the technical and script workers and the producers fall into a rhapsodic and private bubble of familial devotion. A very similar sense is given in *Lost in La Mancha* (2002) by Keith Fulton and Louis Pepe, a description of the ordeals endured by Terry Gilliam and his crew/family while they attempted to film a version of *Don Quixote* in the face of a patriarchal illness.

However, given that the rhetoric of the happy family is useful in film production, in studio/actor relations and in publicity, and given that family relations can be helpful for those who wish to break into the movie business, and given that a kind of family warmth takes over on many actual film productions, we may still usefully wonder, what is onscreen family *for*? The patrons in the movie theatre have left home in order to be there, after all, and this in many senses beyond the simple fact that aside from movie moguls very few people have screening facilities inside their family domiciles. Most of us walk away from the family philosophically, leaving our roots and our connections behind us – at least in a dream of independence – and orienting ourselves to the screen as though we had no socialisation under our belt, no history of family interaction, no heredity, no expectant relations eager to watch our every move (see Arlen 1977). Then, in the glimmering darkness, what do we see in our newfound liberty magnified in silver or in the radiant saturations of Technicolor but imitations of the family life we had apparently escaped. Certainly, in seeing representation in film of so fundamental a social institution, such elemental relationships, we not only enter the realm of drama (because drama is all a story of the family wound, whether in tragedy or comedy) but also return to ourselves in a way that makes for recognition and self-knowledge, and therefore a sense of ultimate truth. To see families is in some sense to look in the mirror, and in accepting this 'thing of darkness' that glows in the glass do we not obtain a key for seeing, knowing, accepting and understanding a whole world?

To the extent that cinema is a tool of the state, it can also operate as an instruction manual. The family as site of ideological production functions ideally, in other words, when its shape and systematic operation are both stringently controlled and bounded; there would otherwise be – as in precapitalist times there were – far too many eccentric forms of the family to guarantee conformity and predictability of behaviour. Consumption, reproduction, aggression – these habits need to be organised to maximise return on expenditure in our multinational postcapitalist world. Whether it is played for sentiment or for catharsis, for laughter or for mystification, the screen family is inevitably drawn as a glowing paragon to behold, an image to which we can in some way aspire. If we cannot inhabit a great aristocratic estate (as Ralph Richardson does in *Greystoke: The Legend of Tarzan, Lord of the Apes* (1984)), then at least we can artfully arrange flowers (as Meryl Streep does in *The Hours* (2002)); if we do not possess an operatic capacity for passion (*The Godfather*), at least we can blow off steam after a beer on a street corner, or learn how to say artfully, 'Fuggedaboudit'. Screen families, then, are relentlessly pedagogical, teaching us how to pose, think, behave, acquire, imagine, remember, fear and anticipate as members of families in real life. In *Saturday Night Fever* (1977), Tony Manero's (John Travolta) experience of the nightclub 'teaches' him behaviour that his mother (Julie Bovasso) does not approve of; a similar moral panic infects many parents, who fear their children will 'learn' from film what children apparently should not know, for instance how, like Leonardo DiCaprio in *The Basketball Diaries* (1995), to stow shotguns beneath one's trenchcoat in high school.

Also, since we are deeply committed to family life in the West, using it as a mode of education and warehousing, a mode of defence and strategising – indeed, a sanctity – we also seem prone to the belief that family is the natural state of humankind: all persons emerge from families and recombine into families; the family is the essential human form; the parent/child bond is the preeminent social relation; the family is the temple of privacy even as it is simultaneously the agora itself, the battleground where economic and emotional forces play out to exhaustion. In light of this belief, the screen family becomes a portrait of humankind at its most essential, natural and spontaneous. For the family is never taken onscreen to be a product itself, a concoction with specific benefits to those in power; it is taken instead to spring automatically out of human passion and confidence, quite as though persons who adored and trusted one another couldn't imagine any other way to be than seeking, making, sharing – and ultimately living and struggling in – a family. The Lords of *The Philadelphia Story* (1940), the Flintstones, the Tenenbaums, Indiana Jones and his dotty dad … they all just materialised that way. Thus, apparently, the family is not shaped and cultured in order to work out a certain form repetitively and predictably; it sprouts like a flower. (Hollywood works as though Engels' *The Origin of the Family, Private Property and the State* had never been written, does not exist.)

From various critical perspectives and scholarly backgrounds, the authors in this volume bring their own passions to the consideration of family onscreen. To begin, a number of authors consider family in the context of film genre and the cinematic auteur. Wheeler Winston Dixon gives an account of the family in film noir, noting various ways in which the darkness of noir is used as a rupturing force in family life. James Buhler surveys the family in Hollywood musicals, where courtship ending in marriage is a staple narrative focus but the representation of family, especially children, is very often held back. Andrew Horton examines 'cross-generational' families in American film comedy, where conflicts in value and attitude are demonstrated within families made up of characters who don't understand one another. Walter Metz analyses the family in the western, especially the 1950s Cold War variant and the way that in post-9/11 westerns a linkage between geopolitical security concerns and domestic morality is reenacted through the expression of land use. Jennifer M. Bean frames a complex questioning of the 'paternity' of D. W. Griffith in the history of American narrative film, including a discussion of the metaphorical and ideological values that we associate with the middle-class family. William Rothman considers the Hitchcockian family: the notable absence of family plots, for example, even in *Family Plot* (1976); the frequent protagonists being typically single and childless; and the striking incidences of married life 'viewed darkly'. And Lucy Fischer writes about the family in melodrama, especially the Sirkian family as exemplified in *All I Desire* (1953), a film in which the conflicted family life of an actress is brought to light.

There follows a group of essays centring on discussions of family in the context of political and social relations. Christopher Sharrett presents quite another look at the family in the American western, focusing on the way family, community and heterosexual relations, 'while often subversive', seem systematically to evince rightist or nihilist positions quite as often as progressive ones; he gives special attention to the importance of *Brokeback Mountain* (2005). Steven Alan Carr examines the presentation of family in a Britney Spears Pepsi commercial from 2001, in which the text 'privileges and subordinates a complex array of ideologies' about family, turning its viewers into one massive family that uses a 'familial gaze' to establish 'family values'. Gwendolyn Audrey Foster shows how the trope of voodoo is used in *I Walked With a Zombie* (1943) to provide a 'devastating critique of whiteness and colonialism' in which colonials are 'enslaved in their own familial dysfunctionality'. Glenn Man's interest is the family in late Robert Altman films; for this scholar, what is central in Altman's work is a persistent problematisation of women's independence and power. Yvonne Tasker considers male parenting as framed in contemporary film; this subject is often presented independently of concerns about nurturing, and in such films traditional formulations of gender are too often secured, with women's work in childcare devalued or disattended. James Morrison examines a recent spate of 'family invasion' films, where the family is in a 'post-crisis' state, portrayed entirely outside ideology; as a social institution, the postmodern family is shown as 'doing just fine, or would be, if it were not constantly beset by forces from without'.

Finally, the screen family is a repeating locus of troubles and dreams. Marcia Landy examines the family in several of the films of Todd Haynes, showing how his films 'have confronted viewers with disturbing scenes of the middle-class family'. For Landy, family functions in these films as a 'killing field, a site of "perversion"'. Harry M. Benshoff examines a group of recent films that use queer theory to 'suggest challenges to the structure of the traditional nuclear family'. If queers still figure in mainstream cinema as 'problem people', homophobia itself is coming to be figured as the problem in more and more independent films. Mary Beth Haralovich studies the tensions and fissures in the family structure portrayed in Michael Curtiz's *Mildred Pierce*, paying close attention to the specific alterations made as the film was adapted from James M. Cain's novel (1941) in a moral climate where concern had to be directed at the characteristics of a female protagonist. Nathan Holmes is interested in the relationship between family and suburbia on-screen, giving close attention to *Rebel Without a Cause* and *Over the Edge* (1979). The former film provides a pretext for 'legitimating teenage extroversion' during a historical period where moral panic about adolescents had been invoked nationally; the latter, omitting the 'reversion to family' of *Rebel Without a Cause*, presents a situation where 'kids stick together, not families'. Jerry Mosher studies the fat-cat patriarchal figure, linking Louis B. Mayer and the Burl Ives performance in *Cat on a Hot Tin Roof* (1958); in both types of case, we see representatives of an 'elite group of men and institutions whose values and system of production were on the verge of extinction'. Adrienne L. McLean gives a meticulous reading of fan magazine discourse to examine the way family values and family relations were used in the 1950s as part of the Hollywood publicity apparatus to establish the personae of screen luminaries: magazines went to great trouble to 'make stars appear to reconcile the competing demands of their careers and those of a married and family life centred on devotion to home and children'. And to conclude, Murray Pomerance gives a typology of dramatised family types, concentrating on *What's Eating Gilbert Grape* (1993) and *The Royal Tenenbaums* (2001), among other films, in order to examine the relationship between constructed appearance and family relations in screen presentation.

While reading this book, you will discover that – even though flat, papery and conceptual – it constitutes something of a 'family' itself, with voices disparate and energetic, passionate and convicted, argumentative and agreeable, mellowed like aged wine and fresh on the street. Our hope is that these essays, looking at family in different kinds of films from different kinds of theoretical and analytical viewpoints, will bring light to a subject that is endlessly fascinating, endlessly obscure; will challenge and provoke; will open doorways for new thoughts; and, like the films they are about, will happily entertain. And one thing more: perhaps the reader in moving through these pages will hear a voice in the head responding, a voice with questions or comments or observations or shards of thought about cinema, and will in that way begin to participate in the kind of analysis that is happening here, begin to – dare I say it? – join the family.

Family, Genre, Auteur

1

House of Strangers: The Family in Film Noir

WHEELER WINSTON DIXON

I will focus here on films in which the darkness of noir is seen as a force of rupture within family life, dealing first with Joseph L. Mankiewicz's superb drama of a spectacularly dysfunctional Italian American family, *House of Strangers* (1949). But as Leo Tolstoy put it in *Anna Karenina* (1873–77), 'Happy families are all alike; every unhappy family is unhappy in its own way'; thus, this chapter also explores the unique desperation of family life as depicted in such films as John Brahm, André De Toth and Lewis Milestone's *Guest in the House* (1944), in which Anne Baxter destroys the family that adopts her out of a sense of charity; and Jean Renoir's *The Woman on the Beach* (1947), in which an alcoholic impressionist painter, blinded by his wife in a domestic battle, struggles against the bottle, her chronic infidelities and his own homicidal rage. Further, Sam Wood's *King's Row* (1942) rips the lid off smalltown American life, while simultaneously exposing the manners of polite society as a sham; John M. Stahl's superb Technicolor noir *Leave Her to Heaven* (1945) presents a psychopath who destroys her own life and those around her through her implacable jealousy; and Brahm's *The Locket* (1946) shows a young woman's kleptomania leading three suitors to their deaths.

Strange Illusions of the Noir Family

Was the image of home and hearth a lie from the start? Traditional romance films end with the ideal heterotopic couple living 'happily ever after'; family noir films show the viewer the real 'ever after'. Frank Capra's sentimental Christmas film *It's a Wonderful Life* (1946) captures our attention most during the scenes of the town of Bedford Falls in social collapse, as the result of George Bailey's (James Stewart) attempted suicide. It seems that the structure of smalltown America needs constant verification in order to survive; pull out a peg, and the entire edifice collapses. In Edgar G. Ulmer's *Strange Illusion* (1945), also known as *Out of the Night*, Paul Cartwright (Jimmy Lydon), the wealthy son of an important California family, is haunted by a dream that his deceased father, Lieutenant Governor Albert Cartwright, has been replaced in his mother's affections by an impostor. In a modern-day variation on *Hamlet*, the dream intimates that Paul's father has been murdered, and that Paul must avenge his death.

The villain is the suave Brett Curtis (Warren Williams, in one of his last roles), a psychopathic sex killer who courts Paul's mother, Virginia (Sally Eilers), with a view towards marriage and eventual control of the estate. Ostensibly a friend of the sinister Professor Muhlbach (Charles Arnt), 'Curtis' is actually Claude Barrington, a criminal well known to Paul's late father as an exceptionally clever and dangerous man. Everyone seems fooled by Barrington's masquerade as 'Curtis', especially Paul's sister, Dorothy (Jayne Hazard); and Paul's only ally is his friend Dr Vincent (Regis Toomey), the family's physician. Paul's father communicates from beyond the grave through a series of letters written before his death, delivered to Paul on a regular basis, that warn him of the potential danger to Paul's mother and sister. Only at the end of the film, when Curtis tries to rape Dorothy, is the killer's real nature unmasked and the sanctity of the home preserved. *Strange Illusion* was made for Producers Releasing Corporation (PRC) in a mere six days on a budget of less than $40,000, beginning production on 10 October and ending on 16 October 1944 (Silver & Ward 1992: 266). Despite the film's tight budget and schedule, Ulmer brings both grace and style to its complex narrative, giving Paul Cartwright's privileged world a genuine sense of substance and splendour. But as a tale of family, the film is eerie: this comforting nuclear family, after all, includes both the living and the dead in constant communication. And what looks like family is the horrid mask of crime and death.

Lewis Milestone's *The Strange Love of Martha Ivers* (1946), on the other hand, is an 'A' noir that documents Martha Ivers' (Barbara Stanwyck) tyrannical control of an entire midwestern town through the local factory that she inherited as a child. As with Paul Cartwright, Martha is a child of wealth and power, but in Milestone's film her unyielding hold on those around her has corrupted her completely. She believes that her money can buy her anything, whether it be the love of old flame Sam Masterson (Van Heflin), who drifts into town on a whim, or that of her putative husband, the weak and ineffectual District Attorney Walter O'Neil (Kirk Douglas), whom Martha despises. When Sam's old affections for Martha are aroused, Martha's husband is understandably annoyed and attempts to have him driven out of town through the machinations of femme fatale Toni Marachek (Lizabeth Scott).

However, Sam realises that what is really keeping Martha and Walter together is a shared secret of murder – the true source of Martha's vast inheritance. In the film's harrowing conclusion, both Martha and Walter, fearing exposure, kill themselves, leaving Sam and Toni to flee Iverstown without a backward glance. Money, power, influence – everything has a price, and Martha's life has been a charade that she and her husband can no longer maintain. Behind the surface, all is rotten. The sleekness of Milestone's *mise-en-scène*, coupled with the dark interiors of Martha's palatial yet claustrophobic mansion, do nothing to persuade us that Martha has made a good bargain in trading murder for instant wealth. What is repressed will inevitably be exposed in a rupture of violence – in this case, violence that destroys Martha's unstable, artificial domestic milieu.

Perhaps the most corrosive portrayal of postwar family life is *House of Strangers*. Here, Italian American old-style patriarch Gino Monetti (Edward G. Robinson) dominates his sons and his banking business with an autocratic and despotic vengeance. Forcing his sons to dine at the family table while he blasts opera from a wind-up Victrola, Gino tyrannises his entire family, save Max (Richard Conte), who is Gino's clear favourite. But, as with Martha Ivers, there is a flaw in Gino's empire. He has been making unsecured loans and charging usurious rates in violation of the banking laws, and at length his crime is discovered. Gino goes on trial for fraud, and his sons Joe (Luther Adler) and Pietro (Paul Valentine) do nothing to help him; indeed, they are now in control of the bank and loot and are eager to see Gino destroyed, both personally and professionally. Max, who is a lawyer, tries to save Gino by attempting to bribe a juror at Gino's trial. But when Joe finds out about it, he gleefully turns Max over to the police: Max is the favourite son no more. Despite Max's machinations, Gino is acquitted, but Max gets seven years in the state penitentiary. Released, he returns home to find that Gino has died and his brothers are in full control of the bank. This sets the stage for a final confrontation that pits brother against brother, as old scores are settled and old wounds are opened, one last time.

In a bravura performance, Robinson takes to the role of Gino with his customary gusto, making him a monster of theatricality and old-world malice. Conte's Max is the dutiful son who will do anything to help his father, but his role remains rather colourless, despite its centrality to the film's narrative. But Joe Monetti, as played by the heavy-lidded Luther Adler, is the film's real centre; a seething mass of hatred and pomposity, coiled and waiting to strike out at all who would oppose him. What is most clear in *House of Strangers* is that these people who are bound by nothing but blood ties have, as the title implies, literally nothing in common. Gino has never tried to understand his sons, nor does he try now; he sees himself clearly and simply as the naturally indomitable force that holds the family together. But in the Monetti household, there *is* no togetherness; this is simply a place in which a group of people, related by blood, live, scheme and seek to dominate and/or destroy each other. As an example of old-world values clashing with postwar American society, *House of Strangers* demonstrates that families serve primarily as the repositories of secrets, lies, ambitions and long-held grievances. There is no sense of family here, at least not in the romantic sense implied by, for example, the conclusion of *It's a Wonderful Life*, in which all the woes and anxieties of the Bailey family are salved by the warmth of a Christmas celebration. Further, *House of Strangers* suggests that the Monetti household is much more representative of postwar American family life than most viewers or critics would care to admit. As with *The Strange Love of Martha Ivers*, it also suggests that no great fortune exists without a great crime, in the past or the present.

Finally, *House of Strangers* suggests that one can never escape the consequences of his actions within the family; and that, indeed, with the passing of time sins of the past become more vulnerable to exposure rather than receding into the mists of unrecorded memory. Gino's domination of his family, like Martha's domination of her factory town, is counterfeit from the start, destined to end in collapse. When we first see Gino at the beginning of *House of Strangers*, lording it over his wife and sons at the dinner table, we get the impression that his reign will continue unopposed throughout the film, that even if trouble emerges, Gino will remain a force to be reckoned with. But when his bank fails – and with it his corrupt schemes – his authority collapses, paving the way for his even more brutally corrupt son, Joe, to take his place. After Gino's death, it is as if he never existed, so complete is his erasure from the 'family's' memory.

Guest in the House is another kind of noir, in which the corrosive force is neither greed nor lust for money and power but madness and possessive jealousy. Evelyn Heath (Anne Baxter, in a portrait of exquisite treachery) is brought to the seaside house of the rich Proctor family to recuperate after a nervous breakdown. Soon, she sets her sights on Douglas Proctor (Ralph Bellamy), who is happily married to Ann (Ruth Warrick). But happiness is a relative word to Evelyn, who immediately begins an effective and insidious campaign to replace Ann in Douglas's affections, with apparent success. As *Guest in the House* unfolds, Evelyn's malice and deceitfulness take a decisive toll on the entire household, while she herself remains the serene centre of the storm she has created. The film's tag line neatly summarises the narrative's inexorable trajectory: 'No girl has ever been called more names! That's Evelyn ... the guest ... who manages to throw her pretty shadow around where any man near must see it – and when it comes to a man she grants no rights to anyone but herself!' As in *The Strange Love of Martha Ivers* and *House of Strangers*, we see a family that is no match for the forces that seek to destroy it, living in a home the domestic tranquility and genteel, well-appointed face of which can easily be torn down. Werner Janssen's appropriately ominous music, coupled with Lee Garmes' moody cinematography and Nicolai Remisoff's baroque production design combine to create a vision of the summer house by the sea as the ineluctable domain of madness; a home waiting to be torn asunder by Evelyn's invading intellect. Director John Brahm was certainly no stranger to this psychological territory.

In many ways, *Guest in the House* can be seen as a parable of the last days of World War Two, when social changes (women in the work place, rising divorce rates and skyrocketing inflation) were threatening the stability of the traditional family unit. Yet, too, as with many of his other films, Brahm was ahead of his time, reminding us with this little-known work that once invited, a guest may easily overstay her or his welcome, with disastrous results; in this respect, *Guest in the House* can be seen as a confirmation of the Isolationist doctrine that preceded World War Two. Whatever is happening in Europe is none of our affair; let's keep this war away from us at all costs; let's not go over and help other people with their problems, and let's certainly not invite the wrong other people to join us in our homes over here. Evelyn is a force that cannot be denied, and until the Proctors finally realise that their home front is in danger of imminent collapse, she operates unchecked by normal social rules, eating away like a parasite at the values they have always held dear. Only a last-minute intervention stops her relentless campaign of destruction, leaving the family members shaken, and arguably scarred for life. Will they be as welcoming to the next stranger who comes to call?

Renoir's American Family: *The Woman on the Beach*

Jean Renoir's American masterpiece, *The Woman on the Beach*, is easily the best Hollywood work by the director of such classic films as *Rules of the Game* (1939) and *Boudu Saved From Drowning* (1932). When Renoir fled France with the advent of the Nazi onslaught, he initially landed at 20th Century Fox, where he directed the torrid melodrama *Swamp Water* (1941), shot on location in Georgia. The film failed to click at the box office, and Renoir left Fox for Universal, where he began work on a Deanna Durbin musical. But after a few weeks he walked off the film, upset with Universal's factory production methods, and landed at RKO, where he was able to direct the noirish French resistance drama *This Land is Mine* (1943), starring Charles Laughton as a meek schoolmaster. The film was marred by a stagebound, Hollywood 'studio' look, in contrast to Renoir's best, more naturalistic films.

Departing RKO, Renoir made a brief propaganda short, *Salute to France* (1944), before creating *The Southerner* (1945) and *The Diary of a Chambermaid* (1946), both independent productions with modest budgets and shooting schedules. His American odyssey was coming to an end when he returned to RKO for his last Hollywood film, the brutally vicious *The Woman on the Beach*, which effectively ended his ties with the American film industry. At RKO, Renoir had struck up an acquaintance with the producer Val Lewton, famous for his series of atmospheric and intelligent horror films in the 1940s. He admired Lewton's method of producing masterful films, such as Jacques Tourneur's *I Walked With a Zombie* (1943), on short schedules. Now, he proposed to shoot a film in the same manner.

Still, the scenario and production of *The Woman on the Beach* bothered him, if only because it was unlike any other film he had ever attempted. As he noted at the time, 'I wanted to try and tell a love story based purely on physical attraction, a story in which emotions played no part ... In all my previous films I had tried to depict the bonds uniting the individual to his background ... I had proclaimed the consoling truth that the world is one; and now I was embarked on a study of persons whose sole idea was to close the door on the absolutely concrete phenomenon which we call life' (in Bergan 1992: 261). This, of course, is the very essence of noir, and whatever his misgivings, Renoir embraced this new emotional terrain with his customary skill and insight.

The Woman on the Beach tells the tale of Tod Butler (Charles Bickford), an extremely successful American artist whose career has been cut short by an accident in which he was deprived of his eyesight. His wife, Peggy (Joan Bennett), loves and hates Tod in equal measure, but remains bound to him because it was she who blinded him during a lover's quarrel. The two live in a seaside cottage near a US Coast Guard base, in a state of perpetual disharmony; Tod keeps his paintings locked up in a closet – his only link to the past – while Peggy wants to sell the paintings and move to New York, seeking the fast life the two once shared when Tod could see. Into this uneasy marriage comes Lieutenant Scott Burnett (Robert Ryan), a young officer who has recently survived a torpedo attack and is now recovering from his physical wounds, while remaining mentally unbalanced. Peggy immediately seduces Scott, much to the displeasure of Scott's fiancée, Eve Geddes (Nan Leslie).

Scott becomes obsessed with 'freeing' Peggy from Tod, who he believes is not really blind but rather manipulating Peggy so that she will stay with him out of guilt. In an attempt to prove his theory, Scott creates a series of cruel tests for Tod, in one instance standing by while Tod walks off a cliff. Convinced at last that Tod really *is* blind, yet unable to free himself from Peggy's grip, Scott battles Tod for Peggy's affections. The film culminates in an astounding scene in which Tod sets his house and paintings on fire in a desperate attempt to free himself of his past life. As the house explodes in flames, Tod renounces his past ways and tells Peggy to go with Scott. But Peggy chooses to stay with Tod, who now intends to pursue a career as a writer. Scott returns to Eve, and domestic tranquility.

Summing up his Hollywood period, Renoir commented: 'Although I don't regret my American films, I know for a fact they don't even come close to any ideal I have for my work … they represent seven years of unrealised works and unrealised hopes. And seven years of deceptions too' (in Bergan 1992: 264). But even if this is so, *The Woman on the Beach* is still a remarkable film, the only noir that Renoir ever made and – along with Jean-Luc Godard's 1963 masterpiece *Contempt* – one of the most economical and relentless examinations of a marriage in collapse ever filmed. As Tod, Bickford gives the most nuanced performance of his career, at once tender and dangerous, while Robert Ryan brings an intensity to the role of Scott that is both haunting and achingly realistic. Joan Bennett's foredoomed femme fatale is essentially a reprise of her role in Fritz Lang's *Scarlet Street* (1945), but in *The Woman on the Beach* she seems more tragic and human than in Lang's much colder moral universe. At 71 minutes, the film has little time to waste, and is harrowingly compact. Not available on DVD or VHS, or even in 16mm rental format, *The Woman on the Beach* is Renoir's one true American masterpiece, into which he distilled all his disdain for the Hollywood studio system and American culture.

The Midwest Family Cut Open: *King's Row*

Sam Wood's *King's Row* is another matter altogether, although it, too, looks behind the scenes of domestic life and finds a great deal to abhor. The film began life as a wildly successful popular novel by Henry Bellamann, published in 1940, and soon the studios were engaged in a fierce battle for the rights to the book. But filming *King's Row* would be difficult. This muckraking novel of turn-of-the-century Americana featured insanity, murder, gratuitous amputations, homosexuality, premarital sex, suicide and incest – not exactly material that Joseph Breen would find easy to work with at the Production Code Administration. Warner Bros. finally secured the rights to Bellamann's novel, but then wondered how on earth they were going to adapt it to the screen. When he was originally assigned the project, associate producer Wolfgang Reinhardt wrote to Warner Bros. production chief Hal Wallis in dismay on 3 July 1940:

> I prefer not to kid myself or you regarding the enormous difficulties that [a film version] of this best seller will undoubtedly offer ... the hero finding out that his girl has been carrying on incestuous relations with her father, a sadistic doctor who amputates legs and disfigures people wilfully, a host of moronic or otherwise mentally diseased characters, the background of a lunatic asylum, people dying from cancer, suicides – these are the principal elements of the story ... in my opinion the making of a screenplay would amount to starting from scratch. (In Behlmer 1985: 135)

Indeed, Joseph Breen wrote to Jack Warner on 22 April 1941 saying that the entire undertaking of filming *King's Row* was inherently suspect:

> Before this picture will be approved under the provision of the Production Code, *all illicit sex will have to be entirely removed*; the *characterization of Cassandra* will have to be *definitely changed*; the *mercy killing* will have to be *deleted* ... [and] the suggestion that Dr Gordon's nefarious practices are prompted by a kind of sadism will have to be *completely removed from the story* ... to attempt to translate such a story to the screen, *even though it be re-written to conform to the provisions of the Production Code*, is, in our judgement, a very questionable undertaking from the standpoint of the good and welfare of the industry. (In Behlmer 1985: 136–7; emphasis in original)

Nevertheless, Warner Bros. pressed ahead, with significant changes in the novel's plot line, and much suggestion, rather then direct explication, of other narrative points in the original text.

In *King's Row*, Parris Mitchell (Robert Cummings) is an idealistic young man studying to become a psychiatrist. His best friend, Drake McHugh (Ronald Reagan),

is the town hellraiser, always in trouble of one sort or another, and a perennial ladies' man. Cassandra 'Cassie' Tower (Betty Field) is the daughter of Dr Alexander
Q. Tower (Claude Rains), who serves as Parris's first teacher; Parris falls in love with
Cassie, but before the relationship can progress, Cassie begins exhibiting symptoms of an insanity inherited from her mother. Parris and Cassie have sex, Cassie
becomes pregnant, and in a rage Dr Tower kills both Cassie and himself. Most of
this is suggested, not shown. As critic Tim Dirks notes, in the novel Dr Tower's
motivation was even more sinister:

> Cassie was afflicted with nymphomania, not insanity. Dr Tower's diary re-
> vealed that the warped doctor had eliminated his wife and then committed
> incest with his daughter in order to study its psychological effects. He then
> killed Cassie when she threatened to leave him and go to Parris. (2003b)

As Breen made clear, *King's Row*'s original source material would never have made
it past the censor's office in 1942, so this element, and others in the story, were
significantly revised in Casey Robinson's still-daring screenplay. In a second main
narrative strand, Drake, who has been living handsomely from an inheritance, suddenly finds himself bankrupt and involved with two women, Randy Monaghan (Ann
Sheridan at her no-nonsense best) and Louise Gordon (Nancy Coleman), the daughter of Dr Henry Gordon (Charles Coburn), a sadistic local doctor who specialises in
performing operations without anaesthesia. Unfortunately for Drake, when he is
injured in an accident at work he is taken to Dr Gordon's clinic for surgery. Knowing of Drake's relationship with his daughter Louise, Dr Gordon amputates both
of Drake's legs as an act of revenge. After the operation, Drake looks down at his
mutilated body and utters the film's most famous line, 'Where's the rest of me?',
which would eventually become the title of Ronald Reagan's 1965 autobiography.

Generally a competent but unmemorable actor, Reagan gives the performance
of his career here. Sam Wood's utilitarian direction concentrates on the performances of the actors, but the film is given a paranoid, claustrophobic air by the alcoholic, gifted set designer William Cameron Menzies. Wood, a lifelong Republican,
can hardly have been in sympathy with the novel's intent; indeed, he kept falling
behind in production because of a laboured, slow pace, and seemed more interested in Robert Cummings' portrayal of Parris than any other element of the film.
King's Row was released to solid business and respectable reviews, but will probably never be embraced as an American classic; even watered down at Breen's be-
hest, it is a stinging indictment of American society. Love provokes not happiness
but revenge; medicine disfigures rather than heals; paranoia lies beneath the most
civilised surfaces.

Indeed, as a dystopian vision of the dark underside of midwestern smalltown
life, *King's Row* has never been equalled. Gorgeously photographed by James
Wong Howe, with a sweepingly romantic score by Erich Wolfgang Korngold, *King's*

Row remains in the memory as a vision of puritan Hell, unrelieved by any ray of light. At the end, Parris, as a budding psychiatrist, offers his chum Drake words of consolation that are sufficient to bring the amputee out of his self-pity and renew his interest in life. But, even as Parris recites the lines of the poem 'Invictus' to Drake in an attempt to make him whole again, in spirit if not in body, and Drake reunites with Randy to plan their future together, *King's Row* remains an unstinting indictment of the ignorance, insularity and small-mindedness of midwestern America, as true today as when it was written and subsequently filmed. The film demonstrates that the spirit of noir is not located only in the big city, but also permeates the rural village. Men and women scheme to gain power, wealth and social prominence, and the local authorities consider themselves bound to give not only legal, but also moral, guidance to all their constituents whether they wish it or not. *King's Row* is that rarest of films, a social commentary made by a major studio, which critiques the very society it so accurately documents.

Domesticity Under Attack: *The Phantom Speaks*

A deeply disturbing family noir from the 1940s, John English's *The Phantom Speaks* (1945), also holds a claim on the viewer's memory long after the last image has faded from the screen. In this brief (69-minute) low-budget film from Republic Pictures, gangster Harvey Bogardus (Tom Powers) murders a man whom he suspects of fooling around with his wife, and is summarily condemned to death in the electric chair. His case attracts the attention of psychic researcher Dr Paul Renwick (Stanley Ridges), a widower with one daughter, who visits Bogardus on the eve of his execution with a startling proposal. Having studied Bogardus's ruthless criminal career, Renwick is convinced that Bogardus possesses a uniquely powerful mind and might be able to reach beyond the veil of death through the efforts of a sympathetic medium. As Renwick outlines his plan, Bogardus becomes convinced that Renwick can, perhaps, effect such a return from the dead, and agrees to participate. As he is led into the death chamber, Bogardus makes a final statement to the assembled members of the press, stating simply, 'OK, so I killed a rat. He got what was coming to him. And I know some others that'll get the same thing. I'm not through yet, hear me? *Not yet!*'

The execution is carried out, and Bogardus is declared legally dead. Renwick immediately returns to his home, where his daughter Joan (Lynne Roberts) awaits him. Brushing her aside, he rushes to his study, and in an attempt to contact Bogardus begins a gruelling regimen of repeated séances which, at length, prove successful. Yet the rematerialised Bogardus is far from whole. 'There are some things I can't do without you,' he tells Renwick. 'I've got hands but I can't pick up anything with 'em. I've got legs but I can't walk around on 'em. These eyes – all I can see is *you*, Renwick. But I've got a *miiiind*.' Renwick is flushed with his success. 'That's a fact I've sought all my life to prove! That a spirit from the dead could take possession of the living. If we can conduct a successful experiment along those lines, we can prove that there's no such thing as insanity. It's a case of a spirit from the beyond crowding out the mind and spirit of the living.' Rejoins Bogardus: 'Wanna try it, Doctor?...' (see Weaver 1993). Renwick agrees to submit himself to Bogardus's will, and in a chilling sequence accomplished entirely through a series of increasingly tight intercut close-ups, Bogardus gradually takes possession of Renwick's mind. While Renwick has a more or less scientific interest, Bogardus has only one objective: revenge. Using Renwick's body, Bogardus's reanimated spirit systematically tracks down and brutally murders all those responsible for his conviction and execution. Renwick's daughter, who is in love with reporter Matt Fraser (Richard Arlen), is kept in the dark by her father, who now alternates between his own personality and that of Bogardus.

As the days pass, Bogardus assumes almost complete control of Renwick, materialising in the doctor's study with steely malevolence, commanding the doctor to do his bidding. Supremely confident of his mastery of Renwick, Bogardus taunts him: 'No, Doc, you're not losing your mind. But then again, maybe you *are* crazy. But what does it matter? I'm here now, and that's all that counts. And we have work to do.' In the film's final minutes, Bogardus sends Renwick out to murder the District Attorney who spearheaded the case against him, but Renwick is prevented from carrying out the mission by the last-minute intervention of his daughter and the police. Coming to his senses as he is captured, Renwick is momentarily freed of Bogardus's malign influence, and looks at his daughter with an expression of amazement and fear. 'Joan!' he cries out. 'What's going on? What am I doing here?'

But in the film's astounding finale there is no trial for Renwick, no suggestion of an insanity defence and no reprieve from society. From the scene of his final capture, the film dissolves immediately to the same death chamber where Bogardus met his end, but this time it is Renwick who is condemned. Although the others never suspect this, we know that it is really Bogardus's reanimated spirit that is being executed. As he is led to the electric chair, Renwick stops for a moment and in Bogardus's voice addresses the assembled company of witnesses, speaking the exact same words Bogardus used before his execution: 'OK, so I killed a rat. He got what was coming to him. And I know some others that'll get the same thing. I'm not through yet, hear me? *Not yet!*'

Thus it is clear that Bogardus will return yet again from the dead, to take over the life and body of another victim, his lust for murder apparently insatiable.

Throughout the film, much is made of the home that Bogardus destroys through his supernatural machinations. Dr Renwick's house is a warm, welcoming place, filled with flowers and music, and the romance between his daughter Joan and Matt Fraser affords him a sense of satisfaction that his life and Joan's will proceed to a happy end. Joan's attempts to help her father are repeatedly underscored by the film's narrative, but as he falls deeper under Bogardus's spell, the succession of breakfast trays and thoughtfully prepared sandwiches she brings to her father are turned away with increasing coldness. It is his insatiable curiosity that ultimately brings about Renwick's horrific end; his work overpowers the domestic sphere until there is no room left for human companionship. As Bogardus becomes increasingly powerful, the others in Renwick's life are shut out, and he becomes a slave to not only Bogardus but also the work he had sought to carry out.

The Phantom Speaks thus offers a truly despairing vision of American small-town family life in the mid-1940s. Although Renwick is a respected member of his community, when he shuts himself off from their care they make no attempt to break through the hold Bogardus has on him, and consign him to death for murders he did not truly commit. Nor is there any interest in an explanation, or in the existence of mitigating factors; Renwick must die – yet his death will not truly protect society. The domestic sphere is continually under attack, and even those whom society respects the most may become the servants of those who would seek to destroy it.

Colourful Blackness: *Leave Her to Heaven*

In the justly famous *Leave Her to Heaven*, psychotically possessive Ellen Berent (Gene Tierney) falls in love with novelist Richard Harland (Cornel Wilde), even though she is engaged to attorney Russell Quinton (Vincent Price). Spiriting Richard away to her lavish family ranch in the desert, Ellen impulsively announces that they are betrothed. When Russell arrives, Ellen coldly sends him away. After their marriage, Richard begins to notice that Ellen is *too* attentive, fixing his breakfast, making his bed, watching him type his new novel – never leaving him a moment's peace. Anyone who intrudes on their relationship is ruthlessly eliminated.

When Richard's paralysed young brother Danny (Darryl Hickman) threatens to monopolise Richard's time and attention, Ellen lures him out into a deep lake and lets him drown. When she becomes pregnant, Ellen is repulsed by the idea that her unborn baby will soon have a claim on Richard's affections, so she throws herself down a flight of stairs and successfully induces a miscarriage. When Richard finally realises what a monster Ellen is, it is too late. In drifting away from Ellen, he has fallen in love with her cousin, Ruth Berent (Jeanne Crain). To respond, Ellen commits suicide, knowing she can never regain Richard's love; but she frames Ruth for her 'murder'. Only a last-minute courtroom manoeuvre by Richard keeps Ruth out of the gas chamber. After he spends a short stint in prison (for not reporting Ellen's infamous deeds to the authorities earlier), Richard and Ruth are reunited at his Vermont hunting lodge, Back of the Moon. The entire story is told in flashback – that time-honoured structural tradition of noir – by family friend Glen Robie (Ray Collins), who has witnessed the tragedy from first to last.

In contrast to the other films discussed in this essay, *Leave Her to Heaven* is shot in gorgeous Technicolor by the gifted Leon Shamroy, with a sumptuous and suitably ominous symphonic musical score by Alfred Newman. The sets, by Lyle

Wheeler and Maurice Ransford, are worthy of a Douglas Sirk melodrama, which in many ways *Leave Her to Heaven* resembles; ornate, carefully colour-coordinated and ostentatiously lavish. Perhaps the most shocking scene is Danny's death in the quiet lake at Back of the Moon. With great cunning, Ellen has been taking him for therapeutic swimming lessons for several weeks, building up his trust in her as well as his confidence in himself as a recovering victim of paralysis. Danny bravely asserts that he can swim to shore, but Ellen, clad in appropriately dark sunglasses, knows that he has gone out too far, and impassively watches him drown as he pathetically screams for her assistance. The brutality and cruelty of this sequence – unaccompanied by any music – in such a bucolic setting is deeply distressing, and made even more disturbing by Ellen's 'desperate' attempts to rescue the drowning Danny at a point when she is secure in the knowledge that he is beyond help.

Worse still, Ellen's pathology is no secret to her mother (Mary Philips), who tells Richard, 'There's nothing wrong with Ellen … it's just that she loves too much … it makes an outsider of everyone else … you must be patient with her … she loved her father too much.' This is the father whom, we discover late in the film, Ellen drove to suicide with her unceasing demands for his attention and her impossibly high expectations. As Ruth tells Ellen during a final, angry confrontation, 'With your love you wrecked your mother's life, with your love you pressed your father to death, with your love you've made a shadow out of Richard.'

What Ellen fears most is the loss of identity that her marriage will bring, a loss of self that matrimony anticipates in the very act of the wedding ceremony itself. Richard and Ellen's marriage is not real, can never be real, because Ellen, a product of postwar American culture, seeks a life for herself above all other considerations and refuses to be subsumed in any relationship. Yet, unable to declare her true intentions because of the social conventions of the period, Ellen must continually lie about her relationships, about her actions and, eventually, even about the manner of her death. As she commits suicide with a lethal dose of poison, she leaves evidence to frame Ruth for the crime, so that Richard and Ruth will be prevented from marrying (and, the narrative implies, having children).

The Home in Peril: *The Locket* and Other Films

But nothing can quite prepare the viewer for the experience of watching John Brahm's *The Locket*, famous for its 'flashback within a flashback within a flashback' structure, perhaps the most convoluted narrative in the history of noir. The plot itself is relatively simple: Nancy (Laraine Day) is a kleptomaniac, driven to steal anything that strikes her fancy (the original title of the film was *What Nancy Wanted*). Nancy's compulsion springs from a childhood incident, in which she is given a locket as a birthday gift from the daughter of her mother's employer. The employer, cruel Mrs Willis (Katherine Emery), objects and takes the locket back. Later, the object goes missing and Mrs Willis acts on the assumption that Nancy has stolen it back, although it is later discovered that the locket simply fell into the hem of a garment. But Nancy is never truly exonerated. Now, twenty years later, she is poised to marry John Willis (Gene Raymond) and thus regain admission to the household from which she was banished as a child; Mrs Willis, having known Nancy only as a child, does not recognise her.

But within this seemingly straightforward narrative, there are numerous obstacles. The film itself begins on the day of Nancy's wedding to John Willis. Just as the ceremony is about to begin, psychiatrist Dr Harry Blair (Brian Aherne) breaks in demanding to see John. Dr Blair, it turns out, was one of Nancy's former husbands; he knows that Nancy is insane, and pleads with Willis not to marry her. As Blair recounts the tale of his marriage with Nancy in a flashback voiceover, he unfolds the story of another of Nancy's husbands, the late Norman Clyde (Robert Mitchum), a moody artist who ultimately committed suicide because of Nancy's compulsive thefts, and her participation in a murder. All this unfolds in reverse, back to Nancy's childhood and the incident with the locket, and then reverses to end in the present, where the still doubting John Willis, having heard Dr Blair's tale, confronts Nancy, who predictably denies everything.

Only Nancy's collapse at the altar, brought on by Mrs Willis's 're-gift' of the locket that Nancy briefly had as a child, saves John Willis from a similar marital fate. As *The Locket* ends, Nancy is taken off to an asylum ostensibly for a cure, but the camera remains within the gloomy precincts of the Willis family's dark Fifth Avenue mansion. What has transpired has left a mark on not only Nancy but all who knew her. For most of the film, Nancy's mania eludes detection, and everyone who discovers her secret is summarily destroyed. Thus, all surfaces are suspect, all appearances deceiving, and nothing is to be taken at face value, especially protestations of innocence in the 'safe haven' of the family. As in all families, dark memories circulate forward from the past, reconfiguring present experience and memory together.

John Brahm effectively stages *The Locket* so that most of it happens at night, on claustrophobic studio sets. Mitchum, a rising star at the time, is oddly convincing as Norman Clyde, a Bohemian artist with attitude to spare, and Nicholas Musuraca's moody lighting leaves the characters, and the viewer, in a state of continual confusion and suspense. Most intriguing, of course, is the triple-flashback structure of the film, which brings into question the reliability of the film's narrative. When Dr Blair bursts in on Willis and begins his recital of Nancy's crimes, Blair's flashback contains Norman Clyde's reminiscences, which in turn contain Nancy's own memories of her childhood – as told to Norman – containing the incident of the locket. Thus, we have only Nancy's word, through Norman, and then through Dr Blair, that any of this is really true, and yet we unquestionably believe in the veracity of all three statements. Why? The entire story is so fantastic that one can understand Willis's lack of trust in Blair's accusations; Nancy seems like a 'nice girl'. The failed wedding that climaxes the film is proof enough of Nancy's affliction, but are all the details of her illness *quite* correct? For this, we have only the word of three narratives that enfold within each other like miniature Chinese boxes, refusing to give up their secrets, opening only when the proper pressure is applied to the correct spot.

In other noirish narratives of family rupture, such as Douglas Sirk's *Shockproof* (1949), in which parolee Jenny Marsh (Patricia Knight) invades the house of her parole officer, Griff Marat (Cornel Wilde), with disastrous consequences; or Otto Preminger's *Whirlpool* (1949), which tells the tale of unscrupulous psychiatrist David Korvo's (José Ferrer) domination of Ann Sutton (Gene Tierney), who is married to reputable psychiatrist Dr William Sutton (Richard Conte), the same narrative tropes play out again and again. Always, it seems, we have the family coming apart at the seams; always a more or less harrowing psychiatric intervention. In Irving Reis's *All My Sons* (1948), based on Arthur Miller's play, Edward G. Robinson is the head of yet another dysfunctional post-World War Two family, this time as a munitions manufacturer shipping faulty airplane parts to the front lines of combat. As Joe Keller, Robinson is all bluster and bravado; when his crime is discovered he frames his partner, so that his family can continue their complacent lives. In Robert Wise's *Born to Kill* (1947), psychotic killer Sam Wilde (Lawrence Tierney at his most brutish) attracts decadent socialite Helen Brent (Claire Trevor); and soon Sam and his obviously homosexual lover Marty Waterman (Elisha Cook Jr) are living in the palatial mansion of Helen's half sister, Georgia Staples (Audrey Long). Sensing an opportunity, Sam moves in on Georgia's affections and soon the couple is married. To exact her revenge, Helen sets into motion a mechanism of betrayal that will eventually destroy Sam, Marty and herself.

In all these films, the message is the same. The home is in peril. The relationship you thought would last forever is doomed. The person you brought into your house as a guest seeks to destroy it, and you. Your friends don't believe you. The police don't believe you. You are powerless before the forces of fate, which have once again capriciously decided to deal you a new, distinctly unpleasant future from the bottom of the deck. The world of the 'family noir' is the domestic sphere under threat, in collapse, existing outside the normative values of postwar society, values that are themselves continually in a state of flux. The family unit is constantly celebrated in the dominant media as the ideal state of social existence, but is it, when so much is at risk and so much is unexplained? The sense of manipulation and despair prevalent in these noirs persists today, and will continue tomorrow, with the representational stakes raised with each succeeding generation. Priests become monsters, teachers assault their students, husbands beat their wives and wives retaliate by murdering their abusive spouses. Notch by notch, the family has become a new kind of Hell, far removed from the ersatz world of *My Three Sons* (1960–72) and *Leave It to Beaver* (1957–63). 'No', say these films 'leave it to Heaven', and in the meantime, let us sort things out here on earth as best we can.

If the 'family noir' seeks to teach us anything, it is that we will never be satisfied; we will never truly come to any definitive point of social or sexual fixed ground. We will always want more, and more again, but we will never have enough. It is our lot to continually seek the phantom reassurance of a new imagistic construct that can never fulfil our spectatorial desires. Lost in a wilderness of conflicting images, moving ever faster, with quicker and quicker editing until the unit of the cinematic shot itself collapses, we are finally stripped of any fugitive identity we may have thought we possessed. The avowal of the self that the construction of the family represents cannot survive without the continual production of images to support it, work that is going on now with a renewed, desperate intensity because the economic and social stakes are so much higher. What will replace the discrepancies of action that constitute straight discourse in contemporary cinema? For the moment, it seems that we are destined ceaselessly to repeat the past, hoping to find there some semblance of security and safety.

But what will we do when we are forced, at last, to see ourselves? What will we do when, finally unable to bear the weight of its own construction, the screen illusion of the family collapses, when it is evident that the home, as construct, can no longer protect us – has never protected us? And these people we are, that family made us: where can we go when we discover that we no longer exist?

2

Everybody Sing: Family, Community and the Representation of Social Harmony in the Hollywood Musical

JAMES BUHLER

Creating Community

When we think of musicals, what is apt to come to mind is Fred Astaire and Ginger Rogers gliding across the floor 'Cheek to Cheek' in *Top Hat* (1935); or Jeanette Mac-Donald and Nelson Eddy finding the 'Sweet Mystery of Life' together in *Naughty Marietta* (1935); or Judy Garland revealing her repressed desire for 'Mack the Black' in *The Pirate* (1948); or Gene Kelly wooing Debbie Reynolds with dance in *Singin' in the Rain* (1952). Music seems the magic that makes us believe in the romance of these films, that just these characters are meant to be together. As Steve (Astaire) sings to Ninotchka (Cyd Charisse) in *Silk Stockings* (1957):

> We were fated to be mated,
> We were slated to be tied –
> Me as the burning bridegroom,
> You as the yearning bride.

If musicals are preoccupied with the stage of courtship ending in marriage, they are also oddly reluctant to include representations of family, especially children. The world of courtship may sing, but apparently the future of its song in marriage is not yet assured. The happy end leaves no hint as to whether the social harmony promised by song can sustain itself. Even in the so-called folk musical, where children do appear, society is generally figured in the form of marriage rather than the family unit. That is, most of these films continue to dwell on the creation of society rather than on sustaining its actual existence. Thus the lead couple – typically both characters are presented as coming of age and so not fully vested in the old community – represents divisions in a nascent rather than actual community. These divisions do not stem from contradictions within existing society, but represent instead blockages to the formation of community. Marriage, then, is the sign that these blockages have been overcome and that the social contract of the new community can be signed.

Yet the contract is not yet in force. That is, marriage remains only the promise of social harmony, a harmony in the process of becoming. Thus, in *Seven Brides for Seven Brothers* (1954), a new community emerges from the unions of the seven socially recalcitrant bothers and the 'civilised' town girls. Born during the estrangement of Milly (Jane Powell) and Adam (Howard Keel), baby Hannah is not a confirmation of existing society but a promise of what might be but is not yet. It is only when she is claimed by all of the women near the end of the film – an act that spares the brothers from the wrath of the townspeople – that the pact of community has been signed. The final scene realises the promise of the title and ends with all the pairs kissing. Despite the presence of Hannah, then, the film remains directed towards successful courtship and creation of a new community rather than towards sustaining an existing one. Likewise, the marriage of Laurey (Shirley Jones) and Curly (Gordon MacRae) in *Oklahoma!* (1955) initiates a new state of society where conflicts between the farmers and the ranchers are resolved not by barbed wire and guns but through a commitment to harmonious society based on the principle of private property:

Brand new state!
Brand new state, gonna treat you great!
Gonna give you barley, carrots and pertaters,
Pasture fer the cattle,
Spinach and termayters!
Flowers on the prairie where the June bugs zoom,
Plen'y of air and plen'y of room,
Plen'y of room to swing a rope!
Plen'y of heart and plen'y of hope.

The final chorus, while celebrating community forged through marriage, remains poised on the cusp of the new state of being: here, too, community is promised but not yet realised.

The emphasis in these two musicals is explicitly on the creation of community, staked on drawing up a social contract designed for reconciling difference. Rick Altman suggests that the Hollywood musical is concentrated in the figure of the dissolve, which operates from the level of the audio dissolve on the soundtrack to the personality dissolve of the central characters (1987: 59–89). The audio dissolve reconciles differences in the actual world by transposing them to an ideal space where those differences have no force. This transposition occurs on the soundtrack with the shift of diegetically motivated sound (say, a piano) into a supradiegetic register (where we hear apparently diegetic singing but a non-diegetic orchestra).

'Good Night, My Someone' in *The Music Man* (1962) illustrates the principle. Amaryllis (Monique Vermont) sits at a piano practising her 'cross hands'. Marian (Shirley Jones), feeling that she may well be on her way to becoming 'an old maid', begins singing to herself over Amaryllis's accompaniment, which soon gives way to an orchestral accompaniment. The presence of supradiegetic music is the sign – indeed promise – of what is not yet present, namely Marian's 'Someone': 'Sweet dreams be yours, Love/If dreams they be.' As usual, the audio dissolve here encapsulates a thematic concern of the film. In Amaryllis's imperfect playing, Marian imagines an idealised place, which is momentarily realised in her song. Similarly, Professor Harold Hill (Robert Preston) will convince the town to imagine itself reconfigured in '76 Trombones'. If Harold at first cynically uses his 'think method' to sell the promise of community, he soon comes to recognise that redeeming this promise is his dream as well. The connection between these two visions is made clear later in the film when Marian and Harold sing 'Good Night, My Someone' and '76 Trombones' in counterpoint. Each has become the content of the other's dream. The promise is then realised in a personality dissolve, where the oppositions and conflicts that threaten to derail the romance are dissolved as each character assimilates the difference of the other. Harold has settled down; Marian has become less inhibited; and the band is no longer imagined, but real. The promised marriage, as a resolution of apparent social difference, thus serves as a figure of social harmony; and the terms on which the marriage is made define the terms of the community.

The logic here is that of the synecdoche: the fate of the couple foretells that of the community. For without a successful marriage between the protagonists, the community cannot be initiated, much less sustained. Whatever obstacles the romance cannot overcome, the community cannot surmount either. Such a situation plays out in *West Side Story* (1961), for instance, where difference can only be reconciled 'somewhere'. Here, the conflicts in the world are so powerful that the audio dissolve is blocked from being realised in the personality dissolve. Difference remains intractable and the romance ends in death rather than marriage. Significantly, the musical ends not with song but with Maria's tearful words of reproach: 'All of you. You all killed him. And my brother. And Riff. Not with bullets and guns. With hate.' (And these words paradoxically offer the possibility of rapprochement as members of both communities escort Tony's body in the final tableau.)

It is noteworthy that the three musicals discussed above – *Seven Brides for Seven Brothers*, *Oklahoma!* and *West Side Story* – centre on characters who are on the cusp of adulthood. The emphasis on couples and coupling in these cases minimises the role of existing family and community. This is especially so when there are few representatives of the adult world. In *Oklahoma!* surrogate parents and thus surrogate notions of community are present in the figures of Aunt Eller (Charlotte Greenwood) and Ike Skidmore (Jay C. Flippen); but it is precisely because these families are surrogate that the sense of community they represent is so tenuous. The union of Laurey and Curly can surmount the divisions between farmer and cowboy because their familial and communal ties to those identities are relatively weak. At the same time, the fact that the farmer and cowboy share the same music suggests that the desired social harmony is blocked by a dissonance more apparent than real. 'The farmer and the cowboy should be friends' just as Laurey and Curly are 'meant' to belong together all along. In essence, the apparent difference of Laurey and Curly – unlike that of Ado Annie (Gloria Grahame), Ali Hakim (Eddie Albert) or most certainly Judd Fry (Rod Steiger) – defines the terms and limits of social identity in the 'brand new state'.

One reason the tragedy of *West Side Story* seems so poignant is because the youths seem to have internalised a pathological commitment to social difference in the *absence* of parental figures. Indeed, representatives of the adult world – Doc (Ned Glass), Lieutenant Schrank (Simon Oakland), even the comically incompetent Officer Krupke (William Bramley) – seem to desire a reconciliation that the kids cannot find it in their power to achieve. The absence of actual family is in this sense the sign of dysfunctional family, which in turn suggests the insecurity of living in a dysfunctional community that can be held together only by an insistence on communal difference. The two communities have wholly different music, 'The Jets' Song' and 'America', with Tony and Maria's lyricism standing outside the opposition. When the two communities sing together, as in the quintet, they give voice to violence and cultural dissonance rather than reconciliation and social harmony. The quintet –

And we're the ones to stop 'em once and for all
The Jets/The Sharks are gonna have their way
The Jets/The Sharks are gonna have their day
We're gonna rock it tonight ...

– soon dissolves into an instrumental dance of death, the rumble.

The unbridgeable cultural difference in *West Side Story* is, of course, race, and a similar theme is explored in *South Pacific* (1958), where Emile de Becque's (Rossano Brazzi) biracial children serve as signs of racial difference. Their presence asks: what are the limits of this difference? Nellie Forbush (Mitzi Gaynor) overcomes her initial discomfort with the children and ultimately embraces them as family, which plays out musically when she joins Ngana and Jerome (Candace Lee and Warren Hsieh) in singing 'Dites-moi', the song that also opens the musical and musically defines the children: 'Dites-moi/Pourquoi/La vie est belle/Dites-moi/Pourquoi/La vie est gaie...' In the end, then, the family takes shape as everybody sings together. If Nellie's acceptance of the children offers the promise of a community no longer held apart by racial division, the fateful relationship between Lt. Cable (John Kerr) and Liat (France Nuyen) – like that between Tony (Richard Beymer) and Maria (Natalie Wood) in *West Side Story* – acknowledges that this promise of society has not yet been redeemed.

Reproducing Community

As the examples of *Oklahoma!* and *South Pacific* illustrate, Richard Rodgers and Oscar Hammerstein II are especially adept at deploying family as a powerful symbol of community. In these two musicals, the happy fate of the principal romantic couple is a microcosm of that of the community. Other Rodgers and Hammerstein musicals likewise draw on the symbol of the family as a marker of community. In *The King and I* (1956), for instance, the son Chulalongkorn (Patrick Adiarte) is the figure in which the culture is reproduced (the continuation of kingly rule) and transfigured (the change of social codes). *State Fair* (1945; 1962), not coincidentally the only one of their musicals written specifically for film, is perhaps the most straightforward example. The family arrives at the fair already constituted as a family, so the romances of the children directly address the issue of sustaining existing society rather than its initiation. If Margy's (Jeanne Crain; Pamela Tiffin) successful romance with Pat/Bobby (Dana Andrews; Jerry Dundee) suggests that the values of the Iowa farm can be transplanted to the urban setting of Chicago, Wayne's (Dick Haymes; Pat Boone) failed romance with Emily (Vivian Blaine; Ann-Margret) implies that she is not the kind of girl who can successfully reproduce the values of the farm. Wayne returns to the farm forlorn, but quickly and enthusiastically embraces his old girlfriend, ensuring that the social harmony of the farming community, represented in the songs 'Our State Fair' and 'All I Owe IOWAY', is perpetuated.

As in *State Fair*, the continuation of the family rather than its initiation is the structuring principle of *Meet Me in St. Louis* (1944). Yet if *State Fair* offers the mild risk of introducing a disruptive element – Emily – into the family itself, the threat to the family unit in *Meet Me in St. Louis* is almost non-existent and it is rather the trauma of social displacement that is the concern. Alonzo Smith (Leon Ames) is offered a promotion that requires relocating his family to New York. When he initially accepts the offer for the good of the family (that is, for an increase in his salary), the family members themselves are distraught, since they recognise that moving will uproot them from the community, disrupting its cycles of reproduction and generation. This latter point is made clear by the two eldest daughters, Rose (Lucille Bremer) and Esther (Judy Garland), both of whom want to stay to pursue romantic interests within the community. Interestingly, the threatened displacements apparently work only one way. John Truett (Tom Drake), 'The Boy Next Door' whom Esther fancies, is new to the community. This suggests that one of the film's concerns is allying the extension of family with the extension of community: John's acceptance in the community is doubled by his (future) acceptance in the family. Consequently, the centre of gravity of the film resides less in the family than in this couple, indeed in Esther, whose command of the soundtrack makes the film very much hers. Musically, the film traces Esther's coming of age as she negotiates a communal place for herself that is staked on performing her emerging identity in terms of romance. 'The Trolley Song', where elements of community and romance momentarily fuse, is thus the musical lynchpin of the film: here, she leaves her home and boards a trolley, whose passengers soon erupt in song. Apprehensive about this unexpected outburst and anxious about John's absence, Esther at first moves fretfully through the car unsure of what to make of the music and dance swirling about her. Soon, however, she is swept up by the energy of communal harmony and joins in. By the end, John has arrived and she has claimed the song as her own:

> And it was grand just to stand
> With his hand holding mine –
> To the end of the line.

In this way, 'The Trolley Song' suggests that Esther has found her voice in a community defined by romance rather than by the limits of her family.

Although romantic elements are present in *The King and I*, *State Fair* and *Meet Me in St. Louis*, none of these musicals is ultimately governed by the usual syntax of the musical comedy, courtship ending in a marriage of opposites. The emphasis in all three falls instead on family as a medium for conserving and extending communal values. Courtship in these films is instrumental to community, so marriage celebrates the continuation of an existing community rather than the initiation of a new one. The endings of *State Fair* and *Meet Me in St. Louis* reflect this. While each of these narratives comes to its end with its primary couple declaring love, neither of the films actually concludes with this embrace. Instead, each has a short coda that re-establishes the family as primary to romance. In *State Fair*, this is sung, allowing communal song to encompass, and so also contain, the music of romance: 'Oh, I know all I owe I owe Ioway,/I owe Ioway all I owe and I know why.' *Meet Me in St. Louis*, on the other hand, resorts to the family tableau, as everyone looks admiringly at the spectacle of the World's Fair. However, the use of visual spectacle to represent the family means that the music of romance is not fully contained by the strictures of social harmony, the community not just limited by what it sees, just as Esther is not contained by the limits of her family.

With a title like *In the Good Old Summertime* (1949) – which with Garland as lead seems to promise something like *Meet Me In St. Louis* – we might expect to find a similar 'charming' picture of old Americana, complete with a strong emphasis on the nuclear family. A musical adaptation of *The Shop Around the Corner* (1940), the film is nevertheless primarily a romantic comedy with the music-store setting serving as a pretence to motivate musical performance. Music, in other words, remains external to the romance and thus also to the conception of community. Still, representations of family pervade the thematic background. Veronica (Garland), who lives with her Aunt Addie (Lillian Bronson), has just passed into adulthood. When the romance between Veronica and Andrew (Van Johnson) moves into domestic space – Aunt Addie's – a neighbour immediately drops off a baby. The appearance of the baby here does not simply foretell the marriage proposal; it also

symbolically extends the stakes of the union to the reproduction of the social structure. Indeed, Andrew is unusually interested in babies, constantly making reference
to his sister's family. It is significant, too, that the film ends with a dissolve to a
family tableau of Veronica, Andrew and their toddler. *Coney Island* (1943), *Easter
Parade* (1948), *Take Me Out To the Ball Game* (1949) and *Wabash Avenue* (1950)
likewise promise a nostalgic image of turn-of-the-century America, but surprisingly
none of these films permits even the rudimentary presence of children that *In the
Good Old Summertime* allows.

Show Boat (1929; 1936; 1951), *Carousel* (1956) and *The Sound of Music* (1965)
offer something of a twist on the formula in that the marriage, the symbol of the
formed community, occurs not at the end but in the middle. The marriage between
Captain Georg von Trapp (Christopher Plummer) and Maria (Julie Andrews) near
the beginning of the second part of *The Sound of Music* marks the point at which
most musicals end. This allows the remainder of the film to address the continuation of existing society, or rather its perversion at the hands of the Nazis. Despite
the film's ending with the audience at the Salzburg Music Festival joining Georg in
singing 'Edelweiss':

Edelweiss, Edelweiss
Bless my homeland forever.

– a moment that suggests an Austrian Volk untainted by the *Anschluß* – the von
Trapp family must first sing 'so long, farewell' to Austrian society in order to per-
petuate its pure, 'clean and bright' traditional values: 'So long, farewell, Auf wieder-
sehen, good night…' (The film presentation of Georg's performance of 'Edelweiss'
is a change from the stage version, where there is no singing Austrian audience;
coincidentally or not, the film supports the Cold War political tactic of absolving
the Austrians of their complicity with the Nazis in order to tip the officially 'neutral'
1960s Austria towards the West. In this way, Austria is welcomed into the family of
'free' nations, that is, those countries 'untainted' by communist ideology.)

Community Lost

If, as Rick Altman says of the show musical, 'to break up a romance is to break up
an act' (1987: 224), something similar holds for musicals staked on the family: to
break up the family is to break up the community. The 1951 version of *Show Boat*,
with book and lyrics by Hammerstein, shares many of the thematic concerns of his
later musicals, and representations of family as a microcosm of community are central to it. It too features a marriage (or perhaps two) at its middle point. Both unions
end up broken. That of Julie (Ava Gardner) and Stephen (Robert Sterling) collapses
due to the pressures of racism that affect the relationship from without, while that
of Magnolia (Kathryn Grayson) and Gaylord (Howard Keel) is broken by internal

pressures, a failure of the couple to work through difference anywhere but 'in make believe'. Only the divisions of this second relationship can be healed; the child, Kim (Sheila Clark), ultimately serves as a catalyst for and promise of reconciliation, which occurs at the end with Gaylord's return. But the pressures of racism persist. Finally, the ideal community that *Show Boat* imagines is one still divided. Not only have Julie and Stephen gone their separate ways, Joe (William Warfield), a hired hand who tends the steam engine, is never integrated into the family of performers. In the 1936 film (but also the stage version), he (Paul Robeson) is supported by a community of black workers as he sings 'Ol' Man River' onshore. But on the boat (and throughout the unduly maligned 1951 version), he sings alone. If Joe has the show-stopping number, he only ever works behind the scenes, labouring to ensure that the engines of society, like Ol' Man River, keep rolling along.

In *Carousel*, the marriage, or rather the pregnancy, is fateful, as Billy Bigelow (Gordon MacRae) is seemingly forced into the impossible choice of inadequately supporting his family or falling back into the world of crime. The impossibility of the family in this case marks the impossibility of the community, and the child, Louise (Susan Luckey), must rehabilitate Billy's ghost in order to 'never walk alone', that is, to achieve what her father could not: integration into a community.

Restoring Community

Incomplete, broken or dysfunctional families are quite common in musicals, especially those focused on children. (Child-centred musicals tended to be the province of film rather than the stage until the 1960s, when *Carnival!* (1961) appeared on Broadway and then *Oliver!* (1968) and *Annie* (1982) appeared onscreen, all three focused on orphans.) The narrative drive in such films is towards completion or correction of the broken or fragmented family unit. Healing the breach, often accomplished through a romance of surrogate parents, stabilises the family so that its members can be reintegrated into a unified whole.

Anchors Aweigh (1945) illustrates well the way the premise of these films plays out. Donald (Dean Stockwell) is an orphan living with his young Aunt Susie (Kathryn Grayson), whose work does not leave her time to provide proper supervision. Although Donald seems peripheral to the main narrative thread, which predictably involves romantic coupling, he is in fact the film's centre of gravity. He is introduced singing 'Anchors Aweigh', the title song, and the plot revolves around the absence of a father figure for him. Clarence (Frank Sinatra) and Joe (Gene Kelly), two sailors on shore leave, run into Donald at the police station, and they are pressed to return the boy home, since, though far too young, he aspires to join the Navy. Clarence takes a shine to Susie, but Donald adopts Joe as a father figure instead, much to Joe's initial chagrin. By the end, the narrative has fulfilled Donald's 'need' for a father figure, as Joe and Susie fall in love. Making a virtue out of necessity – Kelly's and Grayson's voices are not well suited – Joe and Susie never sing a duet; otherwise, such a combination would place the focus of the film squarely on their romance rather than on the way the romance is instrumental to reintegrating Donald into a community.

Of course, there is nothing particularly novel about the situation of a broken or incomplete family that a narrative works to stabilise and complete. What is particular to the musical, however, is that, as *Anchors Aweigh* illustrates, the stability is achieved through music. Music, in other words, becomes a metaphor for and a means of resolving the dissonance of a fragmented (that is, socially constructed as 'dysfunctional') family unit into the consonance of communal harmony. While dramatically effective in and of itself, the narrative emphasis of these musicals on incomplete family units may also be a residue of early melodramatic, 'weepy' film musicals of the late 1920s. The tragic endings of such films as *The Singing Fool* (1928) follow a plot based around 'the plight of the child caught between quarrelling parents or abandoned by a dissolute mother' (Altman 1987: 210). The broken family becomes the sign of a community no longer able to sustain itself. *Applause* (1929) inverts the formula: Kitty (Helen Morgan) works to free her daughter April (Joan Peers) from the community of the stage, scrimping so she can send April away to a convent school. The draw of family, however, proves too strong, and Kitty dies while April takes her place onstage. (After Kitty's death, April's boyfriend, Tony (Henry Wadsworth), whom she had sent away so she could look after her mother, returns, allowing her to escape the stage and join his 'wholesome' farm family.)

Like *Anchors Aweigh*, film musicals from the 1930s often place such young stars as Shirley Temple, Deanna Durbin, Judy Garland and Mickey Rooney in a family setting that is broken – or at least incomplete. If the characters these actors play cannot always fully mend the cracks in these familial situations, they can at least ensure some stability for what is left of the family. As Thomas Schatz notes, Durbin's task in her films is 'not only to integrate different musical styles but also to integrate a father figure into a stable social and emotional context. In fact, in virtually all her films Durbin [is] depicted as a victim of a broken home and fragmented family who [seeks] somehow to restore the traditional order' (1981: 241–2). Indeed, the same could also be said of the others. Temple, for instance, seems always to be cast as an orphan. Although their casting is not quite so consistent, Garland and Rooney likewise play similar characters more than occasionally as well. *Every Sunday* (1936), a musical short starring Garland and Durbin, presents only Judy's 'Pop', a down-and-out musician who can hardly hold onto his Sunday gig conducting band concerts in the park. *The Wizard of Oz* (1939) places Dorothy (Garland) in the house of Uncle Henry (Charley Grapewin) and Auntie Em (Clara Blandick). In *Strike Up the Band* (1940), Jimmy (Rooney) has only a mother; his father has died and an important moment of the plot turns on his mother accepting Jimmy's desire to pursue music rather than a career in medicine as his father had desired. Even in a film such as *Babes on Broadway* (1941), where the families of Tom (Rooney) and

Penny (Garland) do not play more than an incidental role in the film, the plot is centred around raising money to help kids at a settlement house. As late as *Summer Stock* (1950), Garland is cast as Jane Falbury, who has been left to run the family farm alone after the death of her parents.

Nevertheless, it is in the films from the mid- and late 1930s where music most clearly serves a restorative function, a magical balm to heal the wound that fragmentation inflicts on families. *Little Miss Broadway* (1938), for instance, follows the typical Shirley Temple formula, opening with Betsy (Temple) at an orphanage. The Sheas, friends of her late parents, agree to take her in. Somewhat reluctantly she leaves the known community of the orphanage, characterised by music, for the unknown community of this new 'family'. It quickly becomes apparent that the Sheas, who run the imperilled Hotel Variety, are part of a down-and-out community of loveable but somewhat wacky vaudeville performers. Sarah Wendling (Edna May Oliver), the owner of the building in which the hotel is located, wants to evict the performers because she sees them as noisy, unsavoury characters. By chance, Betsy runs into Sarah's nephew, Roger (George Murphy), who also has a major stake in the building, and she charms him with her vivacious song and dance. Roger then works with the residents of the hotel to thwart Sarah's plan. At the end, the whole community of Hotel Variety comes together to put on a show in order to convince the judge to keep the hotel operating. The show thus becomes the means by which the community is stabilised and its future assured. This scenario is quintessential Shirley Temple: the orphan who through song and dance ingratiates herself with a family or with some other character (in this case Roger) who has the power to stabilise her family situation (here, Hotel Variety).

If Durbin does not play the orphan like Temple, her character performs, as Schatz suggests, more or less the same narrative function of stabilising a fragmented family situation. Similar to *Little Miss Broadway*, *One Hundred Men and a Girl* (1937) centres on a group of unemployed performers, in this case, musicians. John Cardwell (Adolphe Menjou), an out-of-work trombone player, is behind on his rent. To gain more time he lies to his landlady, saying that he has been hired by the celebrated conductor Leopold Stokowski. Patsy, his daughter (Durbin), overhears and is elated, thinking her father has finally received his big break. With no heart to dissuade his daughter in her moment of joy, he goes out to seek an audition with Stokowski. While he does not get in to see the maestro, he does find a purse with a large sum of money, which allows him to pay the rent. When Patsy realises what has happened, she insists that the purse be returned. Delivering it, she is persuaded to sing and from this point on, Patsy's voice is the instrument that organises the unemployed musicians into a viable community, that is, an orchestra. This is the voice that opens the door to Stokowski, without whose endorsement the orchestra cannot survive. Yet, importantly, when she sings, she does so without pay. For whereas the instrumentalists play for a living, she sings for her art. This arrangement allows her father to reclaim his traditional position in the family. At the end of the film, Durbin sings to the accompaniment of the orchestra. Everybody plays so that Patsy can make her music; and in making this music her father finds his place in a society where he can support her.

As with *One Hundred Men and a Girl*, one of the concerns of *Everybody Sing* (1938) is the mending of a broken family, but whereas the family trauma of the former is imposed from outside (the Cardwell family's troubles stem from extended unemployment) that of the latter is more or less self-inflicted (the all-encompassing immersion in the work of the theatre threatens the family). The troubles with the play – father (Reginald Owen) as playwright, mother (Billie Burke) as lead, eldest daughter (Lynne Carver) as ingénue – reproduce those of the actual Bellaire family. Meanwhile, Judy (Judy Garland), the youngest daughter and the only member of the family not involved in the production, is neglected. At first seeming a dysfunctional character – she is kicked out of school for singing jazz during music class – Judy proves whole, and it is her family who turn out to be dysfunctional, her parents at each other's throats, her sister preoccupied with learning her part, and no one making time to listen to Judy when she tries to tell them that she's been expelled. In fact, her expulsion is in this sense a sign of her sanity *vis-à-vis* the state of her family: she is the only member of the family who rebels against 'proper' culture and so she is the only one able to escape the dysfunctional economy of the legitimate theatre. It is indeed Judy who, by embracing the values of popular culture, ultimately saves the family from financial ruin. She runs away so that she can secretly work in a revue. The legitimate theatre production that the rest of her family is involved in cannot even come together for a single performance but her show is a great success, and at the end her family joins Judy on the revue stage to comically take final bows. Her success brings success to the family.

In *Little Miss Broadway*, *One Hundred Men and a Girl* and *Everybody Sing*, family and the community it mirrors move from an initially troubled state to one of relative stability. The success of the final performance is important not simply because it testifies to individual triumph but also, and more importantly, because it secures the success of family and community. As Altman points out (1987), the final 'show' typically serves a doubling function, with a fusion of romantic couple and show. The doubling necessarily works somewhat differently with these films because they are centred on a kid rather than a couple, even when, as in *Everybody Sing*, the film contains a romantic couple. In these films, then, the success of the show redounds to the family and community rather than the couple. The display of communal harmony at the end is a spectacle of restoration that venerates the continuity of society.

Remaking Community

The Busby Berkeley MGM musicals starring Garland and Rooney follow a similar script except that the romantic couple is now the focus. Nevertheless, the thematic issue of restoring order to broken or incomplete family situations remains a major concern. Putting on the show to help the settlement house in *Babes on Broadway* illustrates how a romantic couple can be placed at the centre of a film whose thematic focus remains one of restoring community. Here, couple and community are connected not directly but through the show: it takes the romance to put on the show, and the show to help the kids. The show – product of romance – is thus the instrument by which the couple helps the kids. Yet the couple itself only produces the show; they do not belong to the community. The show, indeed, divides them from it. Instead of integrating with the community that they helped *with* the show, the couple pursues the community *of* the show, namely, Broadway.

An intermediary step where couple and community are better aligned can be found in *Babes in Arms* (1939). The first part begins with the birth of Mickey (Mickey Rooney), the rise of the Moran family vaudeville act, and the descent of this family from fame and fortune to ruin as vaudeville theatres close. The collapse of vaudeville shatters the entire community, and the remainder of the film is concerned with Mickey and the kids' attempt to put their society back together by transforming the family act into a communal show, represented by the spectacular finale that closes the film. The Broadway show staged by the kids reaffirms the values of the show business community while acknowledging that a community cannot remain viable simply by preserving older values. The breach opened up by this transformation out of vaudeville remains and is visible in the treatment of Mickey's father, Joe (Charles Winninger). Having soured on the business, which he feels has ruthlessly turned its back on the values of traditional vaudeville culture, Joe is reconciled to the new form of entertainment through a ruse of his son: Mickey persuades the impresario of his show to hire Joe as a consultant to coach the younger generation in the ways of the business. The catch is that Mickey and the others are clearly in no need of such coaching. The job is therefore superfluous, purely symbolic, a way perhaps for Mickey to assuage his oedipal guilt. In this respect, the film is a tale of Mickey's coming of age as he takes the place of his powerless father, who is destitute and unable to defend the family against Martha Steele's (Margaret Hamilton) threat to send the kids to 'work houses' so they can learn a 'useful' trade. The romance of Mickey and Patsy (Judy Garland) grows with the success of the show, and their union is the flip side of the weakened family structure controlled by the father. Family has been displaced by a couple now free to seek its way in the world.

Much the same thing might be said of *The Wizard of Oz*, another MGM production of 1939. Indeed, it *has* been said:

> *The Wizard of Oz* is a film whose driving force is the inadequacy of adults, even of good adults, and how the weakness of grown-ups forces children to take control of their own destinies, and so, ironically, to grow up themselves. The journey from Kansas to Oz is a right of passage from a world in which Dorothy's parent-substitutes, Auntie Em and Uncle Henry, are powerless to save her dog

Toto from the marauding Miss Gulch, into a world where the people are her own size, and in which she is never, ever treated as a child, but as a heroine. (Rushdie 1992: 10)

Miss Gulch resembles Martha Steele in *Babes in Arms* – and not just because both are played by Margaret Hamilton. She is the personification of a demand for a social order that would dictate the terms of community from above, not by a harmonious social accord drawn up and ratified by the members of the community. As such, Miss Gulch functions less to obstruct Dorothy than to reveal the inherent weakness of the family structure, already attenuated by virtue of the fact that Dorothy's parents are absent. It is this weakness Dorothy must grow up to overcome.

The weakness of the family in the face of the moral (and economic) force of Miss Gulch is apparent not just in the inability of Auntie Em and Uncle Henry to protect Toto but in the oppressive (sepia-toned) greyness of Kansas and its lack of song. The control Miss Gulch's morality exercises over the family structure of the farm seemingly extends across all of Kansas, rendering all oppressed persons speechless against injustice. 'For 23 years I've been dying to tell you what I think of you', Auntie Em tells Miss Gulch. But an internalised morality prevents Em from speaking truth to power: 'And now, being a Christian woman, I can't say it.' This morality imposes a stark reality on the farm, and its lack of song is a sign that its community is defined only by economics. Only Dorothy sings in Kansas, and she sings not of community but of escape 'over the rainbow'. Oddly, then, music serves not to bind the family into a community, but to separate Dorothy from it. Oz is the colourful musical world of which Dorothy dreams, but she apparently learns that song (the fantasy world that it brings into being) is no substitute for family. For despite its lack of song, the Kansas she returns to is not the Kansas she left. In her absence, or perhaps through her absence, the farm has evolved into a community bound by the love of Dorothy. This notion possibly redeems Dorothy's otherwise improbable incantation that 'there's no place like home'. What she longs for – her real dream – is the negation of Miss Gulch's Kansas by the transforming strength of 'home' and family. In denying that the dream is Oz, and that Oz is a dream, she gives Oz a reality that supports her wish for a really transformed 'home': if Oz exists in reality, the 'home' she so desperately desires may be no dream, either, but real. Dorothy's wish to leave Oz for 'home' is simply the flip side, or rather the second part, of her dream to escape Miss Gulch's Kansas. She simply cannot be at home in the magical land of Oz, however enchanting it may be, because it is only a way station towards her real destination.

The Magic of Music

If Dorothy's desire to leave the song of Oz behind and return to Kansas seems unconvincing, this is because culture has long invested music with the magical ability to transform social discord into communal harmony. It affirms, Jacques Attali says, 'that society is possible' (1985: 29). From this perspective, it is not surprising that magic takes most overt form in 'family' musicals, that is, those pedagogical films designed to instruct children in the terms of social harmony. Many animated musicals of Disney fit this mould: a child comes of age by learning the song of community. In *Beauty and the Beast* (1991), Belle initially sings outside the community of the town; she and her father do not fit in. But she joins the music of the enchanted castle, breaks the spell, and thus integrates herself into the community of the castle. More pointedly, Ariel in *The Little Mermaid* (1989) exchanges her voice for the ability to walk on land. But her desire to leave the community of the sea to join human society is then blocked precisely by her inability to sing. Although these films, like many of the Disney animated features (for example, *Snow White and the Seven Dwarfs* (1937), *Cinderella* (1950) and *Sleeping Beauty* (1959)), are literally fairytales centred less on family than on romance, the youthful status of the heroines places them in a category similar to the one Garland and Rooney occupy in the Berkeley musicals. The main difference is that, because the members of the couple are not initially part of the same community their romance and eventual union are about the conception of a new community in marriage rather than its reproduction through the extension of family. In both *Beauty and the Beast* and *The Little Mermaid*, the formation of community is blocked by magic, and song is the instrument that dispels the magic, indeed appropriates its power for community. Disney villains typically do not sing, but wield magic for personal gain; their magic is not the communal magic of song, which is the point of their vulnerability. For instance, Ariel regains her voice just in time to unleash a song that breaks Ursula's spell, allowing the mermaid to take her rightful place in a human community de-fined by song rather than being controlled by Ursula's magic.

Other films align music directly with magic and the family. In such films as *Mary Poppins* (1964), *Chitty Chitty Bang Bang* (1968) and *Bedknobs and Broom-sticks* (1971), music itself possesses magical properties. When the children sing Mary Poppins' (Julie Andrews) music, for instance, they suddenly have the power to animate toys, jump into pictures, and so forth. If prior to Mary's arrival the chil-dren had devolved into undisciplined 'little beasts' adept at driving away govern-esses, Mary can easily address their behaviour by teaching them to sing and thus restoring to them the wonder of childhood. Yet the magic of music cannot long persist in the presence of family discord. This is why the film centres on the adults Mary/Bert (Dick Van Dyke) and Winifred (Glynis Johns)/George (David Tomlinson), and why the children often seem almost incidental. The children are a *measure* of domestic harmony, not a *cause* of family discord. Winifred and George are musi-cal even prior to the arrival of Mary, yet they continually sing past one another in songs of bloated egoism; that is, they sing only from and of their own perspective oblivious to how that affects the family as a whole. Mary's primary task is to get Winifred and George to direct their song towards each other and the family. As the family skips off to the park with everyone singing 'Let's Go Fly a Kite', it is clear that Mary's work is done. She has restored harmony to the family.

And so it goes with society as a whole, a point *Mary Poppins* underscores in its finale. The sky is covered with dancing kites, the whole board of George's bank is out participating in the spectacle, and an offscreen chorus picks up the song from the family, transforming it into the song of community. 'The entire history of tonal music ... amounts to an attempt to make people believe in a consensual representation of the world' (Attali 1985: 46). This, too, is the pedagogical function of the musical: it teaches the power of song. Its magical, make-believe world would make us believe in the reality of the social harmony it proffers. Song is a figure of reconciliation, a promise that any discord might be resolved. In the musical, community is family, family community. And song is the sound that joins the individual to the family and the family to the community in one exquisite bond. Everybody sing: the bond of community persists only so long as we believe in the reality of the song. Therein lies the precariousness of its magic.

3

Is It a Wonderful Life?: Families and Laughter in American Film Comedies

ANDREW HORTON

'I want my family to love me.'
– Royal Tenenbaum (Gene Hackman) in *The Royal Tenenbaums*

Is there anything more 'American' at Christmas than families gathering around the television screen – small, medium or super 52"-wide plasma HD – to watch, yet one more time, as if no amount of watching would be enough to drink in all its nourishment, Frank Capra's charming and funny film, *It's a Wonderful Life* (1946)? Capra's film vision of smalltown America is certainly about family and it celebrates Christmas, rural values, angels who come to earth and, yes, LIFE ITSELF. But as customary and joyful a tradition as such a family viewing of Capra's film has become, and American ratings will confirm that it has indeed become a holiday ritual, we should remember that this classic is more drama than comedy, since the plot concerns a man (James Stewart) who, feeling that as husband, father and businessman he is a failure, wishes to commit suicide. 'Is It a Wonderful Life?' we find ourselves asking at the end, and this is perhaps a more accurate title for this classic that skates close to disaster and tragedy only to conclude with a glorious and satisfying seasonal family reunion and celebration.

Families tend to appear in American screen comedies in exactly this equivocal way, as sites of actual or potential disaster and as sanctuaries and reasons for reunion and celebration. As categories, both 'family' and 'comedy' are shifting and multi-faceted, and have received a wide range of attention onscreen in the United States. Yet family as the real *focus* of a film, and especially of a comedy film, is not everywhere to be found. When we go back to the early comedies of Charlie Chaplin, for example, we may recall that the Tramp ended up frequently walking down a highway (in that trademark bowlegged duck-walk), his back to the camera, alone and with no home, no friends, no wife, no family at all. This was the lighthearted image that raised our spirits. Indeed, although Hollywood has made thousands of comedies in the years since Chaplin's films, only a few focus on families or family life. In fact, of the AFI Best 100 Comedy List elected in 2000, only a handful could be called 'comedies featuring family life in some central way'. These would include George Cukor's *The Philadelphia Story* (1940), Preston Sturges's *The Miracle of Morgan's Creek* (1944), Vincente Minnelli's *Father of the Bride* (1950), Mike Nichols' *The Graduate* (1967), Melville Shavelson's *Yours, Mine and Ours* (1968), Hal Ashby's *Harold and Maude* (1971), Norman Jewison's *Moonstruck* (1987) and Chris Columbus's *Mrs. Doubtfire* (1993). To this list, among many others, we could add further pungent examples such as Ron Howard's *Parenthood* (1989), Charles Shyer's lively remake of *Father of the Bride* (1991) and its sequel, *Father of the Bride Part II* (1995), Nancy Meyers' *The Parent Trap* (1998), which was a remake of the 1961 Disney film of the same title based on the 1953 British film, *Twice Upon a Time*, Jay Roach's *Meet the Parents* (2000), Wes Anderson's *The Royal Tenenbaums* (2001), Nia Vardalos's one-woman play-turned-film in Joel Zwick's *My Big Fat Greek Wedding* (2002), Steve Carr's *Daddy Day Care* (2003), Jon Favreau's *Elf* (2003), Christopher Erskin's *Johnson Family Vacation* (2004), Andrew Adamson, Kelly Asbury and Conrad Vernon's *Shrek 2* (2004), David Dobkin's *Wedding Crashers* (2005) and Chris Miller and Raman Hui's *Shrek the Third* (2007). But how exactly *is* family life portrayed as central in such films as these? What is it about the American family that makes it suitable as a nexus for contemporary humour?

I am defining 'family comedy' as embracing some grouping of parents (or a parent) and children (or a child) and 'other relatives', be they grandparents, uncles, aunts or cousins, and, of course, friends of the family and in-laws. The American family comedy is what we can call a 'cross-generational' form of comedy, for it involves characters of different ages and generations who often demonstrate conflicting values and attitudes – whose contention with one another over some issue of value and attitude, indeed, is the motor element of the ongoing joke that the film recounts. *My Big Fat Greek Wedding*, for example, makes us laugh not just because we are watching an outsider to traditional Greek culture (John Corbett) trying frantically and with delicious awkwardness to catch on and catch up in order to marry his beloved, but also because we enjoy the humorous clash between parents who were born in Greece and are trying to maintain their cultural identity on one hand and a daughter who very much wants to become something else, on the other.

The screen family conceived in Hollywood has been watchable, perhaps even more consistently, on television. American television has been the 'showcase' of family comedies from its beginning as a medium that came into the American living room after World War Two to provide family entertainment. *I Love Lucy* (1951–57) and *The Honeymooners* (1955–56) ruled in the 1950s, depicting week after week, with liturgical predictability, the harangues and foibles of American marriages at a time when women were coming into new social powers that men were not openly ready to surrender. Soon later came paeans to paternal wisdom and family harmony like *The Adventures of Ozzie & Harriet* (1952–56) and *Leave It to Beaver* (1957–63), followed by depictions of quirky family relations in *The Andy Griffith Show*

(1960–68), *The Dick Van Dyke Show* (1961–66), *The Beverly Hillbillies* (1962–71), *The Mary Tyler Moore Show* (1970–77) and *The Cosby Show* (1984–92), to mention but a few of the many sitcoms that aired successfully on American networks. The boundary-pushing *All in the Family* (1971–79) managed to present a working-class racist, Archie Bunker (Carroll O'Connor), as a central character and critiqued him as well. More recently, the longest running 'sitcom' in American TV history, *The Simpsons* (1989–), has persistently suggested both our ongoing interest in family comedy and the power of animation to 'stretch' comedy to exaggerated forms while keeping characters from ever ageing as they do in shows with living actors. Unsurprisingly, Hollywood has tried to build on such TV successes with cinematic transformations including John Shultz's revision of *The Honeymooners* (2005) as an updated African American family comedy.

Recent surveys suggest that most American homes today have two or more televisions, not to mention video and DVD players as well as computers and a multitude of video games. Given the multi-faceted activity of families watching television and movies, playing video games and cruising the Internet on a regular basis, it is no wonder many speak of home 'media centres'. But in the early 1950s, as Lynn Spigel has well explained, television was occupying a special place in American homes: 'The introduction of the machine (television) into the home meant that family members needed to come to terms with the presence of a communication medium that might transform older modes of family interaction' (1992: 36). Since in America the move was towards the suburbs, the transformation of family interactions was in part also defined by the concept of having a home with surrounding land away from the centre of the town or city. Charles Kuralt has explained that in terms of numbers, by the end of the 1950s, Americans had purchased over 70 million television sets and produced more than 40 million babies ('When Television Was Young'). Put even more clearly, surveys show that in America, watching television ranks second – after eating meals – in 'the list of activities a family does together' (Tueth 2005: 135). As much or more than films, then, the classic American television comedy based on family life had a profound influence on the way people saw themselves in families, organised their interaction and hoped together for a jointly imagined future (see Leibman 1995).

'Family Comedy'

Since the era of ancient Greek culture, comedy has tended to be classified into one or the other of two distinct categories. First, there are what are called 'anarchistic' comedies, in which one or more central characters have a 'crazy' idea and carry it out (see Horton 1991: 7). The controlling logic, then, deviates from or transgresses against received and dominant social forces, values and principles of organisation. In Aristophanes' *Lysistrata*, for example, the crazy idea is to go on a sex strike to end war. In Monty Python's *Life of Brian* (1979), the crazy idea is an implicit question: what if you were a newborn in the crib next to Jesus? To return briefly to *My Big Fat Greek Wedding*, what if the new member of the family understood absolutely nothing about how life was lived here – did not speak the language, did not understand the culture, did not share our past? This brand of comedy tends strongly towards broad farce, satire and comic surrealism. It is comedy with no compromises and no need to be 'true to life'. Woody Allen's *Everything You Always Wanted to Know About Sex* But Were Afraid to Ask* (1972) focuses at one point on a house-sized mammary gland roving the countryside.

Since late Greek and Roman times, romance has developed as a second large focus of comedy (Horton 1991: 16). Here, what's implied is (a) boy meets girl, (b) boy loses girl, but (c) they find each other again by story's end, where we have a wedding or 'happily-ever-after' wrap up. Important for this form of comedy is a culminating sense of compromise as two very different characters learn to get along with each other. How, we wonder, laughing at the improbability of it all, can these two misfits possibly manage to see their way into a union? Thus, whether we are talking about the middle-aged obsessive compulsive Jack Nicholson and the much younger down-to-earth Helen Hunt in *As Good as It Gets* (1997) or Clark Gable and Claudette Colbert in *It Happened One Night* (1934); about the headstrong Tracy Lord (Katharine Hepburn) and the flippant C. K. Dexter Haven (Cary Grant) in *The Philadelphia Story*, or the hopelessly incompetent Julius Kelp – and his hopelessly arrogant alter ego Buddy Love – (Jerry Lewis) and the kindly and well-meaning Stella Purdy (Stella Stevens) in *The Nutty Professor* (1963), there persists in the background a clear vision of social reality as we know it, against which the 'odd' characters can be defined. (*The Nutty Professor* is not always regarded as a family film at all, let alone a romance; but it can be seen as being implicitly about an extremely eccentric pair (Elvia Allman, Howard Morris) producing a child (Lewis) so very strange by conventional standards that it seems impossible he will ever find a mate and make his own family.) In the end, a 'giving way' on both sides is mandatory in order for two individuals to find a way to actually live together. Buddy Love having more or less evaporated, Kelp becomes just a little less nerdly while Stella becomes just a little more crazy; Dexter and Tracy relinquish a little of their insouciance and hauteur, respectively; and so on.

What we could call 'family comedy' falls somewhere between the anarchic and romantic types, since it is not a 'genre' in and of itself. Like romantic comedy, 'family comedy' is often about learning the art of compromise so that family members with very different personalities or goals can get along together. One cannot imagine a nuttier and more diverse family, for example, than that represented in Ron Howard's *Parenthood* ('Life' says Steve Martin's wife, Mary Steenburgen, 'is messy'), yet by the comedy's end, as the whole tribe looks on at the baby of one of the daughters, family members bizarre and diverse are all accepting each other. Yet at the same time, cinematic family comedies can celebrate a rather anarchistic sense of family, where little possibility of compromise seems to exist and a challenge is being mounted to what we take to be the natural order. Wes Anderson's *The Royal Tenenbaums*, for instance, posits three children born in ten years and then a separation that never became a legal divorce leading to what one child calls, 'two decades of failure, betrayal and disaster'.

The 'comedy of manners' that British and French theatre has given us – in works by such renowned playwrights as Oliver Goldsmith with *She Stoops to Conquer* (1773), Pierre Marivaux with *La Dispute* (1744), Richard Brinsley Sheridan with *The School for Scandal* (1777) and Noël Coward with *Private Lives* (1930) (see Vineberg 2005: 1) – represents the greatest extent of family comedy's progress towards being a full-bodied genre. Comedies of manners involve families of the upper class who are constrained using the 'right' manners of their social class if they are to survive and thrive. Oscar Wilde's *The Importance of Being Earnest* (1895) mocks the comedy of manners: considerable attention is given to – indeed the story turns on – the importance of a man's name (and, by implication, social standing). Steve Vineberg has called such a form, as it appears in American cinema, 'high comedy' (2005: 2) and he points out that although most American family comedies are set in the middle class (in general, Hollywood cinema has disregarded the existence of an upper class in American society) there remain some important – I would add, memorable – representatives of the 'high' category that treat the foibles of the American aristocracy. 'High comedy', he notes, can most clearly be seen in Cukor's *The Philadelphia Story*, adapted from Philip Barry's hit Broadway play.

Consider a significant element in this film that appears in so many subsequent family comedies, the 'wedding-soon-to-take-place' plot, as the young and wealthy Philadelphia divorcée Tracy Lord is about to marry a non-aristocratic simple and honest man, George Kittredge (John Howard). The wedding framework is a perfect set-up for a family comedy since it opens each member of the family to the joys, contradictions and problems of the changes that the marriage of one member will bring to the others. Thus, as we will see in more detail, so many family comedies, from *Meet the Parents* and its sequel, *Meet the Fockers* (2004), to *Father of the Bride* – the original and its Steve Martin remake – to Jennifer Lopez and Jane Fonda fighting it out as future daughter-in-law and frightful future mother-in-law in *Monster-in-Law* (2005), are constructed around the 'wedding-to-be'. What will happen if the wedding takes place and the new social world is created? Could the wedding be interrupted or stopped, and what might happen if it were? Could the wedding-to-be – horror of horrors!, but also pleasure of pleasures! – be founded upon some strange and incalculable mistake?

The Philadelphia Story sets up its family 'high comedy' by showing how Tracy, her high-born but utterly scatterbrained mother (Mary Nash), her much younger and very precocious sister (Virginia Weidler), her cheating but loving father (John Halliday) and the multitude of servants in the Lord estate manage to get along with each other as family and as members of the family staff. Into this mix of warmth and zaniness is stirred Tracy's first husband, C. K. Dexter Haven, who returns to witness the fun of this second wedding. Dexter is as hooked on Tracy as he ever was, and has no charity for the new beau, so his hope, maintained in perfectly casual silence almost to the end of the picture, is that the wedding plans will fall apart. As if we don't have enough comic chaos yet, add a gossip-centred newspaper reporter, Macaulay Connor (James Stewart), and his canny (too canny?) photographer-assistant (Ruth Hussey). Connor proceeds to fall in love with Tracy himself, thus putting Hepburn at the centre of three very different men's wishes and interests.

What develops very much resembles a typical romantic comedy, as Hepburn and Stewart are attracted to each other and have their night-before-the-wedding together (albeit in all innocence). But what is also unfolding in Donald Ogden Stuart's Academy Award-winning script is how much Hepburn and Grant still care for each other. This realisation leads to the glorious ending, in which Hepburn 'cancels' her marriage to Kittredge and marries Grant for the second time! Stanley Cavell has written well about how we can actually speak of a sub-genre of Hollywood romantic comedy, 'the Hollywood comedy of remarriage' (1981: 133), of which this film is a sterling example. *The Philadelphia Story* celebrates how two lovers – ex-husband and ex-wife in this case – can meet up later in life once they are 'smarter', and come to have a successful and loving relationship the second time around. The anarchy in *The Philadelphia Story* is, perhaps, a little harder to detect: the strange, 'unnatural' state of affairs is the hypothetical arrangement by which Katharine Hepburn and Cary Grant might *not* come together in wedded bliss – a state of affairs, further, which appears to be grounding the action of the story from the beginning (when Grant punches Hepburn in the nose) to within a breath of the finale.

Such a 'remarriage' scheme works, too, for straight-on romantic comedy, as in Howard Hawks's *His Girl Friday* (1940) where newspaper editor Walter Burns (Cary Grant) and star reporter Hildy Johnson (Rosalind Russell) remarry. But *The Philadelphia Story* has a dense, variegated and notably visible family surrounding the lovers, with the final exchange between not Grant and Hepburn but Hepburn and her father. He once seemed distant and uncaring, 'Do you know how I feel?' she asks him, 'Like a human being.' And he replies, 'Do you know how I feel? I feel proud.' Thus, Hepburn has remarried the man she realises she truly loves (and suddenly able to see her own history, knows she always did love) but there has been a strong family acceptance and rejuvenation, as well. Similar 'remarriages' can be seen in many of the family comedies. *Father of the Bride Part II* is not about a wedding at all, but about the daughter (Kimberly Williams) announcing her pregnancy and following through to birth; the 'remarriage' becomes the re-uniting of her parents, Steve Martin and Diane Keaton, who push through their mid-life crises with Keaton becoming pregnant and a mother again as the plot is tied up.

Families often have important moments in comedies that are predominantly organised around other topics. The family scene or family moment can thus be an important hiatus in the plot, or a key background against which unfamilial action plays out. The family can be implicit through a film. The Coen Brothers, for instance, often bring a strong family element to their own particular style of comedy. In *O Brother, Where Art Thou?* (2000), loosely based on Homer's *Odyssey*, while most of the film concerns the comic misadventures of George Clooney, John Turturro and Tim Blake Nelson in escaping a Southern chain gang and making good, Clooney's actual goal is to meet up again with his wife and daughters in a hilarious variation on Odysseus's return to Penelope. Similarly, *Fargo* (1996) is clearly something of a crime comedy spoof but by film's end the relationship of police officer Frances McDormand, seven months pregnant, and her work-at-home artist husband (John Carroll Lynch) provides us with a 'happy ending' as they look forward to becoming a family. *Raising Arizona* (1987) is a family comedy, because the central focus is on Nicolas Cage and Holly Hunter, who cannot have children of their own, forming a family by kidnapping one of a set of quintuplets. The culmination, which is Cage's dream of the future, is a glorious family moment in which he foresees a Thanksgiving family feast when he and Holly have become old grandparents!

Variations on the American Dream Family

Given that screen comedies involving family seem invariably to play with the question as to whether family problems can be rectified; whether incomplete families can be completed; whether family wounds can successfully be healed; whether divided families can come together; and whether families that are implicit or profoundly desired can come to be, it can be argued that as a genre the family comedy ultimately holds the family up as an ideal form. Is there an American dream family? Certainly one dream for many viewers since World War Two, at least, has been a particular stereotyped ideal of a successful middle-class Mom and Dad (thus a husband and wife) with careers well under way, parenting two or three children in a comfortable suburban home. But hardly anyone is unaware that statistics show the divorce rate to be roughly 60 per cent of all marriages and that there is a growing gap between those who have a comfortable life and those who do not. Families are divided between blood-related ones and those that form out of need or choice or both under the terms of a broadened understanding of 'family'. Hal Ashby's *Harold and Maude*, based on a strong script by Colin Higgins, exemplifies a fascinating – but far from typical – family-style relationship (that goes considerably beyond friendship while stopping short of legal wedlock) between two perfectly fitted 'misfits', 20-year-old Harold (Bud Cort), who repeatedly attempts suicide, and 79-year-old life-loving Maude (Ruth Gordon). The two are not related, nor do they enter into a legal relationship, and the closeness they come to share recalls that of a strong grandmother-to-grandson relationship more than merely that of two acquaintances of differing ages. Yet something transcends this and seems to make of Harold and Maude's link a wild new kind of marriage: the extreme sensitivity of one to the other; the comfort in one another's presence; the mutual depth of regard.

We can stretch the definition of a 'family comedy' even further by including such films as Leonard Nimoy's *Three Men and a Baby* (1987), adapted from the French hit *Three Men and a Cradle* (1985): three hip bachelors care for a baby whom one of them fathered. Traditional parents Tom Selleck, Steve Guttenberg and Ted Danson are certainly not, but the four do become a loving 'family' by film's end. 'Family' can thus be such a conscious configuration of friends caring enough to raise a child who would not otherwise have had a loving home. A similarly all-male and similarly protective family is to be found in Mike Nichols' *The Birdcage* (1996), where two middle-aged, and very settled, gay lovers, Albert (Nathan Lane) and Armand (Robin Williams) go to extreme lengths to protect the hopes of Armand's son (Val Goldman) for marriage with Barbara (Calista Flockhart), the daughter of a rabidly homophobic senator. In both films – *The Birdcage* was an American remake of Edouard Molinaro's *La Cage aux folles* (1978) – the loving family bond transcends sexual orientation, gender identity, political affiliation and social status, not to say sexuality itself. The men in *Three Men and a Baby* are so busy with the kid they have little time for fantasising their next encounter.

A very different view of America, family and comedy emerges depending on whether families live in small towns and the countryside or in cities and suburbia.

Smalltown, Urban and Suburban Family Comedies

Frank Capra's *It's a Wonderful Life* does end up championing smalltown American values, placing the unified family as a vital support for nationhood, a transmitter of cultural hegemony and a vehicle for personal transcendence. We have certainly had a number of family comedies that nostalgically look back to the simpler 'good old days' of rural America before suburbs and urban life became a reality for most Americans. The family cast in the bucolic, agricultural mode tends to display a rigid and traditional gender hierarchy, a focus on marriage as both revolutionary and apotheotic, and a fondness for stable inter-generational bonds, all this even in the face of encroaching modernity with its thrusts and changes.

Preston Sturges, who never lived in a small town in his real life, cast several of his films in a mythical rural America where no crimes seem to be committed, where people enjoy direct and open relationships with one another, and where families can embrace and put up with nutty relatives and crazy neighbours, no matter how zany, in the name of constancy, neighbourliness, tradition and love. This is notably the case even in films Sturges only wrote for other filmmakers. *Remember the Night* (1940), a Sturges script directed by Mitchell Leisen, has New York attorney Fred MacMurray recuperating shoplifting criminal Barbara Stanwyck by bringing her to his Indiana hometown to meet his mother, his aunt and his stalwart Midwestern community during the Christmas holidays. There is something of the spirit of Norman Rockwell meeting Salvador Dalí in Sturges's comic yet touching portrait of an America that was more myth than reality, but Sturges does suggest there is much that is worthwhile in such rural communities that cities such as New York have missed or never known. Needless to say, once the criminal and her prosecutor are safe in the protective haven of the mythical small town, they fall in love, and the film's problem is raised of how justice and the dictates of romance can both be served.

With two other comedies Sturges returned to families in small American towns. Both are set during World War Two and were filmed while the war was actually ongoing. *The Miracle of Morgan's Creek* (1944) plays with the idea that families have to be intentionally and consciously formed. The film has smalltown beauty Trudy Kockenlocker (Betty Hutton) telling her father (William Demarest) that she is out on a date with the most innocent young man in town, Norval Jones (Eddie Bracken), when she actually goes to a wild party, winding up very drunk, married and pregnant and unable to remember who the father is. Demarest helps to engineer a wedding between Bracken and Hutton when he hears what has happened, and Bracken becomes a nationally acknowledged 'hero' in uniform, even though he has a 4-F draft status, as Hutton heads to the hospital and gives birth to six boys. Sturges followed this deeply ironic comedy with *Hail the Conquering Hero* (1944). Woodrow Lafayette Pershing Truesmith (Bracken again), in a uniform that isn't his own, returns to his small town and his mother with six Marines insisting that he is a 'conquering hero', when he was actually discharged from the Marines because of hay fever! Soon, his family expands beyond just himself and his mother as his old flame Libby (Ella Raines) leaves her husband-to-be to marry Bracken and as he winds up being elected mayor because, once he admits to not being a hero at all, everyone considers him a paragon of honesty. If the bonds of family might seem tenuous in these arch slapstick parodies larded with misunderstandings, false postures and accidents, the smalltown setting offers an atmosphere of ingenuousness and sincerity that works to substantiate the feelings people have for one another, regardless of their 'official' claims to identity. The smalltown family comedy is thus not merely hokey or charming, but invokes the tension between the deepest human needs for family bonds and the more superficial, contingent, vacillating facts of modern life.

Family comedies in the city have a different character – more flavourful, more enigmatic, ultimately more moving. Norman Jewison's *Moonstruck* remains one of the most memorable of these. Winner of three Academy Awards (Best Actress to Cher, Best Supporting Actress to Olympia Dukakis and Best Original Screenplay to John Patrick Shanley), this ensemble comedy is set in an Italian neighbourhood in Brooklyn. The film opens with a skyline shot of New York in the 1980s, with the twin World Trade Center towers glowing in clear sight years before their destruction, and an effusion of the energy and promise the big city carries for relationships however accidental, however strange. This family comedy of 'remarriage' centres on Loretta Castorini (Cher), a thirtysomething widow on the verge of marrying the rather safe, conventional Johnny Cammareri (Danny Aiello), not for love but for convenience. But she falls in love with his younger – and emotionally more tempestuous – brother, Ronny (Nicolas Cage). 'Nothing can replace the family, Loretta', cries Aiello on the phone before the wedding. His mother is dying; the idea of family has taken over his world. 'Do you love him?' demands her mother Rose (Dukakis) when early on Loretta announces she will marry Johnny. 'No', replies Loretta, to which Dukakis rejoins, 'Good! … Do you like him?' To this Loretta replies, 'Yes.' 'Good!' says the mother – no long speech is needed to convey simple truths about trying to live without the pain of being in love.

A rich tapestry of minor characters is woven into this complex Italian American film that keeps us laughing at the same time that tears are evoked by such fine performances as those of Cher and Dukakis. Shanley's finely-honed dialogue makes every scene memorable for the comic insight given to each character and to family relations. 'When you love them', says Rose, 'they drive you crazy.'

The film is aptly titled, for while during daylight each family member plays out one form of deception or other – Rose thinks her husband is cheating on her – at night they become 'moonstruck' and finally come to accept a more forgiving and giving form of 'family' life. As Roger Ebert (n.d.) notes:

> The most enchanting quality about *Moonstuck* is the hardest to describe, and that is the movie's tone. Reviews of the movie tend to make it sound like a madcap ethnic comedy, and that it is. But there is something more here, a certain bittersweet yearning that comes across as ineffably romantic, and a certain magical quality that is reflected in the film's title.

Certainly, no American family comedy better presents and explores the overlapping worlds of romance and familial ties than Jewison's enduring film. Cher's father Cosmo (Vincent Gardenia) is in fact cheating on Rose and Rose herself has a tender 'out-of-marriage' evening when she meets a student-seducing professor, Perry (John Mahoney), who is suddenly taken by this older woman. Meanwhile, Loretta does everything possible to avoid falling in love with Ronny, who lost one love and then one hand in a bread-slicing machine when his brother got him to look the wrong way. 'I've not been lucky', she says to him, tentatively, over the kitchen table, as they sit quietly in what is obviously a mounting sexual tension. 'I don't believe in luck', he answers, bluntly.

With considerably more bluntness and rhythm than we would find in a small-town family comedy, *Moonstruck* brilliantly highlights how romance and family life intertwine and how, despite obvious conflicts, the two contribute towards, and ultimately help, each other. If the 'bottom line' for family comedy is the acceptance of a diversity that seems impossible at first, Cage gives a fresh take on this theme when near the end, crippled and in despair, he cries out to Cher, 'Love makes things a mess' and goes on to affirm: 'We are here to break our hearts and love each other.' They proceed to do so.

'It ain't over till it's over', opines Rose at one point. By the end of the comedy, Loretta is with Ronny as the whole family gathers around, each with a champagne glass in hand – including the now jilted Johnny who has realised that marriage is out of the question for him: his ailing mother has recovered and any actual wedding would kill her! They all toast the 'family', having finally accepted each other, foibles and all. 'A la famiglia!' 'To the family!' The camera tracks through the rooms of the family home, ending on a photograph of the original Italian immigrant great-grandparents. Tears and laughter mix and become the ingredients of an enduring urban and ethnic social bond. In the same way, the accompaniment of laughter by tears marks the urban family comedy in general.

Most American family comedies are of the urban type, set either in cities or suburbs and thus mirroring the living conditions of most Americans. *Meet the Parents* is typical of comedies that bridge both areas, with Ben Stiller playing Gaylord Focker, a Chicago nurse, who heads to the suburbs with his girlfriend, Pam Byrnes (Teri Polo), a school teacher, to meet her suburban parents (Robert De Niro and Blythe Danner). Anarchistic humour and romance cross brilliantly in this 'comedy of bad manners', as Roger Ebert calls it (2000). Stiller, incessantly and immeasurably neurotic, but madly in love with the calm and rational Pam, is caught out in numerous 'lies', it being revealed to the excessively WASPy in-laws that he is Jewish. His ethnicity functions against the conventionalised, presumably non-ethnic character of the Byrneses as a 'deviation', a reason to think of the film as anarchic. Further, he manages to set fire to their house and disrupt Pam's sister's wedding, and also to discover that Pam's uptight father, far from being a respectable citizen, is actually a CIA executive planner. Yet through all the comic chaos romance thrives, leaving the improbable lovers Pam and Gaylord wishing to get married. In the best tradition of American family comedies, *Meet the Parents* reaffirms that families can be really crazy; further, that out of the chaos of dissimilarity, incompatibility and dysfunction, the family can emerge as a kind of panacea.

In such an urban/suburban landscape, the simplicity of smalltown America is no longer visible. Yet because the tone, plotting and genre are within the realm of comedy, the bottom line is always for 'acceptance' rather than rejection: in terms of staging, for hugs rather than slaps, blows or worse. It's quite obvious that many such family comedies are set up for sequels that, following one after another relentlessly, come to constitute something of a 'mini sitcom' series; there was no surprise, for instance, when *Meet the Fockers* appeared and built on the huge success of *Meet the Parents*. With this sequel, we come to know Stiller's folks, the ageing Jewish liberals Rozalin (Barbara Streisand) and Bernie (Dustin Hoffman), in their Florida retirement environment (Florida constituting a kind of meta-suburbia for the urban middle class). The comedy of 'bad manners' continues as a dog is flushed down a toilet and a child keeps uttering 'asshole' and much more, but once again wild and carnivalesque personalities come to a sober understanding and a level of acceptance of each other by film's end. Similarly, *Wedding Crashers* triumphantly celebrates 'bad manners' as Vince Vaughn and Owen Wilson crash a highly respectable Washington DC political family headed up by a very stern Christopher Walken, who, instead of throwing them out as the wedding crashers they manifestly are, comes to see through their bravado to realise that they, as Manohla Dargis in the *New York Times* observes, 'love the ladies, but really and truly, cross their cheating hearts, just want a nice girl to call wife' (2005: B19).

Woody Allen has managed to capture the complexity of urban – and especially Jewish – family relations with wit and insight in several films: *Interiors* (1978) and *Radio Days* (1987) deserve mention as being two profoundly different ways of showing how family unity can be formed out of the most improbable mixture of neurosis, alienation and incomprehensibility; *Another Woman* (1988) for its portrait of family relations gone irrevocably sour. But most memorably in *Hannah and Her Sisters* (1986) he has given us a portrait of the modern urban family *in extremis*. Set in New York, this comedy of friends, family and ex-family, all with intertwined lives, many with lovers, mixes much hilarity with keen perceptions and a bevy of splendid performances from the likes of Michael Caine, Mia Farrow, Carrie Fisher, Barbara Hershey, Lloyd Nolan and Maureen O'Sullivan. In this film, characters seem to head away from one another on tangents that will never be resolved with romantic harmony, but the force of the city seems to draw them together anyway. Although Allen does not say this explicitly in *Hannah and Her Sisters*, New York is portrayed as a family of families, a ground in which even the most conflicted and disparate lines of feeling and action can meet.

We can almost speak of the 'New York family dramatic comedy' as a sub-genre of American family comedy, *Hannah and Her Sisters* holding pride of place at its centre. But another fascinating case is Wes Anderson's *The Royal Tenenbaums*. Anderson, who co-wrote the script with co-star Owen Wilson, takes an engaging mixture of tearful joking about a dysfunctional family trying to come together to a point that *Village Voice* critic J. Hoberman identifies correctly as autumnal:

> More than anything, the movie is redolent of late autumn in New York. The weather is overcast and chilly, but the human relations, however neurotic, have a cheery glow. (2001: 128)

Pushed even further than Allen's neurotic depictions of New York life and the double-edged effect of Capra's *It's a Wonderful Life* and other family comedies, *The Royal Tenenbaums* blends unexpected offbeatness with moments that tug on the heart. Larger-than-life Royal Tenenbaum (Gene Hackman) tries to return to his wife, Etheline (Anjelica Huston), and three neurotic genius children (Ben Stiller, Gwyneth Paltrow and Luke Wilson) after some thirty years of absence. Why did he leave? We never really know. Why does he want to come back, now that he apparently has a terminal illness? Ditto. The resulting 'comedy' so adeptly reflects the rich blend of patterns and influences that New York City offers that no summary can capture it clearly. But Roger Ebert suggests the lasting effect of Anderson's comedy is poignant: 'Trying to understand the way this flywheel comedy tugs at the heartstrings, I reflected that eccentricity often masks deep loneliness' (2001). No warped or disabled personality in this film becomes less warped or disabled by the conclusion. No vacancies, no lacks, are satisfactorily filled or supplied. No failures at communication are suddenly remedied. And yet, we are left with a moment of warmth where earlier there had been only a pervasive cerebral coldness. And once more, we are encountering behind the laughter of family comedy a tough reality that suggests there is no simple 'happy ending'.

Animated Families

Of course, we invoke Walt Disney when we think of the development of animation in American cinema. Yet much could be made of the lack of family life in his films. Disney's empire began with Mickey Mouse and his long cartoon series, but Mickey, like Chaplin, was a stand-alone figure; it is only with Disney's shift into animated features with *Snow White and the Seven Dwarfs* (1937) that we can begin to speak of 'family' and 'comedy' together in his work. There are laughs with these seven dwarf 'children' – ranging from Grumpy to Bashful, Sneezy and Sleepy – but we clearly realise that Snow White is playing 'mother' to a large dysfunctional family of seven 'sons'. Disney pioneered turning serious, dark fairytales such as 'Snow White' into humorous films rather than working from material that is comedic by definition. Instead of 'family' and 'laughter', as Eric Smoodin notes, 'Disney has been responsible for a kind of Tennessee Valley Authority of leisure and entertainment' (1994: 3).

Animated features have become more numerous and more popular than had ever been thought possible. As traditional animation has given way to computer generated work, ranging from Pixar's *Toy Story* (1995) and *Toy Story 2* (1999) to *A Bug's Life* (1998) and *Antz* (1998), not only has the range of visual possibilities increased but the stories have been shaped to attract a wide general audience covering all ages, something most popular films have not succeeded in doing. For example, Leonard Maltin has called *A Bug's Life* 'A treat for young and old alike' (2003: 192).

Shrek (2001) built on this new tradition of reaching out to a wider audience with sly humour and ever more sophisticated three-dimensional and well-shaded figures and landscapes. Produced by DreamWorks, this long awaited tale of an ugly green ogre (with Mike Myers' voice) who falls in love with Princess Fiona (Cameron Diaz's voice) and is helped by an incessantly talking donkey (Eddie Murphy's voice), can be seen as a clever, self-parodying departure from the Disney approach to fairytales and animation. At the time he made *Shrek*, Jeffrey Katzenberg, who had been with the Walt Disney Company, was co-partner in DreamWorks; thus it can hardly be an accident that when Prince Farquaad (John Lithgow's voice) is offered three princesses by the Magic Mirror – (Disney's) Snow White, (Disney's) Cinderella and Fiona – he chooses Fiona. With *Shrek 2*, directed and co-written by New Zealander Andrew Adamson (who also did *Shrek*), DreamWorks not only pulled off that rare feat – a sequel that is as good if not better than the original – but entered the territory of 'family comedy' as we have discussed it. In fact, as the now married Fiona and Shrek head off to the Kingdom of Far, Far Away (a utopia that looks exactly like Beverly Hills), we realise we are in fact watching something of an animated version of *Meet the Parents* and all similar 'live action' comedies. *Shrek 2* is intensely focused on family, steeped in the comedy of sons- or daughters-in-law getting to know the 'other' parents and their world. No need to go into all the misadventures that spring out of this Hollywood satire, but certainly the casting of John Cleese and Julie Andrews as the parents' voices is perfect. As is becoming more common in non-Disney animated features, characters have a resemblance to the famous 'voices' that are animating them, and there is a perfection in this, too.

Certainly animated family comedy in the spirit of DreamWorks and Pixar has built in another characteristic that appeals to a wide range of ages: satirical winks and references to other films. Thus, as *USA Today* critic Claudia Puig (2004) commented in her review, part of the fun of seeing *Shrek 2* for many viewers lies in catching allusions to not only Hollywood as Fiona's parents' 'kingdom' but also *From Here to Eternity*, *Spider-Man*, *The Wizard of Oz*, *The Lord of the Rings* and *Charlie's Angels*. The bottom line for Shrek in *Shrek 2* is that even if you are large, green and monstrous, and not used to such a country as the Kingdom of Far, Far Away, you can finally be accepted by your bride's parents. With *Shrek the Third* (2007), we find out to what degree such a family can live 'happily ever after'.

Race and Family Comedy

Bill Cosby used television to display an intelligent and caring middle-class African American family with a strong father figure. That Cosby in real life has a Ph.D. in Education is well known. Using humour and real-life problems in each episode, *The Cosby Show* became not only a sitcom to watch but a standard to look up to, given that actual statistics point to more than half of the millions of African American families with an absent or missing father and only a small percentage living in the upper middle class as Cosby depicted in his show. Cosby's work notwithstanding, however, mention black family comedy in movies and Eddie Murphy's name immediately appears.

Murphy has cut quite a different figure as a comic father in cinema. He has been more flamboyantly 'silly' than Cosby in many of his performances, playing the likes of Dr Sherman Klump, a 400-pound character in the remake of *The Nutty Professor* (1996). But one could still argue that he too becomes a black American male to look up to. Certainly in *Daddy Day Care* Murphy, like Cosby, plays an upper-middle-class husband and father with a professional wife (Regina King). Murphy gets a lot of laughs as he and friend Jeff Garlin take on the job of running a daycare centre while their wives work. As the story turns, Murphy's daycare centre has become a 'success' only because children are allowed to do whatever they want there. Certainly such a farcical approach to comedy does not come close to the kind of 'pedagogical' comedy that Cosby always worked for and on. Indeed, near the finale Murphy says that the daycare centre 'is not a business, we've become FAMILY!'

Chris Eyre's hilarious Native American comedy, *Smoke Signals* (1998), based on a script by author Sherman Alexie, takes viewers into the problems of reservation life not seen in the Hollywood-stereotyped westerns where cowboys and Indians fight it out in the 'old West'. Eyre's wry film focuses on Victor (Adam Beach), a young Coeuer d'Alene whose mother informs him that his father, who abandoned them when he was a young boy, has died in Arizona and been cremated. She asks her son to go on a journey to retrieve his father, whom he hates, and bring the ashes home. The journey is made with a goofy-looking compadre with eyeglasses, Thomas Builds-the-Fire (Evan Adams), who finances their bus trip to Arizona. Raised by his grandmother, Thomas feels in some way part of Victor's family, not just because they share 'life on the res' but also because during a fire in which Thomas's parents died when the two friends were babies, Victor's father saved Thomas's life. The two young men become more like brothers given this odyssey in which Victor finally accepts his father and even shares some of his ashes with Thomas for all of the help he has given, thus symbolically widening the family circle as the story closes. Asked about the humour in his film, director Eyre said, 'It's simple. American Indian humour is like Jewish humour: it's about survival!' (personal interview with author).

Asian and African characters appear in a family comedy that becomes more melodramatic in its second half in Mira Nair's *Mississippi Masala* (1991). Far beyond slapstick family comedies such as *Monster-in-Law*, that avoid any real contact with social issues, Nair's film starts off in a Uganda that has come under Idi Amin's tyrannical power, where all foreigners, especially those with Indian heritage, are forced to leave. Settling in Mississippi, the family ironically runs into American forms of prejudice. But at first, the romance between the young Indian daughter, Meena (Sarita Choudhury), and Demetrius Williams, a local businessman (Denzel Washington) – he handles the carpet-cleaning for her parents' hotel – is sweet, fresh and, yes, humorous. As Desson Howe writes, the film is a 'serio-comic farce' (1992) that has multiple layers of racial humour and misunderstanding. Even though she is Indian, Meena considers herself Ugandan, for she has never been to India. And when the romance is under way, she attends a barbeque in Demetrius's neighbourhood even though she is from Africa and none of these 'African Americans' have ever been there. Nair and screenwriter Sooni Taraporevala's final triumph is that a sense of family rather than race wins out as Meena and Demetrius accept each other in love as humans who have their differences.

Towards a Comic Ending

Gerald Mast ended his pioneering study of comedy with a number of astute observations, the most central of which is this: 'Comic films are full of pain' (1979: 342). Jimmy Stewart wants to commit suicide in *It's a Wonderful Life* but then angels open his eyes to the triumph of his family and community and soon the spirit of comedy as a way of transcending hardships takes over. We could expand on Mast to say that family comedies are full of a particularly familial pain. Yet each of these films finds its own way to pass beyond the limitations each family endures, to find some condition of joy.

George Roy Hill's adaptation of John Irving's popular novel *The World According to Garp* (1982) is, in a way, a quintessential family comedy and a perfect film with which to conclude this overview. Depicted here is T. S. Garp's (Robin Williams) journey through life. His father, who died in World War Two, was simply a sperm donor to his mother (Glenn Close, in her debut film role), a women's rights campaigner who gathers a motley carnival of followers including the transsexual Roberta Muldoon (John Lithgow). Garp tries to establish his own family within troubled 1970s America. With an English professor wife, Helen (Mary Beth Hurt), and two sons, he struggles as a novelist. Garp's 'world' referred to in the title includes the missing father, the eccentric mother, a busy wife and young sons who do not understand their father. In casting Robin Williams (the comic's first film role), Hill took a chance that paid off with much comic and dramatic impact (see Henderson 1991: 160).

Many of the family scenes are hilarious and zany, and transcendently so. Take a moment, for instance, when Garp and Helen are house-hunting with a real estate agent and a plane crashes into the house they are about to look at. Garp instantly agrees to buy it. Why? Because the chances of it being hit again are astronomically low! Pain is always close by. Garp's mother is assassinated, for one thing; and as the film concludes, Garp is dying and is being shuttled off in a helicopter. He has tears in his eyes but he is smiling. Not only does he have a family that loves him, he is fulfilling one of his biggest dreams: he is flying. *The World According to Garp* shows us the American family in a state of transition during the 1970s with much humour. But because the pain is there too, it has a poignancy that few American family comedies share. The family as we would most desire to imagine it, this film seems finally to say, is impossible. What is laughable, and also touching, is that we continue to dream and strive to make that family real.

4

'Mother Needs You': Kevin Costner's *Open Range* and the Melodramatics of the American Western

WALTER METZ

Introduction

In a scene late in John Ford's *My Darling Clementine* (1946), the citizens of Tomb-stone confirm for Marshall Wyatt Earp (Henry Fonda) that Mr Clanton (Walter Bren-nan) and his sons, who have recently shot two of Earp's brothers in the back, are barricaded in at the O.K. Corral, awaiting the infamous confrontation between the two clans. Here is demonstrated the civic stability of Tombstone: the townsmen offer their aid to Earp and his remaining brother. However, while sitting in the jail-house doodling on a writing pad, Earp issues a deadpan rejection of their help: 'Thanks … but this is strictly a family affair.' This phrase – a family affair – is a frame-work for understanding the melodramatic mode of much of Hollywood cinema, but the classical Hollywood western especially justified the conquest of the frontier as a family affair, as when in *Shane* (1953) a homesteader states that the fertile Wyo-ming valley is 'a place where people can come and raise a family'.

A particularly interesting case is Kevin Costner's *Open Range* (2003), featuring an ultra-violent villain, rancher Denton Baxter (Michael Gambon), who wages war against the heroes, Charley Waite (Costner) and Boss Spearman (Robert Duvall). *Open Range* will be seen as an anachronistic return to the 1950s, Cold War variant of the Hollywood western. At stake in this return is a concomitant re-articulation of the Cold War belief in conventional domesticity as expressed in using the land to raise families, which goes a long way towards explaining the conservative American cultural response to the 9/11 crisis. Post-9/11 westerns re-enact a linkage between the geopolitical concerns of national security and the maintenance of a rigid domes-tic morality (see Corber 1995), returning the western to its classical representations of morally upright men who both save the social order from de-civilising forces and simultaneously engineer the maintenance of traditional family values.

Open Range is ideologically vicious, but more interesting still in its melodramat-ic engagement with the family affairs of the classical Hollywood western, expertly studied by Virginia Wright Wexman in her essay 'Star and Genre: John Wayne, the Western, and the American Dream of the Family on the Land', one of the case studies in her book *Creating the Couple* (1993). Wexman's analysis of the melodramatics of the classical Hollywood western can be used as a reading frame for understanding the remarkable anti-revisionist gestures of *Open Range*. By focusing on the conflict in this film between ranchers and free grazers – cattlemen who make a living by buying cattle young and cheap, roaming them over open, public lands, and then driving them to a market where the now mature herd can be sold at high prices – I will build on Wexman's primary case study (a reading of *The Man Who Shot Liberty Valance* (1962)) to show a history of the New Hollywood western in which the revisionist critique of the family/land use nexus, in films such as *Heaven's Gate* (1980), has been all but expurgated.

Open Range begins when the Irish cattle baron, Baxter, who owns the valley, has one of the free-range cattlemen's workhands brutally beaten. After confronting him and discovering that he has the town sheriff in his pocket, the cattlemen (Duvall and Costner) decide to take the law into their own hands and mete out vigilante justice. Along the way, Charley falls in love with the town doctor's sister, Sue (Annette Bening), who kindly attends to the wounds of another of their hands. At the film's end, after the evil rancher and his cohorts have been brutally dispatched, Charley decides to settle down with Sue. The last sequence of the film finds him herding cattle with Spearman, however; he tells Sue he has a last obligation to fulfil, and soon he will return.

This ending is more than odd for the romantic subplot of a Hollywood film. As Thomas Schatz shows in proposing the formation of the stable family as the most significant marker of social change in the Hollywood western:

> The ideal union of westerner and Woman in the family, the one social institution revered by all of [John] Ford's essentially antisocial heroes, has regressed from a reality (Ringo and Dallas) to a promise (Wyatt and Clementine) to an untenable situation (Ethan and Martha) to an outright impossibility (Tom and Hallie). With the steady enclosure of the genre's visual and thematic horizons, the hero's options are reduced to one single, inexorable reality: Doniphon does not ride off into the sunset or across Monument Valley, but into the Valley of Death. (1981: 80)

By tracing the John Ford western from 1939's *Stagecoach* to 1946's *My Darling Clementine* to 1956's *The Searchers* to 1962's *The Man Who Shot Liberty Valance*, Schatz establishes a history of the genre that unequivocally announces its death. After the revisionist impulse of *The Man Who Shot Liberty Valance*, in which the murder of the idealised westerner (John Wayne) obliterates any possibility of a heterosexual conclusion based on desire, what more can happen? What is remarkable about *Open Range* is that it reincarnates this presumed-dead western hero, neglecting the historically intervening revisionist films. The domestic ending of *Open Range*, in which Charley promises to return to Sue and settle down, exactly replicates *My Darling Clementine*, in which Earp promises to return to Clementine (Cathy Downs) after finishing his manly business. Thus, unlike what Jim Collins (1993) calls the 'New Sincerity', through which Costner's *Dances With Wolves* (1990) eschews Hollywood film westerns to return to an idealised if still fully imaginary West of the nineteenth century, *Open Range* finds a different – I would say worse – sincerity, in the conventional melodramatics of the classical Hollywood western.

Open Range is a proposal, therefore, that Schatz's understanding of the western's family affair needs to be, as Janet Staiger might put it, 'appreciatively revised' (1995). Despite many proclamations of its apocalyptic end, the western – unlike the westerner in *The Man Who Shot Liberty Valance* – did not die. Instead, the genre has continually re-invented itself. What *Open Range* indicates is that the revisionist impulse of the 1960s and 1970s – *The Wild Bunch* (1969) and *Little Big Man* (1970), for example – has been replaced, since 9/11, by a return to the conventional values of the classical Hollywood western, a return that has erased those revisionist gestures entirely.

Central is *Open Range*'s odd engagement with the relationship between family and land use in the American West. The iconic classical film in this regard is *Shane*, which brings into focus the hitherto under-appreciated significance of the Johnson County War within the cinematic western imagination. At some level, the western is built around a conflict over who gets to control the land and for what purposes, a conflict explicit (as in the case of *Heaven's Gate*) or implicit (as in the case of *Shane* and *Open Range*). Three uses of the land are dominant in the western: the small family farm, the large ranching estate and free grazing. In *Shane*, the rancher Rufus Ryker (Emile Meyer) is at war with the farmer Joe Starrett (Van Heflin); in *Open Range*, the rancher Baxter challenges the free grazer Spearman. Both films thus construct a drama about land use. In both films, however, it turns out that, regardless of who controls the land, the characters who are privileged are those interested in preserving the family.

Land Use as a Family Affair in the American Western

Wexman begins her study of the familial issues in the American western with an epigram from Patricia Limerick, one of the crucial figures in the 'new western history', a revisionist historical approach to the American West: 'If Hollywood wanted to capture the emotional centre of western history, its movies would be about real estate' (in Wexman 1993: 67). This radical assertion, that the iconic elements of the American western – honourable men, gunslingers, horses – represent a smoke-screen for the key issues of the domination of the land by a particular form of European familial configuration, offers an opportunity for a new history of the postwar American western. Consider, for example, the plot of *Open Range*: its heroes, inserted into a traditional revenge narrative that culminates in an epic gunfight, are free grazers, usually the villains of Hollywood westerns because they claim a use of the land that precludes small families from settling fenced farms. The use of free grazers as heroes is the only aspect of *Open Range* which makes it differ from the classical western. Instead of denigrating him, the film redeems the free grazer, romanticising his life, but ultimately sutures him into the traditional family life in the town that other Hollywood westerns endorse.

The ownership of land in the American West and its complexities do not become an obsession for the Hollywood western until after World War Two. For example, John Ford's *Stagecoach*, an archetypal prewar American western, is about a journey through Indian country undertaken by a motley crew of Americans inside a stagecoach. When the two major rejects from Eastern society, the Ringo Kid (John Wayne), a wrongfully accused westerner, and Dallas (Claire Trevor), a prostitute, arrive safely at their destination, they flee American society altogether, headed for Ringo's ranch in Mexico. But the postwar American western became obsessed with conflicts over the land, arguing for the centrality of small family farms over both Native Americans' and ranchers' more unrestrained uses, at precisely the same time as contemporary white Americans' flight to suburbia. Canonical postwar westerns, such as *Shane*, *The Searchers* and *Red River* (1948) while being different from one another in many ways, all positioned the homesteader family as the American ideal, largely because this ideal most closely matched the ideological dominant of the postwar social formation, the suburban family (on land use and suburbia, see Nathan Holmes' essay in this volume).

A major film in the canon of postwar westerns to address issues of family and land ownership was Howard Hawks's *Red River*. Tom Dunson (John Wayne again) fights with his adoptive son, Matthew Garth (Montgomery Clift), while driving their cattle the long distance to Abilene, Kansas. When they finally arrive, after a protracted father/son fistfight, they form a familial bond, agreeing to run the cattle ranch together. The film is expertly presented by Robert Sklar as an allegory for Cold War America:

> *Red River* is a film about the issues of empire. It is a film about the territorial expansion of one society by the usurpation of land from others, and the consequences arising there from – in the relations between men and women, in the relations between men and other men, in the social compact that binds people together for a common purpose. (1988: 169)

The celebration of Americans taming the land and producing beef (with scandalous inefficiency) to feed the population would become a central trope of the American western, as in Anthony Mann's *The Far Country* (1954), in which Jeff Webster (James Stewart) attempts to make a fortune by driving cattle from Wyoming to the

Klondike gold fields in order to feed the miners. In her discussion of the western, family and land use, Wexman leads us to a film even earlier than *Red River.*

> The conflict over land typically involves pioneers against Indians or small farmers against cattle barons with property as the prize that goes to the victors. Often the conflict is explicitly posed in terms of the right of private property as when the concept of the open range is opposed to the right to fence in fields or pastures in westerns like *Abilene Town* (1946) and *Man Without a Star* (1955). (1993: 77)

Edwin L. Marin's *Abilene Town* is never studied in detail in film studies literature. It could certainly be looked at in either star or genre terms, since on one hand it is a Randolph Scott vehicle and on the other it is associate-produced by Herbert Biberman, one of the Hollywood Ten and director of the radical 1950s pro-union film, *Salt of the Earth* (1954). But it is foundational for its presentation of land use issues in the western, revealing conflicts that structure the American western from canonical films like *Shane* all the way to *Open Range*. *Abilene Town* begins with an extreme long shot of men on horses running cattle through a valley, an emphasis on landscape that is characteristic of the opening shots of both *Shane* and *Open Range*. A superimposition tells us that the year is 1870, 'five years after the Civil War'. We are then presented with the town of Abilene, a home to illicit gambling and scantily-clad nightclub performers as well as to church-going 'suburban' men and women with children. The film's first event emphasises this split in the town. Dan Mitchell (Scott), the sheriff, is in church with Sherry Balder (Rhonda Fleming) and her father, Ed (Howard Freeman), the town's general-store owner. Dan gets annoyed by gunshots and leaves the church in the middle of a hymn. In a wonderful overlap cut, the last note of the hymn is the first note of burlesque singer Rita's (Ann Dvorak) song, 'I Love It Out Here in the West', interrupted by cowboys shooting off their guns. Dan attempts to intervene, Rita kicks him and resumes her song, annoyed at his interference.

After this introduction of the two sides of Abilene, the film's narrative begins: homesteaders ride their wagon through town, also singing a hymn, thus establishing the compatibility of the homesteaders and the townspeople. The film's villain, Cap Ryker (Dick Curtis), a free grazer, warns the homesteaders to keep off the trail: 'This is cattle country, and it's going to stay cattle country.' Dan confronts Ryker, which angers the townspeople, who argue that their town's economic security is reliant on Cap and his men. Dan goes out to the homesteaders' camp to investigate, significantly lifting a young homesteader boy onto his horse as he rides in. Henry Dreiser (Lloyd Bridges) tells Dan, 'There's land to work, and we're gonna put more into it than we take out.' Dan returns to the town, convinced of the superior life that the homesteaders will bring to the town. 'This is a war, the rider against the settler, the quick drunk against the family', he tells the townspeople. But

Ryker's men act quickly, torching the homesteaders' camp and stampeding it with cattle.

The surviving homesteaders meet in Dan's office. Henry explains the benefits of farming over cattle ranching: 'Cattlemen hate farmers because we make forty acres support a dozen people instead of one cow.' One of the farmers accuses one of the villainous cattlemen, Jet Younger (Jack Lambert), and Dan rides off to apprehend him. In the film's central scene, Jet and Dan have an extended fistfight. After he is victorious, Dan explains to Jet that he is taking him off to jail for twenty years. Jet is confused, and asks Dan what he expects to get out of his actions. 'A little security for my children', Dan explains. When Jet observes, 'You ain't got any children', Dan allegorically explains the future of the West: 'Someday I might.'

Henry rallies the surviving homesteaders. He goes to the general store to buy barbed wire in order to fence off the cattle trail, so that they can use the land for their farms. Ed refuses to sell the wire to Henry, afraid of angering Cap. Henry goes behind Ed's back to his daughter, Sherry, arguing that he wants to have what his father did not have, land for 'growing wheat, enough of it to raise a fine family, with peace surrounding us. Is that a poor thing to want?' This convinces Sherry, who sells the wire to Henry.

Cap's men find the barbed wire on the cattle trail into Abilene and stampede the homesteaders again. This time, the elder of the homesteader community is killed, leaving Henry in charge. Dan tells Henry to bring all the homesteaders into town 'while there still is one'. The townspeople meet to decide what to do. Ed worries that 'this is another Gettysburg', while Sherry argues for helping the home-steaders to defeat the cattlemen: 'They're people like us. Better.' Dan convinces the townspeople to act. 'This is a fight for the State of Kansas. The way the nation's going.' Ed is finally convinced by the potential profits thousands of homesteaders will bring his general store business.

The film's climax features the battle between the town and the cattlemen. The cowboys ride into town, hooting and howling like animals as they destroy the saloon side of the street. The town's brothel owner, Big Annie (Helen Boyce), leads the homesteaders in a chorus of 'Mine Eyes Have Seen the Glory' as they march through town, fanning out to protect the buildings. Dan enters the saloon to arrest Cap Ryker for murder. A gunfight ensues, in which Dan shoots and kills Cap and his men. Dan rescues Rita from the burning saloon. When Rita wants to go back and rescue her pretty burlesque show dresses, Dan replies, 'Leave them. All you'll need from now on is kitchen aprons.' Rita, the burlesque singer; Sherry, the grocer's daughter; and Big Annie, the brothel owner all join arms as the town is redeemed from the sins of the cattlemen. Dan confronts the surviving cattlemen, gloating, 'This is the way a tough street dies. Not with a roar, but with a whine. The tame are taking over', and chases them out of town.

Abilene Town predicts the melodramatics of *Open Range*, the belief that small family units represent the best practices of the American West. While the appropriate family makers – farmers, ranchers, free grazers – might change from film to film, the end result of the American western narrative will remain stable, culminating in the noble and happy production of the normative family unit. It is George Stevens' *Shane*, however, with which *Open Range* has most in common. The plot focuses on a land dispute between the small farmer Starrett and the big rancher Ryker. While he is as villainous as the Ryker in *Abilene Town*, this Ryker is no illiterate animal: he argues clearly his position regarding his family's right to the land. Early in the film, when the Rykers trample Starrett's crops with their horses, Ryker and Starrett reveal the land use question as one of semantics. Ryker calls Starrett and his homesteaders 'squatters', using historical precedent to argue against Starrett's federal government-produced licence to farm the land. Later, Ryker argues passionately for the importance of history: 'When I came to this country, you weren't much older than your boy there', he begins, looking over at Starrett's young son, Joey (Brandon De Wilde). He claims that he invested sweat and tears that the new homesteaders did not. 'I got a bad shoulder yet from a Cheyenne arrowhead. We made this country ... We made a safe range out of this. Some of us died.' But against this argument Starrett observes, 'You didn't find this country', pointing to the trappers who came before even Ryker and his fellow ranchers. Of course, a crucial element for arguing the history of the West is absent from this conversation. Native Americans – those rightful to the land, using the logic of both Ryker and Starrett – have a presence in this dialogue only as aggressive warriors (the Cheyenne who fired an arrow at Ryker). Native American land use, untied to European concepts of private property, is beyond the pale of the classical western.

For its part, *Open Range* features a similar conversation about land use. Here, however, there is no conflict concerning small-homesteading farmers. Instead, Ryker's position in *Shane*, advocating an open range, characterises the film's heroes and the villain, Baxter, is a rancher like Ryker, but one who works on early-established, fenced-off lands. He gives Spearman a lecture that is reiterative of Ryker's in *Shane*, beginning with history, arguing that the ranchers perceive their fight against free grazers as similar to the one they had with the Native Americans, from whom they stole the land. 'You know, folks in Fort Harmon country don't take to free grazers, or free grazin'. They hate them more than they used to hate the Indians.' Also like Ryker, Baxter argues to Spearman that claims to the land should be organised not according to the rule of law but according to sweat equity: 'I got the biggest spread around these parts. Bigger than any three or four put together. Built it up with me own two hands. Piece by piece. Along with this town. There ain't no free graze cattle gonna take the feed off my cattle on this range.'

When Spearman observes that 'Free graze is legal', Baxter retorts with an argument that proves to be the film's theme (despite its emerging from the villain's mouth): 'Times change, Mr Spearman. Most folks change with them. A few holdouts never do.' In making its heroes free grazers and its villain a big estate rancher, *Open Range* seems to argue for unfettered use of the land. However, the film ultimately decrees that the West was destined for land use based on private property, crucially a use in which the small family unit is dominant. Free grazing is seen by everyone as a historically dead occupation; after killing the evil Baxter, Spearman and Charley promise to give it up, Spearman to run a bar and Charley to settle into family life with Sue Barlow. Thus, *Shane* and *Open Range* share the same melodramatic tendency towards western land use – that in the end, and principally, it is for supporting families.

New Visions of Land Use in the Western

The period of the revisionist Hollywood western, so brutally rescinded by the likes of *Open Range*, demands further attention in this regard, particularly revisionist westerns that take Native American land use seriously. Kevin Costner's *Dances With Wolves* is the key film in this regard, since it represents Costner's triumph as a filmmaker (the film won the Best Picture Academy Award, and Costner was named Best Director). Like a number of other prior revisionist westerns, such as Elliot Silverstein's *A Man Called Horse* (1970), the film is an example of a progressive captivity narrative: when the white Lt. Dunbar (Costner) is confronted with comparing European and Native American lifestyles, he chooses the latter, falling in love with a Native American woman, Stands With A Fist (Mary McDonnell). While many critics see *Dances With Wolves* as simplistically liberal, it is worth noting that compared to *Open Range*, it is at least interested in re-envisioning how and why we use the American West to construct our national mythology. Another such film is Jim Jarmusch's *Dead Man* (1995), similarly a progressive captivity narrative and perhaps the most revisionist western ever made in America. Post-9/11 Hollywood is a viciously conservative place where no such film will get made. *Dead Man* is about death from the very beginning – as opposed to a classical western where the hero ventures westward as a foppish dandy from the east and dies or confronts death as a result of tensions he encounters beyond the frontier. William Blake's (Johnny Depp) death is predicted from the outset of the film: there is no other poss-ibility. Thus, *Dead Man* doesn't believe in the sure potential of the white man to tame the west, or any sphere in which an alien Other seems to dominate and threaten America (as Osama Bin Laden seemed to do).

The revisionist western most directly representative of the Johnson County War is Michael Cimino's *Heaven's Gate*, more literally about that event than such films as *Abilene Town*, *Shane*, *The Man Who Shot Liberty Valance* and *Open Range*, which all treat it more symbolically. In 1892, the Wyoming Stock Growers' Association, representing big ranching corporations such as Denton Baxter's in *Open Range*, decided to take the law into their own hands in keeping the range open against homesteaders. The association recruited 'Regulators' – hired gunmen – to eliminate the homesteaders (an act depicted in *Shane* in Wilson's (Jack Palance) cold-blooded murder of Torrey (Elisha Cook Jr)). For their part, the homesteaders

banded together, surrounded the gunmen and defeated them. A corrupt government, acting in the interests of big business, sent the federal cavalry in to rescue
the paid killers. None of the killers or corporate interests who paid them were ever
indicted for their many crimes against the homesteaders. *The BFI Companion to
the Western* claims that the Johnson County War represents 'the most dramatic
encounter between big ranchers and small farmers, a struggle that has some of the
classical hallmarks of class conflict' (1988: 163).

Cimino depicts the major events of the Johnson County War in an epic film
whose disastrous release is legendary for ruining one of the key business enterprises of the classical Hollywood period, United Artists; after losing roughly $38 million
on the release of *Heaven's Gate*, UA was swallowed up by MGM. The three-hour
sprawling film has to stand as one of the strangest westerns ever made. It begins
with a 15-minute sequence at a Harvard University graduation in 1870 and ends on
a fancy yacht off the coast of Newport, Rhode Island, in 1903. The film thus wilfully
violates the two sacred traditions of the western, that it should treat the East Coast
of the United States only as a horrible space from which escape is necessary, and
that it should retreat exclusively into the heyday of the nineteenth century.

In terms of its melodramatics, *Heaven's Gate* is the only film I have examined
that argues that the founding familial myth of American culture is indeed incompatible with our ideological assumptions. Classical Hollywood westerns, like *Shane*,
produce a fantasy in which good gunfighters rise to the defence of the small family. *Open Range*, echoing the burgeoning pessimism of *My Darling Clementine*,
only promises that such families will develop after the end of the film, suspecting
that their stability is not so easy to produce. However, *Heaven's Gate* boldly and
radically states that under the deplorable circumstances of the Old West, and by
extension all of contemporary America, the idea of having a happy family amidst
corruption and horror is impossible.

The film presents its hero, Jim Averill (Kris Kristofferson), as the representative
of classical, Western civilisation. One of the graduates of Harvard, he brings classical knowledge to his job as a Wyoming marshal in the 1890s. In fact, the classical
battle techniques he learned at Harvard are exactly the tools he uses to lead the
homesteaders in their victorious campaign against the hired killers. He has the
homesteaders assemble flaming logs and uses them to encircle the Regulators, a
circular composition that the film has, from the start, associated with civilisation:
at the Harvard graduation, the men and women dance waltzes, circling with the
camera in turn circling them in a wildly bravura long take.

The film, taken from the historical record, refuses to live up to the Hollywood
western's mythology. In a vicious stab at American hypocrisy, when Averill turns
to soldiers of the federal cavalry for help against the Regulators, they refuse, instead playing baseball, the American pastime. The governor, in the pocket of the
Cattlemen's Association, has ordered the cavalry not to help the homesteaders. In
response to their betrayal by America, the immigrant homesteaders have nothing

but despair. In the film's most graphic image, rather than live in such a corrupt world in which all hopes for a future have been ripped away from her, one homesteader shoots herself in the head. Thus, far from the happiness of the farm wife Marion Starrett (Jean Arthur) in *Shane*, this film ends without any potential for familial re-production, except that engineered for the cattle by the ranchers.

Most crucially, unlike Shane (Alan Ladd), who desires but cannot have Marion Starrett because she is already married to Joe – 'Mother needs you!', shouts Joey when Shane plans to leave, unaware in his innocence that domestic morality precludes his hero and his mother from acting on that desire – *Heaven's Gate*'s gunfighter is teased with a familial future. Ella (Isabelle Huppert) is presented throughout the film as Averill's lover. Based on a real figure in the Johnson County War, Cattle Kate, Ella accepts payment in her bordello from cattle rustlers, to the consternation of the ranchers. In real life Kate was lynched, but in the film Ella is brutally raped by the Regulators. Yet the film still preserves the possibility of Averill and Ella having a family; he shows up just in time to kill all of the rapists. However, the film has not taken its final, brutal turn. Canton (Sam Waterston), the leader of the Stock Growers' Association, shoots Ella in the back during an ambush of Averill in the film's penultimate scene.

At this point, the film presents us with its revisionist coda, an image of the birth of the twentieth century that is unprecedented in the history of the western. Averill is shown in 1903, literally and symbolically at sea, adrift in a fancy yacht off the coast of Newport. After walking around aimlessly on deck, he goes belowdecks, to his ornately decorated sleeping chambers. He slumps into a chair. A servant delivers food on a fancy tray. A woman, presumably his new wife, in a sleepy stupor, asks him for a cigarette. He lights one for her, never uttering a word. Here the film finds a brilliant new use for the wordless westerner; whereas Charley in *Open Range* does not speak much because men should act, not talk, here Averill does not speak because to do so in such a corrupt world would be a profane violation of the beautiful ideas of classical civilisation that he learned while at Harvard. All that remains for him is a photograph of his happy life with Ella, buried amid the possessions down in his cabin. He walks back to the deck, and the epic ends with a long shot of him, standing helplessly, with nowhere to go.

The stunning *Heaven's Gate* represents the pinnacle of what the revisionist western achieved between the late 1960s and the 1980s. In the wake of its financial disaster, many pundits pronounced the western dead. The western, of course, was not. In relation to the land-use theme, Clint Eastwood would remake *Shane* as *Pale Rider* in 1985, and that same year Lawrence Kasdan would produce *Silverado*, another western in the classic mould about evil ranchers, good homesteaders and the good gunfighters who protect them. One of those gunfighters, significantly, is a young Kevin Costner. Westerns would continue to be made throughout the 1990s, some of them (for example, *Dead Man*) more revisionist than others (*The Quick and the Dead* (1995)). However, the resurgence of a resolutely anti-revisionist western, one which truly believes that Hollywood had it right all along, seems to be the special provenance of 2003, when *Open Range* promised to hop across the preceding thirty revisionist years of the western and return us to representations of the simpler America of the postwar years.

From the perspective of melodrama, this is deeply lamentable. The land-use ideology on which the classical Hollywood western was built is untenable, both as a way of life and as a framework for understanding American history. As a corollary – and by no means a minor one – the gender assumptions of this melodrama, that women should be the centre of nuclear families around which active men should rotate, is also problematic and untenable.

Conclusion

Drawing on the psychoanalytic work of Klaus Theweleit, Virginia Wright Wexman argues that the westerner's desire for family and land is tied to an incestuous desire for 'the earth itself' (1993: 109). Applying this to film westerns, she argues that 'this symbolic longing for "mother earth" is closely related to two western conventions … the lyrical interlude of the figure in the landscape and the climactic shoot-out' (ibid.), both of which are at the centre of *Open Range*'s masterful reconstruction of the ideological practices of the classical Hollywood western.

Open Range begins with a sequence that directly references the openings of classical Hollywood westerns, the quintessential use of the landscape. Just as Shane rides into the valley of homesteaders where the film's equivalent of the Johnson County War is about to take place; and as the end of the film, when the little boy shouts 'Mother needs you!', visually answers this opening as Shane, wounded and dying, rides away, perhaps to the Valhalla of the westerner; so *Open Range* begins with its two protagonists leading their cattle into a pristine valley. The first shot of the film, indeed, is a beautiful extreme long shot of the cattlemen on horseback in the foreground, with the cattle and the sumptuous valley as a backdrop, which directly revisits the western landscape celebrated in *Shane*'s famous ride. Wexman suggests that the sumptuous music usually accompanying these lyrical landscape sequences also contributes to their ideological effects: 'The sense of oneness … is strongly underscored by the non-diegetic music that invariably replaces dialogue in such interludes. This background music is typically characterised by a rich orchestral fullness and a rhythmical approximation of a horse's leisurely gait' (ibid.).

Sure enough, the opening shot of *Open Range* features this sort of sumptuous orchestral music and reduced dialogue. In the background, far away but in focus, we see cattle slowly moving into the depth of a valley. In the foreground, green grass sways gently amidst colourful wildflowers. A cut reveals a thunderstorm rolling into this valley. A pan right reveals Boss Spearman on horseback. Charley Waite rides up to him. All through this sequence, the music melodramatically telegraphs the beauty of this life of living off the land without binding roots. As Wexman predicts, the dialogue is minimal, allowing the viewer to partake of the visual and musical splendour. When Spearman asks Charley whether the storm will come their way, Charley the minimalist westerner responds simply: 'Might.' Spearman responds in kind with a terse order: 'Best bed 'em down.' A sheepherder's wagon follows the line of steers down into the valley as the credits roll and the image fades to black.

A new historiography, first offered by Richard Slotkin in 1973 (see Slotkin 1992), and then by 'new western historians' such as Donald Worster (1991) and Patricia Nelson Limerick (1991), has clearly and convincingly demonstrated that the American mythology of the West does not match up to its historical realities. They have argued that to truly understand the grim and complex history of the American West, we need to discard the central metaphors – such as 'the frontier' (Limerick suggests 'border' as an alternative formulation) – upon which we have built our misunderstanding.

Film studies of the 1970s relied upon the traditional mythology that Slotkin and Limerick intend to displace. Wexman, for example, uses Limerick to critique Thomas Schatz's structuralist analysis of the western in *Hollywood Genres*, where he argues that the civilisation/wilderness opposition structures experience in the western. In the Ford films, as in the opening and closing shots of *The Searchers*, the wilderness is associated with the westerner, and civilisation with women and the family.

The Hollywood western and its critics adopted a mythological understanding that is not borne out by the historical realities of the West. Indeed, in his seminal postwar study of land use in the American West, *Virgin Land* (1950), Henry Nash Smith builds a careful critique of the 'myth of the garden', instead pointing out that the high plains was in fact an arid desert. At one point, Smith tracks the Congressional debates in the 1870s over land reform, citing how traditional glorification of 'small tracts' according to the Jeffersonian ideal would soon give way to 'baronial estates'. As a result of corruption in the government, land policy in the West would become 'a speculator's dream' (1950: 199).

The real West, for both white settlers and Native Americans, was not experienced within a mythological binary. In different ways for white and Native American women, living in the 'wilderness' was every bit as active and engaging an experience as it was for their male counterparts. My claim about *Open Range* is that by returning to the pre-revisionist representational trends of the classical Hollywood western, the film moves us even further away from what Elliott West (1991) calls 'a longer, grimmer but more interesting story' about the American West. American westerns and their critics need to account for this paradigm shift in the historiography of the American West. If a divide in criticism still exists, we need to mend it, and move towards celebrating new images of the West that capture its historical complexity. If we fail, the 'family affair' of the western will not be restricted to the characters in the films.

5

D. W. Griffith, Families and the Origins of American Narrative Cinema

JENNIFER M. BEAN

'Griffith ... is to the various histories of the cinema what Abraham is to the Bible – the necessary Patriarch.'
– Jacques Aumont (1990: 348)

Introduction

What differentiates one period or phase of film history from another? How small or large must the differences be in order to determine where one element or stage leaves off and another begins? These are questions that any discipline must ask if it is to reflect on its historical parameters, which means that disciplinary knowledge is intrinsically bound to the construction of 'families', to the process of retrospectively organising observable phenomenon into what Charles Darwin calls 'genera, families, sub-families' (1996: 562). What is intriguing from the perspective of American film historical discourse is the apparently irreducible equation linking the origins – the originality – of a properly *narrative* cinema to the Biograph films of D. W. Griffith (1908–13), and beyond that to the metaphorical and ideological values associated with the middle-class, nuclear family unit.

When Jacques Aumont describes Griffith as the 'necessary Patriarch' of cinema's 'multiple histories', he refers to a critical genealogy that relentlessly reiterates Griffith's name as the signature stamp of narrative cinema's artistic and cultural patrimony, even while the core or essence of what that patrimony means has altered over time. But other more revolutionary alterations are currently on the rise. Indeed, given the broader reach of archival and historiographic methods emerging in the digital age, the rash of encyclopedias and reference tools now being written, and a roaring wave of very good work from scholars of varying political and aesthetic perspectives, it seems clear on all fronts that we have only just begun to explore the films and figures that constitute narrative cinema's ascendance in the early 1910s. Anticipation mounts as newly restored or discovered prints mock revered critical assumptions, raising questions that remain as yet unanswered, the ultimate question being whether a positivist film history will ever again be possible or desirable. Then again, in the midst of such intellectual ferment and vitalising possibilities, the most immediate question becomes quite simply: in the face of a substantial body of work about the man and his films, why write on Griffith *again*?

I have two contrary attitudes or inclinations. On one hand, I am firmly committed to the necessity of writing a new film history, of redrawing the cultural and aesthetic lineages of narrative cinema in accordance with whatever 'genera, families, sub-families' one seeks to organise and classify and why. At the same time, I consider it imperative to move cautiously towards 'revisionary' conclusions in an intellectual moment as volatile as ours, to remain wary of writing in reaction to, or against, an assumed critical norm, lest we run the risk of too quickly replacing bad old truisms with bad new ones. My goal, though, in rendering with some precision the role Griffith's films and the middle-class family have played in our critical legacy, is not to provide a comprehensive survey. It is rather to sketch the diverse inflections this particular name and group of films has undergone when viewed through the lens of various critical categories. From classical to revisionist historical discourse, from structuralism's imperatives to genre studies, we find a series of remarkably dissonant perspectives – dare I say, our own kind of 'family affair' – to which an emergent generation of historians remains indebted as heir.

The Rise of the Mythical Father and the Fall of the Realist Text

There is, to be sure, a historical basis in the status ascribed to David Wark Griffith, who postulated himself as a film artist/author *sine qua non* in 1913. Shortly after he left the Biograph Company (where he had been working as a 'director' for five years), Griffith placed an advertisement in the *New York Dramatic Mirror*, blowing his own horn, so to speak, for 'revolutionizing Motion Picture drama and founding the modern technique of the art'. Listing in particular 'the large or closeup figures, distant views as represented first in *Ramona* [1910], the "switchback", sustained suspense, the "fade out", and restraint of expression', Griffith also lists over one hundred film titles, retrospectively 'crediting' himself as director in an era when credits as such rarely appeared onscreen. Indeed, the novelty suggested by this attribution to the individual self as the site of creativity zooms into focus when one considers a similar commentary published in the same journal a year earlier. Ascribing inventiveness of artistic techniques to the Biograph Company *qua* company, one anonymous reporter pronounced:

> Biograph's influence on picture production has been important. It was the first company ... in America to present acting of the restrained artistic type, and the first to produce quiet drama and pure comedy. It was the first to attempt fading light effects. It was the first to employ alternating flashes of simultaneous action in working up suspense. (Anon. 1912: 56).

Leaving aside this writer's qualifying emphasis on national location ('in America'), the nigh uncanny resemblance this list bears to Griffith's broadsheet reveals that the consideration of acting style, lighting effects or suspenseful editing techniques was hardly new to the discourse surrounding cinema in 1913. Remarkably new, however, was Griffith's loud claim to individual creativity and originality.

Baldly put, Griffith's 1913 posting heralds the origins of the 'author function' in film historical discourse, a critical function that Michel Foucault describes as 'result[ing] from a complex operation whose purpose is to construct the rational entity we call an author [in which] we speak of an individual's "profundity" or "creative" power' (1980: 127). To speak of a *film* author, especially one working in a commercial context, most often involves a humanistic operation employed to elevate the individual's films above the grimy morass of the marketplace, to efface the rude machinery of production. That this civilising gesture often summons familial metaphors is particularly intriguing, although hardly idiosyncratic to film studies. As Roland Barthes reminds us, the conception of the Author as a figure of originality and creativity, a figure designed to ensure the homogeneity and unity of a text, emerges in post-Middle Age culture as a crucial tenet in the growing emphasis on individuality, privacy and selfhood in the Western world. That the historical construction of selfhood as such is buttressed by a positivism that finds its epitome in capitalist society, the same society that invents and privileges the nuclear family unit, generates a set of interrelated issues that emerge in the common, now naturalised use of parental – or more specifically, *paternal* – analogies for speaking of authorship. As he observes: 'The Author, when believed in ... is thought to *nourish* the book, which is to say that he exists before it, thinks, suffers, lives for it, is in the same relation of antecedence to his work as a *father to his child*' (1977: 145; last emphasis added).

Nowhere is Barthes' assessment of authorship as a figuration of paternity more visible than in classical film historical discourse, which rapidly enshrined Griffith as 'the father of classical narrative cinema and inventor of narrative filmmaking' (Elsaesser & Barker 1990: 293). In Terry Ramsaye's history of American cinema, *A Million and One Nights*, for instance, we find 'Griffith Evolves Screen Syntax', a chapter dedicated to Griffith's years at Biograph, in which the biological idiom of evolutionary growth images the cinema as a child maturing under Griffith's tutelage: 'The motion picture spent the years up to 1908 learning its letters. Now, with Griffith it was studying screen grammar and pictorial rhetoric' (1926: 508). By reprinting in part Griffith's *Dramatic Mirror* posting (1926: 636), Ramsaye's account impels a line of descent embellished in Lewis Jacobs's study, *The Rise of the American Film*, which reproduced the 1913 ad in full (1968: 117). Passed from the self-professed progenitor of Motion Picture Art to the founding 'fathers' – so to speak – of American film history, Griffith's legacy crossed the Atlantic in 1951, gaining pride of place in Georges Sadoul's *Histoire générale du cinéma* and shimmering across Jean Mitry's prolific writings throughout the 1960s. 'Without exaggerating in the least', Mitry effectively summarised, 'one can say that if the cinema owes its existence as a means of analysis and reproduction of movement (and therefore as an entertainment form and an entertainment industry) to Louis Lumière, it is to Griffith that it owes its existence as an art form, as a means of expression and of signification' (1985: 68).

That Griffith's name attained a nigh mythical status through this critical genealogy is relatively easy to discern, especially if we understand myth as a story told in reverent tones, with broad plot strokes and with little care for empirical data. The remarkable adaptability of this myth to differing critical contexts surfaces forcefully in the work of Christian Metz, whose semiotic approach to cinematic language in 1964 has come to emblematise, in Dudley Andrew's terms, the 'weening of modern film theory from Mitry's paternal embrace' (1984: 58). But Metz, for all the 'weening' he accomplished, remains in full accord with Mitry's embrace of Griffith. Directly quoting his predecessor, and allowing that certain expressive techniques could be discerned among the 'primitives' (Georges Méliès, Edwin S. Porter, George Albert Smith, James Williamson), Metz observes: 'It was Griffith's role to define and to stabilise – we would say, to codify – the *function* of these different procedures in relation to the filmic narrative, and thereby unify them up to a certain point in a coherent "syntax" ... Thus it was in a single motion that the cinema became narrative and took over some of the attributes of a language' (2004: 67; emphasis in original). More than simply a vestigial remnant of earlier mythmaking histories, Metz's peculiar turn of phrase reveals the evolutionary concept implicit to the critical genealogy we have been tracing. In the sudden timelessness of Metz's 'single motion', there is no development, no growth and no history, only an instantaneous and inexplicable break with the past.

Even so, it is important to emphasise that salient elements of this discourse transformed as Griffith's legacy descended from one critic to another, and chief among them was an increasing focus on crosscutting techniques as the salutary mark of originality and, beyond that, on editing's capacity to transform theatrical space through a filmic discourse that could shape the spectator's relation to the visual field. What Jacobs refers to as 'the device of parallel and intercutting' which could 'catch and control the emotions of the spectator' (1968: 98) becomes, by Mitry's account, a technique capable of 'introduc[ing] the audience "into" the drama ... making them participate in the action as though actually experiencing it themselves' (1963: 98). In 1972, Jean-Pierre Baudry explained the origins of cinematic language thus: 'that which the short films of D.W.G. inaugurate and *Intolerance* [1916] rearticulates, is, roughly speaking, the formation of a rhetorical machinery which uses the cinema for effects analogous no longer to those of photography and the theatre, but of the novel' (in Aumont 1990: 348). Irony stains this account when we recognise that Griffith's achievement of an avowedly novelistic technique both forms the bastion of his privileged status as 'the father of narrative cinema' and proves the basis of his later fall from grace, a critical reversal of terms whereby the spectator's interpolation in filmic space comes to be perceived negatively, as trap, delusion or lure.

Treated as an extension of the realist tendency in the nineteenth-century novel, the emergence of a self-sufficient narrative discourse in film was increasingly understood by theorists in the 1970s to satisfy a social appetite or demand for verisimilitude and illusory mastery, to recapitulate the 'oedipal' pleasures that Barthes identified in his 1970 study of Balzac, *S/Z*, as typifying the realist or 'readerly' text. The ubiquity of this model, known as Hollywood 'classicism', gained explanatory power by eschewing specific or local examples in favour of outlining a broad set of traits shared by the realist novel and the dominant mode of commercial cinema. As Stephen Heath wrote in *Questions of Cinema*: 'In its films, cinema reproduces and produces the novelistic: it occupies the individual as subject in the terms of the existing social representations and it constructs the individual as subject in the process' (1981: 127). I quote Heath in particular since his readings remain among the most far-sighted in the field, although the assumptions governing his project are far from idiosyncratic. Hence Dudley Andrew would summarise soon after: 'This [cinema] is an art born in, and as part of, the age of realism. It has known no other norm. Even today, despite the struggle of modernist filmmakers, realist cinema dominates our screens. Semiotics of cinema has, then, felt obliged to deal with the issue over and over. Film semiotics is virtually synonymous with the study of codes of illusion' (1984: 63). These 'codes of illusion', in turn, virtually confirmed that American narrative cinema amalgamated a machine of great homogeneity, an apparatus calibrated to induce the ideological effects that thinkers like Friedrich Nietzsche, Theodor Adorno and Louis Althusser stress: the coercive character of identity, the entanglement of subjectivity and subjection to a dominant norm.

The thinker who has perhaps done most to fix the interrelations of the realist text and Griffith's work at Biograph is Raymond Bellour, whose structural reading of *The Lonedale Operator* (1911) also remains a celebrated instance of what close textual analysis can reveal about the operations of any one film's 'rhetorical machinery'. The film's plot is relatively simple: a female telegrapher (Blanche Sweet), left alone in an isolated station when her boyfriend/engineer departs for work, is first threatened by two bandits attempting to invade the station and subsequently saved when her boyfriend learns of her plight and rushes to the rescue. Of particular interest to Bellour are the ways in which this film moves forward through a system of repetitive echoes that structure and unite the narrative level (with its emphasis on sexual difference) and the formal level (different patterns of symmetry and asymmetry in the composition of the frame, in figure movement, and in visual rhymes). As he explained in an interview with Janet Bergstrom, 'From the very beginning we see the setting up of a diegetic alternation: he/she/he ... And so it continues: the text of the film goes on dividing, joining up and redividing its elements through a succession of varied alternations over 96 shots, until the final joining up which shows us in a single last shot the majority of the elements involved' (1979: 77–9). The perfect balance operating at multiple embedded levels in this film, all geared towards a harmonious equilibrium and goal-oriented resolution, thus discloses a historical locus for 'the systematicity at the heart of the great American classicism' while revealing that system's origins in the 'socio-historical situation opened up by the simultaneous development of the bourgeoisie, of industrial capitalism and of the nuclear family' (Bellour 1990: 360). This situation is shared, Bellour explains, by 'the nineteenth-century novel' (Bergstrom 1979: 89).

Griffith's Melodramatic Imagination and Cinema's Mother Tongue

Such semiotic-structural approaches to narrative cinema as this one have lost their purchase in contemporary film studies, of course, just as the self-same tenets of a doctrine that roared across the fields of literature, sociology, linguistics, psycho-analysis, anthropology and philosophy in the 1960s and 1970s have, with varying degrees of submission, met their demise in humanistic enquiry more generally. It is recognised that even the best of narratological readings derive from an assumption that all meaningful questions are synchronic ones, and that the axiom that any one film or instance reveals the larger system's governing principles betrays a methodology that necessarily produces, rather than identifies, homogeneity in its object of enquiry. As film theorists in the 1970s and 1980s sought alternatives to classical cinema's purported homogeneity, it is hardly surprising that melodrama, a tradition associated with theatricality and hyperbole, with excessive spectacle and overt parallelisms, would emerge as psychological realism's most virulent competitor. What warrants detailed scrutiny here, however, is the critical shift whereby Griffith's films came to emblematise a cinema rooted in melodrama's theatrical traditions rather than in the nineteenth-century novel. Now this 'father of cinema''s 'cinematic language', rather than embody the patriarchy of capitalism's investment in novelistic narrative, was associated with the feminine – the realm of sentiment, fantasy, domesticity – and ultimately with an *embodied semiotics*, a sort of mother tongue. If Griffith's filmed stories had been seen to express eventfulness, linearity and causality, they were now, perhaps, about experience, feeling, the body and moral imperatives.

This shift from Griffith as realist to Griffith as melodramatist took place gradually, buoyed by relatively new historical methodologies. In 1981, voicing a perspective lauded as 'revisionist', Tom Gunning bluntly chastised earlier mythmaking histories: 'D. W. Griffith, the mythical "father" of film as art, haunts film history. All too often Griffith has been an excuse for a lack of scholarship on early film' (1990: 336). Rather than exorcising the paternal ghost *per se*, Gunning fleshes out a more historically informed view of Griffith's narrative experiments in the initial 1908–09 period. Establishing a historically sensitive perspective (that would later inform his well-known recovery of the erstwhile 'primitive' period as a 'cinema of attractions' fully commensurate with *fin-de-siècle* culture and the medium's locus in techno-logical/industrial modernity), Gunning argues for a view of the Biograph films as determined by the local effects of industrial and cultural mores. Linking the onset of Griffith's career in 1908 to the formation of the Motion Picture Patents Company (MPPC), Gunning reveals that the initial objective of the 'Trust' to achieve greater economic stability among its ten allied companies found a corollary by seeking the stability promised by social respectability. This aggressive 'wooing of a middle-class audience' materialised in two ways: by improving theatrical conditions (providing better lighting, comfortable chairs and proper ventilation) and by improving film content (eliminating 'gruesome melodrama or vulgar comedy' and 'lobbying for the happy ending as a requisite for all films') (1990: 338–9).

The textual effects of this stress on what the vernacular now terms 'family values' emerge with vivid precision in Gunning's 1991 study, *D. W. Griffith and the Origins of American Narrative Cinema*, where a micro-archival-based method-ology informs rigorous close readings of key films. Deftly excavating the myriad sources for Griffith's *The Lonely Villa* (1909), for instance, Gunning reaches back to a one-act play by André de Lorde, *Au Téléphone* (1901) and forward through multiple pre-Griffith film incarnations: *Terrible angoisse* (1906, Pathé), *Heard Over the Phone* (1908, Porter) and *A Narrow Escape* (1908, Pathé), among others. As he observes, each of these productions shares the story of a domestic order shattered by outside intruders; each turns on the husband's absence from the home; and each dramatises a pivotal moment in which the threatened housewife telephones her husband, thus emphasising the physical separation of the couple as the news of danger is relayed. Endings, however, differ dramatically. Whereas the 1901 play ends with the husband listening on the phone as his wife and child are murdered (a *Grand Guignolesque* finale repeated in *Terrible angoisse* and *Heard Over the Phone*), the husband in *The Lonely Villa* races to the rescue, arrives in the nick of time and effectively restores the sanctity of the hearth and home. More than simply showing male impotency and gruesome horror transmuting to the period's requisite happy ending and the symbolic reassertion of familial-social order, Griffith's ending articulates suspense through a triangulated editing pattern – victimised women, aggressive thieves, noble rescuer – that provides the basic armature for what Gun-ning terms cinema's 'narrator system', a specifically filmic variation of literary and theatrical narrational strategies. The editing weaves moments in different spaces and different times into one harmonised form.

This detailed revisionist perspective clarifies that any theorisation of cinema's narrative discourse as a simplistic extension of the realist novel is bound for deri-sion. Nor is Gunning alone. In a heuristic move that bears affinity with Gunning's archeological investigations, Rick Altman (1992) observes that Biograph films like *Ramona*, often identified as coming from novelistic originals, might best be viewed in terms of the text's intermediary adaptation for the stage. For Altman, there is no need to think of a stark division between novelistic realism and spectacular melodrama; they are to be seen in terms of one another, as two aspects of a single phenomenon. Peter Brooks's magisterial study, *The Melodramatic Imagination* (1985), often cited as the most influential work for scholarship on melodrama, takes America's *ur*-realist, Henry James, as a key example. Brooks shows that elements of dramatic peripety and the increasingly polarised and oppositional choices that characters such as Isabelle Archer in *Portrait of a Lady* (1881) are forced to make produce a psychic drama closer to the language of dreams than to that of the social world. Geared to express a hidden or repressed meaning, a moral occult, this melodramatic mode originated, Brooks says, on the late eighteenth- and early nineteenth-century European stage as a response to the period's unsettling revolutionary violence and as a mode particularly appealing to a newly secularised middle class, a public for whom the moral coherence afforded by a sacred Being no longer had purchase.

Of utmost importance to the present context is Brooks's assertion that the body claims preeminence in melodrama's system of signs; and that this semiotic system strives to resuscitate an *original* language, rather than 'realistically' attempting to mimic an ordinary one. He hence turns to the aesthetic theory of gesture in eighteenth-century writers like Denis Diderot, whose *Encyclopédie* claims that gesture was 'the primitive language of mankind in its cradle' and Jean-Jacques Rousseau, whose *Essai* construes gesture as 'a kind of pre-language, giving a direct presentation of things prior to the alienation from presence set off by the passage into articulated language' (1985: 66). Yet, as Mary Ann Doane astutely observes in her study of the 1940s woman's film, Brooks seems relatively unaware of the gendered implications underlying this conceptual move. Locating its expressive register in the 'cradle' of 'mankind', trumpeting its relation to the natural world, to bodily plenitude and to non-differentiated signs, melodrama, she argues, theoretically resembles a 'maternal tongue' (1987: 84). Seen from this perspective, the genre's association with the feminine is, in part, explained.

Whether or not Brooks familiarised himself with Doane's analysis is anyone's guess. But in 1992, he turned to melodrama's 'inevitable' encounter with silent-era cinema, specifically to the mode's renewal in Griffith's films, and elaborated a 'convergence in the concerns of melodrama and of psychoanalysis', insofar as both 'conceiv[e] psychic conflict in melodramatic terms' (1994: 22), and both understand the body to be the preeminent site on which repressed matter is acted out, brought to visibility and hence legibility. Moreover, the body most prone to the production of meaning as such is the victimised, or hysterical, suffering female body. And in Brooks's analysis this body proves to be Griffith's most salient representational sign. Attending to Griffith's later historical epic *Orphans of the Storm* (1921), specifically to the overly static pictorial tableau where Henriette, on her way to the guillotine, bids a final farewell to her sister Louise, Brooks writes: 'It is a pure image of victimisation, and of the body wholly seized by affective meaning, of message converted on to the body so forcefully and totally that the body has ceased to function in its normal postures and gestures, to become nothing but text, nothing but the place of representation' (1994: 22–3).

Routed through and across the suffering, feminised body, melodrama's expressive register differs dramatically from the 'realist' norms presumed by Bellour, the 'Grand Syntagmatique' sought by Metz or the 'syntax' alluded to by Ramsaye. Its ideological emphasis differs as well from the generalised 'narrator system' outlined by Gunning, although scholarly attention to the female body's symbolic potency in the Biograph films depended on the textually and historically sensitive revisionist perspective that Gunning's analysis, among others, rendered imperative by the mid-1980s. Through the work of scholars as diverse as Aumont, Altman and Shelley Stamp (see Lindsey 1994), it became clear that Griffith not only staged the hysterical reactions of his many female victims in interior spaces or domestic dwellings, he also developed and relentlessly rehearsed a specifically cinematographic expression of feminine space.

The details are telling. Almost without exception, as Stamp notes (see Lindsey 1994), a single, consistent camera set-up frames the interior space represented in these films. If there is a variation in the camera set-up – the shot of Blanche Sweet telegraphing for help in *The Lonedale Operator*, or the housewife on the phone in *The Lonely Villa* – it tends to be a closer view along the same axis as the initial camera position. The stability of the frame, and the consistency of viewpoint, is reinforced by the visual linkage of walls and other architectural features that often double the edges of the frame so that screen space and room coincide, generating what Aumont terms 'the prison of the frame' (1990: 354). In *An Unseen Enemy* (1912), for instance, the orphaned sisters, played by Dorothy and Lillian Gish, remain trapped in a single room throughout their ordeal, while the 'slatternly maid' and her cohort rob their house and hold the girls at gunpoint. Here the girls' confinement in an enclosed 'space' is rearticulated by the repetitious use of a confining frame, a medium-close shot of the girls' physical immobility and expressions of terror, which Aumont tallies as recurring 15 times in the cutting sequence that relays their brother's race back home to the rescue. In other suspense-laden rescue films of the same period, however, Griffith dramatises the female victims' mobility between rooms in an interior dwelling. As Rick Altman notes in an eloquent reading of *The Lonely Villa*, the mother and her daughters successively retreat from the front parlour to an inner library as the thieves penetrate the mansion from the outside. But, he argues, the match-on-action cuts that link the laterally contiguous rooms, as well as the horizontal character movement between the rooms, emphasise the similarity of the spaces more than their succession in a larger space. The point is crucial: rather than enlarging the space available to the female characters, the progressive movement to narratively 'different' spaces actually refutes linear progression and heightens the sense of interior confinement (1981: 129).

The emphatic stress on the female body's symbolic equation with space does not relegate temporal dimensions to insignificance. On the contrary, the emotional

reverberations of feminine space are intimately bound up with the dramatic significance of temporality; indeed, the very crux of the rescue paradigm is its emphasis
on time: last-*minute* rescue. As Stamp summarises (see Lindsey 1994), the logic
of parallel editing, that of simultaneity, would seem to imply that the alternating
scenes of returning rescuer and victimised womanhood transpire in a comparable
amount of time. Yet suspense is built by expanding the time of the events in the
space under siege, while accelerating and eclipsing the rescuer's frantic return.
Accentuating this spatial-temporal dynamic in one of the boldest studies of melodrama to date, Linda Williams returns to Griffith's reiteration of cross-cutting techniques in the climactic scenario of *Way Down East* (1920), observing that even as 'a
rapid succession of shots specifying the physical danger gives the effect of speed,
of events happening extremely fast, the parallel cutting between the breaking ice,
David's pursuit, Anna's unconscious body, and the churning falls prolongs time beyond all possible belief. Actions *feel* fast, and yet the ultimate duration of the event
is retarded' (2001: 33). Of particular relevance to what Williams is getting at here is
the wildly asymmetrical form of Griffith's rescue scenario, which is commensurate
with the tense and contradictory nature of the viewer's emotional experience. 'The
"main thrust" of melodramatic narrative, for all its flurry of apparent linear action,
is thus actually to get back to what feels like the beginning', Williams explains. Offering 'the hope ... that there may still be an original locus of virtue', Griffith's melodramatic mode is intimately linked to the moral imperative and 'maternal tongue'
of the broader mode outlined by Brooks (2001: 35). At the same time, Williams
reasserts Griffith's primacy and paternity in the production of a cinematic form of
expression: 'This teasing delay of the forward-moving march of time has not been
sufficiently appreciated ... as an effect that cinema realised more powerfully than
stage or literary melodrama' (ibid.).

Coupling Space and Time: Technology's Family

When Williams refers to melodrama as an 'expression of feeling towards a time
that passes too fast' (ibid.), she might be articulating an aesthetic-ideological impulse born from melodrama's roots in late eighteenth-century European culture.
But narrative cinema's capacity to defy time, to subvert or pervert its quickening, at-
tains privileged status in the context of early twentieth-century culture's flagrant affair with technological modernity. Associated with momentary shocks and unprecedented speed, modernity fostered an anxious fascination with ever more powerful and equally unruly machines. It also fed a capacious public appetite for spine-
tingling thrills, for sensational stimuli capable of breaching the body's integrity. Given
the concurrent development of technological inventions like the train in the early to
mid-nineteenth century and the large-scale construction of urban centres, it is relatively easy to see that the threat to individual selfhood suggested by technology's
sensory pummelling is reinforced by the incursion of a mass public, emblematised

by the unruly crowd. Nor is it a stretch to see that the wildly indiscriminate body of the public mass threatens the stability and cultural privilege previously assumed by the integrated and hierarchical structure of the private family.

Although the earliest cinema's position as a crucible in this constellation of terms may seem transparent to us now, it has not always been understood thus. Once the bastion of a film theory debated by Walter Benjamin and Siegfried Kracauer among others in the 1920s and 1930s, cinema's bawdy affair with modernity vanished in the wake of a humanist tradition emblematised by the mythmaking histories of Ramsaye, Jacobs, Sadoul and Mitry, just as a pre-Griffith cinema languished in the face of a heuristic poised to privilege artistic refinement and the humanising touch of an individual author-Father. Nor could the homogenising theoretical models preached by Metz and Bellour permit detailed scrutiny of modernity's historical exigencies. But in the late 1980s, concurrent with a revisionist methodology proselytised most powerfully by Gunning, the conjunction of the terms 'modernity' and 'early cinema' rushed into critical purview. Without opening up once again the illuminating and often competing perspectives of a *fin-de-siècle* 'cinema of attractions', in which Lumière's one-shot actualities, Méliès's trick fantasy films or the popular 'phantom rides' (in which a camera was hooked to the front or back of a moving train) are seen as fully reflecting social and subjective upheavals of modernity, we can ask how this historical perspective alters the constellation of terms – 'Griffith', 'narrative cinema' and 'families' – that most interest us here.

Of particular interest is the critical recapitulation of parallel editing techniques as the *locus classicus* of Griffith's narrative system, even as the explanatory rationale for editing's mechanisms and effects notably shifts. The capacity of editing to disassemble and reassemble elements of space and time, to manufacture the illusion of continuity out of fragmented and otherwise discontinuous moments, is seen as an active participant in the technological culture of which cinema is a crucial part. As Gunning notes, when revisiting his reading of *The Lonely Villa* in an essay that highlights the period's 'terrors of technology', the confusing leaps in space produced by parallel editing depended for their sensibility on plots that incorporated communication technology's capacity to instantaneously link one space or another. Hence, the telephone in *The Lonely Villa*, like the telegraph in *The Lonedale Operator*, gets coded for narrative purposes, 'naturaliz[ing] film's power to move through time and space' (1998: 219). When the isolated housewife telephones her husband to relay the news of impending danger, the image of the phone makes sensible the cut to an entirely different space. However, for Lynn Kirby, whose 1993 study details the disorienting fascination both pre-1908 cinema and the nineteenth-century train elicited for 'out of control' bodies and things, Griffith's narrative mechanisms do not draw from an already naturalised technological function; rather, editing naturalises or 'tames' an otherwise unruly technology. Speaking specifically of the purposeful race of the engineer back to the station in *The Lonedale Operator*, Kirby claims that 'the train in Griffith became an agent and an object made to serve human agents

... his engineer-driven trains are a far cry from out-of-control early train films' (1993: 108). Ultimately, what cinematic technology naturalises in these films, says Mary Ann Doane in her massive study, *The Emergence of Cinematic Time*, is precisely the illusion of a meaningful, directed, energised time (2002: 196).

Although they differ in style and scope, these analyses together foreground the uneasy alliance Griffith forges between modern technologies and the family. Trains and telephones, like editing, earn privileged status by virtue of the capacity to bring together, or 'couple' as Kirby says, husbands with wives, sisters with brothers. But that same technological prowess bears with it the capacity to annihilate the family, to disperse its members. It is hardly accidental, Gunning notes, that Griffith's rescue dramas are predicated on stories determined by absence and separation: it is the husband's or male sweetheart's departure from the isolated home or railway station that inaugurates the dramatic action. More than simply fuelling the plot, the threat that the family may be sundered irreparably, the recognition that the sanctity of the home is neither immutable nor natural but fragile at best is, ironically, the most meaningful dramaturgical element here. Viewed in the context of a technologically altered and disorienting modern world, the paradoxical and irresolvable dilemma at stake in these films lies in the simple fact that the restoration of the family depends on the same technologies that would otherwise destroy it, on the message relayed via telephone or telegraph and on the rescuer's fast-paced automobile or train ride.

A similar paradox holds true for Griffith's innovative use of parallel editing, which generates an expressive system predicated on representational instability, including its potential for destroying the very illusion of continuity on which editing's unique or 'original' configurations of space and time depend. As Doane notes, Griffith's mode of suspense is 'on the side of invisibility, and depends upon the activation of offscreen space, or (what Pascal Bonitzer calls) the "blind spot". In parallel editing, when shot B is on the screen its legibility is saturated by the absent presence of shot A, and vice versa' (2002: 195). The viewer's experience of the dramatic rescue in these films hence depends on what is not seen or represented – on what editing edits out. Doane's insightful analysis gets at this point by illuminating the interrelation between editing's dependency on invisibility and the exploitation of space in the Biograph films whereby the victims' entrapment in an interior and their successive retreats to increasingly confined closets, libraries or bedrooms strain to make the terror of an absent, unseen space, acutely felt. In other words, the representational (what is on the other side of the door, the threshold) becomes a figurative expression of cinema's signifying system (what is on the other side of the frame, the offscreen space). Speaking more generally, the offscreen space is the space between shots, the disfiguration of continuity on which editing is predicated and which Griffith's narrative system labours to hide. In this unseen space lurks fatality, death, invisibility. It is, says Doane, this 'semiotically dense' space that 'makes it possible for the cinema to say anything at all' (ibid.).

Coda

If the cinema does say *something*, then the implication is that cinema has a voice, which implies, in turn, that cinema articulates or enunciates a subjective perspective. As I hope to have revealed, however, the metonymy implied in this logic is dubious at best. Returning to where this essay began, we find Griffith noisily casting himself in the role of artistic luminary, precisely because his films alone could never reveal the self behind the set. Nor is there an individual who speaks in the system delineated by Bellour, for whom dominant ideology occasions both formal system and manner of address, just as the more localised constraints imposed by the MPPC provide Gunning's 'narrator system' its axiomatic pitch. Perhaps it is the suffering female body, as Brooks would say, that expresses otherwise ineffable meanings, or the telephone – an emblem of speech conveyed rather than speech itself – that allows technological configurations of space and time to form a continuous line of meaningful sense. As we listen to the multiple voices chorusing through this by now familiar conjunction of terms – 'D. W. Griffith', 'families' and the 'origins of American narrative cinema' – we find little that resembles an epistemological guarantee for fixing the patrimony of our cultural and aesthetic past. What we find, instead, is a far more provocative critical affair, an ongoing renegotiation of the terms and traditions through which we turn our uncertain, passing contemporaneity into the signs of history.

6

Blood is Thicker than Water:
The Family in Hitchcock

WILLIAM ROTHMAN

'Breakdown' (1955), the last episode of the first season of *Alfred Hitchcock Presents* (1955–62), was the one my third grade classmates and I couldn't stop talking about in the P. S. 181 playground. It has haunted me ever since. Although it is not about family – few Hitchcock works are – it will be a useful starting point for the reflections that follow. It begins, as usual, with Hitchcock's introduction. 'I think you'll find it properly terrifying', he says, 'but like the other plays of our series it is more than mere entertainment. In each of our stories we strive to teach a lesson or point a little moral. Advice like mother used to give: You know, "Walk softly but carry a big stick." "Strike first and ask questions later" – that sort of thing. Tonight's story tells about a business tycoon and will give you something to ponder … You'll see it after the sponsor's story, which, like ours, also strives to teach a little lesson or point a little moral.'

'Breakdown' is, indeed, a morality play. A businessman (Joseph Cotten) scoffs at the weakness of others, and pays dearly for it. He is paralysed in an automobile accident. Taken for dead when the authorities find him, he reveals himself to be alive only when, on the coroner's slab, he gives up trying to control the situation and, breaking down, prays to God. His silent weeping produces a tell-tale tear. When the coroner sees it, he leans over to assure Cotten that everything will now be all right. End of story. Except that Hitchcock appears again onscreen and says, with that inimitable knowing, bored, disdainful look to the camera: 'Well, that was a bit of a near thing.'

There is such disdain in Hitchcock's voice! But is he sharing this disdain with us, or directing it at us? And what, or whom, exactly, does Hitchcock hold in such contempt? His sponsors, who won't let him 'tell it like it is' but insist on a happy ending, and those of his viewers whose eyes need to be opened to the gap between his sponsors' rosy picture of the world and the way things really are? And what won't his sponsors let him tell? That the real world, unlike the world according to his sponsors, is not just, or moral. (If it were, Hitchcock would have no need for sponsors.)

Does Hitchcock really believe that 'Walk softly, but carry a big stick' and 'Strike first and ask questions later' are the kind of advice that mothers do give, or should give, to their children? Or does a mother's love impart a different kind of lesson, the kind of lesson the Cotten character learns when he fails to acknowledge his own humanity, or the humanity of others, and finds himself subjected to a terrible ordeal? Cotten learns, the hard way, that his ability to control his world, or even his own self, has limits. When he stops trying to assert control, the 'miracle' happens, and he is saved (if, perhaps, for a fate worse than death).

And yet, even as 'Breakdown' is pointing this moral, its author is asserting *his* control over Cotten's fate. Hitchcock, not God, arranges the series of unlucky 'accidents' that push Cotten to breaking point. And when Cotten finally breaks down and prays, it is Hitchcock who intervenes to spare his life. In arrogating to himself the power to mete out retribution and salvation, Hitchcock becomes at one level, or reveals himself to be, no different from Cotten, hence no less deserving of punishment, no less in need of learning the lesson Cotten is taught.

Here as elsewhere, Hitchcock's reassuringly impish delivery belies his seriousness. Playing the jester gives him a licence to speak truths that others on television consign to silence. Yet for all his impishness, there is real vitriol in his voice, a palpable cruelty in his expression, as if he is happy that the world is unjust, and happy as well to be the one to be opening our eyes to this truth. 'Breakdown' points to a moral, which it also by its very nature calls into question, even as it calls into question its own self-questioning. This is a paradox at the heart of all of Hitchcock's work.

In 'Breakdown', Hitchcock returns after the final commercial break and prefaces his concluding remarks by saying, 'There, now'. His voice is soothing, as if he were a mother who has just administered medicine to her sick child and is reassuring herself that the ordeal wasn't as bad as the child thought it would be. In *Marnie* (1964), when Marnie's (Tippi Hedren) injured horse finally stops struggling after she shoots it in the head at point blank range, she says 'There, now', with exactly the same intonation, as if she believes she has put her beloved Forio to sleep not merely figuratively but literally, and is praying that the bullet to the brain she has just administered was not such a bitter pill to swallow. The distinct echo of Hitchcock's voice I hear at this moment brings home to me both the sincerity of Marnie's belief that her act of killing was an act of love, and the mocking irony of Hitchcock's suggestion that the 'medicine' his sponsors have just given us not only puts us to sleep, it blows out our brains.

In his appearances on *Alfred Hitchcock Presents*, Hitchcock declares his contempt for the world according to 1950s television, the world as Hitchcock's sponsors would have us believe it really is – a world in which father knows best that morality always pays and crime never does, that marrying, raising children and being good consumers guarantee living happily ever after. It is a world in which 'family values' are enshrined. Hitchcock, too, claims to know best, but what he knows is that in the real world there is no guarantee that good will prevail, that faith will be rewarded. People's true motives – even our own – are unfathomable. And evil exists. 'We always kill the one we love' is a maxim Hitchcock never tired of citing in his interviews, or illustrating in his films. Then, does Hitchcock believe that the world is a foul sty, as another Joseph Cotten character, Uncle Charles in *Shadow of a Doubt* (1943), rather hyperbolically puts it? Or does Hitchcock possess, despite everything, the faith in others – and in himself – necessary for representing with conviction a marriage or a family that is of value in itself?

Hitchcock films – even *Family Plot* (1976) – do not have family plots. They are romances, intimately related, generically, to the Hollywood films that the philosopher Stanley Cavell (1981) calls comedies of remarriage, such as *It Happened One Night* (1934), *The Awful Truth* (1937), *The Philadelphia Story* (1940) and *Mr and Mrs Smith* (1940), Hitchcock's third American film, his own not very successful contribution to the genre. As in remarriage comedies, the man and woman joined together at the end of a typical Hitchcock thriller are not shown as even contemplating raising a family. Hitchcockian protagonists, typically, are not only single and childless; they are not shown as having parents or even siblings. When married life is glimpsed at all, it is usually viewed darkly (the brief glimpse that *Rear Window* (1954) offers us of Mr and Mrs Thorwald (Raymond Burr and Irene Winston) before he chops her body into pieces; the comical scenes of the domestic life of Chief Inspector Oxford and his wife (Alec McCowen and Vivien Merchant) in *Frenzy* (1972); Hannay's (Robert Donat) sojourn at the home of the brutish crofter and his wife in *The 39 Steps* (1935)). The same can be said of family life. How often do we see a happily married couple, or a happy family, in a Hitchcock film? Young Charlie (Teresa Wright) rather sums it up in *Shadow of a Doubt*: 'Do you ever stop to think that a family should be the most wonderful thing in the world, but that this family's just gone to pieces … We just sort of go along and nothing happens … We're in a terrible rut.' She's concerned that everybody else wants to talk about money, but she's talking about souls. 'We don't even have any real conversations. We just talk.'

Marriage

Nowhere does Hitchcock present a bleaker view of marriage than in 'Revenge' (1955), the first episode of *Alfred Hitchcock Presents*, which brilliantly set the tone for the series. When Carl (Ralph Meeker) comes home from work, he finds that his wife Elsa (Vera Miles) was attacked by a brutal intruder who left her in that same catatonic, trance-like state into which Rose Balestrero (another Vera Miles character), in *The Wrong Man* (1956), withdraws after her breakdown. We recognise this state from other Hitchcock films as well. Scottie (James Stewart) is in such a state after he sees (so he thinks) the Kim Novak character fall to her death in *Vertigo* (1958). So is Alice White (Anny Ondra), in *Blackmail* (1929), after she kills the artist who tries to rape her, and Diana Baring (played by Norah Baring) in *Murder!* (1930), after she witnesses a murder she is wrongly accused of committing. Carl decides – his wife emerges enough from her trance to nod her approval – to find the perpetrator on his own, and kill him. Driving into town from their trailer park – unlike Hitchcock's movies of the 1950s (except for *The Wrong Man*), episodes of *Alfred Hitchcock Presents* often have working-class protagonists; they are more 'slices of life' than 'pieces of cake' (as Hitchcock liked to call his theatrical films) – Carl and Elsa pass a man walking on the street who Elsa says is 'the one'. Carl follows and kills him. On their way home, however, Elsa sees another man. 'He's the one', she says of him, too, as we hear the siren of an approaching police car.

Elsa speaks these words with a trace of a smile, the same smile that is on Rose's lips at the end of *The Wrong Man* when her husband Manny (Henry Fonda) visits her in the sanatorium to tell her that their ordeal – he was being tried for a crime he did not commit – is all over because the police have caught the real robber; she replies, accusingly, with a sucker punch: 'That's fine for you.' The intense hostility in Rose's voice reveals that she blames Manny for her madness. (Is it madness for her to think this way? Is there reason to her madness?) Her words cause him pain, and she means them to; they're her form of revenge. I hear in Elsa's 'He's the one' the same hostility, the same vengefulness, towards her husband. But revenge for what? For being a man. If her husband is capable of such violence, is it madness for this woman to believe that the man she fingered for him to kill is not different from the man who attacked her? Any man – and only a man – could have attacked her. If Elsa, who suffers a man's violence, gives the green light to the execution of a man for the crime of being a man, then how could there ever be a true marriage between a man and a woman?

At the end of *The Paradine Case* (1947), Maddalena Paradine (Alida Valli) openly celebrates her humiliation of her lawyer Anthony Keane (Gregory Peck), who fell in love with her and was blinded to the truth of her murderous guilt. She does not mask or disavow her vengefulness, or feel ashamed of it, as Elsa and Rose do; she brazenly declares it to the world. She is dangerous, as they are, but not mysterious. She lacks their clairvoyance and their fragility, their sense of being haunted – the characteristics especially salient in Vera Miles. Except for Nova Pilbeam and Peggy Ashcroft (in her brief stint as the crofter's wife in *The 39 Steps*) and perhaps Sylvia Sidney, I do not sense that Hitchcock was particularly inspired or drawn to – we might say, in love with – any of the actresses in the films he made before moving to America, however much the characters they played – especially Daisy, Alice White and Diana Baring – may have interested him. The same can be said of Hitchcock's earliest American films. Joan Fontaine is perfectly good in *Rebecca* (1940) and *Suspicion* (1941), but she was David Selznick's kind of woman, not Hitchcock's. Nor was Teresa Wright, as wonderful as she is in *Shadow of a Doubt*.

Everything changed when Ingrid Bergman appeared on the scene. Anyone viewing *Spellbound* (1945), *Notorious* (1946) or *Under Capricorn* (1949) cannot but believe that Hitchcock was in love with his Swedish star (whether we believe it was the flesh and blood actress whom he loved or the woman onscreen, the 'real' woman as she was transfigured by Hitchcock's mastery of the art of pure cinema, as he liked to call it). Hitchcock's love for Bergman found expression in the films he made with her, films that are also *about* her. I find it irresistible to view *The Paradine Case*, made between *Notorious* and *Under Capricorn*, as also being somehow about Ingrid Bergman, even though its female lead, Valli, although European, is a very different kind of actress. More precisely, I take it to be a veiled fantasy or allegory about Hitchcock's infatuation with Bergman, how it threatened his marriage, and how his wife's capacity for forgiveness enabled the marriage to survive the threat – but at a cost. It even includes – prophetically, as it were – a European rival who bests the protagonist (Peck) and wins Valli's love. Is it nothing but a coincidence that it was Hitchcock's wife, Alma, who adapted the novel on which *The Paradine Case* is based? Is it a coincidence that it was during the ensuing period that Hitchcock made a series of films (*Rope* (1948), *Strangers on a Train* (1951), *I Confess* (1953)) that are virtually devoid of women? And is it a coincidence that *Stage Fright* (1950), with its sympathetic focus on women, was based on another novel that Alma Hitchcock adapted for the screen? But even *Stage Fright*, one of his most underappreciated works, left Hitchcock in search of a woman onscreen for him to fall in love with. Jane Wyman – whose wide-eyed, deer-in-the-headlights look can no doubt be explained as a lingering hangover from her marriage to Ronald Reagan – gives a brilliant performance in the film, but she was also not Hitchcock's kind of woman. Marlene Dietrich surely was, but fashioning a vehicle for that screen legend, especially given her advancing age, was a formidable challenge he may well have fantasised about, but chose not to pursue. So the stage was set for Grace Kelly. And the rest is film history.

North by Northwest (1959), a monumental landmark of that history, is the first Hitchcock thriller to end, like a comedy, with a romantic couple joined in marriage and unambiguously joyful to be married to each other. (Although it is anything but a comedy, *Marnie* too ends with its leads thankful to be married, but their mood is far more sober.) Evidently, it took the major part of his career for Hitchcock to achieve – or reconcile himself to – such an ending.

For one thing, it required the right actress. As I argue in *The 'I' of the Camera*, Eve Kendall is a composite of all three of the women in *The 39 Steps* (Pamela, Annabella Smith and Margaret, the crofter's wife (Rothman 2004: 241–2)). There's also more than a little of Madeleine Elster, and of Judy Barton, in her situation and her nature. To be believable in the role, an actress has to possess, onscreen, impossibly incompatible qualities. She also has to be able to hold her own with Cary Grant, as Ingrid Bergman and Grace Kelly, in very different ways, had proved able to do (Kelly by dint of her sophistication and youthful beauty, Bergman by her passion and perversity). And she has to possess, onscreen, something of the fragility, and the dangerousness, that Hitchcock saw in Vera Miles. Ingrid Bergman or Grace Kelly could not convincingly have incarnated this impossible composite character.

Neither, actually, could Vera Miles. Viewing *North by Northwest*, I do not find myself able to believe that Eva Marie Saint *is* Eve Kendall. But she is such an intelligent and skilled actress, and so elegant and beautiful to boot, that she does a sufficiently convincing job of impersonating her.

When *North by Northwest* concludes with Roger and Eve about to indulge in the pleasantest perk of connubial life, there's no guarantee they will live 'happily ever after'. What makes theirs an exemplary marriage, one worthy of a remarriage comedy, is their shared commitment to living each day, and each night, in a spirit of adventure.

It is illuminating to reflect on the path by which these characters arrive at this perspective. In comedies of remarriage, as Cavell argues in *Pursuits of Happiness* (1981), in order for the couple to transform their failed marriage into one worth having, the woman must undergo a metamorphosis so traumatic as to be tantamount to death and rebirth. One feature that makes *North by Northwest* different, Cavell observes in an essay titled simply '*North by Northwest*' (2005), is the fact that it is Roger, not Eve, who undergoes such a transformation. It is marked in the film by the symbolic piece of theatre they stage together, in which Eve pretends to kill Roger, and he plays dead. A further feature that distinguishes *North by Northwest* from remarriage comedies, I would add, is the fact that the man's rebirth requires, symbolically, not only a death, but an act of murder as well. In remarriage comedies, the threat to marriage is divorce. In the Hitchcock thriller, divorce, which is always provisional, is replaced by murder, which is always permanent (although *The Trouble with Harry* (1955), in which the Shirley MacLaine character's ne'er-do-well husband keeps popping up, like a bad penny, even after he is dead and (repeatedly) buried, casts doubt on the efficacy of death in terminating a worthless marriage).

Earlier in *North by Northwest*, after Roger learns that Eve knowingly sent him to what she thought would be his death, he finds himself unable to forgive her. At the art auction, he deliberately, and vengefully, places her life in jeopardy. If she dies, there will be blood on Roger's hands, for part of him *wants* her to die. Then again, when she sends Roger to his doom, she has no choice in the matter. But that doesn't mean there isn't a part of her that wants *him* to die – not for being a man, exactly, but for being the kind of man who doesn't believe in marriage. Whether there is, or could be, any other kind of man is a question the film asks itself, and answers in the affirmative. (Thank God for Cary Grant! Where would the American cinema have been without him?) Roger and Eve stand in need of each other's forgiveness, in other words. By the end of the film, they both acknowledge the darkness in themselves that makes them capable of killing, as we all are. And they both forgive each other, and themselves, for the darkness within. In *Notorious*, Devlin (Grant) and Alicia Huberman (Bergman) likewise acknowledge the darkness in themselves, and in each other, and forgive one another, and themselves. And I believe the same can be said of all the men and women in Hitchcock films – *Re-*

becca, *Under Capricorn*, *Rear Window*, *The Trouble with Harry* and *Marnie* among them – who convincingly achieve relationships worth having. They, too, come to forgive each other, and themselves, for the darkness within, the darkness whose existence Hitchcock's television sponsors would have him deny.

I am aware that *Rear Window*'s clever ending – Lisa (Grace Kelly) pretends to be reading a travel magazine, but she has a fashion magazine hidden under its covers – can be viewed as casting doubt on the idea that she and Jeff (James Stewart) are a viable couple. I don't subscribe to that view, however. Earlier, Jeff, confined to his apartment, can only watch ineffectually as Lisa, who has bravely or foolishly climbed into the Thorwald apartment, finds herself in grave danger when the murderer returns. Admiring the way she cleverly extricates herself, Jeff whispers under his breath, 'Smart girl!' It's Lisa's gift for improvisation, her capacity for deviousness and deception, that wins him over. If he knew, as we do, that she is now only pretending to have changed her reading habits, he might well put up an argument, but that argument would inevitably remind him that he loves her the way she is. And the feeling is mutual.

I am also aware that the ending of *Rebecca* can be viewed as the restoration, and affirmation, of patriarchal marriage. I do not subscribe to this view, either. Manderley is burned to the ground, never to rise again – except in the Joan Fontaine character's dream, a dream represented, rhetorically, by Hitchcock's film. And that film ends with the explicit declaration that Manderley is gone, vanished. *Rebecca* asks us to believe that this woman's marriage to Maxim de Winter (Laurence Olivier) has been reborn. But their marriage can no longer be characterised – if it ever could – as patriarchal. The burning of Manderley signifies that from now on this marriage, if it is to continue to survive, must be a partnership of equals – the radically new kind of marriage that remarriage comedies envision and celebrate.

Family

The typical Hitchcock protagonist is not only single and childless, but also not explicitly shown as having parents or even siblings. When Hitchcock shows a married couple's home life, the couple is usually childless. Family life is even less often shown, much less dwelled on, than married life, although a number of Hitchcock films do offer glimpses – yet only glimpses – of it. They include *The Lodger* (1927), *Blackmail, Murder!* (the comical scene in the working-class home), *The 39 Steps* (the birthday party), *Sabotage* (1936), *Young and Innocent* (1937), *Rebecca, Notorious, Stage Fright, Strangers on a Train, The Trouble with Harry, The Wrong Man, The Birds* (1963), *Marnie* and *Topaz* (1969).

Hitchcock sometimes presents family life in a caricatured fashion. I am thinking, for example, of Anne's (Ruth Roman) impossibly stiff and formal family and Bruno's (Robert Walker) impossibly dysfunctional one in *Strangers on a Train*. In other Hitchcock films, family life is represented more realistically, as in *The Lodger*,

Blackmail, *Murder!*, *Young and Innocent*, *Shadow of a Doubt*, *The Birds*, *Marnie* and *Topaz* (where the relationship of André Devereux (Frederick Stafford) and his daughter Nicole (Dany Robin) is presented, quite unusually, from the point of view of the parents, not the child). Typically, as we have said, the protagonists in Hitchcock films, like the couples of remarriage comedies, are not shown as having children, or even contemplating having them. When they are shown as having a family, they are typically represented as *having* parents rather than *being* parents. Family enters the picture mainly through the ways fathers and mothers haunt their children's lives, as emblematised by the portrait of the Joan Fontaine character's late father in *Suspicion*, who seems to look down disapprovingly on his daughter's marriage. The perspective is that of the child, not the parents, although in his later films Hitchcock is always at pains to incorporate at some point an acknowledegment of the parents' perspective as well, as in the very different endings of *Psycho* (1960) and *Marnie*, for example, or the sequence in *The Birds* in which Mitch's (Rod Taylor) mother (Jessica Tandy) drives over to her friend's farm only to find him dead, his eyes pecked out.

The Man Who Knew Too Much is the great exception to the rule that Hitchcock films present parent/child relationships from the point of view of the child (although in the 1956 version, the kidnapped son's perspective is movingly acknowledged in the haunting series of slow dissolves by which the camera makes its way from the ballroom where his mother is singing to the room where he is being hidden). In both the original and the remake, when the couple's child is kidnapped it feels as if Hitchcock has magically turned the mother's fantasy (what she most dreads, or, perhaps, what she unconsciously wishes) into reality.

In the 1956 version, Jo and Ben McKenna (Doris Day and James Stewart) have a son, Hank (Christopher Olsen). In the opening of the film, Jo surprises her husband by announcing that she wants to have another child. She pushes for a second child in part because she feels she got the short end of the bargain when she gave up her career to further her husband's. He vetoes it. In the midst of the surprisingly bitter argument that ensues, Hank is kidnapped. The challenge of getting Hank back provides the occasion and incentive for husband and wife to put aside their grievances and join together in a spirit of adventure. Teaming up to rescue their son, saving the life of a foreign dignitary in the process, rekindles the spark between them. But it is significant that it takes Hank's absence for this man and woman to recognise how much they are capable of enjoying each other's company. Once the three are again living together under one roof (and in Indianapolis, no less), will the couple's adventurous spirit survive? We cannot say.

As is par for the course with Hitchcock protagonists, young Charlie in *Shadow of a Doubt* is plucked out of her everyday routine and thrust into an extraordinary situation. But what precipitates this is the entry, or re-entry, into her family of her Uncle Charles. Except for the opening sequence in a seedy Philadelphia boarding house, the film takes place within the bosom of the Newton family in all-American

Santa Rosa, California. The extent to which *Shadow of a Doubt* constitutes a *study* of the family – the family it studies is posited (ironically but, as is Hitchcock's wont, not simply ironically) as the 'typical American family' – makes this film an exceptional one in Hitchcock's oeuvre. Only *Young and Innocent, Stage Fright, The Birds*, and *Marnie* are at all comparable in this respect.

Shadow of a Doubt is one of several Hitchcock films whose protagonist is a young woman who lives with her parent(s). Others include *The Lodger, Blackmail, Young and Innocent, Suspicion, Shadow of a Doubt* and *Stage Fright*. (To these characters, we might add Guy's (Farley Granger) fiancée Anne (Ruth Roman) in *Strangers on a Train*, although she is not the film's protagonist and is, indeed, a not very appealing character.) In these films, the woman's family life plays a significant role. Such is not the case with all Hitchcock films with female protagonists, however. I am thinking of *Rebecca*, for example (unless we count Mrs Van Hopper (Florence Bates) as the young woman's family). This is a theme that, in Hitchcock's work, can be traced back to *Easy Virtue* (1928). Reversing the more usual pattern, in *The Birds* it is the man, not the woman, who lives at home with mother, as does the villain Alex (Claude Rains) in *Notorious*. But in *The Birds*, also living at home with Mitch Brenner and his mother, Lydia, is Mitch's young sister Cathy (Veronica Cartwright), to whom he is a kind of surrogate father. This, too, is a reversal of a more usual pattern in Hitchcock films, the pattern of having a female protagonist serve as a surrogate mother to her sibling(s). That pattern is exemplified in *Sabotage*, for example, with the Mrs Verloc (Sylvia Sidney) as a surrogate mother to her much younger brother, while in *Young and Innocent*, Erica (Nova Pilbeam), for all her youth and innocence, is a surrogate mother to a gaggle of younger brothers. As the oldest child, one who has learned a sense of duty from her beloved father, she has taken on part of her dead mother's responsibilities within the family. We might also say that in *Vertigo*, Midge (Barbara Bel Geddes) is a kind of surrogate mother for Scottie ('Mother's here', she says when she visits him in the sanatorium). And in *Stage Fright*, Eve Gill (Jane Wyman) lets herself be adopted, in effect, by Charlotte Inwood (Marlene Dietrich) as a kind of surrogate daughter. Perhaps at least in Hitchcock, if not in other cinema as well, mothers and surrogate mothers are indistinguishable.

In *Sabotage*, Mrs Verloc is acts as a mother figure to Steve (Desmond Tester), her teenage brother, who lives under the same roof with her and her unsociable husband (Oscar Homolka). We feel that she could not possibly have had any reason to marry this gruff, unlovable man other than a wish to provide Steve with at least the semblance of a father. When Steve is blown up in a bus as a result of Verloc's traitorous work, she stabs him to death with a kitchen knife. She does so partly, but only partly, in self-defence when he tries to grab the knife before she does. But he only thinks of going for the knife when he notices how intently she is staring at it. She wishes to kill Verloc to avenge Steve's death, to rid the world of the loathsome monster she now recognises her husband to be, and also for her own pleasure.

Mrs Verloc kills the man who caused the death of her surrogate son. Young Charlie and Marnie both kill when they perceive that their mother's life is threatened, Charlie believing that if Emma (Patricia Collinge) ever learned that her brother was a murderer, the truth would literally kill her. In Hitchcock films, motherhood is inextricably intertwined with killing. Then again, we might perhaps expand this principle to say that in Hitchcock films, family relationships in general, like marriage, are linked with killing. 'We always kill the one we love', indeed.

Mothers and Sons

Thanks to *Psycho*, most people associate Hitchcock with perverse relationships between harpy-like mothers and terminally screwed-up sons. And yet, except for *Notorious* (in which Alex and his mother are both Nazis, so their murderousness comes with the territory), *Psycho* is the only Hitchcock film in which a mother is portrayed as monstrous (and even in *Psycho*, the matter is complicated).

In *The Lodger*, the mother of the eponymous character (Ivor Novello), who on her deathbed calls upon her son to avenge his sister's murder, is anything but a monster. Hitchcock's other British films of the 1920s and 1930s are all but devoid of mother/son relationships of any kind. Neither do such relationships figure in his American films prior to *Notorious* and *Strangers on a Train*. In the latter film, Bruno's mother (Marion Lorne) is so ditzy, and so obviously harmless, that he holds his father responsible for making him the way he is. It is only in the remarkable series of great films from *The Trouble with Harry* and *The Man Who Knew Too Much* through to *The Birds* that the mother/son relationship assumes a central place.

In the first two of these films, the mother/son relationship is viewed, exceptionally, from the mother's perspective, not the son's. Jennifer Rogers (Shirley MacLaine) and her son Arnie (Jerry Mathers, of *Leave It to Beaver* fame) are very close, but the film posits their intimate relationship as a healthy one – indeed, as virtually ideal, in no small part because MacLaine, in her first screen appearance, is herself so winningly childlike that we have no difficulty believing that Jennifer is Arnie's best friend as well as his mother.

In the remake of *The Man Who Knew Too Much*, the mother/son relationship is more ambiguous. Jo and Hank are very close, but in this film, unlike *The Trouble with Harry*, we sense disturbing oedipal stirrings. Mother and son dance almost like lovers (not a good sign) as they sing 'Que Sera, Sera' together (definitely not a good sign). When his parents share an intimate moment on the Marrakech bus, Hank seems perplexed at being excluded. A lurch causes him to yank off a Muslim woman's veil. As a line of dialogue reminds us, in the Muslim religion – as in the Freudian religion; as in Hitchcock's religion of pure cinema – there are no accidents.

The Wrong Man, another of Hitchcock's underappreciated works, is perhaps most realistic in representing the mother/son relationship. Mama Balestrero (Esther Minciotti) is no monster, but Hitchcock goes out of his way (as he does in *Shadow* of a Doubt) to show the power that a mother, in all innocence, can wield over her family. Manny's deepest bond seems to be with his mother; his two sons come second; his wife Rose, third. Hitchcock's camera, never more observant, subtly reveals how Rose, who is not shown as having relatives of her own, repeatedly suppresses her own inclinations in order to fit in with Manny's family, and especially his mother. Yet Rose is the only character whose powers of perception, approaching clairvoyance, rival the camera's own. The suffocating presence of Manny's mother contributes to making Rose feel increasingly isolated as, unnoticed by her husband, for all his efforts to be attentive, she inexorably slips towards her breakdown. Significantly, the decisive moment occurs when Manny, tactfully not mentioning his fear that she is becoming mentally unstable, suggests to Rose that she let the boys stay with his mother for a while. When Mama Balestrero later pleads with her desperate son to pray, Hitchcock may seem to be ratifying her authority when he answers Manny's prayer with the famous virtuoso slow dissolve that sets the stage for the apprehension of the real robber. But although this 'miracle' releases Manny from his ordeal, it does not release Rose.

Vertigo is the one Hitchcock film from this period that seems to lack the mother/son relationship. In a way, though, it enters through Midge, who, as we have suggested, has grudgingly accepted a relationship in which she is reduced to being Scottie's surrogate mother, not his lover. When Midge bows to the inevitable and admits to herself that she has irretrievably lost the love of her life, not to a living woman but to a ghost, she walks out of Scottie's life, and out of Hitchcock's film. Hitchcock pays his respects to Midge by holding on her as she walks slowly away from the camera, her footfalls echoing down the length of the hospital corridor until she rounds a corner and disappears from view – one of the saddest, most elegiac passages in all of Hitchcock's cinema.

In *North by Northwest*, Roger Thornhill and his mother enjoy each other so much, and Jessie Royce Landis (Grace Kelly's altogether winning mother in *To Catch a Thief* (1955)) plays Roger's mother so zestfully, that we have no inclination to blame her for any problems with commitment that her son may have. As far as Roger is concerned, his mother is neither part of his problem nor the key to its solution. After doing her small bit to help, she makes an early exit from the film. We're sorry to see her go, but there's no need for her to stick around.

Other than *Psycho*, *Notorious* is the only Hitchcock film that portrays a mother in a villainous light. Alex's mother (Leopoldine Konstantin) conspires with her son to poison his wife, Alicia. She has been suspicious of Alicia, and her suspicions turn out to have been prescient. But it is impossible to separate her maternal instinct, which enables her to sense from the outset that Alicia is not as she appears to be, from her conscious or unconscious wish to discredit, in her son's eyes, this beautiful young rival for his affection. When Alex defies his mother by marrying Alicia, then seeks his mother's help after he discovers his wife is an American agent, her maternal instinct to protect her son (especially given the magnitude of his stupidity, as she rather uncharitably puts it) cannot be separated from her possessiveness and petty jealousy in taking indecent pleasure in the prospect of killing Alicia.

In *Psycho*, it is a complex question whether Norman's mother is really villainous. At the end of the film, the glib psychiatrist characterises her as a spiteful, vengeful woman. This is on the basis of what he takes to be a conversation with her, for he is convinced that the 'mother half' of Norman's split personality has completely taken over and the 'Norman half' is no more. As I argue in *Hitchcock – The Murderous Gaze*, however, we have no reason to believe this blowhard (Rothman 1982: 333). Thus, when at the end of the film Anthony Perkins looks up at the camera with a villainous grin, we don't know who – or what – is grinning at us. Is this, as the psychiatrist's account would imply, mother grinning in triumph? Or is it really Norman, who has put one over on the psychiatrist and is now playing us for suckers as well? When Norman's real mother's mummified face is momentarily superimposed over Perkins' face, she – it? – is also grinning. Does this confirm that Norman's mother is really the villain of the piece? Or is the villain Norman, who has created this monster (to carry out his own murders, perhaps) and is challenging us to acknowledge his creation? Or, indeed, is the real villain Hitchcock, whose art has created *Psycho*? Are artists to be thought of as fathering their works, or as giving birth to them?

The Birds revises in a humane way the stereotype of the monstrous mother that plays a central if ambiguous role in *Psycho*. Mitch's ex-girlfriend Annie (Suzanne Pleshette) characterises his widowed mother, Lydia, as being afraid that Melanie (Tippi Hedren) will give her son the love that she has been unable, or unwilling, to give him. No woman incarnated by Jessica Tandy could possibly be a monster, but Annie understands Lydia's fearfulness to be the source of Mitch's resistance to committing himself to another woman. Annie's characterisation rings true, and she seems to be offering it to Melanie as a friendly gesture. Lydia is so different from Melanie's own mother that Melanie seems genuinely interested in trying to understand her. Both Melanie and Lydia recognise that they are in competition for Mitch's affection. Yet they seem to have a certain amount of respect, even affection, for each other.

Frenzy gives the mother/son relationship a bizarre twist. The serial killer Rusk (Barry Foster) seems fond and proud of his mother (Rita Webb). He's at his most likable, and normal, when he shows off his 'mum' to Richard Blaney (Jon Finch), the film's not particularly likable protagonist. From a psychoanalytic point of view, it is reasonable to assume that Rusk's affectionate relationship with his mother is a cause of his perversity. But how *could* this harmless woman be to blame for Rusk's evil ways? In the gruelling sequence in which Rusk rapes and murders Blaney's ex-wife Brenda (Barbara Leigh-Hunt) in the matrimonial agency that she runs, she believes until the end that he is a sick, pathetic man driven mad by sexual frustration. We, too, believe that Rusk is a human being, not a monster, until he goes over to the dead woman's desk and stands for a moment with his back to the camera.

Still turned away, he picks up a half-eaten apple and takes a hearty bite. Then he puts the apple in his pocket and, with a jaunty step, walks coolly out of the office. He no longer seems like a tormented Adam; he's the Serpent. Is Rusk a true villain, the devil incarnate, whose 'mum' had no part in making him evil? Or is he a human being no different from us? We cannot say. We cannot answer this question because Hitchcock's camera never unmasks Rusk. At the moment he bites into the apple – the bite is on the soundtrack – his face is hidden from the camera.

Mothers and Daughters

A good deal of critical attention has been given to the relationships between mothers and sons in Hitchcock films; but much less to the mother/daughter relationship. And yet this is a central theme in *Shadow of a Doubt*, which Hitchcock often spoke of as his personal favourite among all his films, and in *Marnie*, his last masterpiece. It is also a thread that runs through a number of other Hitchcock films.

I am thinking, for example, of the suggestive moment in *Stage Fright* when Charlotte Inwood tries to explain to the respectful Sgt. Mellish (Ballard Berkeley) what it is that made her goad her boyfriend into murdering her husband. 'When you give all your love and get nothing but betrayal in return', she says, 'it's as if your mother slapped you in the face.' I'm also thinking of *Vertigo*. If father/son relationships are the stuff of tragedy in cinema, father/daughter relationships the stuff of comedy, and mother/son relationships the stuff of horror films, then mother/daughter relationships are the stuff of melodrama. The story of Carlotta Valdes, which haunts Judy in *Vertigo*, is pure melodrama. But why should Judy be haunted by Carlotta's story? What makes her feel that it is particular to her? It helps to think of Judy's bond as being not only with Carlotta, the mother who descended into madness when her daughter was cruelly taken from her, but also with Carlotta's daughter, the little girl whose mother failed to keep her from becoming lost. This provides a key to Judy's psychology. Judy's story, too, is pure melodrama. She keeps a photograph of herself and her mother taken in Salinas, Kansas. After her first husband's death, her mother married a man her daughter did not like (shades of *Psycho*), precipitating Judy's move to San Francisco in search of a man who would love her for herself, setting herself up to be ensnared by the villainous Gavin Elster (Tom Helmore).

And I am thinking of *The Birds*, which dwells more on Mitch's fatherless family than Melanie's motherless one. But the fact that her mother deserted her family gives Melanie a poignant personal interest in learning something about a mother's love that personal experience has not taught her. When Melanie asks Mitch whether, in light of his relationship with his own mother, it might be better not to know a mother's love, he answers, after a pause, that it's better to be loved. Mitch's pause, which suggests that he finds this almost too close to call, always reminds me of Jack Benny's pause, in a famous episode of his radio show, when a mugger gives him the choice, 'Your money or your life?' The mugger has to repeat his question before the notoriously penurious Benny finally answers, with some annoyance at being forced to cut short his calculations, 'I'm thinking it over.'

In Hitchcock films, as I have argued, family relationships are bound up with killing. The mother/daughter relationship is no exception. In *Shadow of a Doubt*, Charlie doesn't want to suffer her mother's fate, yet she loves Emma, as we do, and will do everything in her power to enable her mother's innocent view of the world to remain intact. Believing that if her mother ever learned that her beloved brother Charles was a murderer, the truth would kill her, she kills her Uncle Charles herself, destroying her own innocence in the process. She loves her mother, but surely Charlie must harbour a wish, which she continually represses, to provoke her to change, to open her eyes to the way things really are, even at the risk that the truth will kill her. Hitchcock too, I take it, loves Emma as if she were his own mother. He, too, must harbour a wish to open her eyes, to provoke her to change, even if it kills her. For Emma views the world the way, a decade later, Hitchcock's hated sponsors will come to do.

Young Charlie kills because she perceives that her mother's life is threatened. The same can be said of Marnie. When Marnie asks her mother (Louise Latham), point blank, why she never gave her love, it is one of the most poignant moments in all of Hitchcock's cinema. An equally poignant moment comes at the end of the film, when Marnie finally realises that her mother did love her but was never willing or able to express it, and her mother responds by saying, 'You were the only thing in this world I ever did love.' Even then, she holds back from fully expressing her love for Marnie, first, by referring to Marnie not as a person but as a thing (a thing she acquired when she let a boy have sex with her in exchange for his sweater); secondly, by not being able to bring herself to caress her even at this moment, although her hand is poised a fraction of an inch from Marnie's golden hair; thirdly, by forcing Marnie to pull back from physical contact by saying, as she had several times in the film, 'Get up, Marnie, you're aching my leg.' As Mark (Sean Connery) leads Marnie out of the house, promising to return, Marnie looks back at her mother, sitting alone in the gathering darkness, and says, 'Goodbye.' 'Goodbye...' her mother answers. The camera stays on her as Mark and Marnie exit the house. It is only then, when Marnie cannot hear her, that she adds, in a loving voice that she will never allow her daughter to hear, '...Sugar Plum.'

If Melanie Daniels had asked Young Charlie, rather than Annie Hayworth, whether it's a good thing to know a mother's love, Charlie would have answered, 'Yes', without a pause. If Melanie had posed her question to Marnie Edgar, and while the events of *Marnie* were still unfolding, Marnie, too, wouldn't have needed to think it over. Her answer would have been, 'No.' But if Melanie had asked Marnie the question *after* those events had run their course, Marnie might well have needed to think it over. I like to imagine that Marnie would have answered – with a sigh, perhaps – in the affirmative. Or perhaps a sigh would be her answer.

7

'How Do I Love Thee?': Theatricality, Desire and the Family Melodrama

LUCY FISCHER

What is at stake [in domestic melodrama] is the survival of the family unit and the possibility for individuals of acquiring an identity which is also a place within the system, a place in which they can both be 'themselves' and 'at home'...
– Geoffrey Nowell-Smith (1987: 73)

All I Desire (1953) is one of two melodramas directed by Douglas Sirk that concentrate on the figure of the actress. His more renowned work, *Imitation of Life* (1959), takes as its protagonist a contemporary woman, Lora Meredith (Lana Turner), who moves during the course of the narrative from a model to a Broadway diva to a major film star. Alternately, *All I Desire*, set at the turn of the twentieth century, features Naomi Murdoch (Barbara Stanwyck), a down-and-out vaudevillian who longs for her former days in 'legitimate' theatre. Significantly, rather than situate the actress solely within the world of drama (as in *All About Eve* or *Sunset Blvd.* (both 1950)) both movies place her within a family, establishing tensions between her career and her role as wife and mother.[1] In this regard, both Sirk films link two of the major facets of screen melodrama: a domestic setting and a focus on theatricality. As *All I Desire* opens, these elements merge. Naomi is in a Chicago music hall, conversing backstage with a fellow entertainer and bemoaning the 'broken down' houses in which they are forced to play. She is shocked to receive an unexpected letter from her long-lost daughter, requesting her presence at the girl's high school graduation and senior play. The 'backstory' of the drama reveals that, years earlier, Naomi had fled her children and marriage, running away from smalltown life.

Given that the drama is set in the late Edwardian era, it is tempting to consider a short film of the period that deploys the character of the female performer. *She Would Be an Actress* (made in 1909 by the Sigmund Lubin Company of Philadelphia) depicts an entertainer whose career choice disrupts her connubial universe. Specifically, it portrays a married woman who leaves home to perform in a saloon against her husband's protestations. He follows her there, however, and, impersonating a waiter, surprises her and forces her to retreat. Several aspects of the film help to illuminate *All I Desire*. First of all, female acting is associated with excess, as is evident from the film's initial shot, which depicts the heroine declaiming and gesticulating as she reads a theatre manual. Secondly, the actress is seen as an enemy of marriage, and an emasculator of men. Before she runs away, her husband wears an apron and serves her dinner since, in order to succeed, she has abandoned her domestic chores. Finally, acting is equated with sexual exhibitionism. Thus, we see her dancing shamelessly on the street and flirting with a theatre patron. At the end of the narrative, her surplus is contained: with her husband looking on, she contritely shakes her head to indicate that she will forego her artistic pursuits in the future.

While numerous decades separate this silent film from *All I Desire*, similar attitudes towards the actress and the family circulate in both. Sirk takes pains to represent Naomi's theatrical domain as both failed and sordid (in contradistinction to the moralistic, family-friendly town which she has deserted). In the opening scene, in voiceover narration she describes herself as 'not quite at the bottom of the bill and not quite at the end of [my] rope'. Later, she refers to the theatre world as a 'jungle' and admits that she has had 'no glory, no glamour' there, only 'bruises on [her] illusions'.

Throughout the film, her employment in vaudeville is contrasted to her dashed hopes for work on the dramatic stage – where, she claims, she might have performed Shakespeare. To some degree, Naomi's position stands in opposition to that of Lora Meredith in *Imitation of Life*, who transcends the shallow world of advertising to achieve accolades on Broadway and in the cinema. While Lora (a widow and mother) has much to forego in spending time as a dutiful parent and fiancée (given her professional success), Naomi has little to lose in returning to the fold.[2] When she does, she encounters a woman in Riverdale, Sara Harper (Maureen O'Sullivan), who has made the socially 'appropriate' use of her theatrical skills, becoming the town's high school drama coach. To make the women's inverse symmetry even clearer, Sara has fallen in love with Naomi's estranged husband, Henry (Richard Carlson), the school principal. Clearly, Sara would like nothing more than to marry him and become a benevolent step-parent to his offspring (the next best thing to giving birth).

Like *Imitation of Life*, *All I Desire* pits a woman's acting vocation against motherhood, but does so in a rather complex fashion. While Lora has only one daughter (who is highly critical of her workaholism), Naomi has two – and each takes the contrary stance. Lily (Lori Nelson), the one whose missive ushers Naomi home, entirely admires her electrifying mother (even after Naomi's shocking ten-year absence), and wishes to be an actress herself. She tells her family that her mother was 'smart' to leave town and declares herself 'just like her'. The older child, Joyce (Marcia Henderson), however, is completely judgemental of her parent and shouts, when Naomi returns, 'We aren't your family and you're not our mother.' In scripting Lily as an attractive child who mirrors her mother's nature and pardons her trespasses, Sirk gives more credibility to Naomi's strength and creativity than to that of Lora Meredith. While in *Imitation of Life*, Sarah Jane (Susan Kohner), almost a second daughter, admires and duplicates Lora's theatricality, she is so problematic a figure that her approbation hardly validates Lora's calling. In *All I Desire*, however, Sirk advances esteem for Naomi even further. During the course of the narrative, Joyce is influenced by her mother, albeit against her will. When Naomi arrives, Joyce is a rather prim, authoritarian and subdued individual – having taken on the vacant maternal position within the family at an early age. In the course of the drama, she confronts not only her dislike but her jealousy of her mother (especially when her fiancé, Russ (Richard Long), is bedazzled by her attractive parent). Naomi accuses Joyce of cowardice and urges her to compete – a confrontation which sparks and liberates her daughter's libidinal energy.[3] For example, in a scene which follows involving Joyce, Russ, and her mother horseback riding in the country, Joyce abandons her usual cautiousness and dares to ride a challenging steed instead of the docile one she generally chooses. Furthermore, she seems less prudish in her interactions with Russ, enjoying more the romance of their encounters.

In a similar fashion, Sirk allows Naomi a certain triumph in the resuscitation of her marriage. For, as Geoffrey Nowell-Smith has noted, in melodrama, the attainment of the heroine's goals, rarely entirely 'impossible', does not happen 'without sacrifice' (1987: 73). After Naomi returns to Riverdale, Henry boldly decides to allow Lily to go to New York City with her in order to pursue an acting career. Through the experience of his failed marriage, he has realised the perils of restraining female desire within the bounds of the family and does not want to make the same mistake twice. While it is true that, by the close of the narrative, Naomi has agreed to remain home (her theatrical career in shambles), Henry is not completely victorious. Rather, he admits that he too has been at fault – for having been spineless and conformist, and having lived a 'dull routine'. He literally asks for Naomi's forgiveness (despite her acts of adultery and abandonment) and promises to be a husband who 'has faith in his wife, believes her, loves her'. His contrition is all the more impressive given that, in an attempt to reject her ex-lover, Dutch Heinemann (Lyle Bettger), Naomi has accidentally shot him and created scandal anew, demonstrating, as David Rodowick notes, that in melodrama there is an 'equation of sexuality with violence' (1987: 273). Hence, Naomi has returned home on her own steam, and on her own terms. Rather than Naomi being charged with castrating a man, her husband takes blame for his own meekness and seems ready to change.

Clearly, an examination of *All I Desire* also extends our sense of Sirk's satirical vision of American life – especially as regards its small towns and traditional families. Sirk's analysis is located in the concrete details of the melodrama. Set in the midwest (the original name for the town in Carol Brink's 1951 novel was Placid Lake), the film mocks provincial existence. When Naomi first reminisces about Riverdale, she sighs with exasperation, 'What a burgh!' – reminding us of Bette Davis's line 'What a dump!' in *Beyond the Forest* (1949). Arriving in town, she is immediately the subject of surveillance by Clem, a lascivious townsman. When it is rumoured that she will appear at her daughter's play, the event is suddenly sold out, and as she finally enters the hall there is silence and gaping. When she brings her ex-lover Dutch to the hospital, after having mistakenly shot him, a physician calls the citizens lurking outside 'maggots' and decries their fascination with 'the oldest and the nastiest story in the world'. The petrifaction of the community seems encapsulated in the vision of the family name, 'Murdoch', chiselled into the curb of their street – an indication that they will remain there in perpetuity. More ominously, the lettering resembles that on a granite gravestone. All the more reason for the audience to sympathise when Lily (identifying with her rebellious mother) shouts to her relatives, 'You're not gonna bury me in this provincial burgh!' As though to symbolise this fate, in the room of Naomi's son, Ted (Billy Gray), there hangs a collection of dead butterflies mounted under glass. Finally, one of the reactionary city councilmen is named Colonel Underwood – a moniker reminiscent of the word undertaker (whose profession it is to put corpses in wooden coffins). Though at the opening of the film (when her career is on the skids), Naomi's narration reveals that she has 'not much to look forward to', it is clear that in Riverdale she never did. Sirk himself (revealing his hostility and disdain) calls the milieu of the melodrama an epitome of 'rotten, decrepit, middle-class' America (in Halliday 1972: 89). Not surprisingly, Thomas Schatz has noted that 1950s melodramas are actually among the most socially self-conscious and covertly '"anti-American" films ever produced by the Hollywood studios' (1981: 224–5).

As well as with death, Riverdale (with its attendant 'family values') is associated with inhibition, for, as Rodowick comments, in melodrama sexual identity is 'determined by social identity' (2001: 271). When Naomi returns home and upsets Henry, he confesses that he has not shouted at anyone since she has gone. While she reminds him that they once had 'fun', he grimly recalls that they have 'paid a heavy price' for such enjoyment. Just when they finally kiss, gunshots ring out in the street – a secret signal from Dutch that he desires an illicit rendezvous. The explosions function like the phone ringing in *Imitation of Life*, which repeatedly stops Lora and her lover Steve dead in their tracks every time they are about to embrace.[4] Although the locale of *All I Desire* is wholesome America, the evil or lower-class figures all have foreign names (like Dutch Heinemann) and often exaggerated accents (like the servants Lena Marie Engstrom (Lotte Stein) and Hans Petersen (Fred Nurney)) – and thus signal a trace of xenophobia. As in *Imitation of Life*, it is a marginalised figure – a maid – who nurtures the theatrical heroine (more than does her 'real' family). While in the later work this role is inhabited by the black servant, Annie (Juanita Moore), in *All I Desire* it is filled by the Germanic Lena – an overweight, maternal figure who occupies the position of the domestic, asexual Other (a Teutonic Mammy, as it were).[5] Furthermore, jokes are made at the expense of marriage when the mature, unattractive Lena expresses her desire to marry the elderly Hans – who responds to her advances with grim but passive terror.

Beyond its surface portrayal of woman, *All I Desire* holds theoretical and formal interest as well. In *Imitation of Life*, it is obvious how the character of Lora Meredith comments upon the status of the performer who played her, Lana Turner, one of the major screen actresses of the 1940s–60s. Known, originally, as a glamorous 'sweater girl', she went on to star in numerous noir crime films and melodramas playing against such male stars as Rock Hudson, Clark Gable, Robert Taylor and Kirk Douglas.[6] Especially noteworthy in *Imitation of Life* are the parallels between Lora's struggles with her daughter Susie (Sandra Dee) and Lana's infamous problems with her child, Cheryl Crane, who was arrested in 1958 for stabbing Lana's live-in lover, Johnny Stompanato. To some degree, such self-reference also marks *All I Desire*, attaching equally to Stanwyck's private life and professional history. Thus *All I Desire* can be profitably compared to King Vidor's *Stella Dallas* (1937), the family melodrama for which Stanwyck is best known. As the actress once stated (in commenting on *All I Desire*), 'It's the type of part I've had many times – a bad woman trying to make up for past mistakes' (in Smith 1974: 241). In particular, *All I Desire* reminds one of the Vidor film in the heroine's refusal to renounce sexuality for parenthood (that is, to be nothing else 'besides a mother') and in her banishment from the domestic scene. In the opening of *All I Desire*, as Naomi stands on the porch and peers through the door and windows of her old home (to glimpse her family at the dinner table), we recall the end of *Stella Dallas*, when the protagonist watches her daughter's wedding through a window while standing in the rain outside. As a contemporary reviewer of *All I Desire* aptly noted, 'A mother symbol in America is a mighty potent fixture, and Barbara Stanwyck is its prophet' (Anon. 1953b: 10). Like Lily in *All I Desire*, Stella's daughter Laurel (Anne Shirley) wishes that her mother would attend a key event. Significantly, the scene of Naomi's return home is one of the most histrionic in *All I Desire* (despite its occurrence early in the narrative). A *Variety* review called the film a 'full blown period tear-jerker' and a '79-minute excursion into sentimentality' (Anon. 1953a: 30). She stands on the porch of her home at night, looking into the illuminated family scene. A close-up reveals that tears have welled up in her eyes. She furtively hides in the shadows when her son comes home, but, as she peers again into the house, she is spotted by the shocked housekeeper. As Naomi re-enters the domestic space, Henry refers to the 'years of desertion' she imposed on the family and screams, 'Why did you come back? You hate this town!'

While certain scenes in *All I Desire* hark back to Stanwyck's prior screen roles, other moments more directly engage her status as a star. Born in 1907, Stanwyck became a chorus girl at 15 years old, finally appearing on Broadway in *The Noose* (1926) and *Burlesque* (1927). Movie offers ensued, and between 1929 and her death in 1990, she appeared in some eighty films (including *Meet John Doe* (1941), *The Lady Eve* (1941), *Double Indemnity* (1944), *Sorry, Wrong Number* (1948) and *No Man of Her Own* (1950)) – specialising in roles involving strong-willed independent females. In the opening of *All I Desire*, there is a contrast established between the actress Stanwyck and her fictional counterpart, Naomi. In the credits, the words 'Barbara Stanwyck' appear even before the film's title, which is eventually super-imposed over her name – an emblem of her celebrity power. After an establishing shot of the exterior of the Bijou Theatre, we cut to a close-up of a poster for a vaudeville programme with Naomi Murdoch advertised as 'direct from Broadway'. It is then that Stanwyck's voiceover narration starts and the narrative truly begins. Clearly, Murdoch is a long way from Stanwyck – as far as the Bijou Theatre is from the Great White Way. However, when in the next scene a friend suggests that Naomi return to the legitimate stage 'where you don't have to worry about getting old', we realise that Stanwyck (then 46), is living on borrowed time as a female box-office draw. As Michael Walker points out, she was by this time not prestigious enough a lead for Universal to shoot the film in colour (1990: 32). Stanwyck shares other biographical features with Naomi as well. Orphaned at four years of age, she led a working-class existence before becoming a chorus girl with the Ziegfeld Fol-lies as a teenager. By the mid-1920s, she had made it to mainstream theatre.

Another self-referential scene in the film depicts Naomi observing Lily onstage. As the camera tracks in to a close-up of Stanwyck in the audience, her voiceover is heard musing, 'It was just an amateurish high school play until Lily came on.' Naomi is thrilled to think that her daughter 'could develop into an actress'. Here, we have a vision of a fictional performer confronting a drama within the narrative (all the while being performed by a Hollywood actress who is working in one). It is significant that this scene involves a use of the voiceover trope (as does the open-ing of the film). Both occur at moments when theatricality is highlighted. While in the first example Naomi's voice is temporarily disembodied (with her name on the theatre poster standing in for her corporeal presence), here she is fully visible. There is also an inconsistency in tense between these two sequences that makes the film's point of view enigmatic. In the first instance (when Naomi introduces herself), she speaks in the present tense. At Lily's play, however, she uses the past tense, as though her story were now recalled from a later time. This tempo-ral slippage seems dramatised in Lily's post-production party prank of setting the clock back to make her mother miss her train. Perhaps both stylistic tropes imply that in returning to Riverdale Naomi has personally regressed, as it were. But they may also signify that social clocks are being stopped in the film – with the work-ing women (once liberated by World War Two) being urged to return to hearth and home in the 1950s. As Thomas Elsaesser has observed, in domestic melodrama the bourgeois household functions 'to make time stand still, (to) immobilise life' (1987: 62). The temporal conundrum of Naomi's narration also supports the notion that the female voiceover generally marks a textual 'crisis'.

As the film's title (in addition to its discourse on marital infidelity) would indi-cate, the work is also a consummate treatise on the intricacies of desire. By the phrase 'All I desire', we might mean 'I desire *all*', signifying that my desire is end-less and voracious. On the other hand, the words might suggest that something is 'all (that) I desire', indicating that my wishes are properly limited. It is the tension between, and incompatibility of, these two poles (as registered in linguistic ambiguity) that animates the film. In one scene between Naomi and Sara, Naomi tells the teacher, 'You're the woman he *needs.*' Sara corrects her by noting that Naomi is the woman he *wants.* By the end of the drama, Naomi has bounded her desires (without having utterly resigned them). As she tells Henry, 'We all want things we don't have.' Significantly, the original title of the film was to be *Stopover*, the name of the novel upon which it is based. In the literary plot line, Naomi leaves her hometown again at the story's end, her visit being only a temporary stay. This is the conclusion that Sirk himself desired but was forced to renounce in the name of a more upbeat dénouement. Clearly, the threat of that ending was its affirmation of Naomi's unseemly ambition and her rejection of the familial lifestyle endorsed by the American public. In terms of the culture of the 1950s (in which divorce was still rather unusual), to leave one's husband and children not only once but twice (despite the opportunity to return) was decidedly beyond the pale.

But there is a more subterranean desire that inflects the film and its vision of the family – that between daughter and mother. Lily's passion for her parent is so unlikely and intense that it seems to surpass 'normal' filial devotion. Despite her mother's having forsaken her, she calls her parent 'heavenly' and concocts a scheme to run off with her to New York: 'I always wanted to be with you, always.' Even after Naomi has shot her ex-lover Dutch, Lily is unperturbed. 'Now', she says, 'Mother will be even more famous!' – as though the spectre of a homicidal parent excited her. When the affection between her parents is rekindled and Naomi decides to stay in Riverdale, Lily is furious at her and jealous of her father. 'You let him keep us both in this old town', she screams, 'just 'cause he's stuffy and old-fashioned himself!' There seems an equal passion of mother for child. As Naomi watches Lily perform onstage, she thinks, 'For me, there was only Lily. It was almost magical. I couldn't take my eyes from her.' Significantly, we have just heard a line in the school play in which a male character confesses his obsession with looking at Baroness Barclay (played by Lily).

What is especially interesting about this discourse on desire is that the movie was released in 1953 – the same year in which Alfred Kinsey and his colleagues published *Notes on Sexual Behavior in the Human Female.* The research for that volume is based on interviews with 5,940 'white, non-prison' women in the USA (1953: 43). Chapter Ten of the tome focuses on 'Extra-Marital Coitus', one act that spurred the separation of Naomi and Henry (1953: 409–45). According to research,

> about a quarter (26%) [of the sample] had had extra-marital coitus by age forty … Since the cover-up on any socially disapproved sexual activity may be greater than the cover-up on more accepted activities, it is possible that the incidences and frequencies of extra-marital coitus in the sample had been higher than our interviewing disclosed. (1953: 424)

The researchers also note two more things. First, there is a double standard in so-cial attitudes towards male, as distinguished from female, infidelity:

> It is widely understood that many males fail to be satisfied with sexual relations that are confined to their wives and would like to make at least occasional con-tacts with females to whom they are not married. While it is generally realized that there are some females who similarly desire and actually engage in extra-marital coitus, public opinion is less certain about the inclination and behaviour of the average female in this regard. (1953: 409)

Secondly, obsession with marital infidelity in world literature attests to its prevalence:

> The preoccupation of the world's biography and fiction, through all ages and in all human cultures, with the non-marital sexual activities of mar-ried females and males, is evidence of the universality of human desires in these matters, and of the failure of the existent social regulations to resolve the basic issues which are involved. (Ibid.)

Certainly, Kinsey's findings are relevant to *All I Desire*. They bespeak the high in-cidence of infidelity in America in the era of the film's debut as well as people's tendency to judge adulterous females more harshly than adulterous males. But the fact that Kinsey published his study in 1953 (and that it was a bestseller) also, per-haps, demonstrates that the postwar era saw a weakening of traditional morality and a willingness to confront the realities of sexual behaviour (see Johnson 1983). In fact, Kinsey audaciously lists certain *advantages* to extra-marital coitus including: its offering of 'variety' in sexual experience; its improvement of spousal sexual rela-tions; and its provision of 'a means for one spouse to assert his or her independ-ence of the other, or of the social code' (1953: 432). Certainly, the third rationale is central to Naomi's behavior in *All I Desire*. Her affair with Dutch bespeaks not only an erotic curiosity but a wish to have a life independent of her family. Significantly (in light of the film's mother/daughter 'romance'), the Kinsey report also studied female homosexuality, which it found evident (by age forty) in some 19 per cent of the female population sampled (1953: 453).

Significantly, when Naomi gazes towards the stage, watching her daughter act, the extradiegetic musical theme we hear (and which recurs periodically throughout the film) is Liszt's *Un Sospiro*, a classical motif previously used in Max Ophuls' *Letter from an Unknown Woman* (1948) – a canonical melodrama of the 1940s. In that film, too, the melody swells at moments when the heroine, Lisa Berndle (Joan Fontaine), observes someone performing. In particular, it attaches to the instances when Lisa hears her lover, Stefan Brand (Louis Jourdan), play the piano – initially from her courtyard and then from her apartment window. The lyrical connection made across films cements (for the knowledgeable viewer) the subversive association of maternal and amorous passion. There are other connections to *Letter from an Unknown Woman* that prove intriguing. In some respects Naomi is an 'unknown woman' to all her children, but especially to her son Ted, who, Henry says, was too young when she left to remember her. The narrative of *Letter from an Unknown Woman* hinges upon the illegitimate son that Lisa bears by Stefan. While in *All I Desire* there is no overt mention of Ted's possible illegitimacy, Michael Walker has asserted that the narrative suggests that Ted is the son of Dutch, and not Henry. Significantly, Kinsey's researchers found that a large number of pregnancies resulted from extra-marital affairs and that the progeny were often raised in the marital home without the husband's knowing of the child's genetic heritage (1953: 434). Moreover, *All I Desire* can be read as opening with a 'letter from an unknown woman' – that is, a note from Naomi's long-lost daughter. Some might argue that Lily remains 'unknown'; with the narrative's end, her hopes for leaving Riverdale are quashed when her mother renounces a theatrical career and resumes her connubial existence. The film leaves Lily hanging and her future vague. As Walker puts it, 'Lily is virtually forgotten' (1990: 41) (as is Lisa in the Ophuls film).

My use of the term 'hanging' is not accidental. In the scene in which Naomi first returns to her home, she finds that the house key is still kept in a hanging planter on the front porch. Towards the end, when she tries to leave, she places the key back in the same flowerpot. Ultimately, Henry returns it there when he convinces her to stay. Elsaesser has remarked on the 'symbolisation of objects' in domestic melodrama, given the genre's focus on the bourgeois home (1987: 61). Walker reads the primacy of the key in *All I Desire* in psychoanalytic terms. As he notes:

> [It] would seem to be a significant symbol here … at the very end, Henry takes the key and gives it to Naomi. This clarifies the meaning of the key in the dominant discourse: it was waiting for her and there is no longer any need for it to hang outside. Equally, we can see that symbolically the key is Henry's phallus, waiting, unused, for Naomi's return. (1990: 46)

While Walker's interpretation is plausible, I prefer to read the key in the hanging flowerpot another way – one not so emphatic about depth psychology (sometimes, after all, a key is only a key). The end of the story, relatively upbeat, is qualified in its celebratory tone; it is 'an unhappy happy ending', as Sirk once deemed it (in Walker 1990: 37). We are to believe that Naomi has re-entered a loving home, yet she has also sacrificed her liberty – become a 'potted plant', as it were, instead of one that flourishes wild. Perhaps this transformation of Noami is *our* key to the film. Interestingly, in the beginning of *Stopover*, as Naomi boards a train, much is made of her dislike of domesticated flowers:

> One of her friends had thrust the violets into her hands when she was leaving Chicago; and although she should have discarded them some time ago, she

still made periodic journeys to the water cooler to wet the handkerchief and give them every opportunity for survival. People were always giving Naomi flowers; and while she liked to see flowers growing, the cut ones were an embarrassment to her ... Perhaps because she was so enamored of life, she had a superstitious feeling about death, even for a flower. (Brink 1951: 2–3)

Significantly, the child who most resembles Naomi and who values freedom equally, is named Lily (a bloom associated with both life and death). At the melodrama's close, the fate of both women is left 'hanging', since each may end up discontented and metaphorically 'pot bound'. Sirk noted, when asked to predict Naomi's future, 'What will happen to her? Maybe, maybe a flicker of the old love. But it is impossible. Pretty soon she'll become one of those housewives, inviting the academic crowd in for tea and cake. She'll be lost. She'll disappear' (in Stern 1979: 90). In other words, she will become an 'unknown woman' – to herself, to her vagabond existence and to her admiring daughter. Sirk's quote reminds us that in narrative, women often 'disappear' in more literal ways. In *Beyond the Forest*, for example, Rosa Moline (Bette Davis) is a perverse married woman who flees her small town after aborting a pregnancy and winds up dead on the tracks that lead to Chicago.

While Naomi remains home at the end of *All I Desire*, in her lifelong revolt she is also reminiscent of Ibsen's Nora, a woman who finally leaves. Nora's words of departure to her husband, Torvald, in *A Doll's House* (1879) might have been uttered by Naomi some years before *All I Desire* begins: 'I must stand on my own feet if I am to find out the truth about myself and about life. So I can't go on living here with you any longer' (1966: 97). Nora even pointedly returns a key to Torvald. In the final scene of *All I Desire*, Naomi stands on the porch of her house, the vantage point from which she much earlier viewed her estranged family through a doorway. The doorframe had graphically transformed the interior scene into a picture or, perhaps, a stage tableau. That early scene also foreshadowed the later sequence of Naomi regarding Lily in performance, an ironic parallel between the familial and theatrical realms. Clearly Lily's play-within-a-play references the world beyond the proscenium arch. Like Naomi, Lily's character, Baroness Barclay, is a fascinating woman who (like Naomi) pays the 'penalty' for forbidden, extra-domestic yearnings. The fluid border between theatre and reality is also foregrounded when Lily declares that her mother has made 'a dramatic entrance' into town; and when, as Lily brings her mother breakfast in bed, Naomi jokes that she is getting 'real star treatment'.

Clearly, Brink's novel emphasises this sense of an 'imitation of life'. On the night of Lily's graduation, an encounter between mother and daughter is described in highly dramatic terms:

Lily closed the door behind her and stood against it. Her eyes blazed; the color came and went in her face. She was alive with vigor and beauty and a swift, sure anger. Automatically Naomi began to play their scene, 'Darling, you're lovely! My baby girl, so lovely! And tonight you graduate'. But Lily did not fall into the usual patter of lines, 'Angel! You're lovely too. My own, my little mama!' The blaze and glitter in her eyes was hard, and Naomi saw that Lily was no longer playing a scene but was in deadly earnest. (1951: 130)

In the film version, there is a privileged moment in this discourse of theatricality when Naomi gives a reading of a Browning poem at Lily's post-production party. As Naomi intones, 'How do I love thee? Let me count the ways', she dims the lights for aesthetic effect and stares moistly at Henry, making us wonder if the real question is, instead: '*Do* I love thee?' Here the prodigal actress plays the loving wife on the set of her own home. With this ironic move, Sirk fulfils Naomi's goal to play 'legitimate' theatre, offering her validation of a societal – as against an artistic – kind.

While Sirk's version ends with this compromise, the novel takes a more radical turn. At one point in the film (after Naomi's oration of the Browning poem), Sara asks her to read from Shakespeare at the upcoming high school graduation ceremony. We immediately begin to wonder what her selection will be, dreading that the film will make clichéd comparisons between *The Taming of the Shrew* and the taming of Naomi Murdoch. By the end of the film, however, that possibility is foreclosed, since the graduation ceremony is never depicted (as though the scene had been planned but never shot, or eliminated). Thus, Sara's remarks just hang there – like some porch plant – reminding us of a signifying absence. Clearly, the scene's elision stands as a marker of Sirk's original conception of a dénouement, one more consonant with Brink's striking ending. For in her novel, a shocking scene unfolds when Naomi takes the stage at the high school graduation – just moments before she leaves town forever:

> She saw them all plainly and acutely, as one never sees an audience when footlights intervene … Naomi let the ripple of applause recede and fade away … 'I've been asked to give you a reading from Shakespeare', she said dangerously in a gentle voice, 'and I could do it, too, although I'm not a Shakespeare scholar … No, I'm really not a scholar', she repeated as her clear pale neck and bosom emerged in a white 'V' between the falling barriers of the unhooked bodice. 'I'm just a girl who likes a jolly time…' They all sat frozen, gazing at her with their mouths half open, as she let the black blouse fall, negligently, sensuously, with a slothful and insidious purpose. (1951: 237–8)

Hence, the novel's heroine terminates her stay with an ironic 'striptease'. What Brink accomplishes (and what Sirk must forego) is not only the stripping of Naomi's body, but the paring away of constraints that society puts upon her as virtuous wife and mother within the bourgeois family. For us, however, such a scene remains a mere 'tease' – as we imagine what may have transpired had the tethers been removed from Sirk's directorial hand. At one point in the drama, when Sara asks

Naomi to continue her poetic oration, Naomi replies, 'I'm a great believer in "leave them asking for more".' At the end of Sirk's melodrama, however, it is not only the audience, but *she* who continues to desire more, as her nostalgic 'stopover' becomes a bourgeois 'makeover' and her transitory masquerade a permanent 'imitation of life'.

Notes

1   In *Imitation of Life*, Lora Meredith is a widow when the film begins. During the course of the narrative she meets and becomes engaged to Steve Archer (John Gavin) and her struggles with career vs. love mimic those of a married couple.

2   According to *The New Jewish Encyclopedia* Naomi (in 'The Book of Ruth') returns from Moab to her native Bethlehem after the death of her husband and two sons (Davis & Wolk 1976: 337.

3   As Michael Walker notes, 'Naomi's challenge has already started to transform [Joyce], releasing her suppressed sensuality and taste for excitement' (1990: 39).

4   Walker talks of the motif of the 'interrupted kiss' in Sirk's work and points out how Naomi's arrival by train interrupts some affectionate play between Henry and Sara in the school office. Specifically, the train whistle is heard in the background (1990: 43).

5   Walker remarks on the parallel between Annie and Lena, as well.

6   See the introduction to my own edited anthology on *Imitation of Life* (Fischer 1991: 3–28).

Politics, Family, Society

8

Family, Frontier and the Destruction of the Social Order

CHRISTOPHER SHARRETT

The title of this essay may seem overly provocative, perhaps even absurd to the reader who sees the western, at least in its classical phase, concerned with the valorisation of the American civilising project. Such a view of the genre is obviously sensible. Many westerns, especially the canonical works of John Ford, seem very much involved with extolling the virtues of family, home and community. But I want to argue that the value of the genre might be fully appreciated by understanding its subversive aspect, one that is seldom resolved but remains mostly incoherent and contradictory. We must note that the western's view of the family, community and heterosexual relations, while often subversive (and one hardly has to read 'against the grain' to see this impulse), can be read as coming from rightist or nihilist positions (the two are closely associated) as often as progressive ones.

The western's project of condemning rather than praising social institutions can be found early in the genre's history, represented perhaps most famously by Doc Boone's (Thomas Mitchell) line at the end of *Stagecoach* (1939), as he and Curly (George Bancroft) turn loose the Ringo Kid (John Wayne), so that he and the young prostitute Dallas (Claire Trevor) can begin a new life in Mexico. As Ringo and Dallas ride away in a wagon, Doc says to Curly: 'Well, they're saved from the blessings of civilisation!' The line has been much debated; how could this pivotal western, which gave the genre new legitimacy, end on a note that runs very counter to the ostensible values of the western, particularly given that Ford was among Hollywood's most conservative directors, even in his populist moments? (see Grant 2003). *Stagecoach* indeed seems populist, viewed by some critics as Ford's response to the banking interests (represented by the corrupt Gatewood (Berton Churchill)) that were considered to be the cause of the Great Depression. (It is instructive that Gatewood finally decides to steal in order to escape his shrewish wife.) The film's rejection of civilisation may be read as its rejection of snobbery and elitism (the expulsion from Tonto of Doc and Dallas by the self-righteous citizens' council, composed of ageing biddies: repeatedly civilisation is associated with the evils of the female). The narrative appears to recreate a more democratic notion of family and community from the motley ship-of-fools stagecoach travellers, yet this 'family' is filled with tensions. And what could possibly be the afterstory of *Stagecoach* but the recreation of the bourgeois family and community by Ringo and Dallas? Doc Boone's famous line recapitulates the ideology of the western: civilisation equals the corruption of a purer culture represented by the male adventurer; it is not incidental that the snobs who control Tonto's morality are women. The western, as exemplified by *Stagecoach*, genuflects in the direction of home and hearth (the birth of Lucy Mallory's (Louise Platt) baby, the idealisation of women, Ringo's ranch), but at its core it has a contempt for the family and community viewed as centres of domestic, feminine values, and for civilisation (Lordsburg, the extension of family and home) as symbol of total depravity. Can the depravity be read as other than the culmination of the feminine influence? And at the core of the genre is a profoundly homosocial/homoerotic world, a place of men without women. It is important to note that the genre does not incidentally marginalise women because of its macho worldview; women are simply of small relevance to the genre (except as occasional diversion and symbol of ideals) since its main concern is the emotional bond between men, and the unfettered personal freedom of the male. Ang Lee's extraordinary *Brokeback Mountain* (2005), about which more later, brings these issues to clear light.

Cimarron, *Giant* and the Awfulness of the Domestic World

The irrelevance or evil of the female and the civilising process she represents is evidenced early in the sound era, in Wesley Ruggles' *Cimarron* (1931), another very foundational and rather neglected western based on one of Edna Ferber's typically sentimental 'generational' novels concerned with the rise and inevitable transformation of an American family. *Cimarron* is a 'classic' western in its ostensible celebration of America – its contempt for same can be seen at the level of the 'political unconscious' as the film works through the genre's conventions and addresses their assumptions. One of only three westerns honoured with Best Picture Academy Awards (the other two, *Dances with Wolves* (1990) and *Unforgiven* (1992), both revisionist, appear nearly sixty years later), *Cimarron* is a merger of the 'gunfighter' and 'settler' forms of the genre. The gunfighter mode celebrates the charisma and professionalism of the male shootist, whose skills are admired for their rendering of adventurism and the male's personal freedom. The settler mode is concerned with homage to the civilising process itself in its depiction of the arrival and struggles of families, the tilling of soil, the building of towns and cities (see Slotkin 1992). *Cimarron*'s hero, Yancey Cravat (Richard Dix), is the locus of the settler/gunfighter conjunction, as well as an amalgam of American archetypes. Yancey is a pioneer, an outlaw, a lawyer, a preacher, a publisher, a husband and a father. He is also the embodiment of the film's metaphoric title, the wild, untamed spirit of the West – and of masculinity – that cannot and should not be hemmed in by domesticity. That domesticity is represented by Yancey's wife Sabra (Irene Dunne) and her family, the Venables. The Venables are portrayed as effete, aristocratic and unreconstructed postbellum racists – their young black servant boy Isaiah (Eugene Jackson) sits on a swing over the dinner table, fanning his masters in a moment re-calling the conditions of the pre-Civil War southern slavocracy. Sabra continues her family's aristocratic, white supremacist values. She is in constant conflict with her populist husband Yancey with her talk of 'those dirty, filthy Indians'. Racism's loca-tion in feminine or 'weak' impulses of civilisation is underlined: it is later embodied in Sabra's snooty daughter Donna (Yancey says jokingly when he first admires his young daughter: 'She's a Venable!'), whose posture and racist remarks recapitulate her mother's almost in caricature.

Yancey, on the other hand, is both master of the fast draw (against the villain-ous 'white trash' of the range) and bearer of Enlightenment values. He takes part in the Oklahoma Land Rush ultimately to establish his newspaper, the Oklahoma Wig-wam, whose main purpose, as its title suggests, is to argue for the rights of Native Americans, much to the consternation of the town of Osage. Yancey's strong arm and consoling presence provide shelter for *every* oppressed minority: the Jewish peddler Sol Levy (George Stone), the prostitute Dixie Lee (Estelle Taylor), less-than-masculine types like the printer Jesse Rickey (Roscoe Ates) and the runaway ser-vant Isaiah, who takes refuge with Yancey. Jesse and Sol give Yancey their devoted loyalty; he in turn gives them crucial places in the world that he builds (in which he himself wants no part). Sabra continues throughout her husband's construc-tive, democratic work to project the racism and narrow-mindedness of her family; it re-emerges at regular intervals, as when her son courts a young Native woman originally used by Sabra as, in her words, a 'cheap servant'. It seems sensible, then, that one of the chief characteristics of *Cimarron* is the hero's absence. Yancey's refusal to stay put is portrayed in the film as a virtue; his adventurous nature makes one recall the words of the village elder (Vladimir Sokoloff) to Chris (Yul Brynner) and Vin (Steve McQueen) at the end of *The Magnificent Seven* (1960): 'You are like the wind, blowing over the land and passing on.' Like Chris and Vin (and countless western heroes), Yancey is a primal force. He is masculinity seen as a cleansing agent, creating a vital Culture before its inevitable spiral downward into Civilisation (to use Spengler's notion). While Chico (Horst Buchholz) is encouraged by Chris and Vin to stay in the village with the young peasant woman enamoured of him, one cannot imagine *The Magnificent Seven* endorsing the same choice for its two lead heroes. So, too, Yancey Cravat has virtually anything on his mind but tending children and cooking meals.

Yancey's free spirit is justified as instrumental to the nation's creation – al-though his story occurs in the 1890s, rather late in history, the point is nevertheless clear, particularly since the timeframe takes us into the decadence of the early twentieth century – just as the 'strong wind' of the errant Magnificent Seven is a cleansing agent permitting a community to reclaim itself. Yancey's wanderlust takes him to the Spanish-American War, the first major US attempt at colonialism and empire-building. Later, Sabra reads a note suggesting that the still-absent Yancey fights in World War One. In the final, poignant scene, occurring in 1929 (the start of the Great Depression), just as Sabra is celebrated for her achievements as manager/mogul of the newspaper founded by her husband, Yancey, now an old man, dies a heroic death in an oil field accident as a common roughneck. As he expires in Sabra's arms, he murmurs, with his typically romantic flourish: 'Wife and mother, stainless woman, hide me in your love!' This final paean to womanhood is immediately undercut by the last shot, which is the unveiling of a monument to the Oklahoma pioneer, a statue of Yancey alone – without Sabra – valiantly protecting a Native American. Yancey's frequent praising of his wife doesn't jibe with the evidence of the film, most importantly the extraordinary scene of Yancey's return from the Spanish-American War for the sole purpose, so it seems, of acting as lawyer for the prostitute Dixie Lee, whom the city fathers of Osage want to run out of town via a kangaroo court. Sabra has suspected – and the film has implied in an early scene – that Yancey is attracted to Dixie Lee; he may have had an affair with her during his roistering days with the outlaw The Kid (William Collier Jr). The film's position on this archetypal madonna/whore construct seems clear: Sabra is to be admired for her stalwart determination but she warrants no further interest. Dixie Lee is a rather minor character, but can be seen as a hypostatisation of the world of the erotic, that is, the place where the male is free of the awful fetters of domestic responsibility and able to partake of sex as a transitory, revitalising pleasure. This association of the transgressive female with the unchained, possibly dangerous libido (but even in its dangers infinitely more compelling than wife/home) has its alternate side: repression/oppression is constructed as an entirely female agenda, of a social/political as well as sexual character (the snide anti-semite Mrs Wyatt (Edna May Oliver) snubbing Sol Levy). While at one level the last glimpses of 1929 Osage are supposed to represent the marvels of American progress (Sabra says: 'All this up from raw prairie!') the images of a congested city, complete with Texaco trucks and surrounded by oil derricks, is closer to a Fritz Lang nightmare than a vision from Frederic Remington. Indeed, the images suggest the beginning of the end – and it is a world over which the female presides. The point seems less the female's inability to manage what the male has bequeathed to her than the poisonous influence of the female on the male project. Seen this way, Cimarron, perhaps the most representative of classic westerns, continues the nihilism at the heart of patriarchal civilisation.

George Stevens' Giant (1956), another Edna Ferber adaptation filmed 25 years after Cimarron, may be seen as a bookend to the earlier work, in its similarly generational story of cattle baron Bick Benedict (Rock Hudson) bringing his Maryland-born wife Leslie (Elizabeth Taylor) to his huge ranch Reata in 1920s Texas. Reata is situated in a desert as flat as the proverbial stove lid, a huge, out-of-place Gothic mansion in its centre. The notion of the oddball homestead being out of sync with its wholly inhospitable surroundings is key to the film's sense not only of the bigotry and evilness of Texas (the film tones down the critical concerns of Ferber's novel) but of the empty, desiccated and outmoded sense of domestic life and the civilisation it engenders. A common reading of the film sees it as an embrace of 1950s centrism and reasonableness, as the ageing Bick accepts Leslie's liberal views of child rearing and, above all, race (see Biskind 1983). Bick is an unreconstructed racist who demeans Mexicans and Native Americans while claiming to be a 'fair man'. When his son Jordan (Dennis Hopper) marries a Mexican woman, Bick finds himself defending minorities, less because his vision of race has changed than because, as Jordan tells him, the family name has inadvertently become entangled with racial issues. Nevertheless, the film concludes with Bick, in late middle age, battling Sarge (Mickey Simpson), the brutish owner of a roadside greasy spoon operated according to Lost Cause/Jim Crow regulations that prohibit a feeble Mexican couple from being served. Although Bick loses his Last Stand brawl at Sarge's diner, his beating has a sacrificial cast; he is made noble at long last in Leslie's eyes as the film's final consoling moment shows Bick and Leslie admiring their Mexican American grandson, who stands smiling in a crib next to their Anglo grandchild. A calf and a lamb – rival livestock provoking range wars in earlier westerns – here complete a Holy Family crèche. But the domestic tranquility and reasonableness that bring the story to a happy conclusion are disconnected from the narrative's logic, especially from an element centred on the key character, Jett Rink (James Dean).

Jett is a surly young ranch hand despised by Bick, who shows him a strange animosity from their first encounter when Bick and Leslie return to Reata. The reason for this hatred is obscure. Jett may be seen as socially inferior by Bick; when he strikes oil, he lashes out at Bick and 'all you sons of Benedict'. His curse is a Hawthorne-like condemnation of elitists who have seized power and deformed the future. There is a suggestion, perhaps overread with hindsight knowledge of Rock Hudson's and James Dean's gay sexuality, that Bick is wary of the sexual provocation that Jett represents, the provocative sexuality opposing the respectable straight façade that Bick prefers (indeed, one that corresponds to the life of the Hollywood-groomed Hudson, far more than to the bohemian Dean). Jett is indeed a sexual threat to Bick, but via Leslie.

Jett is an archetypal sexual interloper, popular in the cinema of the 1950s (see *Picnic* (1955)) and in the plays of Tennessee Williams (*Orpheus Descending* (1957), *Sweet Bird of Youth* (1959)), a character whose very presence is threatening enough to be disruptive to the bourgeois community. Jett's attraction to Leslie may be based as much on the young Texan's dream of upward mobility – realised when he strikes oil and becomes a threat to the entire Benedict way of life – as on actual sexual interest (Elizabeth Taylor's charms notwithstanding). The notion makes sense as we see the ageing Jett, a combination of rightist oil mogul H. L. Hunt and wildcatter Glenn McCarthy, wooing Leslie's daughter, young Luz (Carroll Baker), concurrently with his assault on Jordan at the Emperador opening. But Jett is not purely a force disruptive of bourgeois family values. On the contrary, he is a member of the lumpenproletariat who fully internalises the racist values of his employer/oppressor. When Leslie shows sympathy for the impoverished, disease-ridden Mexican workers at Reata, Jett scornfully refers to them as 'wetbacks'. Jett's patron is Luz Benedict (Mercedes McCambridge), Bick's older sister, whose genteel rivalry with her brother for full control of Reata is intensified with the arrival of Leslie. There is a fascinating perversity to the Bick/Luz/Leslie relationship. Luz is taken aback when Bick arrives with his new bride, who is seen as a challenge to not just Luz's role as Reata's overseer but also her emotional bond with Bick. Apart from *Bonjour Tristesse* (1958), an incestuous relationship had never been so bra-zenly implied onscreen. Luz feigns warmth to Leslie, seeing to it that breakfast is prepared for her – although a breakfast Leslie can scarcely eat. When Leslie faints at a barbecue served in the hot Texas sun, the camera shows Luz in tight close-up, nodding knowingly (and with a trace of satisfaction): 'That's what I was afraid of.' Luz is a masculine woman comfortable in cowboy boots and ranch life, with no het-erosexual coding (her butch bearing is furthered by the casting of the tough-voiced McCambridge). Luz's affection for Jett makes sense; like her, Jett doesn't fit nor-mal heterosexual expectation, especially for a westerner. He is blond, slight of build and lacking in self-possession. Interestingly, the land Luz wills to Jett ('Little Reata') becomes not only the basis for his oil empire but a serious challenge to Luz's own brother. Perhaps most important, Luz shares with a vengeance Bick's and Jett's racism. If anything, she is even crueller in her racism than her brother, warning that without her oversight the Mexicans would 'sit on their honkers'. Like Jett's, Luz's characterisation as a sexual outsider is complicated by her base meanness, but this can be read as an outgrowth of her general rage. By inadvertently bequeathing an oil fortune to Jett (it is tempting to read Jett's wealth as Luz's 'curse'), Luz not only brings the *nouveau riche* to Texas but poses a challenge to her brother's form of wealth and a guarantee that her racism will continue to have solid roots through the hated outsider Jett, this undermining Bick's drift towards centrism.

With his achievement of empire, and the crass decadence flowing from it (his kitsch Emperador Hotel complex), Jett's racism comes home to roost, represent-ing the true face of the supposedly 'enlightened' 1950s Texas that is embodied in fully domesticated, centrist Bick. Yet the reign of the oil money of the Jett Rinks of this world, and the attacks on minorities in the fast-food joints of New Texas, owe everything to the Benedict family and their racist roots in patriarchy and capitalism. Wealth changes shape, but not ideological assumptions. While Leslie has refused to allow Bick to put her 'in her place', she has become complicit in the Benedict empire as it shifts from cattle to oil. The attack on her son Jordan (whose wife entered a Jett Rink-owned beauty salon) underscores the falsity of the notion that domestic, centrist values can overcome deeply-rooted prejudice. It may be argued that Jett's racism, enforced with an official apparatus borrowed in part from Bick's own entourage (the judge who writes oratorical 'humdingers' for Jett), is based on his lack of family and his sexual frustration. But it is clear that racism's destructive force as well as class prejudice and various forms of jealousy and competition have their origins in the family structure for which Jett wistfully yearns (or thinks he does). Despite the consoling coda of the film with the ageing Bick and Leslie, it is clear that the original, baronial Benedict family has disintegrated, to be replaced by its bourgeois-liberal manifestation that will be presided over by Bick's innocuous son-in-law (Earl Holliman) and, more importantly, by rightist power brokers like Jett Rink and his ilk, whose sense of compromise is even less than was that of the young Bick. Racism, classism and the quest for extended empire are deadly not only to their obvious targets but to the family structure itself.

Duel in the Sun and the Rise of the Monstrous Family

King Vidor's *Duel in the Sun* (1946) inaugurates perhaps the western's most caustic phase of re-evaluation of family as the centre of civilisation. It is a work that in the words of Robin Wood 'dramatises an ideological system that was rotten at its very foundations and leaves it in a heap of rubble' (1992: 195). Overseen by David O. Selznick as a big-ticket film that would repeat the success of *Gone with the Wind* (1939) while, as Wood argues, continuing Selznick's interest in films about struggling women, *Duel in the Sun*'s repudiation of the family as ideological bedrock of civilisation is total. The film concerns Pearl Chavez (Jennifer Jones), who is sent to live with her father's cousin Laura Belle (Lillian Gish) when her father, Scott Chavez (Herbert Marshall), is condemned to death for the murder of his wife, Pearl's mother (Tilly Losch), a Native American woman whose 'loose' sexuality has compelled him to kill her. Scott is himself a racial other, referred to by the grotesque locals as 'that renegade Creole squaw man'. That the film is centred on Pearl makes it the only western whose narrative concerns the Other twice over: woman and Indian.

The film argues that the female has no place to turn in America: Pearl, like her murdered mother, is an outcast simply for being a woman. What is especially key here is Pearl as a sexualised woman, again like her mother, who violated male property rights by having sex with a man other than her husband. Unlike any number of films wherein the female's sexualisation is the subject of audience delectation, this film, through its very self-conscious stylisation, reflects on popular assumptions about the sexual woman in mass art and the consequences that inevitably face her. As Wood notes, the traditional places of respite for the younger woman offer no respite at all; Laura Belle seems consoling enough, but she is an uncritical product of the Confederate Lost Cause, a crushingly brutal social system that physically and psychologically enfeebles her.

The land baron Jackson McCanles (Lionel Barrymore) is a grotesque whose affections are directed less at his ineffectual son Jesse (Joseph Cotten), who becomes the bringer of industrial capitalism (and, logically, the end of the 'dream' of the frontier), than at the monstrous Lewt (Gregory Peck), often photographed with

Expressionist shadow reminiscent of characters from Murnau or Lang. Pearl's love affair with the murderous Lewt seems the archetypal instance of the woman who can associate affection only with brutality; in this narrative the social conjunction of the two is made clear. The famous *Liebestod* that ends the film, while a bit over the top, makes the point that even as the female realises she must destroy her deceitful oppressor, she can't help but be taken in by the seductions of bourgeois romantic love, even as she faces certain death. In the family structure, be it Scott Chavez's highly romanticised Lost Cause family of the antebellum south or the supposedly forward-looking McCanles family, the female's options are nil, her construction as sexual property total.

John Ford is never able to portray the family institution as totally monstrous. The closest he comes to this perspective is with his treatment of the 'aberrant monstrous clan', as in the Clantons of *My Darling Clementine* (1946) (Walter Brennan, John Ireland, Grant Withers), who are set in contrast to (rather than doubling) the righteous Earp brothers (Henry Fonda, Tim Holt, Ward Bond). Yet, as was the case in *Stagecoach*, there is much about the family of conservative postwar westerns that suggests at the very least its instability as an institution, its role as source of discontent. Even (perhaps especially) George Stevens' *Shane* (1953), one of the most romantic visions of the frontier family, contains this discontent. Shane (Alan Ladd), like Jett Rink, is an outsider whose function is both to enable civilisation (with its dreaded prospects) and to be a sexual interloper (Richie 1970). Clearly Shane's sexual charisma outstrips that of the homesteader Joe Starrett (Van Heflin), a reality so explicit that Joe can't help acknowledging it, seeing in Shane a future for his wife and son should he be killed by the malevolent rancher Ryker (Emile Meyer). Marian Starrett's (Jean Arthur) sense of duty requires her to stay with Joe as Shane rides off to sacrifice himself, but more crucial is the disruption Shane has indeed caused in the Starrett family. As Marian says so clearly, the grubby 'shack' that is the homestead is less than appealing; more important, except for its connections with nature, the images of which could as easily be read as reference to Shane's grace, it is a thoroughly unattractive emblem of constraint as opposed to the freedom – sexual and otherwise – embodied in Shane.

Shane would be expanded upon a decade later by Sergio Leone's *A Fistful of Dollars* (1964), whose source is indeed Stevens' film far more than Akira Kurosawa's *Yojimbo* (1961) (see Magee 2006). The openings of *Shane* and *A Fistful of Dollars* are structurally very similar. In the establishing sequence of *Shane*, the camera's position is behind the blond hero, who is dressed in buckskin, mounted on a pale horse, riding down a verdant, wooded mountain, curiously observed by young Joey Starrett (Brandon De Wilde), Joe and Marian. Shane exchanges friendly glances with the boy. In the opening of *A Fistful of Dollars*, the camera is in the near-same position behind the Man with No Name (Clint Eastwood), who wears a poncho, chews on a small cigar and rides down an overlit, parched hill on a mule. He rides not into a fertile farmstead but towards a bleak adobe village filled with comical portents of doom (a hangman's noose, a man with a sign saying 'adios amigo'). As No Name approaches the village, a young boy (one could say Joey's counterpart) appears; he is being tortured by a fat bandit. The boy's mother watches the savagery from a window, glancing up towards No Name as he satisfies his thirst at a well (a correlate to Joe offering Shane a cup of water). No Name does nothing. This can be read simply as one of Leone's cynical gestures until we place the scene in context. Although No Name rescues the little family, saying, without explanation, that at another time he 'knew someone like you once and there was no one there to help', the scene is marginal to his employment by the Rojo and Baxter families. These clans are both portrayed as irredeemably vicious: No Name kills many of the Baxters, allowing (and watching) their final annihilation as though it were a show, then wipes out the Rojos. Here the frontier family, Anglo or Hispanic, is portrayed as solely predatory, leaving behind a wasteland where the only prosperous business (certainly a dead-end one) is coffin-making.

The frontier family as monstrous has its strongest foundations in the films of Anthony Mann. In *Winchester 73* (1950), *Bend of the River* (1952), *The Naked Spur* (1953) and *The Far Country* (1954), the hero, centre of patriarchal charismatic authority, is obsessive, with more than a little hint of dementia, underscored, especially in *Bend of the River*, by the presence of a *doppelgänger* who signifies the hero's truly destructive potential. The final re-integration of the hero into family and community at the end of the Mann films always seems a tacked-on genuflection to the Production Code that doesn't detract from the films' sense of instability, centred on the hysterical male. The instability of the male and the monstrousness of the family that produced him are clearly articulated in *Man of the West* (1958), Mann's greatest achievement. In this film, the frontier hero, played by western icon Gary Cooper, is both a civilising force (a man looking for a schoolteacher for his adopted town) and a savage killer – most savage of all as the exposition unfolds – produced by a pack of killers strongly associated with the pioneer family. Dock Tobin (Lee J. Cobb), the hero's barbaric 'uncle', at one point speaks of his clan as 'just like a family of old settlers'. The Anthony Mann westerns point to two important tendencies: the need, at some level of consciousness, to strike at or in some sense jeopardise the family, and the recognition of the family's irrelevance as the homosocial world of men and male bonding are foregrounded while the genre goes through a final, convulsive phase before its partial restoration in the reactionary 1980s.

Marlon Brando's *One-Eyed Jacks* (1961), a very oedipal rethinking of the Pat Garrett/Billy the Kid story, concern's Kid Rio's (Marlon Brando) revenge on Sheriff Dad Longworth (Karl Malden) for betraying him. The revenge can be seen to flow as much from broken homosexual love as from the father's betrayal of the son. Rio's killing of Dad also destroys the façade the older man created, the 'good life' his blood money purchased. This kind of betrayal of one man's affection and trust by another becomes obsessive in Sam Peckinpah's *Ride the High Country* (1962), *The Wild Bunch* (1969) and *Pat Garrett and Billy the Kid* (1973), all films where male love is paramount, the family either marginal or totally irrelevant. In an extraordinary scene in *Pat Garrett and Billy the Kid*, Garrett (James Coburn) can hardly bring himself to open the gate in the white picket fence in front of his bourgeois house, a rather surreal 1950s image in the middle of the 1880s town of Lincoln. Once inside, he can tolerate being with his wife for only a few minutes before he tells a lie that will let him rejoin the world of men. In the western's current neoconservative moment, male love and the irrelevance of family is, oddly, even more in the forefront. In the TV mini-series *Lonesome Dove* (1989), the emotional centre is clearly the affection between Gus (Robert Duvall) and Woodrow (Tommy Lee Jones). Perhaps this is not so surprising, as the genre in its revamped reactionary phase is comfortable with women solely as whores or frontier madonnas. Another example is *Deadwood* (2004–06), where Calamity Jane (Robin Weigert) is a foul-mouthed Florence Nightingale. The excuse in both cases is the attempt to give the western realistic grit. Both are still unable to consider clearly the implications of the male bond, the most recurrent feature of the genre.

Afterword: The Achievement of *Brokeback Mountain*

Elsewhere in this collection Harry Benshoff gives Ang Lee's superb accomplishment *Brokeback Mountain* (2005) detailed discussion. I want merely to comment on some of the ways by which this film goes far in demolishing the western's conventions very intelligently while, in the best tradition of the genre, using them to portray the impossible features of American bourgeois life. Fordian celebrations of community are deconstructed in Ennis Del Mar's (Heath Ledger) bleak marriage to Alma (Michelle Williams), their hardscrabble domestic life and their inevitable divorce. The Fourth of July fireworks display, during which Ennis punches out a foul-mouthed biker ostensibly to protect his wife and daughters, externalises the unendurable extent of his sexual frustration – the prospect that he will be permanently separated from his friend and lover Jack Twist (Jake Gyllenhaal), in part due to his own inhibitions. The assumptions underneath the western's 'showdown' moment are economically displayed in Ennis's sudden expressions of rage flowing from his repression. Romanticised tales of frontier violence here become Ennis's 'foundational' narrative of the murder of two gay men, which his father may have helped perpetrate, and then Jack's own death at the hands of Texas homophobes (if this scene, visualised only briefly during Ennis's phone call to Jack's wife, isn't born of Ennis's anxiety-ridden imagination, the editing intelligently leaves the point debatable). The film follows the western's convention of the hero gaining legitimacy first by being the central 'bull of the woods' to family and community. Jack, the more 'feminine' of the two protagonists (because he is open about his feelings), struggles to gain credibility at his own dinner table, winning a tussle with his brute father-in-law only to be disparaged (and finally murdered?) by the community. Ennis is credibly macho, a strong silent type, which counts for very little in the lower-class subsistence to which he is condemned, the condemnation becoming more profound as he fails to sustain heterosexual domesticity. The film's portrayal of gay sexuality is necessarily intricately involved in comments on the horrendous construction of masculinity – what it means to be 'tough' – within patriarchal capitalist society. Its insight rests in its insistence that no alternative sexuality can exist within patriarchal assumptions. Ennis fully internalises these assumptions. While he tries to replicate the pleasure of gay sex in his uneasy intercourse with Alma, his motivations for heterosexual relations are tied to his desire for her to be a breed sow reproducing his tortured male conscience in more children. She refuses, on the grounds that he is not a sufficiently productive workhorse able to 'provide' for the home. Nor is Ennis immune from displays of jealousy associated with patriarchal society: his outburst at Jack over his visits to Mexico (where Jack solicits hustlers) is representative. Capitalist oppression is constantly tied to sexual repression. The two men meet as teenagers trying to eke out a living tending sheep; the cowboy hats, rifles and other romantic accoutrements of the genre are in deliberate counterpoint to the men's circumstances, reminding us of the misery of daily life in the American wilderness, then and now. Ennis cannot permit himself to form a permanent relationship with Jack, using as an excuse, during their later years, his commitment to child support and increasingly burdensome working-class labour. Jack, considerably more upwardly mobile, finds his natural flamboyance put to the use of economic interests over which he has no control (his father-in-law's farm equipment business), and which are simultaneously associated with his need to prove his masculinity (his defiance of his father-in-law, for example, or his need to endure the two redneck farm machine clients scoffing at his 'piss-ant' rodeo talents).

As has been noted by various critics (and by a too cute video montage at the 2005 Academy Awards), *Brokeback Mountain* tends to bring to light the male bond crucial not only to the western genre but to American civilisation. The film details the devastating consequences of repressing this bond, which is to say the transformation of male love into male violence and the thin boundary between the two in a rapacious capitalist civilisation that transforms not only our basic bisexuality but all life-affirming energies into murder and, finally, self-destruction. It is a superb latter-day western portraying American society – the frontier fought for with such ferocity – in a state of collapse. The bleak, empty town of Signal, Wyoming that opens the film, and the faux cowboy culture suggesting a cheesy simulation of the American past, make the point efficiently.

A few distinguished films continue this project. Tommy Lee Jones' *The Three Burials of Melquiades Estrada* (2005) shows the family and community in an utter state of fragmentation and decay (yet presided over by the same racist impulses that saw the winning of the West). The Lone Hero of the film (Jones), while well-meaning, is driven by obsessive delusion and the search for a non-existent utopia that is at the very heart of the American conquest. David Jacobson's *Down in the Valley* (2005), which rethinks *Taxi Driver* (1976) via *Lonely are the Brave* (1962), presents the community (Los Angeles) as post-industrial horror, the little family tenuous at best and nearly destroyed by the Lone Hero (Edward Norton) who seems to grace it, à la Shane, with his charm and good will. Not ironically, for all his lunacy he is indeed a revitalising force in a society at the precipice. In the genre now, the family seems not to offer even a pretence of worthiness, and gets not even a pretence of extolment.

Author's note

My thanks to Murray Pomerance for his support and friendship.

9

How Some Things Never Change: Britney, the Joy of Pepsi and the Familial Gaze

STEVEN ALAN CARR

As the process of globalisation extends towards and encroaches upon more territory, more institutions and more cultures, scholars would do well to remember that
the most important unit of consumption in many developed economies is not the
individual, but the family. Families serve as the target market for everything from
groceries to durable goods such as major appliances and automobiles. However,
what constitutes a family is not fixed, self-evident or independent of the globalised
institutional forces that seek to colonise individuals and to target groups into lucrative markets and commodities. At the same time, institutions do not unilaterally
determine what a family is, or who gets to belong to one. The US Census Report
of 2000, for example, claims that for the first time in the history of the Census, the
number of traditional nuclear families in the nation dropped below the quarter mark
to 23.5 per cent of all households or 55 million, while the number of people living
alone grew, and the number of unmarried couples nearly doubled over the past decade to 5.5 million households. From the standpoint of manufacturing, mainstream
media and advertisers, the most efficient unit of the audience – the nuclear family
that consists of a married heterosexual couple with one or two children – is becoming a depleted natural resource.

Nevertheless, regressive attempts to restrict and delimit the possibilities of
family and individual identity to the rigid template of the heterosexual and heterosexist nuclear arrangement are on the rise, at least within a North American
context. The perceived threat of gay marriage has prompted a number of states to
pass legislation outlawing the practice. The landmark Roe vs. Wade 1973 Supreme
Court decision upholding a woman's Constitutional right to choose whether to carry
a foetus to term appears at risk of being overturned, as recent Court appointments
indicate an appeasement to religious fundamentalists within the Republican Party.
But so-called 'family values', which became a rallying cry for conservatives throughout the 1990s, did not completely succeed in demonising single mothers, African
Americans, those on welfare or even a fictional television situation comedy character named Murphy Brown (see Fiske 1996). While at the beginning of the twenty-

first century the craze for family values seems to have subsided, the notion of faith initiatives seems to have taken many of the core concepts of family values to a logical development, attempting to impose upon the rest of society a narrow, dogmatic and more explicit brand of Protestant conservatism as the 'natural' and 'normal' set of default values. According to this view, women are subservient to men, bear children, tend the home and repress their sexuality. Children are an expendable natural resource, bred either for cheap labour or for military excursions. Men in this schema are the breadwinners, performing and acting decisively in public life in making important and seemingly rational determinations. Unlike their women, these men are to be forgiven if they freely and aggressively express their heterosexuality.

How is it, then, that as the number of traditional nuclear families within the US appears to be on the wane, regressive ideologies centred upon the concept of the nuclear family appear more resolute and more widespread than ever? People often subscribe to ideas and beliefs that are clearly not in their best interest, and ever since Karl Marx, critics and intellectuals have grappled with the question of why this is so. Popular media, in fact, have served as a focal point for this critique. Rather than argue that popular culture simply conveys false consciousness through capitalist, materialistic consumer culture, however, much recent media scholarship has considered popular culture as a sophisticated apparatus of appropriation, in which a wide spectrum of concepts concerning family and sexuality are negotiated through complex visual and rhetorical strategies. At the same time, the complexity and negotiation involved in cultural appropriation has inspired some media scholars to view popular culture as a potentially liberating rather than repressive force, presenting a range of arguably subversive alternatives to the nuclear family. But this popular view of ideology, while acknowledging what is indeed a complex process, misses what one might deem a deep structure of illusions. That is, while the notion of false consciousness might be overly simplistic (and thus itself false), the mere evidence of cultural appropriation and complexity does not automatically guarantee a moment of cultural liberation or resistance.

In considering how a deep structure of illusions might figure within media analysis, this essay performs a close reading of the second of two Pepsi-Cola commercials featuring Britney Spears that premiered during the 2001 Academy Awards broadcast. The first advert, two minutes long, features Spears singing and dancing in a Pepsi bottling facility. Running one and half minutes, the second intercuts much of the performance material from the first with shots of various media audiences encountering Spears's routine. In addition to airing the commercials during the Academy Awards, Pepsi also promoted both versions of the advertisement on their website and arranged to have the second commercial screened in multiplex movie theatres across the United States along with previews for coming attractions. This advertisement appears, at least on the surface, to be somewhat at odds with conservative ideologies. It promotes a highly sexualised image of the pop star, and does so at a moment when she was trying to break away from her earlier image as a wholesome icon for a nine-to-twelve-year-old 'tween' audience. At the same time, it also features former Senate Majority Leader and 1996 Republican presidential nominee Bob Dole who, after a failed bid for the presidency, was in the process of remaking his own image as spokesperson for the male impotence drug, Viagra. The commercial ends with Dole, sitting in a darkened room watching Spears' performance on television, saying 'Easy, boy' as his dog barks at the set. While one ultimately must read both commercials as part of Pepsi's larger and subsequent campaign featuring Spears, or as part of an even larger text about post-Cold War consumerism, this essay considers a deep structure of illusions present only within the second Pepsi commercial. In just a mere minute and a half, this text privileges and subordinates a complex array of ideologies.

Although they are advertisements – especially expensive ones such as the Pepsi commercials I am invoking here – these productions are really micro-movies. In dollars per screen second, they rival the most elaborate widescreen extravaganzas. They contain implicit ideologies. They are shot on 35mm film stock and then transferred to video. They are edited as miniature narratives that are centred on complex visual strategies and organisation. In privileging and subordinating a complex array of ideologies, this particular Pepsi ad furthermore functions in hegemonic fashion. The notion that the vast majority of popular media operates as a contested and negotiated ideological terrain is not new, of course. Antonio Gramsci's conceptualisation of hegemony – which theorises how socially subordinate groups could both influence and be co-opted by a superstructure – offers a much-needed refinement to overly rigid and deterministic models of ideological influence. In 'Ideology and Ideological State Apparatuses: Notes Toward an Investigation' (1977), Louis Althusser further differentiated between repressive state apparatuses (RSAs) relying upon physical force to maintain social order; and ideological state apparatuses (ISAs) relying upon imposing an imagined but highly persuasive set of social relations to maintain this order. Althusser further theorises a process of ideological interpellation, whereby ideologies must call out to, or hail, individuals on the basis of their identification within a particular social group or subculture. The concepts of hegemony and interpellation have been particularly salient to media and cultural studies. For example, John Fiske has defined what he calls the 'clawback' structure of mainstream media, which 'works to claw back potentially deviant or disruptive events into the dominant value system' (1993: 288). Thus, while the dominant value system always exists in relation to both material and symbolic threats, the clawback function of the media works to contain and domesticate these threats within a hierarchy of conformity.

Within media studies, explorations of hegemony and clawback have considered ideologies as distinct interpellations of race, class, gender, and the like. Less attention has been focused upon the deep embedding of emotion and feeling within a structure of illusions. In attempting to analyse to a fuller extent how illusion works within the Pepsi commercial I am studying, I return primarily to Raymond

Williams' notion of a deep 'structure of feeling'. Like the work of Gramsci, Althusser and others, Williams' concept marks a much needed shift away from the more literalist and deterministic Marxist notions of culture as the primary conveyance for false consciousness. Although it has sparked much discussion and many potential interpretations, three significant themes have emerged from Williams' 'structure of feeling': first, that when interpreting culture through cultural products, one must take into account not just explicit meanings but implicit meanings read between the lines as well; secondly, that one cannot discount how an audience experiences popular culture through emotion, a dimension that Marxist determinist critiques frequently dismiss as another iteration of false consciousness; and finally, that when considering implicit meanings and the role of emotion within popular culture, one must locate the cultural text within 'material life, the social organisation, and, to a large extent, the dominant ideas' (2001: 33).

The value of reconsidering a structure of feeling in light of some of the more recent refinements to ideological theory goes beyond simply pointing out the existence of a complex ideological process at work, or noting that this process functions like a well-oiled machine (which it certainly does). Williams reminds us of the deeply felt and emotional dimension of ideology. Ideological analysis perpetually runs the risk of performing its own clawback function, acknowledging the complexity of the process while dismissing emotion and feeling as cheap ploys meant to distract, delude or lull the masses into a complacent false consciousness. Furthermore, in imagining ideology as a complex process of discrete stages, we run the risk of replacing an imagined and ahistorical audience with an actual audience that makes sense and responds emotionally to cultural products given a specific historical context bounded by actual events. Through a 'structure of illusions' a commercial works not because it dupes an audience into something fake or false. A serious analysis of the 'structure of illusions' engages notions of complexity, audience awareness and even the authenticity of the illusion itself. The deep structure of illusions within the 2001 Pepsi commercial works precisely because this structure draws upon both audience awareness of the illusion and an audience capable of distinguishing illusion from authentic lived conditions. At the same time, the commercial depends upon its audience entering into an authentic relationship with mediated illusion, though in ways that hardly operate in either simplistic or linear fashion.

In the commercial, Spears appears in a blue Pepsi jumpsuit between two delivery trucks. As she tears off her uniform to begin dancing and singing, fellow performers suddenly leap from the two trucks. The ensemble moves into what appears to be a bottling facility. The rest of the commercial intercuts Spears' performance with various audiences, all of whom express varying degrees of appreciation and/or arousal.

A deep structure of illusions here engages a series of relationships that are subordinate to one dominant ideological relationship: an actual audience entering into an imaginary affiliation with mediated representation. That imagined primary relationship positions a subsequent set of imagined relationships, both explicit and implicit, that further interpellate the audience. For example, the intercutting between Spears' performance and the mediated representation of various audiences encountering her performance offers a range of possible meanings. A literal interpretation might focus on the graphical difference between the different aspect ratios employed within the commercial. Shots of Spears performing appear letterboxed, while shots depicting the various audiences watching this performance appear in a full-frame 4:3 aspect ratio. Even if a casual viewing might miss how these screen shapes alternate, an interpretation focusing on implicit meaning might consider the dynamic tension between a performative widescreen space, and the more domesticated audience space of the 4:3 frame associated with television. Should the material differences between these frame variations elude a casual viewing, the dynamic tension can still affect the audience emotionally, creating a structure of illusion that draws upon an imagined thrill of attending a live performance, the excitement of watching a movie in a movie theatre, the comparative calm or regularity of the spaces in which audiences watch Spears' performance on television, and the like.

The deep structure of illusions both encodes and organises different possibilities for family, gender, sexuality and politics. Like much of mainstream popular culture, the commercial organises these different possibilities, yet not simply by conveying false consciousness through a literal and stock set of images and sounds. Rather, it is through the subordination of different possibilities that this commercial promotes an opportunity, however illusory, for individual expression. Viewed in terms of individual expression, choosing a cola can have as much consequence as choosing a president. In *A Logic of Expressive Choice* (2000), Alexander A. Schuessler makes an intriguing connection between soft drinks and presidential elections. In asking why people vote, when an individual ballot virtually has no chance of influencing a national election, Schuessler turns to a 1960s Pepsi advertising campaign. People choose presidents like colas, he suggests, not because they believe their choice matters but because they believe the *opportunity* to make a choice matters. In terms of rational choice theory, the opportunity to express one's identity through a personal preference is more compelling than the expectation that making a choice will be rewarded with a specific outcome. Both Schuessler and Thomas Frank (1997) have noted how the 'Pepsi Generation' was born in the 1960s with the emergence of lifestyle advertising techniques. These techniques sought to identify audiences demographically, though the particular demographic would ideally be construed as broadly as possible. In the case of the Pepsi marketing campaign, advertising sought to align its product with an emergent youth culture. Consumers thus did not have to identify with youth culture *per se*, but with the idea of a youth culture; they did not have to believe that drinking Pepsi would make them young as long as they believed that drinking Pepsi would provide an opportunity for youthfulness. By imagining a product as aligned with youth culture and against the more traditional and staid brand of Coca-Cola, consumers could make the expressive choice to drink Pepsi.

The close outcomes of recent presidential elections may provide one indicator of a culture suffused not so much by materialism as by expressive choice, in which the rapid convergence between presidential campaigns and product advertisements reflects not the political aspirations of a nation but the supremacy of a consumer-driven paradigm. Within this frame, politicians, like product brands, provide opportunities for citizens to express a lifestyle habitus. For example, one could address how modern political rhetoric has become defined by the rhetoric of consumerism and expressive choice. Republican candidate Walter Mondale made reference to Wendy's 'Where's the Beef' commercial in dismissing Democratic rival Gary Hart during the 1984 primaries. Ronald Reagan purportedly sang the virtues of Pepsi as the metonym for Western-style democracy, which in turn could serve as the metonym for Western-style capitalism. Meanwhile, the Reagan-Bush advertising campaign of 1984 relied on what the *New York Times* called a 'Pepsi-like advertising strategy', putting together a group of advertising executives known as the Tuesday Team to create the so-called 'Morning in America' campaign. 'That is what we have done in the past with Pepsi, to elicit a sense of feeling', Phil Dusenberry, executive creative director of Batten, Barton, Durstine and Osborn (BBDO) told the *New York Times*. 'It is a sense of optimism, a sense of patriotism' (in Clendinen 1984: A18).

Such examples evidence a correspondence, and perhaps a convergence, between politics and consumerism, but in and of themselves they do not explain how consumerism invokes feeling and emotion. How does expressive choice, working within the schema of consumerism, invoke a sense of deep feeling and commitment to product brands? To answer this question, one must view expressive choice as a set of opportunities for individuals to perform individual identity within a context of a deep structure of illusions.

This is not to suggest that the structure is fleeting, false or a by-product of consumerism. Because it invokes a relationship between real people, and the imagined perception of the very real conditions of our existence, the deep structure activates powerful and consequential ideologies. For example, as Marianne Hirsch notes, these illusions can invoke powerful schematics for family and belonging. She uses family snapshots to show the powerful role they play in both shaping familial identity and mediating historical trauma, describing the familial gaze, not as

> the look of a subject looking at an object, but a mutual look of a subject looking at an object who is a subject looking (back) at an object. Within the family, as I look I am always also looked at, seen, scrutinized, surveyed, monitored. Familial subjectivity is constructed relationally, and in these relations I am always both self and other(ed), both speaking and looking subject and spoken and looked at object: I am subjected and objectified. (1997: 7)

While Hirsch finds this familial gaze operating within the relatively decentred universe of lived family relations, popular culture can appropriate such relations to produce its familial subjects and objects on a grander, more centralised and impersonal scale. To this end, one can read advertising such as the Pepsi commercial as constructing its own relational set of subject and object looks. These looks comprise their own familial gaze in ways that allow the viewer to engage emotionally with a deep structure of illusions. This engagement allows the viewer to make an 'expressive choice', not just in terms of the product advertised but also in terms that subordinate some definitions of 'family' over others.

Whatever so-called family values might advocate superficially, and in whatever kinder and gentler iteration family values might speak, the assertion of traditional family values in cinema and advertising within the past decade seeks to rehabilitate regressive notions of gender, heterosexism and racism to mainstream acceptability within American life. While the deep structure of illusions inherent within the Pepsi commercial may not propel family identity or memory as forcefully and immediately as the familial gaze of the family snapshot does, the Pepsi commercial does turn its viewers into one massive family, and the familial gaze it produces powerfully makes us both look and be looked at in relation to the ideology of so-called family values. In addition to being intimate, this gaze always operates within a broader context of shifting and contested ideological terrain. When the George W. Bush administration came to power in 2000, the battle lines to define what constitutes family had never been drawn so starkly, or in so lopsided a fashion. On the first day after taking office, Bush reversed Clinton Administration policy and restored the ban, put in place under his father's administration, on international US aid to any organisation even advocating a woman's right to choose. At the time the Pepsi ad aired, a little-known provision in Bush's much-touted No Child Left Behind Act began requiring all public schools receiving federal funds to provide to military recruiters the names and phone numbers of all students attending those institutions. The Act empowers military recruiters to contact minors without first gaining parental consent, and requires public schools to furnish the student information on demand – even if a telephone number is unlisted – or risk losing their federal funding. The familial gaze of the Pepsi commercial anchors us within a product-based notion of family amid political and ideological shifts redefining the meaning of family. As the audience dances happily along with the commercial in our spectatorial imaginations, we become exactly the kind of ideal family the No Child Left Behind Act would presume.

At the same time, the identification with family values isn't a matter of conscious rationale but is only as compelling as the emotions and feelings it can evoke. Those emotions and feelings work relationally, appealing to desires for an ideal family as well as managing threats to the family as is. Under the guise of promoting a newfound transgressive sexuality for its young spokesperson, 'The Joy of Pepsi' commercial seeks to situate the viewer familially within an ethos of pleasure, liberality and freedom from constraint. Rather than literally espouse a right-wing agenda, the commercial establishes a set of contrasting relationships between Spears' sexual and transgressive performative space and the domestic spaces within which her performance is consumed. Thus, the advertisement mini-film invokes the emotion of family life in a way that feature-length films exhibited publicly in a theatre cannot. The domestic space in the commercial is not regressive in and of itself, nor, necessarily, is the one in the viewer's home; but the relationships between these spaces – that the former penetrates and subsumes the latter – and how these relationships position the viewer in passivity are what conform to regressive conservative ideologies. While these commercials belong to part of a larger, subsequent Pepsi campaign featuring Spears, and can be understood as part of an even larger text about post-Cold War consumerism, a closer analysis of 'The Joy of Pepsi' will complete this essay. Through a series of subject and object looks, the Spears Pepsi ad rehabilitates traditional family values and the mutual familial gaze through three central subject/object oxymoronic vectors: conformist individualism, horny abstinence and segregated inclusivity.

Conformist Individualism

In 'The Work of Art in the Age of Mechanical Reproduction', Walter Benjamin warns that if the masses do not seize the means of interpretation and criticism of texts for themselves, fascism will seize these means for them, and in a way that gives 'these masses not their right, but instead a chance to express themselves' (1985: 693). The goal of fascism, then, is to create seemingly endless *opportunities* for expressing 'individualism', while ensuring that the brand of individualism expressed reinforces and ultimately conforms to a highly regulated social order. The commercial appears to reinforce this worldview with such lyrics as 'The world turns round and round, but some things never change'. While a consumerist society is not in and of itself fascist, it nevertheless shares some important characteristics with fascism. Both fascism and consumerism bear the primary ideological challenge of organising what Benjamin calls 'property relations' so that individuals have opportunities, rather than a right, to express themselves without interfering with the existing social structure. Thus, one can read the Pepsi commercial as deploying symptomatic configurations of space, performance and gender reinforcing the paradox of conformist individualism so that the world can turn 'round and round' without disrupting the status quo.

A dialectical paradox between individual expression and regulated social order governs the commercial. The ad begins with a shot of a retro Pepsi-Cola marquee on the roof of the warehouse, before a crane shot descends into a loading station to reveal a lone figure with back turned towards the camera and dressed in a blue cap and jumpsuit uniform prominently displaying the Pepsi logo. The transition from Spears' initial asexual anonymity to a situation in which her gendered performance provides an opportunity for individual expression ultimately organises the logic of the rest of the commercial. In a quick, jump-cut montage, Spears turns towards the camera, rips off her uniform and tosses her cap, revealing a short tube top and bare midriff. This gendered, individualist wardrobe offers an opportunity to differentiate Spears from the other performers who, remaining in uniform, perform synchronised dance movements with her. At the same time, Spears' clothing and performance conform to a gendered objectification, reinforcing a heterosexist way of looking that becomes codified within the commercial's subject/object glances.

Central to this paradox is the recurring motif of Spears gazing directly into the camera. While the exchange of subject/object glances in which we watch Spears looking directly at us has the potential, in Benjamin's terms, to alienate the viewer from the cult value of the Pepsi product and from the visual strategies of this particular text, such moments actually become what he refers to as mere opportunities to express individuality, and then only in terms of heterosexist conformity. No mere object, Spears returns the viewer's gaze in the opening montage as she turns towards the camera. The commercial thus begins to construct a familial gaze; in Hirsch's words, a mutual look of an object becoming a subject looking – through a gaze of direct address – at a subject who, in the course of the commercial will become object. In establishing the permutations of who looks where, Spears' gaze of direct address retains almost exclusive prominence. In breaking the fourth wall, this familial gaze does not transgress heterosexist attitudes, but reinforces them. As a subsequent shot reveals, the gaze of direct address in the commercial is distinctly female. One notable shot features another female performer drinking from a Pepsi can before turning to directly face the camera. It is the only one to feature anyone other than Britney Spears in as direct a familial gaze. Distinctly feminine, this familial gaze carries decidedly non-feminist connotations of submission, gendered care-giving and the pretext of looking so as to be looked at.

The commercial further undermines the potential alienation effect of this gaze exchange through its sexually-charged depictions of Spears' performance. One brief, low-angle shot has her thrusting her chest towards the camera before stepping back. Visually, the shot uses point of view to mimic the act of intercourse, in which Spears appears to be on top. One could argue that such depictions of a sexually aggressive young woman might serve a potentially liberating purpose. However, as other aspects of the commercial reveal, the shot offers an opportunity for sexual expression that is bounded by heterosexist and even racist norms.

Just as the familial gaze turns Spears from object to subject, it can also turn the audience as subject into object. When men and women in the commercial look at Spears, they look offscreen and at ubiquitous television monitors. Yet even as this commercial objectifies the audience, it carefully differentiates between various kinds of objectifications. In a number of shots, masculine looking clearly establishes arousal through a number of signifiers: a fire on a grill behind a short-order cook, two elderly men sharing an oxygen mask in a nursing home, the barking of Bob Dole's dog. Feminine looking, on the other hand, appears less clearly delineated.

For example, as a female bowling team, dressed in blue uniforms, presumably watches Spears on an offscreen monitor in a bowling alley, a heavier, older woman emulates one of Spears' pumping arm movements. A subsequent close-up shows Spears smiling and looking directly into the camera, before averting her gaze downward. This permutation of shots suggests what Sander Gilman (1986) has called the double-bind. Unlike horny male desire, female desire for Spears' performance seems limited to a poor counterfeit emulation of her performance. As if to emphasise that this counterfeit attempt at individualism is comical, Spears' smiling familial gaze engages the viewer as a confederate in mocking this sham version of her gendered performance.

Horny Abstinence

The Pepsi commercial asserts a male subject position through a paradoxical vector of horny abstinence. At the time the commercial aired, the popular press was quick to point out the numerous image-substitutes for ejaculation and oral sex. Many also noted how Bob Dole's appearance invoked his other role as spokesperson for Viagra. Fewer, however, recalled Dole's 1996 attack on Hollywood as part of his failed bid for the presidency. At that time, Dole attempted to capitalise upon the so-called family-values rhetoric by criticising rap music and Oliver Stone's *Natural Born Killers* (1994) for 'mainstreaming deviancy'. At the same time, Dole's rhetoric carefully avoided criticising popular films that also garnered controversy, but were closer to the 'family values' rendition of mainstream America. For example, his speech never mentioned the anti-Arab racism of a summer blockbuster, the Arnold Schwarzenegger vehicle *True Lies* (1994). He even praised the military thriller *Independence Day* (1996) as family-values-friendly, perhaps since some of the victims in this science fiction alien invasion film include a gay man, a maternally deficient First Lady and a Vietnam veteran who believes he was anally raped.

Just as Dole's uttering 'Easy, boy' in the commercial demands an intertextual reading connecting him to his role as Viagra spokesperson, his very presence within the commercial recalls the 'mainstreaming deviancy' ploy to help shore up a flagging political campaign in its waning days. His appearance both distances the articulation of family values from the earlier sanctimony of the Republican Party and reasserts the primacy of the male heterosexual subject position in its newfound embrace for popular culture. Dole's sexually-charged gaze upon the mediated image of Spears is not so much a concession to the mainstreamed deviancy against which he once railed as a blunt assertion of a leaner, meaner and more concentrated conformity to the ideology of family values.

As Dole now watches his television within the world of the advertisement, gendered performance and sexuality become mainstreamed, provided they operate within a narrow range of whiteness, heterosexuality and abstinent horniness. The interplay of gazes – the gaze of Spears who invites being looked at, the gaze of an unseen Dole looking at her, the gaze of a slack-jawed fry chef watching Spears and the gaze of the audience – insists upon displaced sexual desire. The visual logic of Pepsi ejaculate seen throughout the commercial – images of caps exploding off of Pepsi bottles and the white pyrotechnics that appear atop the retro Pepsi bottle sign for the commercial's finale – operate as part of a grander logic of a consumerism seeking to instill both desire and abstinence as a means of transformation from personal horniness to horny commerce. Just as fascism alters the right of expression into an opportunity for expression, the consumerist logic of the Pepsi commercial transforms the right of sexual expression into an opportunity for product consumption.

Segregated Inclusiveness

In addition to showing the compatibility of horny abstinence with both family values and consumerism, the Pepsi commercial also asserts a paradoxical logic of segregated inclusiveness. The familial gaze of this commercial includes faces of colour, yet makes sure to keep these faces separate within the contexts depicted. Although darker-skinned performers frequently appear in the shot, they just as quickly move out of the frame. The scene in which the only white female performer other than Spears returns the gaze, for example, is preceded by a tracking shot that insulates the gaze of two dark-skinned performers. The shot crowds out these figures from the lateral foreground. As a black male moving from screen right to screen left averts his gaze, another dark-skinned performer moves from screen left to screen right, holding out a Pepsi can before retreating offscreen. Although these darker-skinned performers are seen within the visual space, their subjectivities get laterally crowded out of the foreground as the shot remains anchored upon Spears in the background who maintains her look directly at the camera.

This visual logic of segregated inclusiveness extends to the way in which the commercial objectifies the diegetic audience. The whiter gazes of the slack-jawed fry chef and the firefighter hew close to the camera axis, as the shot dollies in to exclude an African American patron from the margins of the frame. In another shot, a lone African American male, his back to the camera, step dances before Spears' mediated image. A cut to a closer shot of men at a rival Coca-Cola facility edits out the one black gaze that appears in the preceding wide shot. Tracking from left to right, the shot of elderly viewers either frames black gazes out of the shot, or leaves them darkened, shadowed and in the background.

As part of the familial gaze, these shots both include African Americans and at the same time push them out of the frame. Segregated inclusiveness thus works in concert with horny abstinence and conformist individualism. These paradoxical motifs work to create a deep structure of illusions that at once offers different possibilities for family, gender, sexuality and politics; while at the same time limiting these possibilities. By limiting the presence of African Americans, the commercial appears to create opportunities for expression. Yet the opportunities appear marginal, organised beneath the governing motif of Spears' direct and dominating gaze into the camera.

The deep structure of illusions also organises opportunities for expression in terms of performance and domesticated spaces. Visually, the alternation between the two is represented by masking shots of Spears' performance using the Pepsi red and blue colours to achieve a letterbox effect. The shots of domesticated spaces, such as the diner, the bowling alley, the hallway of a hospital, a nursing home, and others are all shown in full-frame 1.33:1 screen ratio. By depicting groups of people viewing Spears' 'commercial' on television, the advert organises the emotional response to her performance in terms of ad hoc families engaged as 'viewers'. Rather than explore divergent definitions of family, however, the deep structure of illusions inherent within this commercial invites the viewer into a set of relationships with Spears and the familial gaze, but at the same time denies the possibilities of what these relationships and the gaze might bring about. It is through both the offering of opportunity as well as the limiting of possibilities that conformist individualism, horny abstinence and segregated inclusiveness ultimately propel the narrow conservative agenda of family values into the American mainstream.

10

The Corruption of the Family and the Disease of Whiteness in *I Walked with a Zombie*

GWENDOLYN AUDREY FOSTER

EXT. BEACH – DAY FADE IN on two distant figures who walk across a sunny BEACH parallel to the surf: a tall, thin, bare-chested black man and a shorter white woman in a nurse's uniform.

BETSY (voiceover): I walked with a zombie. (Laughs a little, self-consciously) Does seem an odd thing to say. Had anyone said that to me a year ago, I'm not at all sure I would have known what a zombie was.
– *I Walked with a Zombie*

You shouldn't get mad at New York reviewers. Actually, it's very difficult for a reviewer to give something called *I Walked with a Zombie* a good review.
– Val Lewton in a letter to his sister, 1942 (in Weems 2003)

In *I Walked with a Zombie* (1943), the trope of voodoo is used as a devastating critique of whiteness and colonialism in a Hollywood fantasy horror film set on the Island of St Sebastian in the West Indies. The film both supports and subverts the primacy of Hollywood's construction of voodoo and colonialism in its reworking of the plot of Charlotte Brontë's *Jane Eyre* (1847). *I Walked with a Zombie* is, as Erik Weems notes, a 'melancholy tale of a nurse and her experience in the Caribbean … accented by cogent scriptwriting by Curt Siodmak, Ardel Wray, and Val Lewton; moody cinematography by J. Roy Hunt, and a sensitive music score by Roy Webb. The direction is by Jacques Tourneur, and the editing by Mark Robson' (2003). The isolated Holland family that Canadian nurse Betsy Connell (Frances Dee) comes to work for is seen as continually under attack, in constant need of reification from within and without, as the various members seek to escape through drugs, alcohol and voodoo. The film may also be read as a series of postcolonial tableaux that critique, and simultaneously partake in, Hollywood's construction of whiteness against the backdrop of blackness and the film's set of a decaying West Indies sugar plantation. *I Walked with a Zombie* is one of a series of evocative low-budget horror films that producer Val Lewton created for the RKO 'B' unit, films that were made to order from pre-sold titles supplied by the RKO advertising department. As Kenneth Yousten notes, 'RKO executives really out-did themselves when they came up with this title and told Lewton to "make a film to go with it". But in what was to become standard procedure for Lewton, he used the title [to create] the story he wanted to make, a re-working of *Jane Eyre*' (n.d.). Weems suggests that the title came from 'RKO Film Executives who were trying to cash in on the horror film boom that the Universal film studio had brought about with their various Dracula, Frankenstein and Wolfman movies in the 1930s–40s. RKO had set up a special unit under Val Lewton for the production of these films' (2003), films that the studio cared little for, except that they turned a profit. In all his horror films for the RKO unit Lewton, a man of considerable taste and refinement, managed to create a vision of unreal reality in which the everyday and the supernatural coexist uneasily side by side. *I Walked with a Zombie* was not Lewton's first involvement with the Brontë novel, which he had long admired, and it was certainly not his first involvement with literature as the basis for film. As an assistant to producer David O. Selznick before coming to RKO, he had worked on film adaptations of both *Jane Eyre* (1944) and *Rebecca* (1940) (see Yousten n.d.).

Within the brutal constraints of its budget (in the $100,000 range), art directors Albert S. D'Agostino and Walter E. Keller created an entirely convincing West Indian atmosphere on the RKO backlot. The film used RKO contract stars because they were inexpensive to hire and readily available. The film's genesis, as far as RKO was concerned, was a rather sensationalistic article on voodoo in the West Indies, also entitled 'I Walked with a Zombie', by Inez Wallace. It appeared in the popular journal *American Weekly*, and was reworked by Siodmak, Wray and other members of Lewton's writing staff. What Lewton did with this source material was entirely his affair; so long as he didn't go over schedule or budget RKO left him alone, thus affording him and his collaborators an artistic freedom missing from many 'A' productions. Wallace's source material is both condescending and sensationalistic, lacking any real understanding of the culture she hopes to describe, as this brief excerpt clearly indicates:

> Haiti, that dark island of mystery, where such incredible figures as Christophe, the Black Napoleon, rose to world fame as the Negro emperor, where Voodoo rites link man with the supernatural in a manner beyond understanding … has yet another phenomenon that baffles the greatest thinkers and scientists of our age. When I first came to the island and heard the tales I am about to relate, I refused to believe. I cannot blame you for doubting when you have finished reading this account. Yet, in cold type, placed on the lawbooks of the Republic of Haiti, is official recognition of the existence of a brand of metaphysical magic that is abhorrent beyond words. Here is the law, found in Article 249 of the Criminal Code of Haiti: 'It shall be qualified as attempted murder the employ-

ment which may be made against any person of substances which, without causing death, produce a lethargic coma more or less prolonged. If, after the administering of such substances, the person has been buried, the act shall be considered murder no matter what result follows.' In plain words, it is murder to bury a person as dead, and afterwards bring that person's body out of the grave to live again – no matter what result follows. That law was put on the books because it has been proved that time and again the mysterious arts of the black people of Haiti have caused dead persons to rise from their graves and enter a soulless existence as slaves, their bodies moving about without any individual intelligence. These living corpses are called zombies. They are not ghosts, not phantom wraiths, but flesh and blood bodies which are dead, yet can move, walk, work and sometimes even speak.

This description must have pleased Lewton, a man with a decided taste for the morbid and a deep and abiding distrust of the traditional family unit, for he used it to structure a tale of a colonialist family in collapse, clinging to the past, haunted by the twin spectres of social disgrace and fear of the local customs. As noted by Gilles Deleuze and Félix Guattari, this is an ideal location for a true horror film: 'The family expresses more profound social contradictions, for one confers on it a value as microcosm, gives it the role of a necessary relay for the transformation of social into mental alienation' (1983: 361). The complete isolation and alienation of the Holland family in *I Walked with a Zombie* is both geographic and figurative; putative lords of the island domain, they are instead ensnared by their own weaknesses and superstitions, and by their reliance on outdated values to shore up the torn fabric of their futile existence.

Using the usual members of his stock company of actors and technicians, all veterans of the RKO 'B' unit, Lewton concentrated on this corrupted family in his scenario to the exclusion of the more typical tropes of the 1940s horror film, as exemplified by the central performance of the Trinidadian calypso singer Sir Lancelot,

who performs 'British Grenadiers' and 'Fort Holland', written in collaboration with Lewton. According to Jacques Tourneur, the [film's] director, Lancelot functioned as a '...Greek Chorus, wandering in seven or eight times and explaining the plot'. Roy Webb scored [the balance of the] film, which includes three Haitian folk 'voodoo' songs, and a unique counterpointing version of Chopin's 'E Minor Etude', combined with the pulsating drums which dominate much of the movie soundtrack. (Weems 2003)

As Weems also notes, for all of the script's complexity and ambition, the shooting went quite rapidly: begun on 26 October 1942, the film was finished on 19 November. Lewton, who had once worked as Selznick's assistant on *Gone with the Wind* (1939), another tale of a family in collapse, was intent upon concentrating all the film's action around the Holland family home, to keep the tragedy of the film firmly within the domestic sphere. As Weems states,

> the central recurring image [in the film] is of the old wooden figurehead Ti Misery, which is Saint Sebastian, the island's Patron Saint, a tragic emblem of the pain and suffering for the descendents of the slaves that live upon the island, a figurehead that came from Africa on a slave ship. As in Lewton's other films, the past intrudes upon the present in baleful reminders of former deeds which mimic present circumstance ... In *Zombie*, those who came to the island as slaves to European plantation owners are now servants of a different kind of bondage, a bondage that then infiltrates and controls the actions of most of the white masters who control the island. (2003)

Indeed, colonialism and the family are both viewed in *I Walked with a Zombie* as bankrupt, corrupt and immoral. White colonial mastery is perceived as evil and hopelessly mired in images of the collapse of the white colonial family. Alcoholism is rampant, as is the unspecified use of illicit drugs. But the Holland family (around whom the film's plot centres) has a secret that is presented as far more dangerous and evil than voodoo or anything associated with black West Indian culture. Their hidden truth is that the white matriarch has secretly used voodoo to enslave her daughter-in-law as a zombie, after finding that the young woman was carrying on an affair with her brother-in-law. This is a sick, dysfunctional family, trapped in an alien and noirish landscape; the traditional vision of the family as a place of refuge is shown by the film to be an evanescent fantasy. Their home is a prison, replete with menacing shadows and a sense of despair and finality hanging over each member of the family. Paul Holland (Tom Conway), the jilted husband, ceaselessly talks about death and the evils of slavery and continually remarks upon the atmosphere of decay and corruption that surrounds the plantation. Paul's brother, Wesley Rand (James Ellison), is a bitter and angry alcoholic, and the two men are locked in a perpetual struggle for control of the plantation. The brothers spend much of their time bickering, hopelessly bemoaning their loneliness and despair. As Deleuze and Guattari comment in general, here as well, 'the family's mission is to produce neurotics by means of its Oedipalisation, its system of impasses, its delegated psychic repression, without which social repression would never find docile and resigned subjects, and would not succeed in choking ... lines of escape' (1983: 361).

Into this West Indian plantation comes Betsy, who has been invited to the island to care for Paul's wife, Jessica (Christine Gordon), now haunting the Holland home as a walking zombie. As Paul tells Betsy early in the film,

> It's easy enough to read the thoughts of a newcomer. Everything seems beautiful because you don't understand. Those flying fish – they're not leaping for joy. They're jumping in terror. Bigger fish want to eat them. That luminous water – it

takes its gleam from millions of tiny dead bodies. The glitter of putrescence. There's no beauty here. Only death and decay.

It's fascinating to see how Betsy's whiteness is constructed when she arrives at the island. There is a tremendous gap between what she sees and what the viewer sees. While Betsy insists on the beauty of the island, the viewer is treated to carefully constructed studio sets that highlight the film's general atmosphere of decay and indifference towards life and the family. 'They brought you to a beautiful place, didn't they?' Betsy asks the black coachman who is driving her to the plantation. 'If you say, miss. If you say', he replies.

Let us examine this seemingly benign exchange for a moment. The manner in which the carriage driver delivers the line, 'If you say, miss' is patronising at the very least. It's delivered in the manner of one speaking to someone who is incredibly ignorant, childlike, stupid or mad. I suggest that *I Walked with a Zombie* constructs Betsy's white femininity as a form of madness or deliriousness. This is supported by her later behaviour in the film, when she tries to heal the zombified Jessica out of her love for Paul. It is also supported by the sharp contrast between Betsy's reporting of events and the way events are witnessed by the black plantation hands and the spectator.

It is both jarring and bizarre as Betsy describes the beauty of her bedroom (in a breathless voiceover) shortly after her arrival on the island, while the audience sees a frighteningly noirish and claustrophobic chamber patterned with the lighting of imprisoning Venetian blinds and enclosed by numerous French windows that are harshly weather-beaten. Betsy is experiencing a madness of sorts. She is delirious to take on the job of caring for an obviously mad white colonial family, a family that is dishonest both with itself and with her. She falls madly in love with Paul, a positively grim and hopeless figure of white masculinity, who repeatedly tells her, 'This is a sad place', as he talks about the cruelties of slavery under colonialism. Interestingly enough, Paul also tells her that he must have been out of his mind to invite her to the island.

In the form of masculinity or femininity, whiteness is a form of madness in *I Walked with a Zombie*, and madness is troped as an illness of the family that is based on lies, secrets and distortion – anything other than mastery or rationalism. Blackness and voodoo, on the other hand, are associated with health and at least some moments of happiness, and also with rational thinking and witnessing. There is one scene of the celebration of the birth of a black child which stands out with its cheerful lighting. Contrasted with a scene of the white family silently eating dinner at a table lit with only candles, underscored with sounds of the harsh island winds, the scene of the black child's birth celebration constructs blackness as healthy, communal, celebratory of goodness and the procreation of the black race. Betsy is attracted to this scene, caught up in the festivities of blackness, but only for a while. She returns to the illness and depravity of her white employers.

Black West Indian characters are seen as more fully human than whites; as observers, witnesses and judges of the white people who linger under glass in a festering jail of their own making. The maid Alma (Teresa Harris) and a calypso singer (Sir Lancelot) are knowledgeable and caring towards Betsy. They see her as a white figure who can be steered off the island, or at the very least a white woman worth warning; Betsy has arrived, after all, with no idea of the depravity of the Holland family nor any fear of blackness or voodoo. The singer tries to warn Betsy in a song that tells of the Rand/Holland infidelity, and passes grim judgement on them:

> There was a family that lived on the isle
> Of St Sebastian a long, long while
> The head of the fam'ly was a Holland man
> And the younger brother, his name was Rand
> *Chorus*: Ah, woe! Ah, me!
> Shame and sorrow for the family!
> Ah, woe! Ah, me!
> Shame and sorrow for the family!

> The Holland man, he kept in a tower,
> A wife as pretty as a big white flower.
> She saw the brother and she stole his heart.
> And that's how the badness and the trouble start.
> (*Chorus*: Ah, woe! Ah, me!...)

> The wife and the brother, they want to go
> But the Holland man, he tell them no.
> The wife fall down and the evil came
> And it burned her mind in the fever flame.
> (*Chorus*: Ah, woe! Ah, me!...)

As the singer goes on, he is interrupted by Wesley Rand and breaks off with profuse apologies, obviously scared of the phantom Colonialist power that Wesley holds over the island, and, by extension, his person. But as soon as the singer finds Betsy alone again, he continues his calypso, warning her of the Holland family in a much more sinister and insistent manner:

> Her eyes are empty and she cannot talk
> And a nurse has come to make her walk.
> The brothers are lonely and the nurse is young
> And now you must see that my song is sung.
> Ah, woe! Ah, me!
> Shame and sorrow for the family!

Ah, woe! Ah, me!
Shame and sorrow for the family!

This ominous song was, in fact, based on an incident that took place in Trinidad in 1933, and that was already a popular part of the island's folklore. As detailed by Donald R. Hill in his book *Calypso Calaloo*, 'a cuckolded husband paid a [Calypso singer] to compose a song about his wife and the other man – the Inspector General of Constabulary … The song became quite popular despite … attempts to suppress it, and is now best known [under the title] "Country Club Scandal" sung by King Radio' (in Yousten 2003).

Betsy does not give up easily, however. She decides to try to help Jessica and insists on a series of treatments. Shock therapy doesn't work, so she resorts to voodoo, the power of which she learns from Alma, whose knowledge emphasises the rationality of West Indian religion as opposed to the ineffectualness of white medicine. When Betsy tells Alma, 'Doctors and nurses can only do so much … They can't cure everything', Alma replies, 'Doctors *that are people* can't cure everything.' Other, and better, doctors that Alma knows 'even cure nonsense, Miss Betty … The Houngan will speak to the rada drums and the drums will speak to Legba and Damballa. *Better doctors.*'

After Alma carefully gives Betsy instructions, Betsy tries to get help from the Houngan, and fearlessly leads the zombified white woman through the swamps in order to meet with Alma's 'better doctors'. The long atmospheric trip through the night plays upon audiences' fear of the black Other, and especially of voodoo itself. Here, Tourneur and Lewton carefully design and utilise the tropes of voodoo to frighten the audience. There is little dialogue in the scene, only the insistent beat of the ceremonial drums in the distance. The camera glides along in a series of masterfully assured tracking shots, peering through the moonlit marsh with seemingly malevolent disinterest. As the script indicates, this sequence, accomplished entirely in the studio without any exterior shooting, was envisioned from the start as the visual centrepiece of the film. As Alma instructs Betsy on the proper directions to the Houmfort, the script enters a zone of mesmeric ritualisation, in which time stands still and words will not avail. As the screenplay tell us, to protect the nurse and her patient on their journey, 'Alma pulls two voodoo patches from her dress and pins them to Betsy and Jessica's shoulders.' Betsy's is white, in contrast to her dark cape. 'There's a guard there … He keeps the crossroads', says Alma, 'But he won't do you no harm when he sees the voodoo patches. He'll let you pass.' We dissolve to a sugarcane field at night. The seven-feet-tall figure of Carrefour, the voodoo guard (Darby Jones), stands immobile, silhouetted against the moonlight. A stiff breeze shakes the cane stalks. As Betsy leads Jessica through the cane, an 'odd MOANING sound causes Betsy to stop and turn toward it', says the script. She turns her light onto a cow's skull stuck upon a stick, and the noise is coming from the wind blowing through the hollow skull. Soon, there is another noise, 'ominous' and 'vibrating', the wind blowing through a gourd suspended from a scaffold, it turns out. On the ground is 'a human skull … in the middle of a circle of stones'.

The night seems to be getting darker and the cane to be getting thicker, more claustrophobic. The sound of a conch and drums causes Betsy to stop and look around. After a moment, the two women press forward, but Betsy fails to notice that her voodoo patch has caught on a cane stalk and been torn from her cape. She points her light at the ground as they make their way forward. Suddenly, a man's foot appears in its beam. Betsy instantly points her torch at the man's face, revealing the 'spooky, bug-eyed, blank stare' of Carrefour. Betsy is startled, then notices that her patch is gone but Jessica still has hers. She clutches Jessica and the two move cautiously past the guard, who continues to stare at them. Soon, as the script has it, 'The DRUMS grow louder and are now accompanied by intense CHANTING, a call-and-response chant – 'O Legba' – with a male voice answered by a chorus of voices. Betsy and Jessica emerge from the cane field and enter the open-air HOUMFORT.'

The word *carrefour*, of course, means 'crossroads' in French, so Carrefour's name is an indicator of his locus within the narrative: the crossroads between white and black, between the real and the supernatural. When Betsy enters the hut in the Houmfort, she finds to her shock that Mrs Rand, the mother-in-law (Edith Barrett), is some sort of white witch doctor. Apparently, discouraged by the natives' lack of respect for white medicine she has taken on the role of a sort of voodoo priestess, in order to force them to accept the dictates of Western medicine. But Mrs Rand's association with the activities of the Houmfort goes much deeper than mere deception for seemingly altruistic purposes. Falling under the spell of the island's culture, the matriarch has used her knowledge of voodoo to terrible advantage. As she admits to Betsy the next day,

> I entered into their ceremonies. I pretended I was possessed by their gods. But what I did to Jessica … was when she wanted to go away with Wesley. That night I went to the Houmfort. I kept seeing her face – smiling because she was beautiful enough to take my family in her hands and tear it apart. Drums, the chanting, the lights. I heard a voice speaking in the sudden silence. My voice. I was speaking to the Houngan. I was possessed. I told him the woman at Fort Holland was evil and asked him to make her a zombie.

The end of the film asserts to the trope of voodoo as a transgressively inscribed means to destroy the depraved and guilty whites. Wesley, the cheating brother, stabs his lover with an arrow taken from the chest of the statue of St Sebastian. Carrefour paradoxically turns out to be a figure of goodness and a destroyer of evil. He controls Wesley's actions, and forces the young man to walk into the sea to drown both himself and his zombified lover. After this sequence, there is a voiceover by the Houngan, a representative of the omniscient collective black community. As the camera rests on the statue of St Sebastian, he delivers to the audience a prayer that sums up the action of the tale we have just seen unfold.

O Lord God most holy, deliver them from the bitter pains of eternal death. The woman was a wicked woman, and she was dead in her own life. Yea Lord, dead in the selfishness of her spirit, and the man followed her, her steps led him down to evil, her feet took hold of death. Forgive him, O Lord, who knows the secrets of all hearts. Yea Lord, pity them who are dead, and give peace and happiness to the living.

In this film, even if morality is defined in white European terms, black West Indians are ultimately more moral, and voodoo is troped as a force of goodness ultimately aligned with and equal to Christianity. While aspects of *I Walked with a Zombie* are certainly condescending towards voodoo as a cultural practice, these sections tend to be undercut by the construction of whites as deceitful, diabolical and ultimately mad, primitive and associated with death and deception. In the world of *I Walked with a Zombie*, all that is supposedly 'civilised' is in a state of decay and collapse, and only the native culture is seen as living and vibrant. The internecine plottings of the various members of the Holland family are far more horrifying than anything in voodoo practice, a point that Lewton, Tourneur, Siodmak and Wray make over and over in the film. Far from being a refuge, the Holland family estate is a place to escape from, where the only real release is offered by death.

As Deleuze and Guattari comment, 'Who says that the family is a good place? … [it is rather] a race of sick people implored by reaction that they be given back an asylum, or a little Beckettian land, a garbage can, so that they can become catatonic in a corner' (1983: 319). This is what the Holland family has inherited: a small place on an island in the West Indies, a 'home' that creates a series of traps and snares from which they struggle in futility to escape.

Far from the sensationalistic reportage of Inez Wallace that ostensibly inspired the film, Lewton has constructed a characteristic meditation on the power of evil, the omnipresence of death and the hopelessness of human endeavour. Here as in numerous other Lewton films, especially the unremittingly dark *The Seventh Victim* (1943) which followed *I Walked with a Zombie*, death is seen as a release from the corporeal prison of human suffering, a suffering that is mediated only by faith, or alcohol, or, in the best instances, the power of love. But behind every public action, Lewton tells us, there is a hidden motive, and *I Walked with a Zombie* makes this axiom abundantly clear.

Before we discover that Mrs Rand believes in and practises voodoo, we see her publicly dismiss voodoo pursuits, explaining that she began using them merely to convince the West Indian natives to boil the drinking water. As producer and arguable auteur (along with director Jacques Tourneur) of this film, Val Lewton also seemed to take a dualistic approach to voodoo. He employed a technical advisor, Jieno Moxzer, an authority on Haitian folk music and voodoo, in order that the voodoo ceremonies would have the look and sound of veracity unlike what could be seen in any other Hollywood film of the period. Moxzer also played the crucial role of the Sabreur, or sabre holder, who conducts many of the ceremonies depicted in the film. Indeed, one would have to look to Maya Deren's documentary *Divine Horsemen: The Living Gods of Haiti* (1946–85; completed posthumously), which the filmmaker shot in the 1940s in Haiti, to find a more sympathetic vision of voodoo as a practising, living religion. One section in *I Walked with a Zombie* that is particularly accurate is a scene in which the voodoo practitioners stab a sword into the arm of the white female zombie, Jessica; yet, more than accurate, it is also dramatised onscreen to be alienating and terrifying. This comes at the same time that Betsy confronts Mrs Rand at the Houmfort, where she has been masquerading as the high priest.

> The Sabreur confronts Jessica with his sword. He abruptly raises his arm and, as if hypnotized, she raises hers in response. He takes her outstretched hand, turns her to face him, and violently plunges the sword directly into her arm. Jessica doesn't react. The DRUMMING stops. The voodoo worshippers GASP.
> CUT TO:
> INT. THE HUT – SAME TIME
> Mrs Rand looks up, realising something's wrong.
> CUT TO:
> EXT. THE HUT – SAME TIME
> The voodoo worshippers gather around Jessica, whispering in disbelief.
>
> MAN: She doesn't bleed.
> WOMAN: Zombie!

Throughout the scene, Jessica neither flinches nor bleeds. Here is an example of a genuine trait of Loa possession: physical imperviousness to pain and bloodshed. The scene shows respect for the religion of the Other, yet it is also used to frighten the audience, instilling fear of the Other and their religion. Imbued with this duality – not easy to erase or mediate – the film thus moves uneasily between two sites of highly contested ground, in which the dead are alive (the zombies), and the living (the various members of the Holland family) are, for all intents and purposes, dead, lost in a fever dream of Colonial dominion and power which has long since slipped away from them.

Ultimately, however, it is whiteness that *I Walked with a Zombie* portrays as the cultural Other. The Holland family is corrupt internally and externally, through their style of living, their exploitation of the natives, their appropriation of native culture and their lack of self-knowledge and intellectual weakness. These white

American colonials are evil, incapable of goodness, mired in lies and corruption and enslaved in their own familial dysfunctionality. Perhaps because of her Canadian Otherness, Betsy is the sole decent, if often deluded, white character. The others are drunks, suicides, irrational and even homicidal, especially Mrs Rand, who has descended into evil through the ostensible practice of 'good works'. The final voiceover of black maleness, a godlike figure, transcends the evil of the plantation and promises peace and happiness to the living. *I Walked with a Zombie* manages to embrace black Otherness, even as it deconstructs and destroys the primacy of that greater Otherness which is white.

11

Short Cuts to *Gosford Park*: The Family in Robert Altman

GLENN MAN

Robert Altman's attitude towards his characters and human relations has been anything but magnanimous. Instead, his satiric bent and deconstruction of genre subvert the mythically heroic and highlight the foibles of the heart, the vulnerability and limitations of desire, the destructive power of the ego, the reach of institutional distortion and the withering of personal relationships. The institution of the family is an especially rich site for Altman's cynicism to feed upon, given the evidence of films that range from *Nashville* (1975) to *Gosford Park* (2001); indeed, Altman turned his attention almost exclusively to the family in his later work – *Short Cuts* (1993), *Cookie's Fortune* (1999), *Dr T and the Women* (2000) and *Gosford Park*, in each case, reworking genre to suit his own purposes: the literary adaptation, the smalltown film, the melodrama and the Agatha Christie-like murder mystery, respectively.

Earlier films like *Nashville* and *A Wedding* (1978) had opened the Pandora's Box of family secrets, betrayals and dysfunctional relationships long before their blossoming in Altman's second coming in the last two decades. In *Nashville*, Lily Tomlin's Linnea is a loving mother to her two deaf mute children, but her emotional estrangement from her obtuse husband Delbert (Ned Beatty) drives her to a one-night stand with pop singer stud Tom (Keith Carradine); country singer Barbara Jean's (Ronee Blakley) husband and manager Barnett (Allen Garfield) is insensitive to her vulnerability and drives her to a near mental breakdown by overbooking her performances; and Mary (Cristina Raines) openly betrays her husband Bill (Allan F. Nichols) by sleeping with Tom, the third member of their musical trio. But this is just the tip of the iceberg. In *A Wedding*, the lavish reception reveals class, racial and familial tensions within and between the families of the bride Muffin Brenner (Amy Stryker) and the groom Dino Corelli (Desi Arnaz Jr). Dino's father Luigi (Vittorio Gassman) had married into a wealthy Northern industrial family (the Sloans) only after submitting to a blood test for diseases and taking an oath before the family matriarch (Lillian Gish) never to associate with his blood ties back in Italy; his wife Regina's (Nina Van Pallandt) heroin addiction is sustained by the family doctor

(Howard Duff); her sister Clarice (Virginia Vestoff) is having an affair with the family's black servant Randolph (Cedric Scott); their older sister Antoinette (Dina Merrill) runs a sweat-shop factory and likes to think of herself as being in control of the family, a fancy that family members amusedly allow her to indulge in. Meanwhile, the bride's mother Tulip (Carol Burnett) is emotionally starved and has a developing liaison with the groom's uncle MacKenzie (Pat McCormick) during the daylong event; and the bride's sister Buffy (Mia Farrow) has slept with Dino the bridegroom, is jealous of her sister and is pregnant. Dino may or may not be the child's father.

Short Cuts and Carver Country

In *Short Cuts*, the family is a fertile ground for a variety of dysfunctional relationships: Bill and Honey Bush (Robert Downey Jr and Lili Taylor) cannot get it on except by vicariously living through their upwardly mobile neighbours; the policeman Gene (Tim Robbins) uses his job to buy time to cheat on his wife Sherri (Madeleine Stowe); singer Tess Trainer (Annie Ross) is so involved in her self-pity that she rejects her daughter Zoe's (Lori Singer) attempts to communicate with her, unwittingly contributing to Zoe's suicide. None of the characters develops any self-awareness, locked as they are in their obsessions and in Altman's cynical presentation. They are doomed to repetitive patterns of self-absorption. Altman's changes to Robert Carver's short stories in his cinematic adaptation accentuate his treatment of the family as a site for satire rather than for self-awareness and possible transformation. Carver's stories are laced with interior explorations of character and often allow for empathetic responses. They depict the anguish of the individual caught in the grip of a familial crisis or middle-age ennui, at the same time hinting at the possibility for personal insight and change through self-examination. In other words, Carver expands his characters; Altman reduces his.

Two of the central husband/wife duos in *Short Cuts* have undergone an Altman facelift from their counterparts in Carver's stories. In Carver's 'Will You Please Be Quiet, Please?', Ralph, a high school teacher and the story's centre of consciousness, has developed an inflexibility to shield himself from the id of his personality, given free rein during his college years when he was known as the fraternity drunk nicknamed 'Johnson' after a favourite bartender. After years of repression of his past and this dark double, his wife Marian confesses an earlier affair she had during their marriage, a revelation that plunges Ralph into a dark night of self-examination and doubt, a re-initiation into the chaos of his 'Johnson' persona. Painful though this experience is, the possibility exists now for a transformation in Ralph to accept his other self and, more importantly, the complications and unpredictability of an unsheltered existence. The end of the story is fluid and open, suggesting possibilities:

> He tensed at her fingers, and then he let go a little. It was easier to let go a
> little. Her hand moved over his hip and over his stomach and she was pressing

her body over his now and moving over him and back and forth over him. He held himself, he later considered, as long as he could. And then he turned to her. He turned and turned in what might have been a stupendous sleep, and he was still turning, marvelling at the impossible changes he felt moving over him. (Carver 1995: 68)

Altman reconfigures the story. Now, Ralph (Matthew Modine) intersects with the characters from another Carver story 'A Small, Good Thing', functioning as the doctor who attends the injured Casey (Zane Cassidy), the eight-year-old son of Ann and Howard Finnigan (Andie MacDowell, Bruce Davison), who is hit by a car and slips into a coma. Altman's alteration of the characters of Ralph and Marian (Julianne Moore) is revealing. In Carver, Marian's confession of her former affair flows out of a sense of regret and guilt; in Altman, Marian and Ralph are so locked in an adversarial relationship that her revelation of an earlier affair arises out of spite and anger after Ralph badgers her to tell all. At the end of the movie, they are still sniping at one another as dawn breaks over L.A. after an all-nighter with Claire and Stuart (Anne Archer, Fred Ward), a couple from another Carver story, 'So Much Water So Close to Home'. In contrast to Carver, the revelation of Marian's affair in the film doesn't result in self-examination, a dark night of the soul or the possibility of transformation.

In his adaptation of Carver's 'So Much Water So Close to Home', a story about a wife's agonising discovery of her husband's misogyny and her subsequent resistance to him, Altman neutralises the character of the wife Claire and mutes her resistance. In the short story, Claire discovers her husband Stuart's complicity in the defilement of a dead woman's naked body in a river by not reporting its discovery until the next day so as not to spoil his fishing trip with his buddies. To the end of the story, Claire refuses to give in to Stuart's explanations as she strongly identifies with the dead body, an identification made all the more apparent in her own victimisation by Stuart in a continuous pattern of abuse, which includes his threats of violence towards her followed by insincere apologies. In *Short Cuts*, Altman deliberately steers away from weighing the events through Claire's consciousness in order to present both her side and Stuart's side objectively. He says, 'I didn't want to make any judgement whatsoever' (in Stewart 1993: 7). However, this neutrality of presentation flattens Claire's character, waters down her internal struggle and mutes her resistance against Stuart's prevarications. Altman's 'neutrality' along with his characteristic irony underline his intransigence towards his characters' internal dilemmas and struggles for insight and understanding within the bonds of marital commitment.[1]

Women Kin: *Cookie's Fortune* and *Dr T and the Women*

Altman's transformation of Claire in *Short Cuts* merely reminds us of his own misogynist attitude and his resistance to a feminist consciousness. He has persistently ignored the inroads of feminism in his presentation of gender relations, or he has veered from this criticism by saying that he is just being true to the way things are. In the director's commentary on the DVD of M*A*S*H, Altman defends himself from the misogyny in the film by saying, 'I'm showing you the way that I observed women were treated. And that is the way women were treated and still are treated ... the whole point of this film was to show those attitudes toward women'. Tellingly, however, Altman's 1960s counterculture sensibility attacked, rather than just 'show'ed, traditional patriarchal attitudes towards race and war in M*A*S*H (1970), while he chose to indulge the rampant sexism of the times in the same film. Indeed, after Short Cuts, Altman's next two family films, Cookie's Fortune and Dr T and the Women, give him a field day to express a consistent attitude towards the opposite sex. In both films, the women suffer the consequences of conventional moral and marital choices without the benefit of self-awareness or what feminists like to term 'consciousness raising'. Cookie's Fortune has the distinction in Altman's oeuvre of being perceived as warm-hearted and humane. Roger Ebert calls it Altman's 'sunniest film, a warm-hearted comedy that somehow manages to deal with death and murder charges without even containing a real villain' (1999). I'm not sure whether I viewed the same film as Ebert, but before I move to unsettle the Altman icon I must indicate that J. Hoberman balances Ebert's take with his insight into Altman's characteristic tone towards his characters in the film: 'Altman is a filmmaker who aspires to the choreographed and socially astute ensemble humanism epitomised by Jean Renoir in The Rules of the Game (1939). But unlike Renoir, he has a saturnine temperament – he cannot help but condescend to half of his characters and ridicule the rest' (1999).

At the heart of Cookie's Fortune is a Southern matriarchal family presided over by the eccentric Cookie (Patricia Neal) and which includes her two nieces, the bossy and disapproving Camille (Glenn Close) and the dim-witted Cora (Julianne Moore), as well as Cora's black-sheep daughter Emma (Liv Tyler). Two parallel events run throughout the narrative: Camille's rehearsal of the town's citizens in her revision of Oscar Wilde's Salome in the church auditorium and her orchestration, with Cora as an accomplice, of the cover-up of Cookie's suicide. The two events merge when the police arrest Camille for murder just as the scene in which Salome asks for the head of John the Baptist is being performed. Camille has her comeuppance in several ways. Cora does not corroborate her story of the suicide and cover-up, thus exacting revenge on her sister's victimisation of her in the present and in the past; Camille's past comes to light, which unlocks a dark family secret that involves her infidelity to Cora when she had an affair with Cora's husband, giving birth to Emma in secret, passing Emma off as Cora's daughter, and later ostracising Emma from the family for her loose ways. Altman, of course, could have presented Camille, Cora and Emma as victims of the male, of Cora's husband with whom Camille had the affair and who then abandoned the women and his daughter. But no, the monster in the film is Camille. She is alternately viewed as domineering, jealous, silly, cruel, grasping and self-absorbed. Cora, on the other hand, is viewed consistently as meekly obeying her sister and suffering her insults. Even her one great moment of revenge does not presage a change in her life. It exists to tell on Camille; Cora must forever remain the dimwit in order for her story against Camille to stick. The film's narration locates the heart of the family's dysfunction in Southern matriarchy and not in the patriarchy that makes that matriarchy a necessary site of power for its women. Emma's bold indiscretions set her apart from the matriarchy, a privilege she shares with the men in the community who are allowed an untroubled camaraderie and fellowship, figured in the activity of fishing together. If Hitchcock's *Shadow of a Doubt* (1943) transformed the smalltown genre by exposing the darkness beneath the sunny surface of Santa Rosa, California and was ahead of its time in its portrayal of a female hero and the assignment of murder and incest to their origins in a patriarchal brother and uncle figure, then Altman's *Cookie's Fortune* must seem both a continuation and a regression of the Hitchcock enterprise: as it uncovers the darkness beneath the pleasant smalltown surface of Holly Springs, it demonises the matriarchy at the heart of its Southern environment.

Dr T and the Women bristles with family and familial tension. The film centres on the Dallas gynaecologist Sullivan Travis (Richard Gere) and his travails with his 'families' – the immediate family of his wife Kate (Farrah Fawcett), his two daughters Dee Dee (Kate Hudson) and Connie (Tara Reid), his sister-in-law Peggy (Laura Dern), and her three young daughters, and the extended family of his office staff, headed by Carolyn (Shelley Long), and his high-class clientele of patients. The women of Dr T's 'families' are experiencing the consequences of a conventional, consumerist patriarchal society. They are 'hysterical' in varying degrees, and because the Altman presentation is of 'the way things are', his women characters are again denied the opportunity of self-examination and awareness that might give them a way out. Dr T is enthralled with his women. He is caring, loving and understanding, but in a way that is protective and adoring. In the men's locker room at his country club, he tells his golfing buddies, 'Women are … by nature, they are saints; they are sacred; they should be treated as such.' Implicit in Dr T's worship of women is the acceptance of the traditional cultural myth of woman as either angel (of the house) or whore; and it is this attitude that is at the heart of the cause of the women's dilemmas in the film. Indeed, Dr T's wife Kate's breakdown is the result of the 'Hestia complex', a regression into a childlike virginity as a way of rejecting the paternal love and protection that have assigned her the function of goddess of hearth and home. Kate has been given plenty of material luxury and comforts as a wife and mother, but has been afforded none of the opportunities that would allow an outlet for realising her repressed personal desires or energies. Her tragedy lies not in her breakdown and regression but in the lack of a self-awareness that could truly liberate her. The contrast to Kate is the golf pro Bree

(Helen Hunt), who makes choices based on her desires, not on social expectations. When Dr T proposes that they should run off together so that she 'wouldn't have to work; I'd take care of you totally', Bree tells him, 'Why would I want that?' Bree highlights by contrast the degrees to which the other women have bought into the system: Dee Dee is a closet lesbian who is planning a conventional marriage of convenience and a wedding with all the trimmings – bridal shower, bridal registry at Tiffany's, and so on; Connie knows about Dee Dee's lesbianism and assures her father that she is fine and that he is not to worry about her; Peggy is on the brink of a breakdown *à la* her sister Kate, escaping her lot by surreptitiously sipping alcohol, separating from her husband and moving into Dr T's household; Carolyn, Dr T's assistant, has given up her life to serve her boss, suffering in silence for a secret crush on him; and Dorothy (Janine Turner), Dr T's prototypical patient, is a hypochondriac, needing frequent visits to boost her self-confidence from his care and flatteries.

To be fair, two of these women see the light, maybe; Dee Dee realises her personal desire and jilts her fiancé at the altar to run off with her lover and maid of honour Marilyn (Liv Tyler), and Carolyn tells Dr T during the chaos that follows Dee Dee's bolt that she is quitting his service to become what she has always wanted to be, a chef. I say 'maybe', because like Bree's refusal to run off with him after the chaos of the truncated wedding ceremony, Dee Dee and Carolyn's actions seem to be part of a plot by the narrational authority (read: Altman) to contribute to the travails of the male protagonist brought upon by women. They are not the centre of the film's conscience or consciousness; Dr T is that centre, and the ending of the film seems to illustrate and validate his traditional view of women.

Altman engages in magic realism at the end to situate Dr T in a primitive environment where the birth of a baby takes on primordial and archetypal significance. After Bree rejects him and it seems that his world is falling apart, a tornado lifts, whirls and deposits him safely in a desert landscape; three girls discover him and bring him to a huddle of adobe shacks full of women where one of them is in labour and he is called upon to deliver the child; a real birth occurs on film, the camera unblinking in its depiction and celebration of woman as vagina, as earth mother. The baby turns out to be a boy and Dr T shouts joyfully as he lifts him in the air, the camera pulls back into a high-angle long shot of the eight shacks arranged in a perfect circle on the desert landscape surrounded by mountains. This figurative coda reveals what woman's true place is for Dr T and the authority that controls the narration's tone: her primary function is to procreate the earth, and it's especially worthy if the offspring is male. The males in the film have certain privileged sanctuaries where they can congregate, relax and console one another about their problems with the other sex – in their hunting, in their skeet shoots and in their golfing, much as the activity of fishing is a male site of camaraderie in *Cookie's Fortune*. Meanwhile, the women can only feed their frustrations in the shopping malls, as office staff, or in visits to their (male) doctors.

Upstairs/Downstairs at Gosford Park

Gosford Park is Altman's richest film since *Nashville*, and it comes close to being both a critical and commercial success, a rarity in the Altman oeuvre (if one were strict about claims, only *M*A*S*H*, of all of the director's pictures, would be an unqualified critical *and* commercial success). In *Gosford Park*, Altman achieves a density and weight through four interwoven strands that form the film: the framework and conventions of an Agatha Christie murder mystery, the multi-protagonist narrative and its conventions, the hierarchical system of the British aristocracy and its duplication within the downstairs servant class (in the manner of Eileen Atkins and Jean Marsh's *Upstairs, Downstairs* (1971–75), and the various familial interrelations and tensions within and between the upstairs and the downstairs personalities. As in his preceding films that centre on the family, Altman dissects the jealousies, infidelities, greed and self-absorption that result in the dysfunctional relations within the 'families' that congregate for a shooting party one fateful weekend at Gosford Park in the England of 1932.

Altman returns here to one of his most successful forms, the multiple protagonist film, as he had done in *Nashville*, *A Wedding*, *Short Cuts* and *Prêt-à-Porter* (1994), his signature weaving camera and multi-track sound system deftly capturing the dynamic intersections and interplay among the 24 characters. Altman says *Gosford Park* resembles *A Wedding* the most of all his films, since the environment of both pictures is self-contained (see Hohenadal 2001: 52). This is more like what Margrit Trohler calls the 'group film', in which a group of characters assemble within an enclosed setting like a family house, club or meeting place, in contrast to what she calls the 'mosaic film', in which the multiple protagonists operate within the larger network setting of a city, country or the globe (2000: 85–6). But no matter what, in both his group and mosaic films, Altman consistently maintains focus on one of his favourite themes – the individual caught within the grip of social institutions. In *Gosford Park* that dominant institution would be British class society and the drama of its ceremonial relationships, which infects the McCordle family and the surrogate families of guests and servants who gather at their estate for the weekend. In the 'Afterword' to his screenplay, Julian Fellowes notes how important it was to situate the characters in a certain historical period in order to clearly define their social roles. In the year 1932 just before the rise of Hitler, the aristocracy, the *nouveau riche* and their older most senior servants could still rely on class divisions and rituals to give their lives meaning. However, World War Two would signal the breakdown of those divisions and rituals, affording the story's younger servants opportunities to move into other areas of society in postwar Britain (see Fellowes 2002: 169). Situating the characters in 1932 allows Altman to train his satiric vision on a class society that was still fairly rigid; this seems to be the primary intent of the multiple narratives that intersect the upstairs and downstairs worlds of the manor house. Corollary to this intent is the film's exposure of institutional injustices that occur within a hierarchical structure of power and privilege; and thus the plot of revenge and murder whose resolution is secondary to its function in relaying the victimisations and complicities of the past.

Altman dissects the dynamics of family relations in the McCordle circle to expose the dysfunctions and grasping expectations that illustrate the hierarchy of power and the possible motives for murder within the group. The family members and their particular functions, grievances and dissatisfactions include Sir William McCordle (Michael Gambon), head of the clan, a vulgar self-absorbed womaniser and penny-pinching guardian of his finances; he is locked within a loveless marriage to Lady Sylvia McCordle (Kristin Scott Thomas), who is from an old but impoverished family and who married Sir William for the convenience of his title and money. Lady Sylvia releases her boredom in *affaires de coeur*, be they with members of her own class, such as her brother-in-law Lord Stockbridge (Charles Dance), or with servants such as the young Henry Denton (Ryan Phillippe), valet to the Hollywood producer and weekend guest Morris Weissman (Bob Balaban), who wishes to research English manor house society for his next movie, *Charlie Chan in London*. Lady Sylvia's family includes her aunt Constance, Countess of Trentham (Maggie Smith), grand dame of aristocratic attitudes who looks down upon, and undercuts, both the levelling forces of American democracy (in her dismissal of the American Jew Weissman) and the forces of popular culture (in her disparagement of the songs and movies of Ivor Novello (Jeremy Northam), cousin to Sir William). However, the Countess is forced to prostrate herself before Sir William because he keeps her solvent with measured allowances that are not guaranteed while he is alive. Lady Sylvia's two younger sisters and their husbands enhance the tensions within this immediate family circle: Louisa (Geraldine Somerville) is unhappily married to the stolid, irritable, half-deaf Lord Stockbridge and in love with her brother-in-law Sir William; Lavinia (Natasha Wightman) is happily married to ex-Lieutenant Commander Anthony Meredith (Tom Hollander), but her husband has failed in his business ventures and desperately needs Sir William's help in his latest project, an aid that Sir William refuses to give him. Yet another suffering aristocrat is the incompetent and penniless Freddie Nesbitt (James Wilby), who mistakenly expected to gain from his marriage to the daughter of a glove manufacturer, Mabel (Claudie Blakley). A family friend, he is pathetically on the dole. Freddie's disappointment motivates him to blackmail Isobel McCordle (Camilla Rutherford), daughter of Sir William and Lady Sylvia, to intercede with her father for a job on his behalf. Isobel has recently had an abortion, and it is an open question whether Freddie was the father or not.

The servants downstairs mirror their masters and have their own hierarchy, but their tensions and intrigues exist mostly below the surface in contrast to the broiling vibrations within the McCordle family. The butler Jennings' (Alan Bates) stiff formality is appropriate for his station, but it also blunts personal relationships and functions to hide a shameful past secret. The housekeeper Mrs Wilson's (Helen

Mirren) proficiency and organisation disguises repressed feelings of bitter hurt and regret. The cook Mrs Croft (Eileen Atkins) jealously guards over her domain in the kitchen, her territorial conflict with Mrs Wilson a counterfeit of a deeper discord between the two. The head housemaid Elsie (Emily Watson) is having an affair with Sir William, which causes her to bristle under her breath against Lady Sylvia's bitchiness towards him. The first footman George (Richard E. Grant) smirkingly articulates his disdain for the upstairs world among his fellow servants. And the still room maid Dorothy (Sophie Thompson) carries an unrequited torch for the obtuse Jennings. Of the visiting servants, two stand out for similar enigmatic behaviour: Mr Stockbridge, nee Robert Parks (Clive Owen), valet to Sir Raymond Stockbridge, and Henry Denton, valet to Morris Weissman. Of the major servant characters, only Miss Trentham, nee Mary MacEachran (Kelly MacDonald), maid to Constance, is immune to surreptitiousness. She is new to service, an innocent in the ways of both the profession and the world, and not surprisingly, therefore, the moral consciousness in the narrative and, ultimately, the audience's lynchpin to unlocking the mysterious events of the past and present that involve Sir William, Mrs Wilson, Mrs Croft and Robert Parks.

The revelation of the past and its impact on the present in *Gosford Park* play a significant part in carrying on Altman's signature intention of dramatising the interconnectedness of his characters in film after film from *Nashville* to *Short Cuts*. Here, he demonstrates this interconnectedness in a more convincing and successful fashion than ever, in his picture of a self-sustaining society of dependency and power where family blood, legitimate and illegitimate, blurs the lines between masters and servants even as class conventions dictate their separate spheres. David Denby gracefully articulates Altman's accomplishment in his *New Yorker* review: 'He achieves his dream of a truly organic form, in which everyone is connected to everyone else, and life circulates around a central group of ideas and emotions in bristling orbits' (2002: 93). Denby locates Altman's achievement in the amalgamation of form and content, where form confers meaning and analogises the theme of interconnectedness. This achievement occurs over the whole narrative of *Gosford Park*, and one particular sequence stands out as exemplary. Ivor Novello is entertaining the household with his songs, a sequence that brings together various themes and plot strands and that culminates in the discovery of Sir William's dead body, a finding that precipitates the various exposés that pockmark the narrative in the last third of the film, giving the term 'extended family' of masters and ser-vants a new meaning.

Before this sequence, several significant actions have taken place: Sir William has refused to help Freddie and Anthony in their insolvent positions, and he has resisted Lady Constance's solicitations about her allowance. Mrs Wilson has taken a special interest in Lord Stockbridge's valet, calling him 'Robert Parks' when she addresses the other visiting servants only by their masters' names, and reacting with recognition to his orphanage background and to a picture of his mother. Mrs Wilson and Mrs Croft have continually sparred with one another in games of territory and one-upmanship. And Elsie's feelings for Sir William have impetuously spilled over at dinner when she defended him against Lady Sylvia's derision of his money-making wartime activities in contrast to the brave service of Lord Stockbridge – 'That's not fair, is it Bill?' – an *in extremis* out-of-place remark that shocks everyone for its indecorum (not for what it suggests about their already known affair) and that presages her automatic dismissal from the household staff. Sir William has been so upset by Elsie's indiscretion that he has ensconced himself in the library whence 'he won't come out again tonight', as one of the servants notes.

It is after Elsie's indiscretion in the dining room and Sir William's retirement to the library that the Novello singing sequence takes place in the drawing room. In a series of scenes constructed through parallel editing and the moving camera, Altman deftly develops the murder plot while dramatising the interconnectedness of the upstairs and downstairs personnel by means of the entertainment of Novello's songs. The panning and tracking camera captures the movements of those who may have a motive for doing Sir William in: Robert Parks, Freddie, Anthony, even the smirking servant George exit the company of others and return only after the murder of Sir William has taken place. Parallel editing juxtaposes the scene in the drawing room with scenes in other parts of the mansion. One chronicles Sir William's murder: Mrs Wilson bringing Sir William coffee and then pouring a whiskey (in retrospect, poisoned) for him in the library; someone filmed from the waist down putting on a pair of rubber boots, taking a carving knife from a hiding place, walking into the library from a concealed bookcase door, stabbing Sir William, and exiting from the same door; Freddie, then George, Robert Parks and Anthony returning to the company; finally Louisa's shrill, frightened scream heard in the drawing room when she discovers Sir William's dead body slumped over his desk.

Interlinked with the scenes of the murder is another series of scenes that link the upstairs drawing room to the downstairs staff. As Novello sings five songs, the parallel editing cuts from his performance to various groups of servants who listen enraptured by his music and voice. As the music drifts from room to room, the servants gather at doors off of the drawing room and on the stairs leading from downstairs to upstairs. Novello's music unites the two worlds at the same time that it marks their difference: the moment is one of great poignancy for the servants, who relish a rare opportunity to be entertained by a matinee idol and to indulge in the desires and dreams his lyrics and melodies suggest, this powerfully underlining the confinement of their class; meanwhile, in contrast, Novello's singing provides background music for the card game and jaded chit-chat of those in the drawing room and somewhat eases their boredom.

After the discovery of Sir William's body, revelations and exposures pop up with surprising speed, not to resolve the murder in the traditional way but to further the development of characters and relationships and, centrally, to lay bare the past injustice caused by the power of class and patriarchy. Stephen Fry's bumbling and inept detective Thompson assures us that there will be no Agatha Christie-like solution to this murder. He compromises the evidence from the murder scene, dismisses the servants as suspects ('I'm not interested in the servants, only people with a real connection with the dead man'), and permits all the guests to leave after only one day of questioning. The irony of his remark about the servants becomes clear as Miss Trentham (Mary) herself uncovers the secrets harboured by Robert Parks, Mrs Croft and Mrs Wilson, all keys to the real motive behind the murder of Sir William. Other motives and enigmatic behaviour turn out to be smokescreens: that Anthony would be assured of an earlier agreed-upon investment from Sir William if Sir William was dead and could not change the arrangement; that Lady Constance would be assured of her monthly allowance with the fickle Sir William out of the way; that Henry Denton's ruse in pretending to be a servant was merely to help him research his next role as a Hollywood actor; that Jennings' secret is innocent of motive as it involved a past arrest for refusal to go into service during the war; and that Freddie's only hope of a patronage job rested on Sir William's influence.

The clues to the true motives for the murder are the interest Mrs Wilson shows in Robert Parks and the scattered information about Sir William's bastard children from girls who worked in his factories. Mary learns from Parks that Sir William was his father, who gave him away to an orphanage when he was two months old; he has taken service to Lord Stockbridge, Sir William's brother-in-law, to afford him the opportunity for revenge. And so it was he who stabbed Sir William. Mary informs him that Sir William had been poisoned first and that he stabbed a dead man and so did not murder him. Later, when Mary learns from Lady Sylvia that Mrs Wilson's former name was 'Parker, Parkis or something', she confronts Mrs Wilson about her role in the murder: 'Why did you do it?'

The revelation seals the connection between upstairs and downstairs on the familial, if bastard, level, while it testifies to the power and privilege of a callous employer and peer of the realm to inflict with impunity the seduction of his employees and the cruel relegation of their offspring to orphanages rather than to the middle-class families that he had promised for them. Mrs Croft turns out to be Mrs Wilson's sister, and she had opted to keep her child by Sir William, which meant losing her position as a cook in one of his factories. Her child eventually died of scarlet fever. Meanwhile, Mrs Wilson gave her child up, causing a rift between the sisters, which widened when an envious and humiliated Mrs Croft was hired into Sir William's household through the influence of her sister.

Mrs Wilson had guessed the reasons why her son had recently taken a position with Lord Stockbridge and the motives for his presence in the household, and so she poisoned Sir William as an act of maternal sacrifice to free 'Parks' from the murder. She explains to Mary: 'Not much of a crime to stab a dead man. They can never touch him. That's what's important, his life.' But when Mary asks her if she intends to tell Parks of her actions to save him, she says, 'Why? What purpose would it possibly serve?' In other words, the primary consequences of the murder have nothing to do with plot; they have everything to do with theme. The murder leads to the discovery of the web of blood connections that infect vertically the whole of Sir William's household, and it also reinforces the strict divisions and locked-in nature of the working class despite those connections. That is all, but it is enough in assessing *Gosford Park* as yet another one of Altman's unforgiving looks at systemic conventions that control the individual. Mary's moral consciousness and uncovering of the wrongs of the past function as revelatory devices rather than as instruments of justice and change. As a servant, she gains very little power with the knowledge that she has displayed; she can only contemplate with apprehension that any traditional legal justice against Parks and Mrs Wilson would be to compound the injustices of the past. To Lady Constance's apprehensive remark about testifying in court, 'Imagine a person being hanged because of something one said in court', Mary replies, 'I know, and what purpose could it possibly serve, anyway.'

Altman's dispassionate tone towards his characters caught up in the British class system and in family squabbles that link the upstairs with the downstairs falters in a memorable scene of deep empathy. It is the penultimate scene in the film, in which Mrs Wilson releases her long-repressed feelings for her son and the victimisations of the past. Mrs Croft witnesses this epiphany and the moment moves her to empathise with her estranged sister, effecting an unexpected but long overdue reconciliation after years of jealousy and resentment on her part. The moment belies Mrs Wilson's earlier remark to Mary about her personal life: 'I am the Perfect Servant. I have no life.' The outpouring of feelings for her son gives expression to an inner life which affords her a personal space within the restrictions and demands of her role as housekeeper. The scene is filmed in a medium two-shot of the sisters to underline their reconciliation. As the guests and their servants, including Robert, are leaving, Mrs Wilson retires to her room and begins to cry. Mrs Croft, on hearing her sobbing, comes into the room and says, 'Don't cry, Jane, they'll hear you.' Mrs Wilson catches herself and attempts to stifle her tears, but is unsuccessful. Mrs Croft says, 'Come on. You did what you felt was best for him at the time. I see that now.' Mrs Wilson replies, 'I've lost him, Lizzie. I've lost him. He'll never know me, never.' Mrs Croft reaches over to her sister and says, 'At least your boy's alive; he's alive. That's what matters.' On this empathetic note, Mrs Wilson releases another cry, reaches both hands to her sister's face, cradles it, and falls into her arms. The camera discreetly pans and cuts away from their embrace.

This moment of epiphany and empathy is all the more powerful and moving for its singularity not only within the narrative of *Gosford Park* but within all of Altman's oeuvre. It is just the kind of understanding or generosity or forgiveness that Altman's auteur persona resists and denies towards those in the family circles of *Short Cuts*, *Cookie's Fortune* and *Dr T and the Women*, especially in regards to the female characters: Marian and Claire in *Short Cuts*, the sisters Camille and Cora in *Cookie's Fortune* and Dr T's wife Kate, her sister Peggy and the gaggle of women patients in *Dr T and the Women*. What accounts for such an anomaly in *Gosford Park*? The screenwriter Julian Fellowes may provide the clue. He writes that this meeting between the two sisters was not even in the shooting script, that 'The decision was made on the day to shoot it and I wrote the scene but ... apart from the opening line, "Don't cry, Jane, they'll hear you", it is substantially the work of those two great actresses' (2002: 174). One suspects strongly, then, that the scene is the felicitous enunciation of Helen Mirren and Eileen Atkins, more than a statement by the satiric auteur. The deep understanding and emotion that the two great performers generate supply the scene with its power of epiphany and empathy captured by Altman's camera. It is to his credit that Altman included it in the final cut.

Does this moment in *Gosford Park* presage a sea change in the attitude of Altman's narrational persona towards the characters in the families and surrogate families of *The Company* (2003) and *A Prairie Home Companion* (2006)? Given Altman's death on 20 November 2006, his last two films may take on the awful mantle of a summation or consummation of a remarkable career; certainly they will be grouped with Altman's other performance/musical films *per se*: *Nashville, Buffalo Bill and the Indians, or Sitting Bull's History Lesson* (1976) and *Kansas City* (1996), or those in which performance, though not generic, plays a key role: *Short Cuts, Prêt-à-Porter, Cookie's Fortune* and *Gosford Park*. Suffice it to say, *The Company* seems to follow the convention of the musical genre in its presentation of performances that transcend the conflicts within the surrogate family of dancers and unite it in a celebration of talent and artistic integrity. But Altman returns to form in his final and appropriately elegiac film, *A Prairie Home Companion*, in which the figure of death overshadows the proceedings of the last broadcast of a radio show – its own kind of family – and in which several of the performances express rather than transcend the frictions and emotional baggage of the singers and Garrison Keillor, the show's host. But that's another story.

Note

1   In an interview involving Altman and Carver's widow, the poet Tess Gallagher, published in the *New York Times* upon the film's release, Gallagher tactfully praises Altman's art and accomplishment, assenting occasionally when he talks about his 'collaboration' with Carver. At the same time, however, she honestly appraises the differences between her husband's fiction and Altman's adaptation. She says that after viewing *The Player* (1992), she understood that Altman's great gift is irony, but that 'Ray eschewed irony ... he didn't distance himself from his characters and their dilemmas' (in Stewart 1993: 3). Towards the end of the interview, she says: 'I would try to protect the integrity of your and Ray's vision. At the same time, I would say that I missed a certain interiority of the characters in the film. The suffering in Ray's stories is more palpable; the empathetic qualities in Ray's characters are more present' (1993: 9).

12

Practically Perfect People: Postfeminism, Masculinity and Male Parenting in Contemporary Cinema

YVONNE TASKER

My starting point for this essay is my belief that contemporary gender culture can be productively framed through the concept of 'postfeminism'. In asserting this I am not arguing that postfeminism offers a coherent account of gender and power within media culture today. Instead I use the term to refer to a range of contradictory ideas and discourses about gender that have achieved cultural prominence and that, through their persuasiveness and perhaps their sheer repetition, have been incorporated into cultural common sense. In particular I wish to think about the ways in which fatherhood and male parenting are figured within postfeminist media culture. In this endeavour I'm drawing on well-known work by feminist scholars such as Tania Modleski, whose landmark study, *Feminism Without Women: Culture and Criticism in a 'Postfeminist' Age* (1991) sketched dynamics of gender and power that remain in evidence in contemporary cinema. The character and political significance of recent representations of masculinity and the family is evidently open to debate; in this context, Modleski's insight is to underline how some sense of crisis is integral to postwar constitutions of masculinity in general. She argues that, faced with economic, symbolic and political challenges to patriarchal authority, 'men ultimately deal with the threat of female power by incorporating it' (1991: 7). This suggestion of fragility as a context for aggressive or appropriative techniques is also applicable to much conservative political rhetoric, which seeks to consolidate the fantasy structure of 'the family' through a double move that points to its disintegration whilst simultaneously appealing to its supposedly eternal values.

Within the mainstream of Hollywood fictions and entertainment journalism, in which the notion of a cultural 'crisis of masculinity' has been willingly embraced – or so it would seem – this analysis has a definite purchase: from well-regarded, somewhat quirky films such as *Fight Club* (1999) and *Magnolia* (1999) to more generic comedies including *Jerry Maguire* (1996), *What Women Want* (2000), *Cheaper by* the *Dozen* (2003) and *Daddy Day Care* (2003), Hollywood masculinity presents itself as subject to change in ways that are either informed by or respond to feminism. With respect to discourses of fatherhood and male parenting, perhaps the central point of Modleski's analysis has to do with the way in which postfeminist culture centres a male subject within emotional, familial narratives. That centring of the male subject is typically achieved at the cost of women, with mothers marginalised or even absent from various father-centred films. Both Susan Jeffords (1993) and Kathleen Rowe (1995) point to comparable structures operating in 1990s cinema through their analyses of, respectively, figures of male transformation towards an identification with the family and a paternal role, and the new centrality of men within postclassical melodrama.

The specificity of male parenting as a prominent feature of postfeminist media culture has to do with a seeming response to feminist calls for equity in childrearing, a task typically undertaken primarily by women, accompanied by the marginalisation or pathologisation of mothers and other women. Male parenting is rarely conceived in terms associated with maternal nurturing. Films and other texts instead cast the father (biological or otherwise) as initiating a different sort of adult/child interaction, one that serves to secure not only male masculinity but traditional formulations of gender more broadly. Through discussion of a series of film examples I want to explore here some of the parameters of male parenting within contemporary postfeminist culture.

In the first part of the essay I approach these contemporary concerns through a somewhat earlier film, the highly successful Disney musical *Mary Poppins* (1964). A consideration of that film provides a cinematic context within which to situate my comments on more recent movies. In particular, the ways in which male parenting functions to introduce emotion and fun into the life of a hitherto distant patriarch in both *Mary Poppins* and the following year's *The Sound of Music* is indicative of future trends. The trajectory of male transformation prefigures the examples referred to by Jeffords, although male transformation occurs on the margins of *Mary Poppins*, rather than serving as the central narrative concern as in so many recent films.

Building on this context, I explore the ways in which work/family conflicts are represented with respect to male parenting in recent narratives. I do this in a historical context – the early 2000s – framed by economic and employment insecurity and associated with a competitive working culture of long hours that has proven a significant obstacle to workplace gender equity.[1]

Thirdly, I offer some further thoughts on this topic through a discussion of two 1990s films which figure gay male parenting, *The Object of My Affection* (1998) and *The Next Best Thing* (2000). I frame these films in a context of controversy and debate with respect to the legitimacy and legality of lesbian and gay relationships, debates which once more turn on a perceived need to champion and extol conventional models of family and parenting.

Mary Poppins: Bringing Magic to Masculinity

Mary Poppins made Julie Andrews a star, earning her an Academy Award amongst other honours. The commercial and critical success of *The Sound of Music* the following year consolidated a developing star persona associated with asexual mothering (both scenarios find her caring for other people's children). Although Andrews is at the centre of both films, each also features a stern male character who, during the course of the film, is mellowed through parenting and exposure to the charm or magic that Andrews' characters embody. Both films are set in a European past (Edwardian England and prewar Austria, respectively), suggesting that the distant male parenting that defines the films' patriarchs is inherently both old-fashioned and far removed from the context of contemporary US society.

Mary Poppins tells the story of two seemingly unruly children, Jane (Karen Dotrice) and Michael (Matthew Garber), who work their way through a succession of nannies. Their father, George Banks (David Tomlinson), is a distant figure, bound by rigid convention and defining himself through his work at the bank. By the end of the narrative he will be transformed into a fun-loving figure who delightedly skips down the street with his wife and children to fly a kite. For much of the film, however, George is unaware that his remote parenting poses any concerns. 'How pleasant is the life I lead!' he sings early on, praising the virtues of routine, order and consistency. 'It's the age of *men*', he firmly proclaims in the same number, a certainty undermined by our tickled knowledge that, once again, his children have escaped their nanny and are running free of adult supervision. Jane and Michael are brought home by a local policeman (Arthur Treacher) who refers to them as 'valuables' and counsels the father not to be too hard on them. Yet George simply cannot see his children as valuable. Indeed his conception of value is a monetary one, as if his role as patriarch-provider had taken him over completely. Later in the film this conflict will be acted out during a visit to the bank in which Michael's reluctance to hand over his tuppence to his father's employer for a suitable investment opportunity triggers chaos and a run on the bank. As a suffragette, Winifred Banks (Glynis Johns) is a figure of fun in a somewhat different fashion, too busy campaigning for votes for women to care for her children and indeed, by implication, too scatter-brained and privileged to understand what such care might involve. A mild class critique is evidently mobilised here: on the one hand we see Winifred proclaiming women's rights to the female servants whose labour maintains her life of ease, while on the other she hurriedly hides her suffragette sashes from her husband in case he objects.

With their father too preoccupied with work and their mother too preoccupied with votes for women, the children must manage for themselves, their seeming unruliness thus framed by a narrative of inadvertent neglect with definite resonances in the mid-1960s context of the film's release. Throughout its course the film works to define gender-appropriate parenting and adult care in terms far removed from (upper) middle-class austerity, whether in the form of the police constable who speaks fondly of his own son and clearly demonstrates disapproval of George Banks's harshness as a father, the romanticising of chimney sweep Bert's (Dick Van Dyke) 'Cockney' persona, or, most spectacularly, the magical form of Mary Poppins herself. Thus it is no surprise that, in one memorable moment, Winifred Banks entrusts the care of her children to the friendly but somewhat bemused chimney sweep, it being Mary's day off and none of the other servants being willing to take on the task. This passing on of childcare suggests that the structuring opposition at work here is not so much between adults and children as between adult responsibilities and childish fun. Responsibilities are complex and wearisome, fun is simple and direct – regardless of the age of those who engage in either.

Mary Poppins is an intermediary in this opposition, just as she is between the middle-class Banks and Bert's cheery working-class character: familiar with both but belonging in neither's space, she is (explicitly) a magical figure. Though a prim disciplinarian in some respects – she insists on manners and presentation, disapproving of the general hilarity in the mid-air tea party scene, for instance – Mary Poppins generates the fantastic and liminal contexts in which fun can happen, whether it is stepping into a picture, dancing on the rooftops or bringing inanimate objects to life. Of course, Mary Poppins is primarily concerned with bringing fun (and discipline) to the lives of her charges. Yet the film is in many respects paradigmatic of more recent narratives centring on fathers who are transformed by their contact with the world of children.

Initiating a series of events that will lead to George (temporarily) losing his job, Mary 'tricks' the father into taking his children on an outing to the bank, in which dreary world Mr Banks's confidence seems somewhat diminished as his subordinate status becomes apparent. Following the chaos his children bring to the ordered world of finance, Banks is summoned back to the office to be dressed down, a process plainly literalised as his buttonhole is torn from him, his umbrella inverted and his bowler hat punched through. The demise of the banker produces a revival of the father, however, as George, now a comedic dishevelled figure, finally understands the importance of childhood and of fun. Finally he sees the hilarity in Mary's nonsense expression, 'supercalifragilisticexpialidocious', and embraces his wife and children in a newfound enthusiasm for life.

While the magical figure of Mary Poppins appears in the film in response to the children's desire, her work also enacts a reconciliation between father and son/daughter through a transformation of the former.[2] His wishes are set aside, but George Banks does not lose patriarchal power. Indeed, his status is even boosted at the film's end when his sacking is rescinded and he is offered a partnership in the firm. As in more recent scenarios, then, a temporary distance from the public world of paid work allows both a redefined imagery of male parenting and a new (and augmented) authority to assert itself. This process of (spectacular) redemption also requires the construction of George Banks as a figure deserving sympathy and care, rather than rejection. Thus Bert, having promised to look out for Jane and Michael as a father, counsels both father and children as to the difficulties and demands of family life. 'The one my heart goes out to is your father', Bert tells the children, pointing up the isolation of the male, middle-class provider: 'A father can always do with a bit of help.' In his interaction with George, Bert alerts him to what he is missing as his children grow, through a double-edged commiseration with the place of paternal responsibility ('You've got to grind, grind, grind at that grindstone'). Thus Mary's no-nonsense manner and Bert's whimsy combine to bring magic to the father as well as the children. As in more recent narratives, this process is achieved through separating the father from the working life that defines and limits him.

Just as significant as the redemption of the father is the position of Mary Poppins herself, the figure most associated with female parenting in the film. She is left behind in a bittersweet conclusion that stages her regret at her own exclusion as she watches the Banks family skip off to 'fly a kite' together. A brief exchange ensues between Mary and the parrot-shaped handle of her umbrella, an animated object indignant on her behalf:

UMBRELLA: That's gratitude for you. Didn't even say goodbye!
MARY: No, they didn't.
UMBRELLA: Look at them. You know they think more of their father than they
            do of you!
MARY: That's as it should be.
UMBRELLA: Well, don't you care?
MARY: Practically perfect people never permit sentiment to muddle
            their thinking.[3]

In her precise manner, Mary silences the unruly umbrella and the sentiments it expresses, its knowingness as to her true feelings. Flying away with her carpetbag and umbrella, Mary departs the scene. Her magical mothering is no longer necessary now that George Banks has discovered the importance of parenting in person. Indeed, despite her association with witchcraft, Mary Poppins' pleasant yet firm manner has much in common with cultural conceptions of good male parenting. Thus, the film ensures that its magical nanny works to endorse the patriarchal family, centring the father as a figure deserving sympathy and respect.[4]

Men, Masculinity and Work/Family

Conflicts between work life and family responsibilities are central to feminism. The issues at stake turn on both the unpaid labour of care that women typically perform, whether for dependents or within a domestic environment, and the paid childcare and domestic labour, also typically undertaken by women, that underpins the functioning of many middle-class households. Since this work – and feminist perspectives on it – often remains invisible in cultural terms, it is perhaps no surprise that some of the best known films that do render it visible typically do so through the comic spectacle of men negotiating the complexities of childcare and working life, as in the successful melodrama *Kramer vs. Kramer* (1979) or comedies such as *Three Men and a Baby* (1987). It is not the case that women's experience of work/family conflict is never figured within Hollywood cinema, yet it is relatively rarely played for comedy. Such conflicts are evident in the much discussed yuppie comedy, *Baby Boom* (1987), for instance, the humour here deriving from a privileged woman forced to clean up after not only herself but also a child; and rather differently in the woman's picture, as in *Erin Brockovich* (2000) or the romantic comedy, *One Fine Day* (1996), in which Michelle Pfeiffer and George Clooney both play single parents.

Male parents in Hollywood cinema do face conflicts between the demands made by jobs and families on their time, yet these conflicts are typically presented in rather different terms than are those experienced by female parents. Specifically, male parents are frequently presented as *failing* their children as a result of an unhealthy commitment to paid labour (as does George Banks in *Mary Poppins*). Broken promises are the stock-in-trade of fathers in Hollywood films of the 1990s and since: indeed the broken promise forms the premise of *Liar, Liar* (1997), a comedy which grants lawyer Fletcher Reede's (Jim Carrey) son a wish that his father not be able to lie for a whole day. When Eddie Murphy's character Charlie Hinton says, near the beginning of *Daddy Day Care*, 'I will not be late', we know with certainty not only that he *will* be late, but that he will ultimately learn the value of being on time. There is no question that Charlie's wife will forget or be late, so the problem is not that Charlie's son will be alone or in danger but that he will be disappointed. The mother's presence thus allows the father space (and time) to fail their child; she witnesses such disappointment but is unable to effect change within the family dynamic. A similar pattern can be seen in Steven Spielberg's *Hook* (1991).[5]

As with the magical arrival of Mary Poppins, transformation is enforced on the fathers in contemporary narratives through circumstances that position them in an at times involuntary proximity to their own, and others', children. In *Daddy Day Care*, Charlie and Phil (Jeff Garlin) lose their jobs and open a day care facility in the Hintons' substantial family home. In *Cheaper by the Dozen* the sudden (albeit temporary) departure of Kate Baker (Bonnie Hunt) on a book tour leaves husband Tom (Steve Martin) comically attempting to manage their twelve children and the college football team he coaches. Circumstances force these cinematic fathers into an appreciation of what they have in their families and their responsibilities with respect to their children.

Clearly these narratives are shaped by (and consumed within) a postfeminist cultural context in which the heterosexuality of marriage is presented by politicians and others as in need of defence and in which, as Anna Gavanas (2004) details, the diverse 'fatherhood responsibility movement' has had a significant impact within the US, placing fatherhood firmly on the political and policy agenda. For instance, such a context frames the irrational prejudice on the part of the mothers (and one father, who deems the idea 'unnatural') who are reluctant to leave their children in the charge of men in *Daddy Day Care*. This question is staged in terms of gender equity, crediting women with gender prejudice and, presumably, social power over men. Yet these are small setbacks and the conventions of the family comedy are familiar enough for the audience to be certain that the positive benefits of male parenting will be in evidence soon enough.

Whilst intensive male parenting is presented as transformative for both men and children, it is fathers who are our primary focus in both *Daddy Day Care* and *Cheaper by the Dozen*. In *Daddy Day Care*, Charlie finally comes – and it is very late in the day – to a realisation that his son's preferred interactions are artistic and creative, not the horseplay he so routinely and thoughtlessly offers. Nevertheless, both boys and girls are seen to thrive within the informal care environment of 'Daddy Day Care', while the troubled older children of *Cheaper by the Dozen*, Nora (Piper Perabo) and Charlie (Tom Welling), resolve their disputes with their parents by coming around to their father's point of view (Nora rejects an 'unsuitable' boyfriend with whom she has been living; Charlie agrees to graduate from high school).

When Charlie first loses his paid job in *Daddy Day Care*, it is clear that he finds the prospect of caring for his own son demeaning: no longer defined by a 'real job', he mourns his former status as 'a big shot'. As a sign of diminished stature he must give up the keys to the Mercedes (to his lawyer wife, recently returned to work) and the prestige associated with having a child at the overly rigid Chapman Academy (directed by an authoritarian figure of female loathing, Miss Harridan (Angelica Houston)). The scene of childcare becomes manageable or pleasurable only when it is transformed into a site of paid labour, a process that points to a significant cultural anxiety around constructing a suitably masculine form of male parenting. Thus the transformation of Charlie's relationship with his son does not take place until the home has become a workplace. The chorus of 'loser' provided by Bruce (Kevin Nealon), Charlie's former colleague and father to one of the day care children, continues even to the final scene, suggesting that the status anxieties associated with running a day care centre require continuous management. Similarly in *Cheaper by the Dozen*, Tom attempts to resolve his work/family conflict by merging domestic and professional responsibilities – coaching the football team from his suburban home.

In the coda of *Daddy Day Care*, Charlie surveys with satisfaction a fantasised family/workspace in which both children and parents are present; the distinction between paid and unpaid careers is blurred even while Charlie's command of the scene is evident, coded in a look of ownership and satisfaction and his comment to his son, 'I'd say this wasn't a bad trade-off.' First, the family home becomes a place of work; subsequently, with the launch of a lavish new day care centre, the values learned through parenting have allowed Charlie to forge a new workplace (and public presence) for himself. Moreover, this conversion of a potentially low-status caregiving role into a commercial venture is framed by a sequence in which Charlie earns his old job back but rejects it, understanding that 'my kid, that's the most important thing'. His decision to quit (as against his initial sacking) and his success in business both function to shore up Charlie's masculinity, underlining his ability to choose. Moreover, the significance of Charlie's transformation into a responsible dad, emotionally involved as well as labouring, deepens when framed by discourses of 'crisis' so prominent in relation to African American fatherhood.[6] Similarly, while Tom steps down from his high-profile role as Stallions coach in *Cheaper by the Dozen*, he goes out on a high, having secured a decisive victory with the team. Moreover, neither Charlie's nor Tom's household seems to feel the economic consequences of their decisions about employment.

Of the two 2003 films, *Cheaper by the Dozen* stages work/family conflicts more explicitly, as Tom is literally forced to choose between commitment to his family and the job of his dreams. A celebration of fecundity, family and fatherly commitment, the film presents both father and mother as having chosen to compromise their career goals in order to have the large family they both yearned for. Professional opportunity comes to both Kate and Tom almost simultaneously, challenging their commitment to family: following the family's reluctant move to Chicago, Kate travels to New York and subsequently makes a rapid tour to promote her book, *Cheaper by the Dozen*. She effectively turns her reproductive achievements into a commodity via her writing, and her absence and Tom's work commitments combine to produce chaos at home. Kate's celebrity motherhood – we see her on talk shows – is mirrored by Tom's high-profile job and the insistent media coverage that frames both his professional and personal life. Away from home Kate is evidently troubled by her newfound solitude, ordering up pillows to substitute for her children. This scenario ultimately results in the debacle of a planned feature on *The Oprah Winfrey Show* ('One Big Happy Family') being abandoned. Like Kate's maternity, Tom's parenting/professional conflicts are also mediated: 'Can Baker coach two teams?' asks a newspaper headline, contrasting images of Tom with the football team and with the family, and projecting domestic turmoil onto a public stage. Indeed, Kate finally returns when her children call her on a radio phone-in (telling her to 'come home immediately'). Once again, private lives are conducted in a mediated public space.

As both team and family fall apart, the college authorities confront Tom with his options, either to commit fully to his position (that is, set aside family responsibilities) or to resign. As one administrator puts it: 'You have to decide who's making the bacon and who's cooking it.' Although framed as problematic within the film, the iteration of this sexist logic is not openly challenged by Tom who responds quietly with his resignation, telling his old friend: 'If I screw up raising my kids, nothing I achieve will matter much.' Tom's potency as father to twelve children and his sense of responsibility towards them contextualise his ultimate decision to step down as coach. Moreover, his association with the masculine world of sports functions to guarantee his gender identity and to underline the specificity of what he brings as a male parent.[7] Significantly, this choice is presented in relation to the figure of a broken promise. The warring family is brought together in the search for a missing member, Mark (Forrest Landis), who has run away. Having finally found his son on a train, Tom apologises for the cost his family has paid for his professional ambitions. Mark's rebuke ('You said we'd be happier – you didn't keep your promise') effectively makes Tom's decision for him. Thus, both the small African American family of *Daddy Day Care* and the extensive white family of *Cheaper by the Dozen* are secured by fathers who learn to keep their word. The symbolic power of the broken promise echoes the evangelical US men's organisation, the Promise Keepers, who advocate for men's role in marriage, in Christianity and in relation to each other through the promises that members vow to keep.[8] The rhetoric and imagery of transformative male parenting finds much wider resonance in a fatherhood movement that has conservative, mainstream and liberal manifestations. Across diverse formulations, fatherhood movements emphasise the joys and responsibilities of male parenting as practice, position and process.

Despite their fantastic character – in terms of both the narratives themselves and the extravagant wealth of the surroundings in which these film families reside – these scenarios doubtless speak to both male and female parents operating within a culture of employment insecurity, mounting levels of personal debt and an expectation of ever-increasing commitment to longer working hours. The growth in home working and of the home office as a feature of domesticity for many workers suggests a continuing blurring of these spaces and of the gendered roles supported by compartmentalisation of working and domestic lives. In this context, these family comedies work to figure male parenting in terms that are conventionally masculine (earning an income in *Daddy Day Care*; being allied with sports in *Cheaper by the Dozen*) and sufficiently distinct from the female parenting that is effectively superceded through the course of the narrative.

Masculinity, Transformation and Gay Male Parenting

The erasure of women/mothers and the focus on fathers so characteristic of post-feminist discourse suggests rather different issues in the context of gay male parenting. As Gavanas notes, the fatherhood responsibility movement typically disassociates itself from gay male parenting, framing lesbians and gay men as a prospective threat to marriage as an institution founded on heterosexuality and gender differentiation. It is perhaps no surprise that representations of gay male parenting are few and far between within popular culture, too. The 1996 comedy *The Birdcage* (based on *La Cage aux folles* (1978)) is rare in having two gay men, Armand (Robin Williams) and Albert (Nathan Lane), co-parent their college-age son Val (Dan Futterman), who was conceived by Armand and Katherine Archer (Christine Baranski) during a one-night stand. A comedy of disguise and deception, *The Birdcage* revels in its opposition of an anarchic gay world, in which gender is performed rather than assumed, and the conservative Christian parents of the woman Val wishes to marry. This very scenario secures Val's heterosexuality, of course, allowing an indulgence of humour at the expense of the right-wing senator (played by Gene Hackman). The figure of the 'gay best friend' or gay male helper is far more common within contemporary media culture, as a variety of critics have noted.[9]

Where they do appear, films featuring gay male parenting negotiate a complex of cultural and political anxieties with respect to the agenda of influential conservative Christian movements, the fear of feminisation and the erosion of a specificity to male parenting, suggested and averted in the films discussed above. *The Object of My Affection* and *The Next Best Thing* are both postfeminist romantic comedies framing a choice made by the female leads, having failed to find suitable romantic partners, to raise children with gay men. The former shows Nina (Jennifer Aniston), who finds her lover Vince (John Pankow) stifling, inviting her roommate George (Paul Rudd) to co-parent with her. The scenario in *The Next Best Thing* is somewhat different: best friends Abbie (Madonna) and Robert (Rupert Everett) have a drunken sexual encounter after which Abbie announces her pregnancy and the two agree to raise their son Sam (Malcolm Stumpf) together. Neither scenario progresses as the couples envisage. In *The Object of My Affection*, Nina falls in love with George and both must deal with their different and shared desires. *The Next Best Thing* has Abbie marry another man and refuse Robert access to their son, even revealing that she had lied about his paternity. As the latter film's title suggests, co-parenting for Abbie and Robert is a compromise rather than a life choice. Lacking the directness and immediacy of true connection and romance, their sexual encounter is presented as a disorienting and destructive brawl (in contrast, Nina and George's relationship is framed in terms of an intense, at times physical, intimacy). The subsequent bitterness of the court case that ensues suggests the perversity of their arrangement, even as these scenes mobilise sympathy for Robert, rehearsing and critiquing notions of gay male fecklessness. While *The Object of My Affection* presents Nina's predicament with care, Abbie emerges in the other film as deceitful and vindictive.

Ultimately both films move towards a compromise through which gay men are involved in parenting. Thus, Sam's misery causes Abbie to relent in *The Next Best Thing*, allowing father and son to be reunited in the film's final scene. *The Object of My Affection* concludes with a more extensive kinship network that binds together friends, lovers, biological family and queer family. As Karen Quimby argues with respect to *Will & Grace* (1998–2006), it is certainly possible to read such scenarios as an acknowledgement of 'straight women's dissatisfaction with the norms of masculinity and the kinds of relationships that such gendered conventions demand'

(2005: 715). Yet, as various critics have noted, centring on Grace's desire 'for a different kind of intimacy with men' (2005: 727) means sidelining gay male desire, including the desire to co-parent. Quimby contrasts the 'potentially unthreatening' prospect of Will and Grace co-parenting (a scenario that was proposed and then rejected) with 'the alternative: that Will would decide to have a child with another man' (ibid.). That scenario is firmly rejected via the formulation of gay-straight co-parenting within the films considered here.[10]

Both films formulate models of parenting that include gay men, but each also works to delineate the distance between straight and gay masculinities. Thus, *The Next Best Thing* contrasts the security and ease of Ben's (Benjamin Bratt) performance of heterosexual male parenting (captured in an image as he walks with Abbie on the beach, Sam on his shoulders) against the fragility of Robert's relationship to his child as a gay father. That the film must ultimately negate his biological status as father before moving to include him as Sam's dad in the final scene is highly suggestive. In such moments, popular cinema colludes in the very dynamics to which feminism draws attention, presenting male parenting as a site of specific and distinctly masculinist pleasures. And in *The Object of My Affection*, George agrees to co-parent with Nina following a scene in which he silently watches a young boy and his father playing catch; this cliché of father/son interaction alludes to the supposed distinctiveness of heterosexual male parenting, a definition of masculinity from which gay men are rhetorically excluded. As Gavanas writes, 'By casting fatherhood in sports metaphors', the fatherhood movement works to 'masculinize domesticity and male parenting into something men can do without being perceived as feminine', a gendered anxiety that also speaks to a desire to secure fatherhood for heterosexuality (2004: 115). Speaking to Nina of this image and of the power it holds for him, George talks of his realisation that he 'could be the guy who says goodnight'; that is, he could occupy the position of father that he explicitly associates with 'real guys' (that is, straight men; biological fathers) like Vince. In the film's coda we see George involved in the child's life, but not in the form of a sporting encounter; Nina's child is a girl, Molly (Sarah Hyland), who excels in the show that George, now principal of the nursery school where we first encounter him, produces to great acclaim. Like *The Next Best Thing*, the film associates gay male parenting with performative, rather than sporting, expertise, preserving the distinctiveness of heterosexual male parenting in the process.

The broader context for these textual strategies, in terms of current policy debates, has to do with the extent to which lesbians and gay men are inscribed within the mainstream: with mundane questions of health care, employment benefits and partnership rights and, of course lesbian, gay and queer parenting. Many campaigns regard lesbian and gay marriage as a neutralisation of the challenge to heteronormativity posed by queerness, a bid for inclusion that reiterates the exclusion of those who seek alternative patterns of community and kinship (see, for instance, Butler 2002). Of course, lesbian and gay parents enter into all sorts of arrangements with each other, with straight donors and with surrogates (see Bernstein & Reimann 2001). Unsurprisingly, little of this complexity appears within the Hollywood cinema with its repeated figuring of lonely women and unsatisfactory men, and its reinforcement of gender differentiation as a marker of the importance of male parenting. In *Feminism is for Everybody*, bell hooks writes: 'A disservice is done to all females when praise for male participation in parenting leads to disparagement and devaluation of the positive job of mothering women do' (2000: 76). This observation provides a context for both feminist and queer dissatisfaction with the portrayal of male parenting, as a performance of and insistence on heterosexual masculinity, which is so regularly centred within contemporary postfeminist media culture.

Notes

1   A recent British survey suggested that up to a third of workers failed to take their full annual leave, producing a ripple of reports concerned with the national culture of overwork. See http://jobsadvice.guardian.co.uk/officehours/story/0,,1499811,00.html. For more on the British context see Bunting 2004; for a campaigning US perspective see De Graaf (2003).

2   The contemporary resonance of these themes of magical transformation is exploited in the film *Nanny McFee* (2005) and, somewhat more prosaically, in what Laurie Ouellette (n.d.) terms 'Nanny TV' (she refers here to shows such as *Supernanny* (2004 and 2005) and *Nanny 911* (2004–)).

3   The umbrella's 'voice' is provided by David Tomlinson, the actor who plays George Banks, a doubling which reinforces the exclusion of Mary Poppins from the scene of familial reconciliation she has worked to stage.

4   We might contrast this bittersweet conclusion to Andrews' role as Maria in *The Sound of Music*. That film, too, centres on seemingly unruly children who desire love and attention from their father. Maria brings music (rather than magic) into the Von Trapp home, magically mellowing Georg's (Christopher Plummer) austere demeanour, personal bitterness and distance from his seven children. Her incorporation into the patriarchal family as virginal wife offers an alternative.

5   See Fred Pfeil's useful discussion of this film in *White Guys* (1995: 63–9).

6   I'm indebted to Hannah Hamad for her insightful observations on the place of fatherhood in Eddie Murphy's developing star persona.

7   As Gavanas shows, sport and religion are central metaphors within contemporary discourses around fatherhood in the US (2004: 99–125).

8   The Promise Keepers website proclaims that 'Real Men Matter'. See http://www.promisekeepers.org/home.

9   See for example, on *Queer Eye for the Straight Guy* (2003–), the 'Queer TV Style' section edited by Chris Straayer and Tom Waugh (2005); and on the gay best friend theme in cinema, Dreisinger 2000.

10 Gay male parenting appears as a storyline in the final series of HBO's *Six Feet Under* (2001–05) in which David (Michael C. Hall) and Keith (Matthew St. Patrick) foster two boys. The lesbian parenting featured in *ER* (1994–) was swiftly followed by the death of one partner.

13

Hostages and Houseguests:
Class and Family in the New Screen Gothic

JAMES MORRISON

A recent spate of American movies depicts families taken hostage in their homes by invading marauders. As a rule, the families are rich (but presented as contemporary variations on a speciously generalised 'middle class'), the homes are remarkably opulent, and the marauders constitute an anthology of menacing types held over from the feckless demonologies of Hollywood history. The most characteristic films of this cycle are domestic melodramas such as *The Glass House* (2001), *Panic Room* (2002), *Hostage* (2005) and *Firewall* (2006), but the sequence encompasses multiple variations across the action film – *Collateral Damage* (2002) or *Cellular* (2004) – and the horror film – *Cold Creek Manor* (2003), *Saw* (2004) or *When a Stranger Calls* (2006). And Michael Haneke's *Funny Games* (1997, remade in an American version in 2007) represents a particularly extreme example of the form.

For better or worse, this group of films is representative of the styles and attitudes of Hollywood cinema in the first years of the twenty-first century, not least in the way that it points back to the earliest trends of American film. In one way or another, each of these movies is a variation on the themes of D. W. Griffith's *The Lonely Villa* (1909), which has claims to being the first family hostage melodrama in American cinema. A story of a hapless middle-class family held captive by stock villains until they are rescued by the triumphant father, this film established the basic template of this sub-genre and was taken by no less a figure than Sergei Eisenstein to initiate the whole bourgeois ideology of American film in its thoughtless indulgence of the family and its complacent reproof of the crooks (1949: 226–36). A century later, the same dynamic repeats itself, in a form modified by the temper of the time.

In earlier treatments of this theme the class stakes were clear. The family represented upright middle-class values of virtuous conformity to social convention while the invaders were resentful, licentious, unprincipled and debauched refugees from the underclasses. Their breach of the class system inaugurated a crisis overcome in a final victorious confirmation of that system as protector of those values and of the family as its principal mainstay. At various points in the evolution of this template, this sense of crisis was located either in class oppression or in the family structure itself, but recently films are eager to detach it from either foundation, resulting in a kind of free-floating crisis rhetoric. Mingling a conventional 'eclectic irony' and hybridity with forms of what has been called 'the new sincerity' (see Collins 1993), these movies are post-ideological, insofar as they juxtapose highly readable meanings about the societies they aspire to portray against countercurrents that disturb the certitude of their dominant signifiers without quite producing doubt. Moving beyond the redemptive confusions of the 'incoherent texts' that Robin Wood identified as definitive of Hollywood in the 1970s (1986: 46–69), these films achieve an expedient synthesis of hysteria and smugness. It is this synthesis, I think, that makes the films seem current.

The paradoxical mixture of smugness and hysteria still takes shape around themes of family and class. The films' commitments to family as a stabilising force anchor the smugness, while the residual implications of a largely disavowed class consciousness stoke the hysteria. If *The Lonely Villa* precedes class consciousness in American cinema, these films survive it, assuming that it has run its course and is, in any case, futile in the new world order. In the most characteristic of these films, the family is in a kind of post-crisis state, portrayed as a non-class phenomenon, outside ideology.[1] Although they depict the family under siege and trade in a putatively 'dark' or 'edgy' sensibility, these films serve an ultimately reassuring function. In their diagnoses, the postmodern family is doing just fine, or would be, if it were not constantly beset by forces from without.

The Desperate Hours

Just what these forces are varies from film to film, but in all their guises they reinforce an understanding of the family as a type of the new small social groups that, as Fredric Jameson argues in his discussion of postmodern populism, 'arise in the void left by the disappearance of social classes and in the rubble of political movements organised around those' (1991: 319), completing the evolution of power as centralised in economic production (as in Marx), distribution (as in Friedrich Pollack), or consumption (as in Thorstein Veblen), only to end in a totalised sphere exceeding any of these (as in Adorno and Horkheimer or Michel Foucault). An earlier cycle, at the height of the Cold War, continued to narrate the family hostage scenario as a parable of working-class resentment, but added an ingredient of middle-class guilt to the mix. In *The Desperate Hours* (1955), perhaps the quintessential example, a trio of escapees from prison invades a middle-class home and holds the family captive, awaiting money for a getaway. The film adapts the scenario to emergent attitudes of its time: a growing sense of the middle class as universal, leading to a heightened demonisation of the working class as aberrant and threatening; a new conception of the middle-class home as privatised fortress; and an increasing fear of the vulnerability of this domicile to invasion by foreign elements.[2] Yet it also 'humanises' the invaders and implies the culpability of the privileged in the perpetuation of inequity as well as the fearsome ire of the underclass in its haphazard recognition of this situation.

Jameson hastens to add that this alleged 'disappearance of social classes' is something like a postmodern optical illusion, enabled by the 'global restructuration of production and the introduction of radically new technologies' (ibid.). In the Cold War cycle, 'organisation men' and white-collar conformists were typically shaken from their enfeebled social compliance to assume a more potent paternalism, one still fully compatible with prevailing social conventions, in reaction to the encounter with class invaders from below. In *The Desperate Hours*, for instance, a liberally permissive father (Fredric March) learns to exert greater discipline after the ordeal of his family's captivity. In the advent of the service economy and the information age, such films suggest how the family served as a vehicle for emerging identity categories that, for writers like Jameson, displaced class once and for all as defining social markers, some time in the 1960s. While the family in its 'traditional' form emerged as an economic unit with the rise of industrialisation, it was quickly co-opted for nascent categories of simultaneously emerging ideas of psychology in a shift, broadly speaking, from Marx's domestic ideology to Freud's family romance, from thinking of the family as being 'about' class, to thinking of it as being 'about' gender. In this sense the family prefigured the increasing importance of interests based in sexuality, race or ethnicity that so often substitute for questions of economic class in postmodernism, a transposition that, coupled with new cultures and technologies of simulation, enabled global expansions of capital insofar as an erosion of class distinctions effaced the validity of more local interests.

The Desperate Hours sets the stage in the Cold War cycle by beginning as an atavistic class parable and successively deflecting issues of material class onto those of consumerist status. The central family in the film illustrates the rise of the 'new middle classes' being defined at the time by writers like C. Wright Mills (1995a; 1995b), concurrent with 'an underlying conception... of America as a middle-class society in which some people were simply more middle-class than others' (Bottomore 1966: 103). On one hand, the film is careful to note that the middle-class family, despite its trappings of privilege, is not *too* wealthy, as when, in one scene, one of the invaders commandeers the father's bank book and openly ridicules the modest sum in the family savings account. On the other, it is less a study in class conflict than in 'status panic' (in Mills' phrase), as the hostilities turn mostly on outward displays of genteel sensibility. For instance, the most pronounced contempt of the head thug (played with robust crudity by Humphrey Bogart) is directed at the mother for properly using the word 'whom' instead of 'who', even while the audience is prodded to note that the thug himself says 'libary' for 'library'. The mitigated class consciousness of the invaders has everything to do with their recognition of the artificiality of the status claims of the 'new middle classes', rooted in cultural factors such as education rather than economic wealth. This distinction confers a potent resonance on a key moment, when the head thug's younger brother (Dewey Martin), conscripted into the crime – and moved by the hominess of the modest bourgeois sanctuary they have invaded – turns on him with the accusation: 'You never taught me to live in a house like this!'

For many in America, the clearest threat to the family after World War Two was an economic expansion, brought about by a consummated transformation of an industrial to a service economy, a shift that, it was thought by many on the Left, could destabilise the family unit by requiring more labour, moving mothers and children increasingly into the workforce, and depriving families of the leisure and privacy in which their bonds could be reinforced. At the same time, this expansion continued to produce forms of supposed prosperity, revamping American consumerism in such a manner that patterns of status, defined in terms less material than formerly, began to influence class lines in new ways. The class structures of the more recent cycle of family hostage movies culminate these tendencies. By comparison to the Cold War cycle – *The Desperate Hours*, *Key Witness* (1960), *Cape Fear* (1962), *Lady in a Cage* (1964) – the recent cycle at once heightens the class stakes (perhaps only inadvertently reflecting ever more severe class inequities in American society) and denies them all the more fiercely. These new films depict a world in which relative wealth is taken as a norm, and their odd cybernetic gloss, indicative of both the 'global restructuration' and the 'radically new technologies' that Jameson mentions, functions as an armament to insulate this neo-aristocracy, posing as a latter-day version of the 'new middle classes', from contact with lower classes. This armament appears concretely in the form of the intricate home security systems that are presented as spectacular, audience-pleasing gimmicks in most of the films.

Such extremity accounts for the cycle seeming both stylishly quasi-futuristic and thematically archaic, excluding pressing realities of contemporary American life. It is in the name of the latter cause that these family hostage films revert, in all their generic manifestations, to 'that boring and exhausted paradigm' (Jameson 1991: 289), the Gothic mode. According to Jameson, the Gothic is

> ultimately a class fantasy (or nightmare) in which the dialectic of privilege and shelter is exercised: your privileges seal you off from other people, but by the same token they constitute a protective wall through which you cannot see, and behind which therefore all kinds of forces may be imagined in the process of assembling, plotting, preparing to give assault. (Ibid.)

As a contemporary manifestation of the Gothic in just this sense, the family hostage film is rooted in pervasive otherness and creeping paranoia. During the Cold War, films objectified these principles in a false consciousness of class; more recent films extend their suspicions, acknowledged only in the correlatives of tactical plot contrivance. The invading others of these films stand in for a heady range of threats, representing both locally disenfranchised parties seeking violent restitution and contingent or arbitrary alien powers that personify the postmodern condition as such.

The family hostage cycle was revived in the early 1990s in remakes of *The Desperate Hours* (as *Desperate Hours* in 1990) and *Cape Fear* (1991) that 'modernised' their materials by emphasising the dysfunction of the families taken captive. In these remakes, by Michael Cimino and Martin Scorsese respectively, the invaders seemed less like class warriors than like figures from a collective middle-class id, goading the family to heal itself. In movies like *Nick of Time* (1995) or *Ransom* (1996) the family was seen as both source and victim of the same ills, which were typically portrayed less as social than as personal or psychological, reflecting a post-Freudian sense of the family as a system of repression. Wedding the family melodrama to the cynical crime movie, these films tapped into the mood of rakish dejection that appeared more frequently in the mainstream as a pledge of a given film's degree of 'honesty', and took the form, most often, of a stylishly 'dark' or 'edgy' sensibility. This turn accompanied a new wave of prosperity in the socioeconomic sphere as the information age gave way to the digital era, and it is easy to read as an expression of anxiety about the precariousness of this boom. Such anxiety persists in the recent Gothic revival, though in the constant acceleration of the commodity form of the movies it combines an ever greater sense of dread with mounting confusion about its sources. In the new 'dark' films, social consciousness is both a given and a sucker's bet, both what confirms 'the new sincerity' and what must be seen through to maintain the *sangfroid* that is a constituent part of the sensibility. Accordingly, the new Gothic of contemporary film assures us that the faults that proliferate everywhere lie in the system, not in ourselves. But it takes this standard Hollywood ideology to a new level in suggesting that, in the post-digital age, this system does not really exist.

Panic Room

Panic Room exemplifies the Gothic in Jameson's sense quite exactly, but what is most striking about the film is its evacuation of the vestigial forms of social commentary that marked such recent and definitive films by the same director as *Se7en* (1995) and *Fight Club* (1999). As one of the key figures to popularise 'dark' sensibility as a potentially desirable commercial staple in American movies of the 1990s, David Fincher proceeds from the assumption that the great projects of unmasking in modernity – whether personified by Marx, Nietzsche or Freud – have reached their end and demonstrated their failure, with the ideologies they sought to demystify now thoroughly exposed even while the systemic mechanisms those ideologies concealed proceed unabated. The dystopian temper of Fincher's films derives from their sense that we are finally in a position to perceive these operations clearly, even though we are deprived of the illusion that such recognition empowers change.

This presumption conditions the theme of class at every level in *Panic Room*, enabling the contemporary hybrid of class consciousness and false consciousness that results once it is assumed that both categories are obsolete. Fincher's film reconstructs the family hostage scenario as a deracinated allegory of groundless ethical conflict. Set almost entirely inside a single house, the film pointedly excludes social backgrounds and thus refuses corollary explanations rooted in economic determinism. Initiating a key aspect of the current cycle, the confrontation the film works out is less a broad struggle between opposed economic groups than a local squabble under the invisible hand of an impersonal techno-bureaucratic will.

The setting is a neo-Gothic townhouse that systematically exercises in its architecture the Jamesonian dialectic of privilege and shelter, shot through hues of murky green that signify that provisional 'darkness'. At the beginning of the film, Meg Altman (Jodie Foster) and her daughter Sarah (Kristen Stewart) move in after the former occupant, a millionaire, dies. From the start, the two express perplexity and wonder about the 'panic room', the one incongruously modern feature of the otherwise charmingly old-fashioned house. A dungeon-like space with a mechanical metal door, stocked with a hotline to the police and a bank of monitors that provides views throughout the house, it is intended to provide a permanent refuge from potential intrusions. The existence of such a room takes the 'status panic' of the 'new middle classes' to its logical and extreme conclusion.

The film implies a certain distaste for the faddishness and privilege the room represents, but equivocates on this point by showing that the room's ultimate failure to protect, when a trio of interlopers inevitably invades on the family's first night in the house, resides not in technological breakdown but in human error: Meg neglected to hook up the hotline. Due to this neglect, Meg and Sarah are confined helplessly in the panic room as the marauders rove freely through their house. A story of the failures of human agency, *Panic Room* realises an ultimate implication of Fincher's work: that every refuge is also potentially a trap. The protective panopticon, outside the control of any individual, becomes the prison-house of privilege.

It also becomes the cloister of the underclass. As an architectural technology, the panic room acknowledges a fear of invasion as a constant threat that requires standing security measures as a constituent feature of the domestic space rather than as a supplementary set of accessories within it. It stands as a sign of the privileged class's panicked awareness of the enduring menace of the underclasses, and this sense of the perilous permeability of the social sphere is worked out in a dramatic and lurid reversal of the plot: in the second half of the film, after Meg attempts to retrieve medicine to keep her diabetic daughter from slipping into a coma, the intruders make their way into the room with Sarah, while Meg is locked out. The invaders have come to steal a fortune they know to be hidden in the panic room, and they thus find themselves ambushed by their own unwholesome fantasies of ill-gotten riches. To the extent that the panic room functions as a symbolic space, it indicates a common, rotating entrapment of contending groups, suggesting an overlap between status panic and underclass covetousness.

The thieves know the money is there because one of them is the grandson of the dead millionaire, a point that further complicates the already compromised class narrative. Another of the crew is a security technician whose role is to penetrate the room and unlock a hidden safe. In the company of the heir and the service professional, only one of the three can meet stereotypes of the proletarian thug – and it is significant that he is also the only one of the gang to conceal his identity with a ski mask. Two of the three also bear ambiguous markers of ethnic identity. The heir wears his hair in dreadlocks and disports himself in hip-hop style, while another has a name (Raoul) that connotes Hispanic identity. Yet both are played by white actors (Jared Leto; Dwight Yoakam), this rendering them, in effect, empty signifiers. In an earlier strain of the postmodern Gothic, as Jameson pointed out, threat came from generic 'madmen and terrorists' – 'vessels' in which 'any type of social content can be poured at will' (1991: 290). In the recent cycle, despite lingering indicators of a residual racism, the meanings of these vessels appear only on their unreadable surfaces.

The masked invader (Forest Whitaker) is African American, and the film takes considerable pains to de-stigmatise his character once the initial function as demonised Other has been established. In the much earlier *Lady in a Cage* – the Cold War film that *Panic Room* most resembles, in which Olivia de Havilland plays a wealthy matron trapped in an elevator while terrorised by intruders – no apologies are offered for demonising the intruders as racial or cultural others (a Hispanic and a beatnik, respectively). Perhaps the best that can be said of the recent cycle – as of much of contemporary American film – is that it constitutes one long, feverish apology for propagating ideologies it still cannot renounce. In *Panic Room*, the Other is redeemed through ethics as a veritable martyr. Against the entreaties of his co-conspirators, he humanely administers Sarah's medicine and later returns to the house, impeding his own escape, to save the family from his crazed accomplice. He is killed by the accomplice in a slo-mo sequence, the emotional barometer of which is pumped up by a spotty allusion, in a climactic moment, to the final shot of Stanley Kubrick's *The Killing* (1956), in which stolen money flutters lyrically yet fatalistically skywards and then rains back down to earth. It is typical of this cycle of films that one cannot quite be sure, replaying this scene, if the money is meant to be seen as filthy lucre or manna from heaven.

Hostage

In most other recent family invasion films, the house typically appears as a sprawling, zany collaboration of Frank Lloyd Wright and Frank Gehry, a postmodern structure of steel and glass combining cubic and slab-like forms in imposing horizontals embraced by vast corrugated frames, always pointing back explicitly to Vandamm's hilltop aerie in Alfred Hitchcock's *North by Northwest* (1959). Now, architecture has theoretically solved the problem Jameson notes of the traditional Gothic mansion, in which protection produces danger, walling off the outside and rendering it invisible, thus a potential site of unseen conspiracies. By contrast, the alien lair is converted into a domestic fortress as the architecture produces an opulent spectacle of visibility, with walls replaced by plate glass windows, giving a general impression of both vulnerability (due to the openness of the structure) and impenetrability (due to the superabundance of the building itself). Typically wedged precariously into hillsides, these glass houses seem to court danger brazenly: in rendering the outside visible, they also render the inside exposed, but they compensate through the implementation of highly advanced surveillance technologies, usually presented as covert and innate to the materials of the structures. In their incorporation of panoptical technology, these houses illustrate not the shrinking of class paranoia but its enlargement to the point of invisibility as the labyrinthine, enclosed mansion of Gothic lore turns into the lavish postmodern enclave that any postmodern family would be proud to call home.

Such a house appears at the centre of *Hostage* as a bridge to fantasy images of the 'market' or the 'system'. The plot of the film turns on dual hostage situations involving parallel families, one associated with an increasingly pressurised lower middle class, the other associated with the new technocratic elite, seemingly insulated from class pressures. Jeff Talley (Bruce Willis) is a hostage negotiator for the Los Angeles Police Department who fails, in the opening scene, to prevent a beleaguered working-class father from killing his own family and then shooting himself. Traumatised by this defeat, Talley leaves the city for a less taxing job in a remote small town, where he quickly finds himself drawn into another hostage situation after a trio of small-time hoods on a joyride invades the postmodern fortress of a wealthy family and takes them captive. As it happens, the father of this family is a corporate criminal in possession of a computer disc containing information coveted by a shadowy organisation that, forthwith, takes Talley's own family hostage in order to coerce his retrieval of the disc from the fortress on their behalf.

The seeming intricacy of this plot is something of a ruse, as the point of each successive narrative turn is to trump the previous one. The effect is to vacate meanings rather than to multiply them, and the movie thus illustrates the structure of denial that defines this sequence of films, if not contemporary American cinema *tout court*: its mechanisms are devoted almost entirely to revealing what it is *not* about. In the first hostage situation, reversing the cycle's conventions, the father murders his family to protect them from what he sees as the rampant vice of the modern world, but these shadings of a 'dark' parable of reactionism against moral decay – *à la Se7en* or *Saw* – are abandoned, apparently, in favour of a more typical, though equally 'dark', melodrama of class conflict. The latter, however, is strictly fortuitous, the hoods' invasion of the house prompted less by class resentment as such than by capricious, youthfully masculine thrill-seeking. This segment of the plot is quickly eclipsed by what appears to be the real crux of the matter, the quest for the disc and the endangerment of Talley's own family. At nearly every level the film indulges in such tactics of disclaiming. The shadowy group, for instance, may or may not be a government agency, so the film itself may or may not be about state complicity in covert power and local violence, or about corporate corruption in the digital age.

Yet as any student of the workings of the unconscious is aware, and as contemporary American movies are uniquely positioned to demonstrate, to deny is inevitably to assert. Like many films of the cycle, *Hostage* would have us see how the 'primal' psychology of the family bond trumps the socio-economic claims of class interests. Whether stranded at the lowest rank (like the working-class father), entrenched in the middle class and aspiring to upward mobility (like Talley), or perched squarely in the upper echelon (like the corporate criminal), the besieged father immediately surrenders any class desideratum in the face of the hostage scenario, in which the violators target psychology to usurp wealth, or exploit psychological duress to achieve socio-economic advantage. Talley identifies across class lines with both the working-class father and the wealthy father because they all have families in common. Thus the film positions the family as an entity that promotes a sense of unity across class lines, a solidarity almost never available, as these movies would have it, within class categories, except in terms of the family. The violence of the first father displaces class exigency into a generalised moral panic, while the plight of the second, secluded in the bastion of his privilege, crystalises the most basic fear these films express, that privilege does not protect, that all efforts to insulate oneself from the scourge of social predation amount to nothing so long as the fundamental covenant of family persists, as it must, as a source of vulnerability. The postmodern domicile of *Hostage* is the most fortress-like structure in the whole sequence, but it is also the most easily transgressed by a gang of penny-ante thugs with no evident resources to assist in their invasion.

Firewall

Across the cycle, in reaction to the concurrent notion of the family as a source of vulnerability, the films exert pressure to position the family as a site of refuge from the sprawling and interlocking forces now embodied by the invaders. These are forces which, though contingent and arbitrary, continue to perpetrate psychological manipulation. *Firewall* is at particular pains to demonstrate the family's successful adjustment to the conditions of postindustrial life. The father works outside the home as a high-tech banker, a role seen not as that of a faceless functionary but as that of a humane administrator, while the mother works in the home as a po-mo architect, an occupation that allows her to double as a dependable soccer mom. In keeping with contemporary cliché, the film's opening scene depicts the family's hectic morning preparations, and although it emphasises the comical repleteness of the upcoming day's schedule of events, this circumstance is treated as energising, not burdensome, a sign of that bracing 'busyness' that in late capitalism becomes an all-but-reified commodity of status, attesting to the family's continued role as producer of vivifying activity if not of consumable products. The parents confer warmly at the kitchen sink about their sundry custodial duties, casting wryly indulgent glances at the children, who are absorbed in their iPods, laptops and micro-TVs with an engrossment portrayed not as narcissistic but as merely typical. The wryness of those glances is as noteworthy as the indulgence, since the film follows recent custom in promoting this attitude as an indispensable coping mechanism for a world in which the chief definition of fulfilment resides in having too much to do.

The *ordinariness* of this wealthy family is quickly secured. If the dominant myth of Cold War Hollywood was the universality of the middle class, with unusual wealth presented as a spectacle of aberrant excess whenever it appeared in tandem with more moderate bourgeois lifestyles, and with the working class as nothing but a way-station on the road to prosperity, a prevailing myth since then, evident in most of this cycle, has certainly been that of the upper class as standard or median. In *Firewall*, the abundance of the family's lifestyle is purposively soft-pedalled, to the extent that we are denied a full view of their opulent house until late in the movie. Throughout, the luxury in which they live is seen neither as a form of privilege nor as a sign of birthright, nor even as deserved affluence. Any class resentment that the family's extravagant lifestyle might produce in the audience is meant to be neutralised, in a familiar appeal, by the earthiness of its members. On the day we join them, the family is avidly planning to reconvene that evening for 'Pizza Night', a weekly ritual to which the most proletarian audience could relate if the film were willing to acknowledge the existence of any such constituency.

Pizza Night goes awry when a gang of thugs forces its way into the house, taking the family hostage to extort the father's (Harrison Ford) cooperation in a plot to use his bank's computer network to divert millions of dollars into 'off-shore accounts' held by the leader of the ring, an urbane Briton (Paul Bettany) who has been pretending to be a visiting businessman. The clearest indication of the movie's eagerness to divest this confrontation of its class connotations is the refinement of the intruders, who far from class warriors seeking restitution for economic exclusion, are a tony cartel of fellow bluebloods thirsty for even greater wealth. In this way, the movie styles itself as a tale of the gentry's greed, not the underclass's resentment.

What is most uncanny about the hostage situation in *Firewall* is how comfortably the intruders comport themselves in the family domicile, calling members of the family by name, making themselves at home, and generally behaving as if, unlike that younger brother in *The Desperate Hours*, they really had been taught to 'live in a house like this'. So opaque are their underlying motives, given their obvious sophistication, that they continue to be questioned about them even after their digital heist plot has been fully revealed. 'Why do you hate us?' the daughter asks

– an inane question given some weight by its way of echoing a common query in America ('Why do they hate us?') regarding Islamic fundamentalists, after 9/11. 'I don't hate you', a well-mannered intruder replies, 'I just don't care about you.'

This expression of indifference reverses the affect of the Cold War cycle. In *The Desperate Hours*, the claim of the captors is closer in spirit to a contemptuous plaint such as '*you* don't care about *us*'. This reversal indicates a shift in the class dynamics of the recent cycle. If *Hostage* juxtaposes working-class crime against white-collar rapacity only to dismiss the former as a red herring, a minor symptom, *Firewall* goes even further in dispensing with cross-class conflict altogether. In the world system of corporate expansion, the film implies, *intra*-class conflict at the top is where the real action is. This turn reflects, in its way, the ever-growing class divide that the world system of multinational capitalism produces. As classes continue to become more insulated from each other in material or spatial terms they really *could* be said to disappear, theoretically, insofar as their existence depends on their relation.

In *Firewall*, this reversal has everything to do with the new, dematerialised wealth of postindustrial economies, evident in plot turns involving transfers of virtual money at the click of a mouse or the stroke of a keyboard. The film exploits its Seattle setting not just for the steady supply of rainfall that becomes this movie's bid for a share of the cycle's stylistic 'darkness', but also for its associations with the rise of digital culture and subsequent transformations of corporate culture. *Firewall*'s treatment of these developments is double-edged. The plot is predicated on streamlined forms of theft and corruption made available by such alleged advances. At the same time, what Microsoft giveth, Microsoft taketh away: the criminal plot is ultimately foiled by the same technologies that enabled it, when Dad reduces the bad guys' virtual fortune with a few taps at the same keyboard he used to endow it, or when he manipulates the camera built into his daughter's cell phone to snap furtive shots of incriminating information.

When we finally do see the family's house, we note that it is yet another in the line of postmodern Gothic mansions. Not least in the casualness of its presentation, this house moves beyond the image of the uncanny fortress. To the invading others, it is not an enviable manifestation of conspicuous consumption but a site of pure instrumentation. They negotiate it with great familiarity, at ease with the security systems, high-concept computer games or plasma TVs that comprise it. We can recollect that throughout the cycle, in its high-tech design the home remains a site of contest between alienation and familiarity. In *When a Stranger Calls*, for instance, a tormented babysitter is assaulted by an intruder who boasts an uncanny mastery of the house's secret mechanisms, and she must learn to become equally versed in this intricate gadgetry to defeat him. In *The Glass House*, the house in question inspires awe because of its strange trappings of class privilege, with a 'home gym' and a 'home theatre'. As one of its new occupants exclaims, 'You never have to leave it!'

In this sphere of dematerialised wealth, the home and the family become the residual forms of money, and that is what now makes them the targets of the invading others. In most of the films of the cycle, the criminals could just as easily put a gun to the father's head to force his cooperation, but that would only be as effective as stealing whatever cash happens to lay in a vault. To gain access to the virtual wealth they covet, extending beyond material space, they must extend their threat beyond the body of the father to his own supplemental, symbolic wealth. This symbolic wealth is what the family has become as the Cold War dream of individualism edges into the postmodern nightmare of bellicose isolationism.

The tendency in the family hostage films to subordinate class to psychology squares with the earliest conceptions of the 'new middle classes' as a phase towards a foretold American classlessness. Before World War Two, writers like Albert Bingham argued that class groupings were rendered increasingly nebulous by the primacy of psychological arrangements in social life, perhaps most significantly family structures shared across classes (see Mills 1995b). Economic status may have remained the central objective determinant of social status, but in many accounts psychology replaced it ever more powerfully as the material constraints of second-wave industrialisation receded in the wake of the service economy and the information age. Even in the Cold War era, however, commentators like C. Wright Mills mounted persuasive counterarguments that remain relevant for the recent cycle of family hostage films:

> Because men are not 'class conscious' at all times and in all places does not mean that 'there are no classes' or that 'in America everybody is middle class' ... [I]f psychological feelings and political outlooks do not correspond to economic class, we must try to find out why, rather than throw out the economic baby with the psychological bathwater, and so fail to understand how either fits into the national tub. No matter what people believe, class structure as an economic arrangement influences their life chances according to their position in it. (Mills 1995b: 208)

The family hostage film exposes precisely the mutuality of class and attitude in an America in which conservative 'family values' make common cause with the adaptations of the postmodern family. Both, combined to render class invisible, only succeed in turning it into yet another Other, bent on forcing its way back in.

Notes

1   Current debates on the American family 'crisis' tend to take shape around conservative calls for a return to 'family values' and liberal entreaties to accept the new circumstances of the 'postmodern family' (a category including single-parent and gay/lesbian families) as an inevitable social adaptation. For an example of the former, see Popenoe 2005: 72–87;

for an example of the latter, see Stacey 1996: 57–64.

2   Elaine Tyler May presents an illuminating discussion of the emerging paradigm of the home as fortress in the Cold War (1988: 16–20). She emphasises the role of technology in this paradigm, a point with striking application to the reconstruction of the postmodern home as fortress in the recent cycle, to be discussed later. A fascinating discussion of *Suddenly* (1954), another home-as-invaded-fortress film of the 1950s, is in DeAngelis 2005 122–5.

Troubles, Dreams, Family

14

Very Far from Heaven: Todd Haynes' Cinematic Family

MARCIA LANDY

The family is a battleground for the hearts and minds of Americans, a disciplinary unit in the interests of social and political power. Conceptions of childhood, femininity, marriage and sexuality are at stake there. Todd Haynes' films relentlessly mull over the manifold connections between family and the social milieu. From *Superstar: The Karen Carpenter Story* (1987) through *Poison* (1991), *Dottie Gets Spanked* (1993), *Safe* (1995) and *Velvet Goldmine* (1998) to *Far from Heaven* (2002), Haynes' films have confronted viewers with disturbing scenes of the middle-class family. Family functions in these films not as a safe haven from the depredations of public life but as a killing field, a site of 'perversion'.

In this struggle for the power over life and death that Michel Foucault has termed 'bio-power', the family becomes a privileged site; bio-power entails the employment of medical, juridical and governmental technologies in the interests of controlling life, and the family is a major site for constructing and disseminating conceptions of normality and pathology, but family also affords means of escaping from 'the techniques that govern and administer it' (1978: 143). The battle is fought on the territory of the masculine and feminine body, disease, ecology and forms of power. The family is no longer confined to the domestic arena but is determined by – and also determines – the public sphere of politics and culture. Haynes' films explore these lines of flight. In their engagement with the forces that impinge on the family, his films also explore how the technologies of audio-visuality, film and television are connected with constructing, disseminating and potentially subverting dominant images of the American family.

Superstar: War and the Family

Singer Karen Carpenter's death in 1983 from a heart attack brought on by anorexia is the pretext for *Superstar*, but the film quickly reveals that it involves more than merely a biopic or an elegy for the singer. The film opens with a question intoned in voiceover: 'What happened? Why, at the age of 32, was this smooth-voiced girl from Downey, California, who led a raucous nation easily into the seventies, found dead in her parents' home?' The film poses an answer to this question in a series of flashbacks involving Karen's relationship to her parents, her rise to fame and her increasingly deteriorating anorexic body. The events that led to Karen's death are played out between the initial moment that introduces the singer's death (shown in unsteady camera shots of the Carpenter house overlaid with a female voice intended to sound like Karen's mother shrilly calling her daughter's name) and a reprise of that moment at the end.

References to Karen's anorexia are juxtaposed against fleeting Holocaust images of bodies, the bombing of Cambodia, the Vietnam war and the Nixon and Reagan White Houses. The film's quest for an answer to Karen Carpenter's demise is thus tied not merely to the family's role in her illness but also to the external arena of national and global politics. The self-punishment enacted on her body has its parallels in a larger war on the human body that entails an exploration of the multiple forces that impinge on the family and are related to the catastrophic expressions of a disregard for life in the twentieth century.

The film tampers with wholesome media images of American middle-class family life through the use of Mattel doll protagonists rather than live actors. On the soundtrack, what we hear are actors' voices speaking the lines as if in a television sitcom, radiating an effusive aura of 'healthy' concern and ambition. As the film progresses, the dolls become disfigured, discoloured and maimed, while the soundtrack features Carpenter's popular songs – 'We've Only Just Begun' and '(They Long to Be) Close to You'. The images and sounds are, in Haynes' description of the film's style, 'alienating':

> You laugh, but you're not really interested in the story or the ideas or the emotions. It's not helping you identify with the film; in fact, it's keeping you outside of it in ways that provoke ... thought. (In Wyatt 1992: 2)

Karen's illness becomes the enigma for the viewer to unravel, since it is presented not merely as a purely individual physical or psychological problem but as an attribute of the culture and politics of America.

The war between Karen and her family involves the daughter's submission to her mother's insistence that she become a performer and to her mother's control over whom she befriends and what she wears, eats and sings. The mother's managing of Karen's life includes keeping her at home: 'You are not going to get big-headed ... you are to continue living at home.' She is insensitive to Karen's 'eating problem', refusing to recognise the illness she reinforces by insisting that Karen eat. And when Karen finally acknowledges that she is ill and needs to get away to New York for treatment, her parents cannot accept Karen's dire physical condition despite signs of the young woman's deteriorating health.

Our view of the familial battlefield on which Karen's body is fought over is further developed through her relationship to her brother, Richard, who angrily and paternalistically berates his sister for trying to ruin their act. He, too, is indifferent to her physical suffering, interpreting her behaviour as willful. And in a sense her behaviour is obstructive, and intentionally so. It is her way of expressing the exploitation of her body by the media – another 'family', as the manager of A&M Productions describes his record company. However, the more pressure that is exerted by the parents and by Richard in trying to get Karen to conform, the greater and more determined become her efforts to maintain power over what and how she eats. Her battle with anorexia is introduced through a chain of images: food, boxes of Ex-Lax and a bottle of Ipecac, a toilet, and the bare buttocks of a Barbie doll being spanked in response to a male voice shouting, 'Come back here, young lady!' The images of spanking (further developed in *Dottie Gets Spanked*) underscore images of physical and psychic discipline of the body. Karen's anorexia mirrors the battle for control over her body. Through it, she establishes herself as both master and victim. In the words of one of the film's commentators, one answer to Karen's illness is traced to 'a highly controlled familial environment'.

Ironically, the concatenation of family images of war devastation, rampant consumerism and popular entertainment are resolved in the film's focus on the meaning and nature of femininity. Haynes literally says as much in a title: 'As we investigate the story of Karen Carpenter's life and death, we are presented with an extremely graphic picture of the internal experience of contemporary femininity. We will see how Karen's visibility as a popular singer only intensified certain experiences many women experience in relation to their bodies.' In Haynes' films, femininity becomes a contested site – not a bodily essence but an image of the body, as we shall see in the discussion of *Far from Heaven* below. Femininity is a floating signifier looking for a referent in the war over the gendered body.

The film is a feminist text that 'educates' audiences to the threat of anorexia and its destructive effects on the female mind and body. It is a critique of standards of conformity; it is an exposé of celebrity culture and its power. Like a crystal, it has many facets not the least significant of which is an exploration of the 'complex, fraught, symbiotic relationship between image and "reality"' (Andrew 1999: 234). Using a mélange of horror, documentary and avant-garde styles, Haynes questions the media practices that produce fractures in the existing modes of rationalising, legislating and representing 'reality' that are relevant for rethinking 'family values'.

The Carpenter family and A&M Records instigated legal action that removed the film from circulation, ostensibly on the basis of the film's unwarranted non-continuous use of popular Carpenter songs. However, it is more likely that the motive was connected to the film's irreverent treatment of the Carpenter family, locating the demise of Karen Carpenter within the politics of the Vietnam War and the Nixon era. The legal action testified to the contentious character of the substance and style of the film's critique of the tyranny of bourgeois family life and its complicity with other social institutions and the media.

Dottie Gets Spanked: Childhood, Sex, and the Family

Haynes' television production of *Dottie Gets Spanked* (see Stevens 1995: 79), made for the Independent Television Service (ITVS) programme 'TV Families' and aired on PBS, focuses on a seven-year-old boy, Steven Gale (Evan Bonifant), who is fascinated by a television programme, 'The Dottie Frank Show', to the consternation of his father (Robert Pall). His schoolmates taunt him and call him a 'feminino'. Steven spends his free time drawing pictures of his idol Dottie (Julie Halston) and other female TV stars. His father is contemptuous of the boy's interest, and refuses to mail a contest form that Steven and his mother (Harriet Harris) have filled out to win a trip to the set of the Dottie show. Upset at his father's cold and disapproving response, the boy dreams the first of two dreams set off in black and white, where he appears as a monarch refusing to grant Dottie's request to have him visit her show ('I cannot leave my kingdom'). The dream includes Steven viewing a boy being spanked, with close-ups of the boy's behind accompanied by the title, 'A child is being beaten on its naked bottom.'

Having won the invitation despite his father, Steven, the other children (all girls) and their mothers are greeted at the television studio by Dottie and her male co-star, but the episode being shot turns out to be another instance of spanking: in consternation Steven must observe his ideal Dottie getting spanked by her TV husband. To transcend the moment, to rebel, he makes a drawing of it. Much as in *Superstar*, the film augments its investigations of familial relations by linking them to the world of entertainment, in this case, the family situation comedy. The scenes of Steven with his parents are supplemented by surreal images of Steven's fantasies, including advertisements for feminine products such as Revlon 'Fabu-Lash' and reiterated images of women and children being beaten. Included is a scene of a father beating his son on the way to school, as observed by Steven.

Sitting in front of the TV at home, Steven is twice ordered by his father to turn down the volume while his mother sits nearby. Mrs Gale, looking at her husband and then at the boy, asks Steven to watch something his 'Daddy likes watching'. Steven runs from the room and in a second dream appears again as a monarch. In this dream, he is pronounced '100 per cent guilty' (of what, the accuser does not say). As a cage is lowered over Steven, the strongest man in the kingdom sentences him to a spanking. The spanking in this surrealistic landscape is intercut with a montage: the strong man dragging Steven from the cage, the man's metamorphosis into a mustachioed Dottie, a close-up of a hand raised to the child's body, images of Steven and of his family. Awakening, the boy takes his drawing of Dottie getting spanked, folds it up tightly, covers it in tin foil and buries it in the garden. The last shot is of his hands spanking down the soil over the buried object. Steven has learned a lesson and buries his rebellion.

The family relationships occupy only one line of the narrative here. Another involves the boy's fantasies, increasingly centred on being spanked. Significantly, his mother tells a friend that she and her husband do not spank their child, yet Steven's fantasy life is nonetheless tied to spanking. While the family is associated with bodily discipline in the interests of social conformity, the film's strategy turns the physical threat to the child into fascination with the rhythmic striking of his body. *Dottie Gets Spanked* suggests a more complicated view of the child's captive body in relation to subjection and resistance, which emanate from not only the family but also the culture more broadly and its saturation in forms of sexuality.

Although *Dottie Gets Spanked* leaves the viewer with a painful image of Steven's attempt at repression in his burial of the drawing of Dottie's spanking, this ending is not the film's final word on family and sexuality. Haynes has said:

> What was most fascinating about 'A Child Is Being Beaten' is the masochistic subtext Freud reveals behind his patients' fantasies/memories of witnessing beating scenes: a subtext that reveals the person of the child being beaten, as opposed to being an observer, and watching it gleefully from the sidelines. That's so interesting to me how sadism becomes a more acceptable version of masochism culturally. (In Stevens 1995: 77)

Spanking, as described by Freud, is a 'phantasy ... cathected with a high degree of pleasure and ... an act of pleasurable auto-erotic satisfaction' (1955: 180). The spanking is thus not merely a form of discipline successfully enacted but also a potential source of bodily contact and perverse pleasure. The image of spanking, like Steven's dreams, is suggestive of the culture's complicity in repressing sexuality and in linking and proliferating mechanisms of power and their relation to pleasure. The fantasy is intimately connected to expressions of masochism and sadism that Haynes will develop more elaborately in *Poison*. Through Steven's fantasy world, the film shifts its exploration of family from the role of the parents onto the world of the child, and onto forms of sexuality that involve rethinking conceptions of childhood femininity and masculinity.

Poison: Flight from Family

Poison links the family romance to various expressions of guilt, crime and punishment. In it, the male body is the venue for acts of violence raised in connection to sexuality and to the family. The film consists of three interwoven narratives, 'Hero', 'Horror' and 'Homo'. In the first, a young boy, Richie Beacon (role not credited), flees from home after shooting his father (Edward Allen). His crime and his escape mobilise the community to investigate the causes of his action and disappearance. The narrative is replete with 'interviews' about the child's 'deviant' behaviour, his penchant for self-punishment and exhibitionism as described by social workers, teachers, classmates and neighbours. Presented in the form of a hastily constructed newsreel, 'Hero' utilises 'experts' who seek to 'interpret' Richie's behaviour in his absence. The camera movement is slightly jerky, as though produced through a hand-held technique; the shots of the various interviewers – teachers, social workers – and of Richie's mother Felicia Beacon (Edith Meeks) are grainy, as are flashbacks of Richie prior to his escape, his viewing of his mother in bed with the gardener, and the father's beating of her that leads to Richie's murdering him. What links 'Hero' to the other two segments is its exploration of brutality, sexuality and violence. The prurient interviewers of 'Hero' are proleptic of the bloodthirsty crowds in 'Horror' and of the prison guards and inmates in 'Homo'.

'Horror' focuses on Dr Graves (Larry Maxwell), who 'since he had been a child' was 'hungry for knowledge'. He becomes a scientist but is rejected by his scientific peers with the exception of a young woman, Dr Nancy Olson (Susan Gayle Norman), who wishes to work with him and has fallen in love with him as well. By accident, Graves drinks his sex-drive potion and becomes visibly deformed and contagious, thus facilitating Haynes' invocation of connections with AIDS and injection of a 'queer meaning into the homophobic discourses of film history' (Burdette 1998: 69). The 'Horror' narrative is reminiscent of a 1950s 'B' horror/sci-fi film, shot in black and white and featuring images of Graves' laboratory and equipment and close-ups of the visible disfigurations of Graves and his 'victims'. But the film is less invested in parody than in exploring the problem of what is safely permitted to be seen and what must remain hidden from the community. The strange and lengthy close-ups of Graves' disfigurement, his expressionist somnambulistic movement, the flat, almost absent-minded quality of his and Nancy Olson's movements and gestures, and the panning shots and close-ups of the angry mass of people gathered on the streets to ogle him and urge him to jump from his window inject a grotesque perspective on conceptions of normality. Moreover, since 'Horror' is intercut with 'Hero', its narrative is overlaid with nuances that shed a different light on the family narrative.

'Homo' is a conflation of three Jean Genet novels, *Our Lady of the Flowers* (1944), *The Miracle of the Rose* (1946) and *The Thief's Journal* (1949). It takes place in a prison, with flashbacks to a reformatory where John Broom (Scott Renderer) and Jack Bolton (James Lyons) had been inmates. The characters in the prison are introduced by a voiceover that could be the voice of Richie Beacon who, 'in seeking prison life … could reject the life that rejected me'. Broom's voiceover intones: 'There in the counterfeit world of the prison, I found my family.' The narrative focuses on Broom's desire for Bolton. The 'Homo' narrative is shot differently to the other two segments. It is poetic in its linking of the beauty of flowers to scarred bodies and prison rituals of homoeroticism and humiliation. The dark side of sexuality, only indirectly alluded to in 'Hero' and 'Horror', is visually highlighted in 'Homo', the prison world a dark dreamscape – reminiscent of Steven's dreams of the obsession with, fear of and fascination with beating in *Dottie Gets Spanked*. The prison also rekindles searing images from *Superstar*'s linking of the Holocaust and war to Karen Carpenter's anorexic body.

The three narratives of *Poison* function like a palimpsest. Richie Beacon's world in 'Hero' seems the most familiar to the viewer in its focus on the family as the object of public psychiatric and medical examination. However, in its focus on a childhood psychodrama it shares the alienating dark elements of the 'Horror' narrative: Richie is beaten, repeats the beatings with classmates and finally kills his father, the oppressor of his mother and himself. The science fiction world of Dr Graves is reminiscent of the *monde* of Dr Jekyll and Mr Hyde, dramatising Graves as both predator and prey, aggressor and victim, and involving both masochism and abjection. The sadistic violence and beauty of the prison world of 'Homo' is also alien to the viewer. In the dark world of homophobia and homoeroticism, the prison has not only replaced the family but offers an unfamiliar and subterranean perspective on it. Here, the family is unremittingly violent, desperate and dark.

The film concludes with an inter-title derived from Genet: 'A man must dream a long time in order to act with grandeur, and dreaming is nursed in darkness.' This dreaming that is nursed in darkness takes place within a cinematic world also experienced in darkness, one that is isolated from clear distinctions between the real and the imaginary, the subjective and the objective, and where

> we run in fact into a principle of indeterminability, of indiscernibility: we no longer know what is imaginary or real, physical or mental, in the situation, not because they are confused, but because we do not have to know and there is no longer even a place from which to know. It is as if the real and the imaginary were running after each other, as if each was being reflected in the other, around a point of indiscernibility. (Deleuze 1989: 7)

Presenting the viewer with three different protagonists situated in different settings, drawing on different cinematic styles and interconnecting its three 'movements', the film unsettles any familiar interpretation about the identity of its characters and what happened to them, introducing disturbing portraits of family, childhood, heterosexual romance, marriage and homosexuality. The portrait of Richie Beacon, his family and his community bleeds into the horror world of Tom Graves and his disfigurement and the abjectly sadistic homosexual world of the reformatory and prison. Finally, what is 'indiscernible' in *Poison* derives from the images of beauty, particularly in the 'Homo' narrative, that convey the power of desire, the dream of the gesture, that runs counter to the constraining societal conceptions of normality and social health pressed into service through limiting and abject conceptions of femininity that affect men and women alike.

Safe: The Biopolitics of Family

Vision and hearing, conventionally assumed to be 'safe' guides to knowledge of our culture, are rendered unsafe in the context of 'explaining' feminine abjection in the family and society. Through the figure of Carol White (Julianne Moore), *Safe* probes the problematic nature of diagnosis and treatment of bodily ailments afflicting the female body. If femininity in *Poison* and *Dottie Gets Spanked* is peripheral, Haynes' *Safe* places it in the familial foreground. The film is a relentless exploration of the abject female body, set this time in the family milieu of 1990s America. The film does not present a conventional scenario of romance, conflict and resolution; rather it explores Carol's descent into an un-diagnosable illness that leads to both her abandonment of family life and her family's abandonment of her. Haynes rejects the melodramatic formula of inflicting his female protagonist with a *definable* disease from which she either recovers or expires. Illness is the cipher, Carol the instrument for exploring symptoms, examining clues connecting her body to the domestic and public world she inhabits and, further, questioning reigning conceptions of normality.

The biopolitics of the film are expressed through Carol's illness. She is the medium through which the film relentlessly explores forces – medical, psychiatric and ecological – that impinge on the family and have 'assumed responsibility for the life processes and [that] undertook to control and modify them' (Foucault 1978: 142). Uncomfortable questions proliferate about 'what happened' to produce Carol's illness and about the strategies adopted by her husband, Greg (Xander Berkeley), friends and the medical profession to restore her to normality in middle-class family life. But Carol's body slowly revolts against the proffered 'treatment'.

Carol is a modern wife, living in a large ultramodern house in the San Fernando Valley, with a Latino maid who cooks and cleans. Her daily routine includes going to the dry cleaners, taking gymnastics classes, having her hair done, enjoying luncheons with friends, being entertaining at dinners with her husband's colleagues and satisfying her husband's sexual appetite. Nothing in her house is out of place; everything is up to date and everything matches everything else. Her life is a middle-class dream of affluence, status and normality. But this tidy middle-class life begins to unravel when she develops dizziness, headaches, shortness of breath and nose bleeds – a collection of symptoms that defies diagnosis. Her 'illness' is progressive and her symptoms intensify.

A dramatic disjunction is presented between Carol's physical responses and her orderly and sheltered domestic world. Clues to her discomfort multiply as she begins to withdraw from Greg, adducing the clichéd headache. In response to his anger at being denied his conjugal rights, Carol responds: 'I know it's not normal, but I can't help it.' Her frequent declarations, 'I'm fine' (reminiscent of Karen Carpenter's and her family's initial responses to her 'illness'), serve to ward off uncomfortable questions about her 'condition' from her mother, husband, friends and even from herself. In an attempt to cure her illness, Carol goes to see her family physician only to be reassured that she is 'normal'. When her condition continues to deteriorate, she is hospitalised. When the doctor insists that there is nothing physically wrong with her and that her malady may be psychological, she visits a psychiatrist. Eventually, after visible changes in her physical condition and behaviour become undeniable and untreatable by conventional medicine, she acknowledges that something 'is wrong'.

As the routine of Carol's life disintegrates, background sounds of radio programmes and images from television talk shows warn of environmental disintegration and of social disruption (for example, rising crime rates and failing familial relations). Posters on walls bear similar messages, and on the television she hears about the Wrenwood Centre for treating environmental illnesses. The broadcaster asks: 'Are you allergic to the twentieth century?' This question poses yet another 'explanation' for her condition. After visiting an allergist and reacting adversely to patch tests, Carol joins an environmental group where she encounters others who suffer from similar and equally mystifying illnesses vaguely attributed to the urban environment. It seems that she now has a possible response to her malaise and she creates a 'safe' environment, moving into a room barren of objects, carrying an oxygen tank and adopting a special diet – all to no avail. While maintaining her residence in the family, she becomes increasingly estranged from her husband and his son by a previous marriage, who express annoyed indifference about the disruptive effects of her symptoms.

The final segment of the film is set at the New Age Wrenwood Centre where Carol has gone for treatment. The Centre specialises in treating individuals with Carol's panoply of symptoms and other unspecified 'twentieth century' diseases. The Centre's ominous greeting to Carol comes from a woman who, having smelled fumes from the taxi bringing her, shouts, 'Get back!' Carol is, however, soon warmly welcomed by the Centre's director who has AIDS and is 'chemically sensitive'.

The routines of life at Wrenwood involve community rituals, gender division at meals, moderation in dress and sexual abstinence, all expressing a form of substitute familialism. The Centre's philosophy is tied to the 'power of positive thinking', its therapy geared towards getting patients to recognise that they themselves are the source of their illness and that they must learn to develop self-love rather than express anger towards society in the form of symptoms. Carol's treatment at the Centre does not bring her any closer to arriving at an understanding of what's wrong with her or her world. Nor does it produce a cure that enables her to return to the family. Her relation to her husband and his son further deteriorates. When they visit her, they are impatient to leave, expressing no interest or concern in her condition.

Her subjection to her mother and husband are now transferred onto her New Age 'family'. Carol tries to assimilate the Centre's philosophy and advice, but her health continues to deteriorate and she moves to a windowless 'igloo' designed to shut out 'pollutants' entirely. The final image in the film shows her staring blankly into the mirror/camera, repeating, 'I love you. I really love you.' This suggests two alternative scenarios: that the self-help therapy at Wrenwood will lead her to health and adjustment or that she is now an empty shell, like her igloo, lost to the world.

As played with minimum affect by Moore, Carol embodies the film's opaque method. She is a somnambulist. Her impenetrable character reinforces her abjection, her lack of boundaries and her paralysis. She is unable to articulate a complete sentence, and is reduced to repeated clichéd asseverations that she is 'fine'. The film is an assault on the multitudinous clichés that inhere in conceptions of the normal family and of contemporary femininity, inviting the viewer to contemplate less reassuring images of the family, the body and the environment in order to see '*how and in what sense* school (and family) is a prison, housing estates are examples of prostitution, bankers killers, photographs tricks, literally without metaphor' (Deleuze 1989: 21 emphasis in original). Carol becomes a cinematic embodiment of what Gilles Deleuze has termed the 'time-image'. In this cinematic regime, character has undergone a transformation and the viewer is confronted with the challenge of how to understand the situations in which the character finds herself that admit of no well defined or clear action.

> [T]he character has become a kind of viewer. He shifts, runs and becomes animated in vain, the situation he is in outstrips his motor capacities on all sides, and makes him see and hear what is no longer subject to the rules of a response or an action. He responds rather than reacts. He is prey to a vision, pursued by it or pursuing it, rather than engaged in an action. (1989: 3)

The inscrutability of Carol's role calls attention to the clichés that would conventionally be marshalled to restore agency to a character and ameliorative actions to her dilemma. Instead, the film invites the viewer to contemplate the various clichés of family and femininity, raising uncomfortable critical questions about their meaning and efficacy, questions that require a different order of analysis.

Velvet Goldmine: Supplanting the Family

Velvet Goldmine ponders the role of the family and familial surrogates as a force in maintaining heterosexuality and its subversion. In its treatment of history and memory, the film moves back and forth in time from the 1850s with its first 'pop star', Oscar Wilde, to the 1970s and the 1980s. The film offers a mystery to contemplate in the faked death onstage of rock superstar Brian Slade (Jonathan Rhys Meyers), engineered by him and his unscrupulous agent Jerry Devine (Eddie Izzard). The film relies on a mixture of styles – song and dance routines, dreamlike sequences and conventions derived from the detective film.

With homage to the style of *Citizen Kane* (1941) – reporter, interviews and flashbacks – *Velvet Goldmine* focuses its analytical strategies on the flamboyant bisexual bodies of the superstars during the glam rock era. Their rise and fall is developed through the commentary of an investigative reporter, Arthur Stuart (Christian Bale). 'What was so interesting about the glam era', Haynes has said in an interview with Keith Phipps (n.d.), was 'that it was about bisexuality and breaking down the boundaries between gays and straights, breaking down the boundaries between masculinity and femininity with this androgyny thing'. This breaking of barriers 'drastically changed, or reverted to something different, or went into hibernation'.

Throughout the film, images of familial surveillance and discord are juxtaposed with the spectacle of glam rock sexuality. Arthur Stuart is no disinterested reporter; the film provides clues to his troubled struggles over sexuality, struggles associated with his parents and his 'straight' contemporaries. In one scene Arthur, having bought a Brian Slade album, bars his door with a chair and listens to Slade's music. His parents grimace disapprovingly as he leaves the house. On another occasion, as he listens and masturbates to the music, gazing on the album cover images of Slade, his father (Jim Whelan) bangs on the door, pushes it open and, seeing his nude son, begins to shout, calling Arthur's actions 'shameful' and 'dirty'. After this episode Arthur is seen leaving home, boarding a bus to London as his more sympathetic mother (Sylvia Grant) waves to him in the distance.

Familial conflict is also invoked in the case of Curt Wild (Ewan McGregor). After being discovered by his parents having sex with his younger brother, Curt is 'shipped off' for electric shock treatment. The families' violent reactions to Curt's 'perverse' sexuality and to Arthur's 'dirty' fascination with glam rock and Slade's body are paralleled by the hostility of Curt's mates to 'poufs' and 'pansy rockers', highlighting the longstanding, aggressive boundaries between gays and straights that glam rock momentarily transgressed and thereby threatening conceptions of normality as propagated under the aegis of the heterosexual family. The film offers yet another image of family in the marriage of Slade and his sidekick, Mandy (Toni Collette), that begins in camaraderie and shared adventures in the music world but gradually disintegrates under the pressure of Slade's growing relationship to Curt and a life associated with orgies and drugs.

Velvet Goldmine is a double critique, of normative positions concerning family, gender and sexuality and of the technologies of audio-visuality that are instrumental in reproducing the contours of a familiar world. In an interview with Stephen Dalton (n.d.), Haynes described the film as 'an out-right attack on a lot of unexamined assumptions of what films are supposed to be. It's an attack on the things people hold dear about film, which is that it's real. That was always my target, which I think is what Glam Rock's target was.' In the uses of zooming, rack focus, dramatic lighting, filters, costuming, choreography, settings and flamboyant acting, the style of the film, again in Haynes' words, conveys 'a sense of surface, this beautiful almost caressing surface of the screen'. *Velvet Goldmine* plays with theatricality, with the expressive body of the stars and with the medium of film, inviting speculation about how to comprehend the nature and effects of artifice.

Arthur's role as a reporter allows the film to enter not only the pasts of the various stages of Slade's and Wild's transformations but also his own personal and historical investment in uncovering Slade's whereabouts. His investigation is an invitation to the spectator to explore the limits and possibilities of memory not only for rethinking the past but also for contemplating the future. At stake in Haynes' film is the use of cinema as a medium of reflection upon buried dreams and desires. *Velvet Goldmine* enacts 'the powers of the false [where] narration ceases to be truthful, that is, to claim to be true ... because it poses the simultaneity of incompossible presents, or the coexistence of not-necessarily true pasts' (Deleuze 1989: 131). In its quest to rethink cinema through its focus on the body, the film is dependent on the coexistence of different layers of time that calls into question received and habituated conceptions of truth about the body, and sexuality. The film explores the politics of the gestural, the potential of the body for forms of communicability that are something other than a means to cultural, economic and political control. Relying on music, dance and spectacle, the glamorous bisexual body communicates the power of returning 'images back to the homeland of gesture' so as to break 'with the false alternative between means and ends that paralyzes morality and presents' (Agamben 2000: 56). If the heyday of the glam rock movement escaped the oppressive disciplinary role of the family, taking the spectators 'somewhere they had never been before' (Krach 1998: 4), its demise suggests a return to a familial gendered world.

Far from Heaven: Assaulting Family Clichés

Haynes' acclaimed *Far from Heaven* places the family at the hub of sexual and racial conflicts, and once again femininity is critical to his enquiry. The film has recourse to the cinematic language of 1950s melodramas and 'women's films', especially Douglas Sirk's *All That Heaven Allows* (1955) and *Imitation of Life* (1959), and to later works such as Rainer Werner Fassbinder's anti-melodrama melodrama *Ali: Fear Eats the Soul* (1974) . Critics have focused on detailed descriptions of the style of *Far from Heaven*, its uses of colour, music, costuming and *mise-en-scène*. But *Far from Heaven* is not a parody of 1950s melodramas, or a mere homage to other filmmakers. It is an investigation of popular cinema and its expressions of family and gender, in the 1950s and in the new millennium.

From the start, the viewer is introduced to the range of clichés that characterise the family milieu – the mother, Cathy Whitaker's (Julianne Moore) controlling her children, the black maid, Sybil (Viola Davis), taking the grocery parcels into the home, and the father, Frank (Dennis Quaid), working late at the office. The ostensible 'normality' and tranquility of the domestic situation is ruptured by a telephone call, announcing that Frank is being held at the police station. The film relentlessly pursues Cathy's determination to maintain an appearance of harmonious domesticity, despite Frank's 'lateness at the office', his arrest for homosexual soliciting and his avoidance of sexual contact with her. The quotidian quality of her interactions with Frank and the children motors the early episodes – Cathy's congenial relations with her friends and Frank's with his colleagues at work. Slowly, strains in the 'perfect' lives of 'Mr and Mrs Magnatech' appear. Their world is caught up in a vortex of time that links the diegetic past of the 1950s to the extradiegetic present, namely in the treatment of homosexuality and race.

Contention over race is introduced through the gardener, Raymond Deacon (Dennis Haysbert) and contention around homosexuality is introduced via Frank. Audiences familiar with Sirk's *Imitation of Life* recognise precedents in film melodrama for the injection of race in *Far from Heaven*; however the explicit treatment of homosexuality in Haynes' film makes it different from the cryptic masculine conflicts in Sirk's films (for instance, Robert Stack's role in *Written on the Wind* (1954)). Race and sexuality are brought to the surface through the film's characters, colour, camera angle, editing, costuming and *mise-en-scène*, and through the studied recreation here of the style of Max Ophuls' and Sirk's melodramas. While the film's quotations from 1950s melodramas are significant, they are, in Laura Mulvey's terms, a sign of Haynes' film trying 'to find a voice for melodrama's silences while also paying tribute to [Sirk's] styles' (2003: 41). These 'silences' are challenged through Frank's homosexuality and Cathy's sexual desire for a black man. The revisionist treatment of Sirk's films is evident in *Far from Heaven*'s giving 'voice' to conflicts concerning gender, race and homosexuality that would have been out of place within the 1950s cinematic milieu. Anyone familiar with these 1950s melodramas and their uses of sound and visual imagery can appreciate how Haynes' film evokes that milieu and complicates it by altering the characters' conflicts. Furthermore, the film introduces an unsettling sense of time. In its transformation of familiar and commonsensical situations, the film confronts the viewer with the possibility that 'we no longer know what is real and imaginary' (Deleuze 1989: 6).

The interior domestic world and the exterior working world are brought face to face as Cathy discovers Frank in an embrace with a man in his office when she visits his workplace to bring her hardworking husband his missed meal. The aftermath of Cathy's discovery takes place at their home as Frank confesses that, 'once a long time ago, I had problems … I never imagined'. In response, Cathy introduces the possibility of a 'cure' for Frank's 'problem' and their marriage. Frank desperately claims: 'I can't let this thing destroy my life and my family.' The introduction of the psychiatrist (James Rebhorn) adds yet another clue in the film's mounting portraits of the forces that serve to maintain the social integrity of the middle-class family through techniques involving the delinquent body. Yet, as in *Safe*, psychiatry's cure proves illusory, though it exposes another dimension of the forces that circulate to maintain stable images of the family. In *Far from Heaven*, sexuality is critical for understanding the darker side of the forces marshalled to control the family. It is through Frank's homosexuality and Cathy's pursuit of Raymond that pressures are made to erupt in the film.

Cathy's relationship with Raymond presents a different set of problems parallel to, but not isomorphic with, Frank's homosexuality. According to Haynes,

'It became clear as I was writing the script that the theses of sexuality and race were counterbalances with the woman as the force separating them. One was condemned to secrecy and the other to a public backdrop; one was buried within the domestic setting and the other was visible and open to rampant projection' (in Lim 2002: 2). Psychiatry is introduced in the film in the form of diagnosis and treatment for homosexuality; countering racism presents different and more hopeless strategies.

Homosexuality is for Cathy and her social world an 'illness' that can be privately treated and made to disappear in the interests of restoring heterosexual domesticity or at least its 'appearances'. Racism, however, involves a prohibition on what can be seen and a visible punishment for violation of permissible boundaries. As in *Poison*, the leering gaze of the crowds (black and white) on the streets observing Raymond and the shunning of Cathy and her daughter at the ballet recital after she has been seen to be linked to him do not merely constitute a nod to voyeurism. They are an acknowledgement of the disciplinary power of the crowd. The film's confounding of past and present, of boundaries between interiority and exteriority, race and sexuality, and onscreen viewers and offscreen spectators, is its strategy for inviting the spectator to contemplate differences.

Far from Heaven offers a doubled perspective in relation to the issue of race. On one hand, Sybil the black maid and Raymond the black gardener are indispensable to the appearance of comfort and prosperity associated with white middle-class family life. On the other, sexual encounters between the family and its servants are prohibited, controlled by the community's policing gaze, a gaze that erupts into violence against Raymond, his daughter and his business. While Cathy's friend Eleanor (Patricia Clarkson) makes clichéd condescending remarks about homosexuality, she expresses nothing but contempt for racial mixing. Similarly, Frank's expression of rage at Cathy's besmirching his 'reputation' by merely being seen with a black man even while he submits to a 'cure' for the social stain of homosexuality is a further indication of how the texture of the film delicately identifies differences of sexuality and race that act as points of social control.

These differences are evident in the film's overriding emphasis on visualisation, on colour and lighting, in its exquisite recreation of 1950s melodrama through the contrasting uses of warm and cool colours to convey the tension between restraint and affect. Cathy's costumes alternate between warm oranges and cool blues. Her deep orange dress at luncheon with her friends as the (similarly dressed) women talk about their sex with their husbands, the red dress that she wears at the party celebrating Mr and Mrs Magnatech, and her orange coat (set off by a blue scarf) as she waves goodbye forever to Raymond are juxtaposed against her blue dresses and the blue station wagon she drives. The cooler and more sombre colours identify her with the restrained domestic role she has learned to play as a pillar of hearth and community but the warmer colours identify her with the world of sexual desire. The alternation between sombre and bright colours not only epitomises the social and cultural distinctions that adhere to race and sexuality but also creates a delicate but revealing canvas on which Cathy's conflicts are enacted with her husband and Raymond.

Lighting also assumes a critical role. The scenes display nuanced and contrasting forms of lighting to underline different milieux and different encounters that define the characters' struggles. For example, the gay bar uses magenta, as well as green and deep purple, to highlight the difference between this place where emotional restraint is not present and the Whitaker house where bright lighting is employed to ironically convey the unsettling aspects of 'normality'. Orange and reddish hues are identified with daylight scenes in the home in contradistinction to the darkly-lit night scenes that convey the underlying and increasingly erupting tensions between Frank and Cathy.

At the centre of *Far from Heaven* are conceptions of femininity, the force that, in Haynes' terms, separates race and sexuality. Cathy is the film's instrument for probing these terms and the burdens they impose on women and, more extensively, on the culture at large. As guardian of domesticity, Cathy protects her family, and fiercely fulfils what is expected of her as mother and wife – to be beautiful, to have a perfectly designed and managed home, to inspire and meet her husband's sexual demands, to discipline her children, to support her husband's career and to submissively confront the domestic crises that inevitably arise. Like the film itself, femininity is the composite creation of a society that celebrates feminine virtues and is capable at the same time of disciplining women if their behaviour departs from accepted norms.

The narrative abandonment of Cathy as perfect model of femininity exposes the fact that femininity is not an unchangeable essence. Instead, a *concept* of femininity is bound to specific material and historical forms. Femininity is not the universal property of woman but an *attribute* assigned to women who fulfil its prescribed character. Identified positively with woman and negatively with men, femininity is made to appear visually seductive through the woman – provided that she conforms to its requirements. As long as she conforms, Cathy is the embodiment of femininity, but the film develops the consequences of her deviating from its norms and requirements. Her deviation is expressed through her sexual attraction for Raymond. As Eleanor asserts in her final conversation with Cathy, the 'problem' of a homosexual husband is tolerable: a relationship with a black man is not. Femininity can absorb male 'deviance' within the masochistic and melodramatic scenario of the family. But racial mixing cannot be absorbed.

For the community, race threatens prevailing conceptions of femininity and sexuality. First, Cathy's relationship with Raymond troubles femininity, identifying it as sexualised. Secondly, this relationship disturbs the secrecy associated with female desire, making it public and visible rather than confining it to domestic privacy. Finally, by drawing the line between race and sexuality through Cathy's role, *Far from Heaven* exposes the illusory character of femininity; that it is labile and dynamic rather than immutable and static. Thus, the film's closure is hardly a resolution. The Whitakers' two children, a boy and a girl (Ryan Ward, Lindsay Andretta), are relegated to the background, leaving ambiguous the question of whether they are doomed to repeat their parents' roles or whether they will escape. Cathy's isolation becomes another instance, among many in Haynes' films, of open-endedness and indeterminacy, suggestive of the possibility of a different life or, conversely, of another, more threatening instance of repetition, a remake of a remake.

Todd Haynes' films constitute 'a pedagogy of the image that critically evaluates its relations to time and history' (Rodowick 2001: 198). The films do not merely offer 'an illusion of the world', an 'imitation of life', but confront the impossible task of restoring 'belief in the world' (Deleuze 1989: 181–2) through confronting the cynicism of reproducing an unthinking acceptance of inherited values. His penetrating images relentlessly expose the constellation of forces that impinge on the family – gender, sexuality and race – and belong to a 'process of making a means visible as such' (Agamben 2000: 57). His cinema creates 'categories of problems [by] introducing reflection into the image itself' (Deleuze 1989: 186). These cinematic (and televisual) portraits of the family constitute a complex venture into the limits and conditions of possibility for the body of cinema and, hence, for cultural change.

15

Queers and Families in Film: From Problems to Parents

HARRY M. BENSHOFF

Queers and families are two concepts often diametrically opposed in our popular imagination. Throughout the last several decades, right-wing politicians and religious leaders have used the term 'family values' as a semantic club with which to bludgeon all things homosexual, attempting to separate queer people and their concerns from the realm of 'morality' allegedly represented by the traditional nuclear family. Similarly, many queer activists of recent years have also sought to distance themselves from the term family, attempting to deconstruct what they understand to be the traditional nuclear family's outmoded and oppressively heteronormative formulations. Yet, as one recent historian asserts, 'Lesbians and gay men have always been at the heart of family life. Nor has this role been restricted to being uncles and aunts and children. We have always formed families and been parents and grandparents' (Dawidoff 1999: xii). Clearly, queer people cannot be separated from their families in any easy way, a situation compounded by the fact that queers and families are themselves highly variable things. Although some gay kids are still thrown out of bigoted homes (often ironically in the name of 'family values'), many more families are increasingly learning to love and value their queer members, whether they be children, siblings or parents. And as the times continue to change, gay marriage, adoption and surrogacy are creating more and more options for the creation of queer families.

In fact, in the last ten years or so there has been an explosion of gay and lesbian parenting in real life, on television and (to a lesser extent) in the cinema. According to one recent survey of over five thousand lesbians and gay men aged 18–24, 'two thirds of women and a third of the men plan to have or adopt children in the next three years' (Vasquez 2006). Lesbian media personalities like Melissa Etheridge and Rosie O'Donnell are raising children in highly publicised ways, as well as lobbying for adoption and marriage rights. Gay actor B. D. Wong chronicled his successful attempt to become a father in his 2003 book *Following Foo: (The Electronic Adventures of the Chestnut Man)*. In 2006 the Family Pride Coalition, a gay and lesbian parenting advocacy group, organised 250 queer families to attend the White House Easter Egg Roll. Indeed, mainstream family-friendly gay rights groups such as HRC (Human Rights Campaign), PFLAG (Parents and Friends of Lesbians and Gays), and GLSEN (Gay, Lesbian, and Straight Education Network) have to a great extent superceded the previous generation's activist groups which were more narrowly focused on health care, AIDS or legal reform. Now that states no longer have the Constitutional ability to outlaw consensual sex between same-sex adults, the struggle for gay and lesbian equality has become more family oriented, focusing on issues of marriage and child rearing. Somewhat paradoxically, getting married and raising children is perhaps one of the more radical things that twenty-first-century queers are doing (see Goss 1997). And while on one level such families may appear to mimic the heterosexist institutions on which they are based, the very act of gay and lesbian parenting cannot help but queer the idea of family itself.

What follows is an overview of how American films of the last several decades have figured queers and families. These representations have varied both historically and industrially, with older (and Hollywood-produced) images of queers and their families regularly constructed within heteronormative parameters. These films frequently drew upon pre-existing stereotypes of queer people and did little to challenge the assumed prerogatives of the 'straight' family. In them, a queer son, daughter or spouse is represented as a sort of problem with which the other (straight) family members must deal. In offering such representations, these films affirmed binary oppositions between straight and gay, male and female, the 'normal' family and its queer Other. But at the same time, numerous more recent films produced either outside or on the fringes of Hollywood have begun to draw upon queer theory in order to suggest challenges to the structure of the traditional nuclear family. Mirroring recent judicial and legislative decisions, a new crop of documentary films is also insisting upon the rights of gay men and lesbians to form legally recognised pair bonds and raise children together. While queers as 'problem people' still figure in mainstream cinema, more and more independent films are starting to figure the problem as homophobia itself.

Problem People: Queers in 'Straight' Families

As a heterosexist institution, Hollywood cinema has almost always told stories about gay men and lesbians from within heterosexual perspectives, when it told them at all. This means that if and when queers and families do appear in Hollywood films, their stories have generally been scripted from the perspective of the presumably straight family. While this formula allows for the inclusion of token queers in the space of Hollywood filmmaking (as in countless recent films such as *Mrs. Doubtfire* (1993), *Home for the Holidays* (1995), *Dr T and the Women* (2000) and *The Family Stone* (2005)), it also tends to figure the homosexual character as a problem or crisis with which the family must deal. (Arguably, this formula was present even in older Hollywood films that were not officially about homosexuality, such as *Cat on a Hot Tin Roof* (1958), wherein Brick's (Paul Newman) mysterious attachment to his football buddy Skipper causes much drama for his wife (Elizabeth Taylor) and father (Burl Ives).) This 'problem queer' formula has been especially prevalent in social problem films and TV movies of the week, genres that gently attempt to inform a mainstream – that is, white, straight, middle-class – audience about some given social issue without ruffling too many feathers. For example, the first TV movie to deal with any aspect of the homosexual experience, *That Certain Summer* (1972), centres on a white, middle-class father (Hal Holbrook) coming out to his teenage son (Scott Jacoby). Other TV movies like *A Question of Love* (1978), *Consenting Adult* (1985) and *Doing Time on Maple Drive* (1992) follow the same formula, turning the discovery of a family member's homosexuality into a key dramatic crisis. The 'groundbreaking' Hollywood melodrama *Making Love* (1982) takes a similar path, placing its tale of a married doctor's (Michael Ontkean) coming out firmly within white, middle-class, family surroundings. (It didn't help, though; straight audiences of the era could not handle the subject matter, no matter how gauzy and soft-peddled the film was.)

The 'problem queer' formula was also used in some of the first AIDS films, both on television (*An Early Frost* (1985)) and in Hollywood (*Philadelphia* (1993)). As *Making Love* did with a gay man's coming out, these films framed AIDS as a problem for white middle-class families forced to confront the issue because of their wayward gay sons. While such films served a purpose in bringing AIDS awareness to the bourgeoisie, they have also been forcefully critiqued for remaining within heterocentrist paradigms. *Philadelphia* was excoriated in many queer quarters because its producers had deliberately done everything they could to make the film as palatable to mainstream audiences as possible, marginalising gay intimacy, romance and community as well as the broader political implications of the AIDS crisis. Both *An Early Frost* and *Philadelphia* represent AIDS as a personal crisis that the white nuclear family must cope with through love and tolerance, not as a political crisis exacerbated by an entire range of discriminatory social, religious and governmental institutions.

Older Hollywood films often turned their problem queers into spinster aunts or mysterious uncles, as with Aunt Fanny (Agnes Moorehead) in *The Magnificent Ambersons* (1942) or Uncle Charlie (Joseph Cotten) in *Shadow of a Doubt* (1943). More recent Hollywood comedies grounded in this tradition attempt to normalise queer relatives by insisting that they too share 'family values'. A good case in point is *The Birdcage* (1996), a Hollywood farce about a middle-aged homosexual couple (Robin Williams and Nathan Lane), based on Édouard Molinaro's *La Cage aux folles* (1978) with Ugo Tognazzi and Michel Serrault. Although one of the men has a son from a previous heterosexual liaison (thus potentially queering at least one aspect of family life), the gay couple is so overly invested in their son's happiness that they are willing to hide their problematic homosexuality from the bride-to-be's right-wing parents (Gene Hackman and Dianne Wiest). True to the heterocentrist assumptions of most Hollywood filmmaking, the straight couple's wedding is shown as being more important than the gay couple's dignity. The makers of *The Birdcage* – mostly liberal heterosexual men and women – were determined to situate their film with the 'family values' debate of the 1990s. Its press book claims (with no small amount of treacle) that 'With a large helping of laughter and more than a measure of truth, Mike Nichols's newest comedy, *The Birdcage*, demonstrates that the value of family is far more important than anyone's notion of family values.'

The Hollywood comedy *In & Out* (1997) operates in a similar fashion, its mostly heterosexual makers drawing on the usual gay stereotypes and generous helpings of liberal sentiment. *In & Out* is about a closeted gay man (Kevin Kline) so clueless that most of his home town accepts his homosexuality before he himself does. A true Hollywood fantasyland, this Norman Rockwell town is populated by understanding and sympathetic straight families, including the gay man's own, and the film even ends with his parents, Debbie Reynolds and Wilford Brimley, renewing their wedding vows. Both *The Birdcage* and *In & Out* whitewash queer politics with light comedy, and end with onscreen heterosexual marriages facilitated by the films' central gay characters. As to those noble gays, no one bothers to ask about *their* marriage rights.

This is not to say that comedies about queers and families cannot be made, or that they must invariably be insipid. One simply has to look outside of Hollywood. For example, Jamie Babbit's candy-coated farce *But I'm a Cheerleader* (1999) makes the very idea of the 'problem queer' the central target of its satire, skewering the narrow and/or homophobic attitudes of the straight family itself. In the film, two misguided parents (Bud Cort and Mink Stole) ship their teenage daughter Megan (Natasha Lyonne) off to a homosexual de-programming camp run by Cathy Moriarty and RuPaul (in a rare trouser role). The 'True Directions' camp is colour-coded in pinks and blues because its naïve directors think they can cure homosexuality by teaching the girls how to do housework and the boys how to fix cars. Rather than being cured, Megan falls in love with Graham (Clea DuVall), another 'inmate' at the camp whose parents are even more hostile and homophobic. At the end of the film, Megan gets the girl and realises it is OK to be both a cheerleader and a lesbian. In *But I'm a Cheerleader*, it is the straight and narrow heterosexual world that comprises the problem, not any of the film's young queer lovers.

Other recent more-or-less independent films also suggest that the problem with being queer is not in queerness *per se* but in the pressure exerted by the larger heterosexist world and the many restrictions it imposes upon queers. These films expand the usual social problem film formula to suggest that the true social problem afflicting culture is homophobia, not homosexuality. Often set in previous eras and/or remote rural settings, films such as *Boys Don't Cry* (1999), *Far from Heaven* (2002) and *Brokeback Mountain* (2005) examine the various tragedies that can and do result when queers come into conflict with dominant heterosexist society. In *Boys Don't Cry*, a film based upon an actual incident, the price for being transgendered in smalltown America is rape and murder (not the warm and fuzzy acceptance that Hollywood films like *In & Out* would have us believe in). *Far from Heaven* and *Brokeback Mountain* are two historical dramas that focus on the psychic damages that can occur when queer men deny their own same-sex desires and marry women. Although many contemporary queer men and women still allow themselves to be wed at the heterosexual altar, such situations were probably more common in previous decades when gay options were fewer and heterosexual imperatives stronger. In *Far from Heaven* and *Brokeback Mountain*, such 'mixed marriages' end in separation and/or tragedy for almost all involved.

Far from Heaven was written and directed by Todd Haynes, one of the most important filmmakers of the New Queer Cinema movement. Like much of his previous work (including *Superstar: The Karen Carpenter Story* (1987), *Poison* (1991) and *Velvet Goldmine* (1998); see Marcia Landy's contribution to this volume), *Far from Heaven* uses queer theory to interrogate film form, the social construction of sexuality and the relationships between the two. As a gloss on the form and content of the Douglas Sirk melodramas (its title and narrative situations refer directly to Sirk's *All That Heaven Allows* (1955)), *Far from Heaven* centres on Frank and Cathy Whitaker (Dennis Quaid and Julianne Moore), a married couple who appear to be the embodiment of Eisenhower-era heteronormativity. However, in addition to his lovely wife, home and kids, Frank also has secret homosexual desires that he explores in shady gay bars and cruise-y movie houses. When Cathy discovers Frank in the arms of another man, her world begins to crumble, and she begins to form a romantic attachment to her black gardener Raymond (Dennis Haysbert), an equally scandalous development in white New England circa 1958. Although Frank's homosexual desires are at the centre of the film's dramatic core – arguably they are still the problem with which the 'normal' wife must deal – Haynes is careful to situate Frank's dilemma within its social and historical context. Compared to today, Frank's options are extremely limited, as are Cathy's and Raymond's. And that is exactly the point. Although *Far from Heaven* takes place in the late 1950s, it asks its audience to think about how much things really have (or have not) changed. Smalltown gossip and hypocrisy, marriages of convenience and the closet and *de facto* if not *de jure* segregation are all still a part of twenty-first-century America. The film argues that it is exactly such social and cultural factors that determine how anyone is able to define and experience his or her sexuality.

Brokeback Mountain also centres on a family forced to deal with the 'problem' of a queer husband and father but, as with *Far from Heaven*, the film uses a historical setting to reveal and condemn the rampant heterosexism of our not too distant past. *Brokeback Mountain* is as much about the social constraints placed upon them as it is about the relationship between Ennis Del Mar (Heath Ledger) and Jack Twist (Jake Gyllenhaal). The film creates a palpable sense of place and time, conveying the very feel of the closet in which many queers were then trapped. Regardless of the debates over whether or not *Brokeback Mountain* was 'gay enough' for queers or else intentionally 'de-gayed' for straight America, its most powerful effect may be precisely that evocation: it affords straight audiences a vicarious experience of the closet, a concept all too familiar to queers but mostly foreign to heterosexuals. Like *Romeo and Juliet*, *Brokeback Mountain* is an epic tragedy about star-crossed lovers whose social and familial obligations prevent them from realising the true potential of their love. It is not a 'gay cowboy movie' as the popular press has it, as neither character would claim a gay identity. It is a *queer* cowboy movie, though, one in which (homo)sexual desire is explored in relation to social and historical discourses of class, region, religion, gender and the nuclear family.

As such, *Brokeback Mountain* dramatises the processes and effects of both social and internalised homophobia, as well as how those processes and effects relate to traditional concepts of masculinity (and by extension, the family). While traditional patriarchal culture has always praised men for remaining unemotional and aloof, *Brokeback Mountain* makes such unresponsiveness pathological. Although he loves Jack intensely, Ennis cannot state that fact forthrightly, nor can he even begin to conceive of the possibility of a life with Jack, having been forced at age nine (by his father) to witness the mutilation-murder of a local gay man. Even after Alma (Michelle Williams) divorces him, Ennis is still unable to imagine a family that might include both his children and his lover. Although he cannot admit or express his fears, Ennis is terrified of what might happen should the straight world discover his secret, and he grows increasingly paranoid as he ages. His internalised homophobia ('You know I ain't queer') not only destroys his chance for happiness with Jack but ultimately works to incapacitate him entirely. While the younger Ennis is already taciturn and terse, the older Ennis suffers from an almost complete emotional blockage, unable to communicate even to his children. Much of this trait is conveyed by Ledger's Academy Award-nominated performance: Ennis's furrowed brow, firmly set mouth and almost inaudible tones convey a man who has repressed not only his sexuality but any and all capacity to connect with other human beings. The film also dramatises how such repression can lead directly to explosive violence. When he is confronted with Alma's knowledge of his affair with 'Jack Nasty', Ennis erupts with physical violence that is first expressed towards her and then displaced onto a random motorist outside a bar.

Furthermore, *Brokeback Mountain* figures the idea of the traditional American family as itself neurotic, cold and ultimately hostile to its own members. Every family unit in the film is disordered in significant ways. Ennis and Alma produce two children but their marriage is empty and unbalanced because of his desire for Jack. Their heterosexual life together is a vision of domestic hell, complete with sick and crying babies, and cramped and dingy apartments (as opposed to the open ranges where Ennis and Jack's relationship transpires). Jack's marriage to Lureen (Anne Hathaway) perhaps looks better on the surface, but he tells Ennis that it could be conducted over the phone equally as effectively. Importantly, Lureen's father (Graham Beckel) never hides his contempt for Jack, suggesting that even so-called 'normal-looking' families are themselves filled with tension, rivalry and jealousy,

especially between 'alpha males' competing for dominance within the family circle. Ennis's childhood is revealed to be another saga of domestic trauma: when
his mother and brutal homophobic father died in a car accident, Ennis was raised
(briefly) by his sister and brother, both of whom abandoned him when they married
others. The film saves the revelation of Jack's frighteningly dysfunctional parents
for its climax. Earlier in the film Jack had told Ennis how his father never taught
him anything or supported any of his efforts. When this bad father (Peter McRobbie) is finally revealed, he is as surly, silent, cold and remote as the stark off-white
farmhouse in which he lives. On one level, he seems to know all about Jack and
Ennis, but his inscrutable demeanour is haughty and hostile. Although Jack wanted
his ashes to be spread on Brokeback Mountain (and Ennis has come to get them
in order to comply), Jack's father insists instead on interring the ashes in the family
plot, where presumably he can at last keep Jack under his ultimate control.

Brokeback Mountain was a critical hit and the movie phenomenon of 2005–06,
partly for the ways in which it queered traditional masculinity and the genre most
closely tied to its representation, the Hollywood western. Much of its power lies
in its ability to blur the borders between straight and gay, between homosocial and
homosexual. (What 'normal' straight guy doesn't long to get away from his wife and
kids and spend a few days camping in the woods with his best buddy?) Brokeback
Mountain causes one to wonder just what that stoic Marlboro Man cowboy icon of
our national past might have been repressing. One mark of the film's success is the
very fear and consternation it caused among many American men dedicated to traditional ideals of masculinity. By changing the focus of the social problem film from
'problem queer' to 'problem culture', Brokeback Mountain effects a paradigm shift,
one reflective of those occurring in the culture at large over the place and meaning
of queer people in American society.

Queering the Traditional Family

As a film like Brokeback Mountain dramatises, both before and after gay liberation,
lesbians and gay men have been discriminated against in ways both physical and
mental. As queers were booted out of various social institutions (including their
families), they often formed their own pseudo-familial groupings. Historically, these
groups of friends and lovers provided a necessary safe space for queers to begin to
self-identify and organise for social change. Documentaries like Word is Out (1978)
and Last Call at Maud's (1993) attest to the importance of these family-like structures in liberation-era gay bars and lesbian meeting places. The gay pseudo-family
was also the subject of Boys in the Band (1970), one of the first Hollywood films to
deal with homosexuality in the pre-liberation era. While the film has been critiqued
as stereotypical and maudlin, it does dramatise the close ties shared by gay men
of the era, how they could both support one another and bitchily tear one another
apart. In more recent years, gay and lesbian independent films have continued in

this tradition, representing closely-knit groups of gay men and/or lesbians as families in and of themselves. These films, which include *Longtime Companion* (1990), *Bar Girls* (1994), *Go Fish* (1994), *Love! Valour! Compassion!* (1997), *The Broken Hearts Club* (2000) and *Punks* (2000), dramatise a variety of issues such as fidelity versus sexual freedom, friendship versus love, the AIDS crisis, drug use and/or abuse, coming out and discrimination. In each film, families of friends and lovers provide emotional support for queer individuals, offering a model of familial interaction relatively free from heteronormative assumptions and demands.

When Hollywood filmmakers use this queer pseudo-family formula (which happens only rarely because it requires central queer relationships rather than token queers), they tend to simplify the complexities of queer life. A good example of this strategy is Beeban Kidron's *To Wong Foo, Thanks for Everything, Julie Newmar* (1995), a film that borrowed heavily from (some might argue, 'stole the plot of') Stephan Elliott's Australian film *The Adventures of Priscilla, Queen of the Desert* (1994). Although both films centre on three drag queens making a cross-country road trip, the more stereotypical Hollywood version is squarely aimed at straight America, while the Australian film allows its drag queens greater depth and complexity. For example, in *The Adventures of Priscilla...* Terence Stamp's character is transsexual, while Hugo Weaving plays a gay man with a son. In the Hollywood version, the three central characters are all asexual gay men going to a drag contest, a plot that comparatively trivialises the issues raised in the earlier film. Furthermore, *To Wong Foo...* stars macho Hollywood stars Patrick Swayze, Wesley Snipes and John Leguizamo, all of whom are known to be heterosexual; the film was advertised as a sort of stunt-cast freak show.

To Wong Foo...'s drag queens seem more interested in validating heterosexual relations than affirming queer ones. They help steer a teenage boy (Jason London) towards heterosexuality (and, thus, away from themselves), and rescue a straight woman (Stockard Channing) from her abusive husband. Observing that this trend extended well beyond *To Wong Foo...*, Suzanna Danuta Walters has noted that in the 1990s 'cross-dressing, straight-talking drag queens emerged as our national Dear Abbys – providing sassy but affectionate insight into the vicissitudes of heterosexual romance' (2001: 140). Although Swayze's Vida Boheme has been thrown out of his/her wealthy family, and the 'girls' tangle with a homophobic cop, the film never dwells for long on institutionalised heterosexism. And as with *In & Out*, the denizens of smalltown America rather improbably grow to love their drag queens, accepting them as part of their (straight) families rather than allowing their families to be 'queered' by them. Indeed, if the drag queens have made any impact on the small town at all, it is mostly a cosmetic one, similar to their 'Queer-Eyed' brethren on TV.

Far more complicated queer families – ones that actually challenge and/or re-work the traditional nuclear family – can be found in various independent films of the last two decades. For example, Jennie Livingston's New Queer documentary *Paris is Burning* (1990) reveals how cross-dressing queers of colour formed their own family-like subcultures during the Reagan-Bush era. The film explores the complex intersections of race, class, gender and sexuality, showing how images of wealthy white glamour were idolised by many of the era's poor urban queers. Thrown out of their parents' homes in many cases, the documentary's subjects formed their own families – extended social groupings called Houses, complete with a Mother or a Father, and named after famous fashion designers. Similarly, in Gus Van Sant's *My Own Private Idaho* (1991), a group of queer boy street hustlers form their own pseudo-family around a Falstaff-inspired father figure (William Richert). In *Hedwig and the Angry Inch* (2001), a glam-rock punk band comprises its own intersexed queer family, complete with a male/female diva 'created' by a botched sex change operation (John Cameron Mitchell) and a biologically male companion-lover played by a woman in drag (Miriam Shor). *Transamerica* (2005) centres on a transgendered person (Felicity Huffman) with a son; although comedy and drama ensue when the entire family gets together, the film maintains a relatively queer perspective.

Other queer families appear in independent films like *The Incredibly True Adventure of Two Girls in Love* (1995), *The Hours* (2002) and *A Home at the End of the World* (2004). In the first, a 'baby dyke' (Laurel Holloman) lives in a warm and welcoming extended family made up of her queer mother's friends, relatives and ex-lovers. In *The Hours*, Meryl Streep plays a contemporary urban lesbian with both a partner and a daughter; their lives are compared throughout the film to those of women from previous eras who had far fewer social options. In *A Home at the End of the World* (also based on a book by Michael Cunningham, author of *The Hours*), Colin Farrell, Dallas Roberts and Robin Wright Penn play three characters whose more fluid sexualities allow them to create their own unique form of family.

Hollywood has had difficulty finding success when trying to expand notions of family in relation to queers. While pseudo-families of fantastic creatures (like X-Men or Hobbits) are wildly successful at the box office, mainstream Hollywood films that try to queer the family's sexuality have generally failed. *Three of Hearts* (1993) and *Threesome* (1994) attempted to expand the notion of romantic and family relationships, but they fell back into heterosexist moralising, pleasing neither straight nor queer audiences. *Ed Wood* (1994) and *The Rules of Attraction* (2002) have developed cult followings, but also failed to ignite the box office. The more usual (and more usually successful) formula for queering the family in Hollywood these days is the updated 'fag hag' routine between a gay man and a woman. While *Will & Grace* (1998–2006) perfected this formula on television for middle America, other films about gay men and straight women have fallen back into the old social problem formula. *The Next Best Thing* (2000) implies that the bonds between gay men and straight women can only lead to heartbreak and ugly courtroom drama, while *De-Lovely* (2004) more or less presents Cole Porter's homosexuality as the problem his 'True Love' wife must endure. Only one Hollywood film of recent years – *The Object of My Affection* (1998) – comes close to representing a more successful extended queer family, one comprised of gay male lovers, straight female friends, gay male friends, straight male lovers, fathers, daughters and assorted relatives. Of course, it takes money and support to break the rules of traditional heterosexual matrimony, so the characters in most of these films tend to be wealthy, white, urban and well-educated. To find queer families of varying colour and class, one must once again turn to the independent sphere.

Cable television and documentary filmmaking come far closer to representing the reality of twenty-first-century queer families than do either network television comedies or Hollywood melodramas. The groundbreaking series *Queer as Folk* (2000–05) and *The L Word* (2004–) each focus on queer pseudo-families, and include among their members gay and lesbian parents creating and/or raising children. HBO's *Six Feet Under* (2001–05) features an interracial gay couple adopting two African American foster children. Bravo's *Gay Weddings* (2002) also features a diverse group of gay and lesbian families, some with children and some without. Similarly, gay documentaries have always addressed the issues of lesbian moms: this is a topic of discussion in *Word is Out* and the central subject of *In the Best Interests of the Children* (1977). A range of more recent documentaries including *Daddy & Papa* (2002), *Caught in the Crossfire: Children of Gay and Lesbian Parents* (2002), *Making Grace* (2004) and *All Aboard! Rosie's Family Cruise* (2006) have revealed the wide variety of actual gay and lesbian families that exist in America. They come in all colours and sizes, and have been created in numerous ways. As would be expected, these films explore issues pertinent to gay and lesbian parenting, including marriage, adoption, surrogacy, sperm donation, divorce, single parenting and the prejudice faced by the children of queers. *Caught in the Crossfire* poignantly reveals a little girl's fears that her mother may be harmed because of the homophobic violence that surrounds them. A similar segment of *All Aboard! Rosie's Family Cruise* shows what happens when the titular gay family cruise ship is met at one port by Bible-thumping protesters. Ultimately each of these films asserts, as the title of one of the earliest of them attests, that *Love Makes a Family* (1991), no matter the sex or gender of the parents.

Conclusion

This essay ends where it began, with the realisation that twenty-first-century families are becoming increasingly queer. A few mainstream films and television shows, but more regularly documentaries and other types of independent films, are revealing the diversity and complexity of today's families, as well as the heterosexist institutions that continue to limit their freedoms. For decades, gay and lesbian people have been coming out to their families, and now increasing numbers of them are coming out as queer families. Obviously, these seemingly personal acts have much larger social and political meanings, for as gay men and lesbians are open about themselves and the way they live their lives, they are transforming the very meaning of the term 'family'. Laws may be passed to define marriage as strictly between a man and a woman, or to limit gay adoption and/or surrogacy, but queers will go on getting married and having kids. This seems to be a 'problem' mostly for those who still believe – as many in previous generations did – that homosexuality is a sickness, a perversion or a sin; or for those who see it as an expedient political issue to be exploited. Such individuals, rather than learning how to accept queers for who they are, continue to reject them outright, even when they are their own children.

Arthur Dong's documentary *Family Fundamentals* (2002) explores that tragic situation. Dong decided to make the film after noting that having a gay or lesbian child did not necessarily change the anti-gay politics of high-profile conservatives like Pete Knight, Sonny Bono, Phyllis Schlafly or Dick Cheney. A small and intimate film, *Family Fundamentals* centres on three families. The first is comprised of Kathleen Bremner (who runs a fundamentalist Christian group espousing reparative therapy), her lesbian daughter Susan and her gay grandson David. The second centres on Brett Mathews, the son of a Mormon bishop. The third family is comprised of gay Republican Brett Bennett and his father *figure*, the ultra-right-wing homophobe and former California Congressman Bob Dornan. Each family, which was once very close, is now divided by both sexuality and geography, and communication is extremely limited because the parents can relate to their kids only from within their religious belief systems. The film shows how some fundamentalists are so concerned about the next life that they ignore the realities of this one, even choosing to subject their queer loved ones to shock treatment or drug therapy (as the Mormon parents counsel).

Family Fundamentals, like Dong's earlier film *Licensed to Kill* (1997), demonstrates how the anti-gay rhetoric of the religious right is tantamount to hate speech: in *Family Fundamentals* it 'merely' destroys families, whereas in *Licensed to Kill* it helps justify acts of cold-blooded murder. And in a world where religious fundamentalism of all persuasions appears to be on the rise – when more and more people in this world commit atrocities for which they believe they will be rewarded in the next – we would do well to heed Dong's warning. Ultimately, *Family Fundamentals* suggests that there is an epistemological crisis at the heart of many debates involving religion and politics, and especially the gay rights debate. Fundamentalist religious *beliefs* (including books on reparative therapy written by disbarred psychologists and published by crackpot ministries) are felt by some people to express more valid 'truths' regarding homosexuality than studies vetted by medical, psychological and sociological professionals and published by respected university presses. As the film's queer children ruefully realise, their parents' fundamentalist prejudices cannot be argued against in any logical, rational way. Perhaps one bit of solace lies in the hope of a less dogmatic future: studies suggest that gay and lesbian parenting helps children 'learn the importance of tolerance and the necessity of respecting individual differences in others' (Bigner 1999: 61). As queer families continue to form, and as media images of them continue to multiply, the world family itself will continue to change, hopefully into something more welcoming and inclusive.

16

Adapting the Family to Murder: *Mildred Pierce*

MARY BETH HARALOVICH

When a novel becomes a Hollywood film, one expects the film will not be able to duplicate the book. The different natures of movies and books require the film to order narrative events differently from the novel, to eliminate or collapse secondary characters, and so on. For a Hollywood adaptation during the studio years, one expects the film will be less daring, less socially aware, less exploitative than the book from which it is drawn. In a letter to James M. Cain, the author of *Mildred Pierce* (1941), on 22 February 1945, Warner Bros. producer Jerry Wald acknowledged the reality of adaptation to film:

> From past experiences, I know that authors shudder and grunt and groan every time there is an adaptation of one of their properties; and I must admit that there is many a slip between the script and the screen. My sincerest hope is that 'Mildred Pierce' isn't one of them.

While Wald's letter expressed his hope that Cain would not be aghast at the studio's adaptation of *Mildred Pierce*, he allowed that 'many a slip' between novel and film is an essential part of the process when a book is adapted to Hollywood cinematic entertainment. The studio apparently knew what it was doing. *Mildred Pierce* (1945) received six Academy Award nominations: producer Jerry Wald for Best Picture; Joan Crawford for Best Actress; both Eve Arden and Ann Blyth for Best Supporting Actress; Ranald MacDougall for Best Screenplay; and Ernest Haller for Best Black-and-White Cinematography. Crawford, in her first screen role after leaving MGM in 1943, was awarded the Oscar. Director Michael Curtiz was not nominated. James C. Robertson observes in *Casablanca Man: The Cinema of Michael Curtiz*, 'It is difficult to see why their contributions (the nominees) were rated above those of [Jack] Carson, [Zachary] Scott, and above all Curtiz himself' (1993: 91).

In making *Mildred Pierce*, Warner Bros. adapted a contemporary popular novel that, as Albert LaValley observed in his introduction to the published script, was 'a troublesome property' (LaValley 1980: 9). Production Code Administration (PCA) and Warner Bros. files are replete with correspondence about the novel's numerous 'sordid and repellent elements[:] immoral propositions ... illicit sex ... blackmail' (Joseph Breen to Jack Warner, 2 February 1944). Yet the studio produced a successful film by shifting the straightforward chronology of the novel to a flashback structure that intertwines the adventure of a murder plot and the catharsis of a woman's film, the story of a grisly crime with the melodrama of the destruction of a family. In fact, this film has fascinated scholarship for years.

Indeed, the film's variety has made it a rich subject for film studies for more than three decades. Some essays examine Mildred (Crawford) as an independent woman, a film character who exhibits contemporary tensions between a career and home life. June Sochen (1978) uses an American Studies approach in her assessment of *Mildred Pierce* in relation to the circumstances of women's lives. Finding only 'sorrow' in the endings of women's films, Sochen sees the fate of independent women as a means of 'social control' of women in society. Christian Viviani (1976) considers how each woman character in the film fights differently for survival in a masculine world; he finds in the film's pessimism a critique of injustice to women. Andrea Walsh's 1984 study continues the tradition of the 'independent woman' approach to film criticism. Adding the psychology of the mother/daughter relationship, Walsh explores how the style and structure of the film reinforce Mildred's failure at independence and at mothering.

Psychoanalytic approaches offer interpretations of psychic structures and patriarchal ideologies in film, and how sexual difference informs the film's style, structure and meaning. Joyce Nelson (1977) demonstrates how the film's flashback structure is set up to explain not 'who killed Monte', but 'why did Mildred kill Monte'.[1] Pam Cook (1978) investigates the male and female voices in the film, arguing that the female voice is silenced in order to reconstruct a failing patriarchal order. In a modification of the psychoanalytic method and its findings, Pamela Robertson (1990) re-examines the flashbacks in *Mildred Pierce*, contending that the female voice 'speaks' in the way the film presents and suppresses the threat of female empowerment. In an application of psychoanalysis to history, Linda Williams (1988) examines how *Mildred Pierce* both ignores and mediates historical conflicts about motherhood, work and wartime unity. Judith Roof (2002) explores identification and spectatorship in *Mildred Pierce* from the vantage point of Ida (Eve Arden), Mildred's 'mentor' and 'aide-de-camp' in the restaurant business. As the 'female comic second', Ida 'provides knowing but cryptic commentary on characters and events' and an alternative to Mildred's femininity – 'the possibility of living generally without any male interference' (2002: 86, 82, 86).

Industry essays examine the studio production of *Mildred Pierce* and its reception. In her analysis of the music motifs which structure *Mildred Pierce*, Claudia Gorbman (1982) considers the role of the music director in interpreting the film, finding that Max Steiner's score provides unambiguous cues for situating the viewer in relation to characters and story. Albert LaValley's (1980) history of the screenplay traces the process and debates involved in developing a script for *Mil-*

dred Pierce, illustrating links between character motivation, genre and screenwriters' expertise. My own study of the film's promotion identifies what the studio considered valuable in promoting Mildred Pierce (film noir mystery in advertising; maternal melodrama in publicity) and explores the adoption of the studio-produced press book by local film advertising. In an essay on the working mother in public discourses about Joan Crawford and Mildred Pierce, I compared the presentation of the film and the star in the 1940s to their revision in light of Christina Crawford's autobiography on child abuse in the 1980s (Haralovich 1992).

To these discussions of women in film and industry practices, this essay adds a consideration of how the adaptation of the Cain novel revised the mother and daughter characters to accommodate the needs of entertainment and morality expressed in studio memos and PCA files about the film. Warner Bros.'s adaptation was governed by well-established practices of the Hollywood entertainment film: the textual needs of Hollywood entertainment – genre conventions, limited and well-defined character traits, coherent and motivated narrative; and Hollywood self-censorship, institutionalised through the Production Code. Further, the adaptation illustrates studio assumptions and perceptions about the audience for film: how a film offers a pleasurable experience to moviegoers; and how morality and meanings are carried by narrative structure, character traits and character relationships. In the adaptation process, the Pierce family of the novel – in particular mother Mildred and daughter Veda (Ann Blyth) – were redesigned to support the murder mystery and the woman's film.

The chronological events of Cain's Mildred Pierce and the film are similar. Mildred labours in the kitchen, baking cakes and pies for sale. Her husband Bert (Bruce Bennett) is unemployed and spending time with a woman friend, Maggie Biederhof (Lee Patrick). The Pierces have two daughters: haughty and proud Veda and unspoiled tomboy Kay (Jo Ann Marlowe). Fed up, Mildred and Bert separate and Bert moves out. In novel and film, Wally (Jack Carson), Bert's former business partner, seizes the opportunity with Mildred. In the film, she rebuffs his advances; in the novel, Mildred and Wally have an ongoing affair.

After a long search for a job, Mildred becomes a waitress at a diner, where she meets Ida (Eve Arden). Mildred begins to bake pies for the place. When Veda discovers Mildred's waitress uniform, Mildred covers her humiliation by claiming she is learning the restaurant trade. Mildred works and saves, providing dance classes for Kay and piano lessons for Veda.

As she plans her restaurant, Mildred divorces Bert to be free from community property entanglements. She begins a relationship with Monte (Zachary Scott), a Pasadena socialite without income or job. During her first weekend with Monte, Kay becomes ill and dies. Mildred pursues the restaurant dream. Monte and Veda meet at the opening. Their friendship begins, supported by their shared interest in upper-class recreation. In the novel, Veda, but not Mildred, meets Monte's family and spends time at his mansion, playing piano and tennis.

Mildred develops a successful restaurant chain. In the novel, her restaurants are each run by one of her women friends, Ida and Lucy, who become her board of directors. In the film, the financial power rests with men.

Mildred supports Veda's lifestyle financially and then begins to subsidise Monte as well, despite the ill effects this spending has on her business. In the novel, Mildred and Monte's relationship is affected: 'Your paid gigolo thanks you', he says (1941: 135); 'You look down on me because I work', says she (1941: 137). In a torrential New Year's Eve rainstorm, Mildred leaves Monte, having learned that Monte talks to Veda about his attraction to the legs of working women: 'The very best legs are found in kitchens, not in drawing rooms' (1941: 146). Cain's Mildred begins to gain weight and develop a 'matronly look' (1941: 167), while Warner Bros./Crawford's Mildred remains chic and stylish.

Veda and Mildred become estranged when Veda admits to defrauding a wealthy young man by claiming to be pregnant. In the novel, Bert and Mildred contemplate an abortion for her. But Veda is not pregnant; with Wally's help, she extorts money from the young man's family. Disgusted with Veda's deception, Mildred throws her out.

Later, Mildred learns that Veda is singing professionally. In the novel, Veda is a respected colouratura soprano singing on the radio. In the film, Veda performs music hall songs in Wally's waterfront bar. Yearning to have Veda back in her life, Mildred marries Monte and they move into his derelict Pasadena mansion. She pours money into fixing it up and Veda returns. In the novel, Mildred and Monte have separate bedrooms: 'Since the night Veda came home, Mildred had been unable to have him near her, or anybody near her' (1941: 216).

Mildred continues to drain the business to support Monte and Veda. In the novel, Veda's performance at the Hollywood Bowl coincides with the threat of receivership for Mildred Pierce, Inc. Although well paid for performing, Veda does not contribute financially to her lifestyle. Mildred refuses to ask Veda for money and seeks to protect Veda's income from the receivers. Searching the house for Veda to talk to her about this, Mildred finds the girl in Monte's bed. Veda rises and flaunts her naked body. Enraged, Mildred attacks her, grasping her throat. Veda claims to have lost her voice as a result, blames Mildred in the press and breaks a singing contract with the company that gave her career its start. Discovering that this publicity is bad for her career advancement, Veda has a public reconciliation with her mother at Mildred's remarriage to Bert. As Mildred begins to think she is settling into reunited family life, Veda reveals that she faked her throat injury and engineered the publicity so that she could be free from her old contract and accept a lucrative offer to sing in New York City, whither she departs with Monte. After some tears, Mildred accepts Bert's invitation to 'get stinko' (1941: 238) with a bottle of rye.

In the film, on the night of the receivership, Mildred discovers Veda and Monte, fully clothed in evening wear, in a lovers' embrace. When Monte refuses to leave with Veda, an angered Veda shoots him dead. To protect Veda, Mildred attempts to set up Wally as the murderer. At the end of the film, the police arrest Veda. Mildred and Bert leave the halls of justice together.

The studio, always already cognisant of the fact that the PCA would have to approve the script and the release print, developed the adaptation with the Hollywood censorship process in mind. As Annette Kuhn (1988), Lea Jacobs (1991) and others have shown, film censorship is neither imposed from outside the film production process nor is it fundamentally opposed to the needs of Hollywood cinema. Awareness of self-regulation, audience and social context is fundamental in film production. In her study of the fallen woman film of the 1930s, Jacobs describes Hollywood self-censorship 'as an attempt to compromise between the aims of the MPPDA (to eliminate potentially offensive material) and the aims of producers (to preserve this supposedly profitable material)' (1991: 22).[2] Jacobs concludes that the PCA process became 'thoroughly integrated with conventions of narrative, and in this sense censorship became both more subtle and more pervasive' (1991: 131). In her study of British silent sex education films, Annette Kuhn (1988) finds censorship to be one 'contending force' in production, rather than an imposed mandate. My study of 1930s proletarian women's films shows how the Warner Bros. promotional campaign for *Marked Woman* (1935) acknowledged and tempered the film's gruesome and difficult content, providing exhibitors with ideas on how to exploit the film within the bounds of good taste (Haralovich 1990). In his history of the Production Code in the 1930s, Richard Maltby (1995) describes how the Code became a 'convention' of Hollywood film production. Studios – well aware of censorship concerns, the Production Code, and audience – adapted novels and produced films that would serve the interests of Hollywood entertainment as well as satisfy the PCA. The adaptation of *Mildred Pierce* illustrates the integration of censorship with entertainment. PCA concerns about morality and studio concerns about dramatic effect were not so much contending forces as compatible and intertwined allies.

The *Mildred Pierce* adaptation shows that the PCA and the studio both operated from a concern for clarity: moral ambiguity can lead to material that is considered offensive, but moral ambiguity can also produce narrative ambiguity. Clear villainy, clear victimisation and clear atonement served the needs of Hollywood cinematic entertainment as well as those of self-censorship. In a memo to Roy Obringer, Warner Bros. general counsel, assistant story editor Tom Chapman remarked: 'It is commonplace in this business that authors who sell us stories often feel that their material has been destroyed by the vultures of Hollywood' (1950).[3] However one may feel about this sentiment, an examination of the *Mildred Pierce* adaptation allows us to discern the 'occupational ideologies' of the Hollywood film industry (see Bennett & Woollacott 1987) and 'the conventions that rule classical cinema' at work in the film text (Bordwell 1982: 6): the industry's perceptions of its audience, how a film was designed to harmonise with those perceptions, how meanings in films were negotiated in the production process and the social effects that were considered to be at stake. What was at stake with *Mildred Pierce*, in the end, was audience sympathy for Mildred's motherhood.

As LaValley observes, the Cain novel posed challenges for the adaptation. In his thorough discussion of the various versions of the film's screenplays, LaValley lists the significant differences between novel and film:

> Briefly put, in the novel (1) there is no murder, though Mildred in the penultimate chapter nearly strangles Veda when she discovers her in bed with Monte; (2) the narrative is told without flashbacks in standard fashion, chronologically; (3) the period of time covered is longer, from the early Depression to 1941 rather than from 1941 to 1945; (4) the narration is third person not first, though there is much close attention to Mildred's thoughts and feelings; (5) Veda achieves a successful career as a colouratura soprano with a climactic performance in the Hollywood Bowl; (6) the setting is much more tawdry and lower-class – Mildred, though she has shapely legs and some sexual attractiveness, is no Joan Crawford and by the end of the book is fat on booze; and (7) the narrative is very episodic in structure with events linked loosely, much less dramatically. (1980: 15)

To LaValley's list, I would like to add an eighth point: at the end of the book, Veda and Monte go off to New York together.

The adaptation of the Cain novel to the screen illustrates the emphases of Hollywood cinematic storytelling: (1) the primacy of narrative clarity and economy (the story is told in a series of flashbacks, as Mildred recounts her rise and fall to the police); (2) the dramatic value associated with character design and narrative causality (Veda is steadfastly ungrateful and manipulative, poised against Mildred's persistent hard work and failures to win her daughter over); and (3) the making available of meanings and moral positions through a film's narrative structure and the traits and actions of the characters (the adaptation trims Mildred's sexual activity and her drinking, in an effort to gain audience sympathy for her plight as a sacrificing mother). The *Mildred Pierce* adaptation had to cope with problematic character traits of the woman protagonist – her enjoyment of extra-marital sex and liquor; conflict motivated by economics and social class, such as the snobbery of wealthy Pasadena matrons and Mildred's social insecurities; and an ending that allowed miscreants to escape unpunished while the heroine wallowed in booze. The gender traits of the novel's central woman character – her sexual affairs, her enjoyment of sexuality, her pleasure in her body and her legs – had to be redesigned (that is, repressed) so that Mildred could be a sympathetic figure onscreen. Daughter Veda had to become an unambiguous villain, without redeeming attributes such as musical talent. With murder added to haughtiness, selfishness and depravity, Veda's bad character could be properly compensated as the Production Code required, punished by narrative, morality and legal justice (see Jacobs 1991 and Maltby 1995). *Mildred Pierce* handily made use of two genres (film noir and the woman's film) and a flashback frame story to drive the narrative to resolution, leaving behind the novel's morally ambiguous ending, in which Veda, having humiliated and manipulated her mother, goes to New York with Monte while Mildred, witnessing Veda's treachery and venality yet again, has a good cry and then accepts Bert's offer that they hit a bottle together.

LaValley attributes the decision to change the novel's chronology to a murder mystery told in flashback to several contemporary conditions of production, including the Warner Bros. traditions of crime drama, women's films and working-class heroines (*Marked Woman* (1937), *The Maltese Falcon* (1941), *Now, Voyager* (1942)) and the popularity of film noir and Cain's novels, especially Paramount's adaption of *Double Indemnity* (1944) (see Chapman 1949b). The combination of the flashback structure and the murder produces the combination of film noir and melodrama discussed in much of the critical writing on *Mildred Pierce*. Now playing roles in a murder investigation, the characters could be refined and limited; narrative clarity could be achieved, a relatively unambiguous morality could be encouraged and a distinct resolution could be motivated.

Studio discussions of the adaptation of *Mildred Pierce* addressed these challenges: the achievement of narrative clarity; designing characters to support the murder story and elicit appropriate audience sympathies; and encouraging audience interpretations that would support the film's centre, the mother Mildred. In his lengthy summary of the production history of *Mildred Pierce* Chapman (1949b) commented to Obringer that the adaptation began with the knowledge that 'the general moral level of the story would have to be raised before it could be gotten by the Breen office'. Indeed, there are numerous pages of correspondence about *Mildred Pierce* in the Production Code case files. Yet issues of morality were not the sole motivation for the form that the adaptation of *Mildred Pierce* took. The novel was also subject to revisions necessary to produce screen entertainment. In this regard, much of the discussion in studio memos about *Mildred Pierce* centres on how the adaptation could increase dramatic effect and suspense.

Warner Bros. changed the narrative structure of *Mildred Pierce* because the chronological ordering of the events in the novel was a straightforward telling of the Pierces' lives. The studio saw in the novel 'dramatic problems [that] could be solved through the use of a flashback for suspense and a murder for the climax' (ibid.). Exploiting the hermeneutics of suspense was a significant influence in the adaptation. The Cain novel 'did not rise to a big dramatic action' (1949a). Instead, Mildred and Bert drink while Veda lives happily ever after, in New York with Monte. In the film, Veda is led away by the police and Monte is dead. The studio regarded the flashback and police inquiry as a narrative strategy with more entertainment value, one that 'serves to keep the audience interested and provides the suspense element which was necessary to the story' (ibid.). Monte's murder initiates the flashback structure and is a primary motivation for redesign of characters and the moral conclusions of the film. By providing 'a dramatic climax which the book lacked', the murder makes it 'necessary to blacken Veda's character' and 'to make Mildred less vulgar than she is in the novel' (1949b).

With this change in narrative structure and genre came the need for characters whose traits could participate economically in this murder story. The decision to have Veda murder Monte, for example, had several important ramifications for the character traits of both Veda and Mildred. It was necessary to establish a 'clear distinction' between Mildred and Veda to underscore the placement of Mildred as the heroine and Veda as the villain (ibid.). The direction that this character refinement took was guided by three intertwined influences: Production Code tenets on morality and punishment, which required that 'the sympathy of the audience shall never be thrown to the side of crime, wrong-going, evil or sin'; the dramatic intensity of the storyline; and perceptions that class identities can make characters too complex and thereby distance audiences from them. Chapman's history of the adaptation of *Mildred Pierce* reports that 'the immoral activities of Mildred [in the novel] actually were unscreenable because of the Production Code. Since it was clear that Mildred must be the heroine of this story it was necessary to clean up her character' (1949a). The character attitudes and actions that concerned both the Production Code and narrative clarity were not limited to moral issues such as Mildred's affair with Wally or her drinking.

In addition to motivating conflict and resolution, character design also results from studio perceptions about how characters elicit sympathy from audiences. Characters in Cain's *Mildred Pierce* have desires explicitly rooted in contemporary social conditions as well as in personal goals and desires. The lower-class identity of Mildred is clearly articulated and important to her character in the novel. For the studio, such an emphasis on Mildred's class inferiority would adversely affect audience sympathy for a sacrificing mother who spoiled her daughter beyond redemption. Studio perceptions about Mildred's class attributes bring to mind another sacrificing mother, Barbara Stanwyck as Stella Dallas, in the eponymous film. *Stella Dallas* (1937) hinges on the inability of the lower-class woman to cross class lines and the barrier that Stella's 'irredeemable vulgarity' (Jacobs 1991: 137) presents for her daughter's future and happiness. Stanwyck's Stella is coarse in speech and vulgar in dress and manners. The adaptation of *Mildred Pierce* does not take this route to class distinctions, allowing Joan Crawford to comfortably wear Mildred's successful businesswoman wardrobe. With class snobbery and class cruelty securely seated with Veda, and Joan/Mildred at ease in contemporary suits and big shoulders, the murder and the sacrificing mother remain the focus of the narrative.

Cleaning up Mildred's character to ensure the security of her role as heroine involved shifts in her class identity: 'For this reason she was made a member of the upper middle class instead of the lower middle class; vulgarisms were dropped from her speech; she was made more the victim of circumstances than a sinner' (Chapman 1949a). It is hard to discern, from a reading of the novel, the 'vulgarisms' that Chapman reports were dropped from Mildred's speech. In the novel, her speech seems uncontroversial by PCA standards. However, PCA files do contain requests that *Mildred Pierce* screenplays remove language such as 'for God's sake' or 'to hell and gone' or 'I wish to God' or 'I went through hell' or 'hot number ... when applied to a woman' (Breen 1944). The files do not attribute these lines to specific characters, thus Mildred is not identified as speaking them. In the novel, the male characters – Bert, Monte and Wally – are more likely to speak in the vulgate.

Studio perceptions of the social context of the Hollywood film inform the construction of Hollywood cinema. One assumption in the perception that Mildred had to become 'more victim of circumstances than a sinner' is that people in the lower classes are somehow active in the production of their misfortunes. It follows that an audience would be expected to have less sympathy for Mildred if she were portrayed as a crude lower-class woman whose daughter murdered her husband.

A second studio assumption is that the traits of the lower classes would interfere with the clear delivery of the murder story. They complicate the meanings in the film by making character motivation and desires more complex than entertainment can afford. For example, the novel establishes a socio-economic distinction between the locales of Glendale and Pasadena. Wealthy Pasadena matrons treat Mildred with disdain. Monte's patronising pet name for her successful restaurant business is 'that Pie Wagon' (1941: 154). Veda abhors the house in Glendale and Mildred's working life. Monte refuses to live in Glendale after he and Mildred marry. Mildred is uncomfortable at social events with people above her class. In the film, Veda's loathing of Mildred's working life ('everything that smells of grease') is offered as another marker of her villainy. She fakes pregnancy to extort money to escape 'this shack with its cheap furniture' and 'this town and its dollar days and women that wear uniforms and men that wear overalls'. Despite their economic rise, for Veda, Mildred will 'never be anything but a common frump, whose father lived over a grocery store and whose mother took in washing'. The adaptation of *Mildred Pierce* needed to focus on the murder, not on the details of Mildred's struggle for class mobility. The montage sequences of Mildred's job search and the benefits to Kay and Veda of her ever-growing bank balance efficiently acknowledged economic barriers and material conditions while avoiding depiction of Mildred's life as a working mother. For the studio, Mildred's rise in class was made easier on audiences because the adaptation situated her on the edge of the middle class.

Thirdly, the studio's need for cleaning up Mildred suggests a perception that audiences and characters shared identities. Perhaps the studio considered the audience for the Hollywood film to be broadly middle class, and thus the studio redesigned Mildred to be broadly middle class herself. Perhaps the studio understood the audience for the film to be heterogeneous (urban, suburban and rural; uptown, downtown and ghetto; upper class, middle class and working class; male, female and of every ethnicity). Thus, the demographics of the heterogeneous audience might better engage with a broadly middle-class woman character than with one restricted to the lower classes.

As with the redesign of Mildred's character, the rationale for changing Veda's singing abilities from a talent with opera to exploitative music hall performance derives from perceptions of the relationship between morality and class. For the studio, lowbrow music was more effective than opera for retaining narrative clarity and encouraging audience sympathy for Mildred. Chapman explains that Veda singing in Wally's juke joint 'was more in character with her villainous role' (1949b) and allowed the film to avoid the highbrow music of the Cain novel. Producer Wald was afraid audiences would not respond favourably to opera. Replacing Veda's operatic talent with only passable singing was intended to underscore her villainy and reduce the complexity of her character. This reasoning suggests several studio assumptions about music culture and the audience for *Mildred Pierce*. That the Hollywood film audience might not appreciate or respond to the high-art music implied by opera was a risk the studio did not wish to take. Concurrent with the fear that audiences would find opera off-putting, the studio asked the film audience to recognise the entertainment of the lower classes as a signifier for the downward slide of a character. Veda's passion and talent for opera from the novel were 'saving graces' (Chapman 1949a) and thus incompatible with 'her villainous role' in the film (1949b).

The adaptation of *Mildred Pierce* presented the music culture of the lower classes as vulgar, allowing Veda to be punished through irony. As she sings on the stage at Wally's for an audience of howling sailors, she is shown up – for her elitism, for her nouveau riche affectations, for her ingratitude and for her undeserved class rise. This narrative economy places Veda in a cheesy bar where she is leered at, her agonised mother looking on. Warner Bros. explained how presenting Veda's fall in this way encouraged moral interpretation through narrative causality. The scene in the bar 'threw sympathy to Mildred, for the audience was bound to sympathise with a mother whose daughter deliberately and recklessly left her home to engage in such a vocation' (ibid.). An assumption that guided the studio's argument is that signifiers in the *mise-en-scène* and narrative causality could direct the audience of *Mildred Pierce* to empathise with Mildred's motherly emotions. Veda's choice of music was designed to support and underscore sympathy for Mildred. Wald argued that audience sympathy might be lost for Mildred if Veda had operatic talent and ability. He therefore insisted that Veda become a singer in 'a low dive' (ibid.). As the heroine and the centre of the film, Mildred was protected from uncomfortable class attributes and audiences were encouraged to understand her predicament. For Veda's character, on the other hand, the murder was another in a string of bad decisions made by an incorrigible and ungrateful daughter. While the PCA approved the scene in the bar, censors expressed concern about the details, asking the studio to take care with Veda's costume, the song lyrics and dialogue that described her as singing a 'hot number' (Breen 1944).

In addition to clarifying character relationships and guiding audiences through the meanings of a film, limited character traits encouraged a logical conclusion to the narrative. In the resolution of *Mildred Pierce*, the last flashback reveals the murderer to be Veda. Returning to the frame story, the police arrest her, and a reunited Mildred and Bert leave the halls of justice, as day dawns. All of these elements were carefully and redundantly motivated.

Of all the characters in the novel, 'Monte was selected as the [murder] victim because he deserved it' (Chapman 1949b). The adaptation motivated the murder, provided several suspects and redundantly ensured that Monte deserved his fate, due to his defects as a person. Chapman's summary singled out two motivations introduced by the adaptation: 'We introduced a scene in which Mildred Pierce openly buys him as a husband, and further made him responsible for Mildred's losing her business' (1949a). Thus, the adaptation attempted to build audience understanding of the depths of Monte's degeneracy, in terms of moral and narrative clarity.

While Veda's criminal potential was thoroughly established through her character traits, the adaptation used several strategies to make the reconciliation between Mildred and Bert appear plausible and logical. First, Mildred's 'affair with Wally was dropped' (ibid.). This elimination prevented intimations of immorality that might have interfered with Mildred's reunion with Bert and it also streamlined the number of her potential suitors. Secondly, Bert makes occasional appearances in Mildred's life throughout the film 'so that the audience could feel, when the end of the film was shown, that there was a real basis for Mildred and her husband Bert to find happiness together' (ibid.). Finally, Monte's death leaves Mildred a widow and thereby removes Bert's only competition for Mildred's affections, thus 'prepar[ing] the way for the implied reconciliation between Mildred and Bert with which we closed our picture' (Chapman 1949b).

To ensure successful cinematic entertainment, the adaptation of *Mildred Pierce* worked from established conventions of Hollywood storytelling. As Chapman put it, 'All the characters [in the novel], including Mildred, were unpleasant. It is well known that in a successful motion picture the audience must be able to identify itself with the interests of certain good characters as against certain bad ones' (1949a). The flashback structure and murder engendered dramatic intensity and suspense, and also required refinements in characters. Immoral characters (Veda, Monte) were given well-articulated villainy and suitable punishments, while audience sympathy for Mildred and for her reconciliation with Bert was encouraged.

The poster advertising for *Mildred Pierce* shows that the studio focused on the murder mystery to entice audiences to the film: 'Don't tell anyone what she did!' was the tagline, with a drawing of a woman holding a smoking gun. The promotion of a film can be revealing about its value for the studio. The *Mildred Pierce* press book touted the film's high production values, the stellar performance of its lead and especially the murder. The studio clearly saw in *Mildred Pierce* an opportunity for promoting the expertise of Warner Bros. within the film industry and for engaging audiences through genre. The poster campaign focused on film noir – to the exclusion of the woman's film – and was punctuated by an appeal to the entertainment value of suspense: 'Please don't tell anyone what she did! We know our patrons will thank us if no one is seated during the last 7 minutes. No One Seated During Last Seven Minutes!' This promise of thrills and sensation continued in the nearly ubiquitous reminder that *Mildred Pierce* was an adaptation of the Cain novel. The studio-prepared advertising contained a small drawing in which a book lays open, steam rising from its pages: 'from the daring book by James M. Cain!' or 'from that sizzling best-seller' (see Haralovich 1997).

Through murder genre requirements for narrative clarity and character, the unambiguous morality safeguarded by Production Code self-censorship became compatible with the needs of cinematic entertainment. These dramatic and self-censorship concerns intersected with studio perceptions about audiences for film. *Mildred Pierce* demonstrates how the adaptation proceeded from several assumptions: that Hollywood audiences and films share values, attitudes and expectations about characters and narrative logic; that class attributes can be managed and manipulated to elicit audience sympathies in profound ways – class attributes can pull audiences towards characters, or distance audiences from characters; that the meanings of a film are embedded in the moral and social consequences implied by narrative causality and character relations. As characters, it turns out in the end, Mildred Pierce and her daughter onscreen were written by the studio process itself.

Notes

1 This character's name is spelled 'Monte' in the published screenplay and 'Monty' in the novel.

2 The MPPDA was the Motion Picture Producers and Distributors of America, founded in 1922.

3 Generous excerpts from the Warner Bros. production files on *Mildred Pierce* can be found in Behlmer 1985: 254–61.

17

Playing House: Screen Teens and the Dreamworld of Suburbia

NATHAN HOLMES

These offices, furnished rooms, saloons, big city streets, stations, and factories are ugly, incomprehensible, and hopelessly sad. Or rather, they were, or
seemed to be, until the advent of film. The cinema then exploded this entire
prison-world with the dynamite of its fractions of a second, so that now we can
take extended journeys of adventure between their widely scattered ruins.
– Walter Benjamin 1999a: 17

One of the (many) memorable moments from Robert Zemeckis's *Back to the Future*
(1985) occurs as Marty McFly (Michael J. Fox), still elated from his travel through
time and not really sure where he is, stumbles upon the yet un-built housing development in which he now (much later) lives. Stopping his time-machine/De Lorean
in the middle of a country road he jumps out and, in a craning aerial shot, is shown
standing in front of the concrete gates to 'Lyon Estates'. Earlier in the film, Marty
was shown skateboarding through these very same gates on his way home from
school in an aerial view that this shot explicitly matches. The gates he confronts
now, however, lead to only a dirt road, some construction equipment and an empty
field that stretches away to the horizon. A billboard next to the gates shows a man,
a woman, a boy and a girl outside one of the homes soon to be erected there:
'Live in the House of Tomorrow … Today! Ground Breaking this Winter.' The model
domicile on the billboard is, in fact, an exact representation of the one Marty lives
in with his family in 1985.

The narrative function of this scene is to provide a cue that Marty has travelled
back in time. The viewer, of course, privileged – unlike Marty – to know the title of
this story, might already suspect what has happened here. Knowing the plot does
not lessen the power of the moment, however. Marty is confronted with the physical presence of his past: that these gates through which he 'later' so unthinkingly
glides homeward 'once' led (i.e., now lead) to open space; that the place he calls
home 'once' existed (is now reduced) to mere *real estate*.

The scene is doubly powerful because we have already met Marty's family and
seen the inside of that perfect house promised on the billboard. Around a dinner

table crammed with junk food, Marty's homely sister Linda (Wendie Jo Sperber) pines for boys; his brother Dave (Marc McClure) prepares to rush off to work at a fast food restaurant; his mother Lorraine (Lea Thompson), a frumpy alcoholic, smokes and reminisces about her romantic coupling with Marty's father (Crispin Glover), a skinny geek in horn-rimmed glasses who, at the opposite end of the table and never in the same frame, is too distracted by a rerun of *The Honeymooners* to respond to his wife's queries. Each member of this suburban nuclear family seems self-interested, on a private trajectory, and the family itself is atomised. While not lacking affective bonds, the McFly family is fragmented and anomic, an aggregation of people who are talking but not really listening. Lorraine's nostalgia serves only to highlight the dinner as an empty dream. Like so many other families in 1985, the McFlys seem to be on the brink of divorce, not because George and Lorraine harbour any ill will towards each other but because anything else might be better than marriage in this time and place.[1]

The promise once made to the McFlys, the film asks us to imagine, comes in the form of this putative 'House of Tomorrow', both a wink to the spectator (since the 'tomorrow' of the past is the present we have already seen) and an accurate replication of the promises made to middle-class families during the height of sub-urban development in the United States. As the nuclear family of the billboard looks on, they are promised their future: a domicile that will enclose them together, solidifying and securing the family bond against the torrents of modern life. While *Back to the Future* makes no real pretence to social critique, it does ask us to consider, in this scene, the unfulfilled dream of American suburban life. The past that Marty confronts on the billboard is an alternative – perhaps a forgotten – future.

Cinema has offered numerous mediations on suburban life. Standouts (canonical, non-canonical, should-be-canonical, soon-to-be-canonical and never-to-be-canonical) include: King Vidor's *The Crowd* (1928) (where a suburban home is seen only in advertisements and in the fantasies of the protagonist), Max Ophuls' *The Reckless Moment* (1949, remade in 2001 as *The Deep End*), Douglas Sirk's *All That Heaven Allows* (1955), Leo McCarey's *Rally 'Round the Flag Boys* (1958), John Erman's *Making It* (1971), Michael Ritchie's *Smile* (1975), Bryan Forbes' *The Stepford Wives* (1975, remade in 2004), Michael Ritchie's *The Bad News Bears* (1976, remade in 2005), Amy Heckerling's *Fast Times at Ridgemont High* (1982), Tobe Hooper's *Poltergeist* (1982), Steven Spielberg's *E.T.: The Extra-Terrestrial* (1982), Tim Hunter's *River's Edge* (1986), Allan Moyle's *Pump Up the Volume* (1990), Tim Burton's *Edward Scissorhands* (1990), Richard Linklater's *Dazed and Confused* (1993), Ang Lee's *The Ice Storm* (1997), Sam Mendes' *American Beauty* (1999), Sofia Coppola's *The Virgin Suicides* (1999), Larry Clark's *Bully* (2001) and Andrew Jarecki's *Capturing the Friedmans* (2003), among many others. The suburbs onscreen have sometimes been a barely foregrounded location, other times an expressionistic backdrop, and often the stage upon which middle-class anxiety, desire, perversity, frustration and alienation are performed. Rarely considered, however, are the suburbs as a landscape comprehensible in itself, a place that affects people and experience, a place that is actually *lived in*. But this relative invisibility of the suburbs is something to be reckoned with. They determine experience in some way, yet are not shown to be determining; they are a shared experience rarely circulated as one.

The suburbs are often represented in films excessively or ironically in an attempt at 'postmodern' referentiality in broad, flippant strokes that resemble the billboard in *Back to the Future*. *American Beauty* typifies this approach: even as it attempts to sketch the breakdown of the family in relation to suburban life in discrete psychological sketches, it condescendingly exaggerates the psychic landscape of the suburbs as a surface of roses and picket fences, a dream-world which masks and stifles desire and which is identical to typical commercial presentations of suburbia (on billboards; in developers' brochures; in magazine layouts); and also displays the suburbs as a horror. A quick scan of academic volumes in the section on suburbs in my university library suggests that suburbia really is a horror for many: *The End of Innocence, Suburban Backlash, Creeping Conformity, Troubled Suburbs, Trouble in Paradise*.[2] Suburbia, in short, has come to represent a mass-produced sameness, an utterly failed utopian project.

A dream of family has failed, too; above everything, suburbia was constructed for the family. Indeed, the suburbs have become the fullest architectonic expression of what Lawrence Stone names 'the closed, domesticated, nuclear family'. Prior to the emergence of merchant capitalism, Stone points out that

> members of the nuclear family were subordinated to the will of its head, and were not closely bonded to each other by warm affective ties. They might well feel closer to other members of the kin, to fellow members of a guild, or to friends and neighbors of the same sex whom they met daily in an ale house. (In Fishman 1987: 33)

Robert Fishman writes that the increasing autonomy and longevity brought on by capitalism intensified relations between family members, strengthening emotional bonds between husband and wife, and between father, mother and child. This was a family 'closed in around itself, separated from its environment, focused especially on mutual intimacy and on child raising' (1987: 34). In tension with this new kind of family, however, is the modern metropolis. According to Fishman, 'just as the traditional urban ecology was unable to cope with the demands of urban growth, so the traditional urban form and domestic architecture were contrary to the needs of the new family' (ibid.). In the suburbs, safely away from the dangers and distractions of the modern city, the bourgeois household could freely work on forging intimate bonds.

The naturalisation of the family as an emotional nexus requires eliding the material economic and industrial forces (the automotive industry, for example) that led people to migrate away from the urban core and emphasising the unity and natural genetic affinity of family members for one another. In aspiring towards, and indeed constructing, a segregated pastoral existence, suburbia mystifies the capitalist function of its inhabitants, primarily through space and distance. Walter Benjamin writes of the urban bourgeois interior:

> The private individual, who in the office has to deal with realities, needs the domestic interior to sustain him in his illusions. This necessity is all the more pressing since he has no intention of grafting onto his business interests a clear perception of his social function. In the arrangement of his private surroundings, he suppresses both of these concerns. From this derive the phantasmagorias of the Interior – which, for the private individual, represents the universe. (1999b: 19)

In suburbia, I would argue, the exterior, now protected by distance from the threatening forces of urban life, also assumes the phantasmagoric quality described by Benjamin. House fronts and back yards are arranged as a universe to sustain the many illusions of property ownership: dominance and control over a parcel of land (through fencing and landscaping), an entitlement to privacy (achieved with blinds covering the windows; hedgerows and other plantations) and individual autonomy and independence (freedom to repaint the house in different colours; or to face both its surfaces and grounds with decorative stones). Both interior and exterior are expressed through an arrangement that disguises the social functions of the patriarch, wife/mother and children (the reproduction of labour, for example). The suburbs themselves become a sort of extension of this design, protected by distance from the lower classes. Suburbia, Fishman argues, is 'a natural world of greenery and family life that appeared to be wholly separate from the great city yet was in fact wholly dependent on it' (1987: 134).

In that the house separated from society played no small part in *constituting* the modern, twentieth-century family, we might also say that it encouraged people to *play* at being a family. This is particularly evident in the years following World War Two when large-scale housing developments became the primary option for a majority of Americans. A housing shortage after the war meant that people were 'doubled up with relatives, friends and strangers', and that 'war workers and veterans lived in rooming houses and camped out in cars' (Hayden 2003: 131). To a wartime society unused to atomised living arrangements and the social formation appropriate to them, an idea of 'family' as shown in the spheres of advertising for consumer goods or on television programmes like *The Adventures of Ozzie & Harriet* (1952–66) or *Father Knows Best* (1954–60) was something that had to be re-learned and thus played with. While mass culture provided normative cultural models for family, it was in fact in the suburban home, as much as in the television studio or the sandbox, that 'playing house' assumed its most important, if not complex, rehearsals.

As Benjamin surmises, cinema is the prism through which we make sense of modern spaces (1999a). Cinema is in a position, then, to show us suburbia and render it comprehensible, but instead it operates comedically, as in Joe Dante's *The 'Burbs* (1989); expressionistically, as in *Edward Scissorhands*; or by naturalising the suburbs as *the* ineluctable location of middle-class life. Exceptions to this rule, where the suburbs are presented as a particular and historically specific space, can be found in some relatively few instances, for example in a pair of Michael Ritchie's films from the 1970s, *Smile*, a funny and affectionate episodic story about a beauty pageant in a Californian town, and *The Bad News Bears*, another California-set story revolving around a little-league team; and in *Poltergeist*, where a family's house is terrorised by supernatural forces because it is built on a Native American gravesite. In *E.T.: The Extra-Terrestrial* the suburbs are depicted – particularly as the viewer takes on the subjective point of view of E.T. – as large and menacing; eventually, it is the teenagers' knowledge of the labyrinthine byways of their housing development that allows them to evade capture by the police. In *Bully*, teenagers' lives are shown to transpire on green lawns beside suburban shopping plazas, and to end, violently, in the empty swampland behind these plazas. In these films, suburbia plays a role of thematic importance and is also photographed poetically. The space which for so much of contemporary society has been considered a lost cause and devoid of meaning is, in these films, invigorated.

To explore this idea further, particularly for an improved understanding of the relationship between the social construction of family and the social space of suburbia, I will consider two films: Nicholas Ray's *Rebel Without a Cause* (1955) and Jonathan Kaplan's *Over the Edge* (1979). One film is a major work, known primarily for its iconic presentation of James Dean as Jim Stark (a presentation that in today's image economy persists in connoting rebellion, youth and the 1950s generally (see Slocum 2005)), and the other, a little-known cult hit on the basis of only a limited release, is about the revolt of young people in a planned housing development. *Rebel Without a Cause* may not appear to have much to do with suburbia, *Over the Edge* not to have much to do with family; but both of these films are complex filmic responses to ideas about family and home. Specifically, I will closely analyse key scenes that depict groups of characters temporarily inhabiting abandoned houses. The abandoned structures not only give respite from the drama occurring outside them but also say something about the relation between individuals and groups, families in particular and the spaces that are built for them to dwell in.

Rebel Without a Cause and the Spaces of Teenage Play

It would be difficult to overstate the importance of *Rebel Without a Cause* in cinematic history and the history of popular culture. The mass-produced image of James Dean insouciantly smoking a cigarette in a red cotton windbreaker, t-shirt, jeans and black boots is as well known as images of Marilyn Monroe and Elvis

Presley, even outside the circuits of youth, gay and baby-boomer image economies within which it commonly circulates (with different meanings). At a time when the newly invented category of 'teenager' was still coming to be understood by American society at large (see Doherty 2002), *Rebel Without a Cause* offered grandiose cinematic expression to young people's alienation. This grandiosity was achieved, technically, through the use of Twentieth Century Fox's relatively new anamorphic lens system, CinemaScope. In that CinemaScope was typically reserved for 'A' features, *Rebel Without a Cause* was telegraphed to audiences as an important picture from the beginning. The characters and scenarios were afforded a status, not to mention a magnitude, on par with those of Henry Koster's *The Robe* (1953), Vincente Minnelli's *Brigadoon* (1954) or Howard Hawks's *Land of the Pharoahs* (1955). The film therefore plays the pivotal role of launching the teenager into the cultural imagination of the 1950s (and, as we have now seen, beyond) and gives dramatic weight to forms of juvenile delinquency – knife fights, car culture – that had previously been reserved for 'B' features. Through cinema, *Rebel Without a Cause* commands that the teenager be seen and at the same time shapes the teenager into a cinematic presence.

The social alienation depicted in the film is seen through the breakdown of nuclear families residing far from the urban core of Los Angeles – 'a bunch of suburbs in search of a city', as we hear in *He Walked by Night* (1948) (see Dimendberg 2004: 29). In the case of Jim Stark (Dean), it is the inability of his parents to give him direction that drives his confusion and his movement towards delinquency. His parents are 'tearing [him] apart', first saying one thing and then another, encouraging and then discouraging his behaviour. In short, they lack the solid foundation of morality desperately sought by Jim: his father (Jim Backus) encourages him to draw up a 'pros and cons' chart to make a decision that Jim sees in terms of clear absolutes. This lack is displayed primarily through the feminisation of Jim's father, who appears, famously, on his hands and knees at the top of the stairs adorned in a frilly apron, hastily cleaning up a spilled tray of food before his wife (Ann Doran) can see. Jim implores his father to stand up to his mother and let her see the mess, but soon resigns in frustration and abject disappointment (see Pomerance 2005b). The key moment in this family breakdown occurs after Jim returns home from the 'chickie run' that kills Buzz (Corey Allen). For most of the scene, Jim and his parents are poised on the landing, and the stairs come to represent a path to a higher morality. Jim, towering in the frame, moves upwards as he announces that he is going to go to the police to inform them of his role in Buzz's death. His mother, however, blocks him and, as the camera angle cants, he is once again at the lower point of a triangle, bracketed in by his parents. As his mother announces that none of it matters anyway because 'We're moving!' she ascends herself, reversing the valence of the stairs from 'higher morality' to 'evasion'. When his father cannot stand up to her to defend the intentions of his son, Jim descends to the landing once again to violently grab his father by the collar of his housecoat. Oedipal conflict looms as his mother yells, in an insert shot, 'You want to kill your own father!' Jim runs out. 'There are few other directors', V. F. Perkins has noted of Nicholas Ray, 'who have as great an appreciation of the suggestive powers of décor and locale' (1976: 253). Here, Ray gives the neatly arranged surfaces of the middle-class interior expressive weight through CinemaScope framing. A see-saw effect occurs whereby conflict is registered through low-angle shots of different characters dominating from positions at the top of the wide frame. When the camera angle cants it seems as if, suddenly, the stairs no longer ascend but lead off laterally so that any movement upon them now seems futile.

The triangulation of characters in this scene is matched in a subsequent scene with Jim and Judy (Natalie Wood) followed by Plato (Sal Mineo) playfully, and temporarily, inhabiting an abandoned mansion and 'playing house' there. The haven is nestled in protective greenery, suggesting a proximity to the Hollywood Hills. Appearing at the bottom of a grand staircase, and taking on the role of a real-estate agent, Plato lights candles and leads Jim and Judy, who are taking on the roles of husband and wife, through the(ir new dream) house. This play routine is first a satiric caricature of 'adult concerns' (such as property and money), but soon turns into a skit about children. 'We really don't encourage them', Plato says, loftily, still playing the agent, 'They're so noisy and troublesome.' Leading Jim and Judy outside, he points out the 'nursery' – an empty swimming pool. In turn, it is they who play in the pool like children, running around hilariously, Jim pretending to stay 'underwater' and Judy dumping a bucket of real water onto him. This particular sequence ends with the trio converging in the gazebo on a lounge chair. Here, a layering of bodies – Jim's head on Judy's lap, Plato at Jim's side – depicts a physical proximity and harmony unseen in any of these characters' home lives. Indeed, these affective bonds might seem to implicitly connote family: Judy mothers Jim and sings Plato a lullaby as he falls asleep; later, alone with Jim by a fire, she proclaims her love for him again and again.

This reverie is disturbed as Plato is awakened by Buzz's gang, who chase him around the pool. Grabbing a gun he stole from his parent's house, Plato escapes into the house and shoots one of the gang members before he is wrestled to the ground by Jim. Plato flees the house, shouting, 'Why did you leave me?' and 'You're not my father!' To re-emphasise the preceding moments as filial, Judy, hiding out with Jim in the bushes, recounts to Jim that Plato was talking to her about him as if he 'was the hero in the China Sea' (an earlier reference Plato had made to his father). Jim replies, 'You know what he wanted? He tried to make us his family. I guess he just wanted us to be like his...' Jim stops short of saying 'parents'.

The creation of the social category of 'teenager', related as it is to a definable age rather than explicitly to race, class or career, involves, in 1955, a negative definition. Without the full weight of a youth culture through which they might positively identify – a culture about, for and because of a mass youth audience; a culture that would take shape over many years *after* this film – the characters in *Rebel Without a Cause*, who do not yet have the privilege of watching people like themselves onscreen in the full grandeur of CinemaScope, must define themselves and be defined in terms of simultaneously not being adults and not being children.[3] They must instead deal with both residual and anticipated social identities. As they play house on the stage of an abandoned suburban mansion, their in-between-ness becomes clearly registered if not for themselves then at least for the viewer: they play both at being adults and at being children, never fully comfortable in either role. In that they can play at being adults, they are still children, but in that Judy can say to Jim, 'I love someone', over and over as they lie by the fire, she is very much thinking like (and therefore being) an adult by identifying her desires through the vocabulary of romance. The struggle of Jim, Judy and Plato is a struggle for self-constitution in a world that suddenly notices them. But notices them as what, exactly?

Being seen is not the same as *being* (even if being is more a feeling than something more constitutive). If Jim, Judy and Plato's interactions in the mansion represent, as Murray Pomerance argues, affective relations and sexuality un-registered in a contemporary schema of 'economic and military organisation of kinship towards child-production, socialisation, and marketable labour' (2005b: 49), that is, as relations outside the scope of their – and perhaps our – immediate understanding, then we must understand that it is, in the end, the fact of being away from the downtown core in this house, the solid construction and spatial signification of which both initiate their play and sustain a feeling of bondedness – 'He wanted you to be his...' – that makes what occurred in the house something like 'family'. Even if the layering of desire and cross-hatching gazes we see onscreen constitutes something that exceeds the frame of filial relations, it must be recuperated later by Judy as a re-constitution of family so that the sins of unfocused longing may be expiated and she may move towards something more tangible (parenthood).

To play house is to relate to a space, and to take on – or rather, play – a role deemed appropriate to this space. Far from becoming deterministic, however, this space merely allows for a play that momentarily (perhaps even restrictively) frees agents within it. Yet when we talk about cinema, to say 'space' is to refer to a sense of diegetic space created by set design, background, props and lighting: an illusion of space. Although the abandoned mansion has a clear geographical location within the diegesis of *Rebel Without a Cause*, it is still very much a place that exists in abstraction, almost a type of illusion. It is, therefore, foregrounded in a way, *as* a set, becoming a mythic locale. Like the Griffith Observatory it is shown as being planted in the hills high above the rest of Los Angeles and so takes on almost superterrestrial qualities (in fact, the filming location was further away). Both edifices exist away from, though not completely outside of, the domains of school, authority and family. They are spaces of refuge and imagination. Moreover, the abandoned mansion is contradistinguished from the middle-class homes of the principal teens. Instead of containing the power struggles, confusions, repressions, anxieties and – for Plato specifically – the disinvestment of modern families, the mansion, in its aura of the aristocratic and eternal, sanctions a momentary release of pent-up nervous energies. This abstraction of setting is necessary in order that the characters' alienation, their contradictory impulses (to both satirise family and think of themselves as family), be brought to centre-stage. The source of their frustrations is clearly located in their homes, with their parents – for all of them, a very different kind of place. It is the family exactly – its neglect for Plato, its sudden lack of affection for Judy, its overindulgence and absent morality for Jim – that tears these teens apart. And so there is something frustrating in the characters' casting of their mansion experience as a reconstitution of family.

That *Rebel Without a Cause* could not account for the myriad reasons that these characters felt marginalised is no fault of the film itself. It is a film, after all, which first and foremost asks us to see the teenager as a social being who is the effect of the modern family. It premiered just as suburban development was at its height; with the help of federally subsidised mortgages and highway development, a middle-class exodus from the metropolis in the 1950s – 'white flight' – redefined the urban landscape of mid-twentieth century America. While the residential West Los Angeles setting of *Rebel Without a Cause* is surely categorically 'suburban', in that it surrounds a more densely populated urban core, it lacks the mass-produced homogeneity now associated with the pan-American phenomenon of 'suburbia' proper. As this transformation was taking hold, the post-World War Two 'baby boomer' generation was anticipating its teenage years. Just as a mass audience was coming of age, therefore, so too was housing becoming mass-produced. In the film, however, these parallel developments would seem to be unrelated. For a film that so implicitly uses space to structure its drama – the mythic interiors and exteriors of the observatory, the distance of the chickie run, the shadowy decay of the mansion – there are relatively few references to the contemporary built forms that would come to define the spaces of youth experience, what Vivian Sobchack might call the 'material premises' of youth (1998: 130).[4]

Over the Edge and the Suburban Landscape

Since *Rebel Without a Cause*, the trope of the abandoned house has been revisited many times, particularly in films related to youth culture. This is seen in obscure teen comedies like *Making It*, where the protagonist attempts to woo a girl with a candlelit dinner in an abandoned trailer home, to one of the first episodes of the popular teen television drama *The O.C.* (2003–07) where an abandoned mansion temporarily occupied by one of the main characters is accidentally set on fire. Even Bernardo Bertolucci's *The Dreamers* (2003) featured a trio of rebellious, cinephilic youths holed up in a decaying Paris apartment, a faint echo of *Rebel Without a Cause*'s trio in their decaying mansion. It is in *Over the Edge* however, a teen drama from the late 1970s, that both a true homage and reconfiguration of *Rebel*'s abandoned-house motif are played out.

Over the Edge was never released theatrically across North America, but showed briefly in New York and Colorado and won the Outstanding Film Award at the 1979 London Film Festival; it was seen more widely when it was shown, repeatedly, on HBO in 1981. Its first image shows a billboard that reads, 'Welcome to New Granada Tomorrow's City ... Today'.[5] Beneath the text are four icons: a sun, a sailboat, a group of pine trees and a roller skate. Zooming out, the camera reframes to reveal an empty intersection and a row of roofs lining the horizon. As the opening guitar chords of Cheap Trick's 'Speak Now or Forever Hold Your Peace' play on the soundtrack, text scrolls up the screen:

In 1978 110,000 kids under 18 were arrested for crimes of vandalism in the United States.

This story is based on true incidents occurring during the 70s in a planned suburban community of condominiums and townhomes, where city planners ignored the fact that a quarter of the population was 15 years old or younger.

The true incidents referred to here are a youth crime spree and riot that took place in Foster City, California in the early 1970s.

The film itself is primarily a picaresque tale revolving around Carl (Michael Kramer) and his friends Richie (Matt Dillon), Claude (Tom Fergus), Claude's mute brother Johnny (Tiger Thompson), Cory (Pamela Ludwig) and Abby (Kim Kliner). In the opening sequence, the 'rec' centre, a corrugated steel hangar with pool tables, foosball and couches, is closing for the day and the kids are kicked out. Discussing the merits of KISS and of various girls, the principal boys exit the centre and are passed in a car by Cory, who coolly blows cigarette smoke and stares into space. Crossing the street, the boys move from the dirt lot of the centre to the manicured lawns of the townhouses on the other side. This sharp contrast between developed real estate and undeveloped land is a recurring motif, and a boundary traversed by the characters throughout the film. *Over the Edge* chronicles the day-to-day activities of these teens: going to house parties, drinking and doing drugs, the monotony of high-school classrooms, extended walks across empty fields and dirt roads. As the film progresses, the characters' activities – mostly different forms of vandalism and drug use – increasingly draw the attention of the police. The concern of the community escalates after Richie uses a gun to terrorise a drug dealer for snitching on Claude and then later, when Richie is shot and killed by Officer Doberman (Harry Northup) after he pulls the gun on him. The climax of the film occurs as a mass of kids converge in the school's parking lot while inside their parents, who have been called to a community meeting, fruitlessly debate what should be done about the 'youth problem'. Locked in the 'cafetorium', the parents, teachers and officials are forced to stare in horror as the kids stage a frenzy of destruction. Classrooms are trashed, windows are smashed, guns are shot and cars are blown up. The film ends with Carl being loaded with other kids onto a school bus with barred windows that is presumably bound for 'the hill' (a juvenile detention centre referred to often in the story). Cory, Claude and Johnny wave at him from an overpass as the bus sweeps by underneath.

The film's particular cinematographic style helps to transcend the blunt 'realism' often associated with communicating a social message as well as to distinguish it from being just another sex and drugs 'teensploitation' flick. Like *Rebel Without a Cause*, *Over the Edge* is both a product of its time and an exemplary aesthetic achievement. Whereas the earlier film uses locations to connote mythical qualities, *Over the Edge* stresses the more poetic qualities of modern landscape, a landscape of empty lots and fields, highways and viaducts, modular architecture and half-built houses. This is achieved through Andrew Davis's naturalistic photography, a mode clearly influenced by the soft-focus and sun-dappled effects first practised by cinematographers like Conrad Hall and Nestor Almendros in the mid-1960s. The characters in this film walk through a landscape that is designed to be moved through rapidly, a landscape built for cars. Often visible in the background is the multi-lane highway that passes by New Granada. The camera, often stationary, mirrors a perception that comprehends space at walking speed. The perceptual mode that is simulated here thus contradicts the modern visual experience produced by the rapid movement across space in trains and automobiles (what Wolfgang Schivelbusch calls 'panoramic perception' (see 1977: 52–69)). It is a mode that also penetrates the suburban spectacle and its empty spaces – spaces often only just moved through – to show how the suburbs really are for those who inhabit them, and what they look like.

In the first of two scenes that take place in the unfinished interior of a condo, Carl and Richie have invited Cory and Abby to hang out and be shown around. They have outfitted a space among the framed, but unplastered, walls for themselves with a rug, an old mattress, a bean-bag chair, a tape player and, curiously, a poster of Vermeer's 'The Milk Maid'. Throughout the scene, and unlike what we see in *Rebel Without a Cause*, the characters are rarely in the same frame. Family is never explicitly mentioned, but it is a formation that is subtly rejected. When Carl asks Cory out on a date, she says, 'I don't go out on dates.' Asked what she does do, she replies, 'Just see my friends.' Mentioning that they also stole some shells with the gun, the quartet plans to hold 'target practice' in the field the next day. 'Have a Sunday picnic!' Carl exclaims. 'Alright, a picnic with a gun!' says Cory, who grabs the gun and, to the beat of Cheap Trick's 'Surrender' playing on the tape player, runs into the adjacent room and starts to dance around, playing air guitar with the weapon. Carl gazes at her adoringly, even as she begins to wave the gun at him, while Richie and Abby exchange puzzled glances. Then as Cory waves the gun in circles in front of Carl, BANG. A gunshot. Carl falls to the floor and the music stops. As the group rushes to his side, Carl sits up, smiles, and says 'Boo!' The teens then exit the house towards their respective homes, cutting through an expansive field.

Cory's dance with the gun is a performance that for a moment stands time still, or, at least, stops the film in its place. It is a display that mimics the surrealism of the idea of a 'picnic with a gun', an evocation of a passive pastoral pleasure combined with the potential for violent destruction. Whereas the abandoned mansion sequence in *Rebel Without a Cause* illustrates the antinomy between teenage desires and the social frameworks that contain them, this abandoned condo sequence in *Over the Edge* illustrates the ability of these 1970s kids to display their desires openly. We are skewed away from family and towards self-determination and desire. In a subsequent meeting at the house, as Carl hides out after Richie is killed by Doberman, Cory informs him that someday she'd like to become a 'gypsy of the road' (a truck driver). The next morning, a solitary truck is shown driving through New Granada. As the scene cuts to a shot of Cory watching it, the motivation for Vermeer's 'The Milk Maid' becomes clear. In the shot, Cory stands looking out towards the road, the Vermeer painting and its classic depiction of a woman's domestic role hanging on the wall where a kitchen might have been constructed. Cory is momentarily poised between an image of domesticity and a more progressive, self-determined vision of her life.

Whereas the mansion in *Rebel Without a Cause* connotes decay, the condo in *Over the Edge* connotes something unfinished, incomplete and abandoned. Even as the painting of the milk maid calls up domesticity, it does so from an empty frame of a house. Earlier, presumably looking at a developer's pamphlet she finds lying on the condo floor, Cory asks what 'European Living' means. 'It means it's always going to look bombed out like this', Carl replies. The house is hence marked as a simulacral design in an ersatz 'European' style that is never achieved, or that is achieved, following Carl's sarcastic remark, only indirectly. The unfinished condo functions as a metonym for New Granada as a whole, an unfinished project that is more accurately described as a war zone than a garden utopia. The dream of suburbia, and the dream of family, become together a hollowed out fantasy, scoffed at by the youth. Carl, like Jim Stark, eventually seems to unite with his family. In the end, just before he is shipped off to 'the hill', both his mother and father affectionately embrace him. This is a bond many of the other teens do not enjoy. Richie is parented by his mother, and no mention of a father is made. Claude and Johnny's mother exists only when he makes reference to her being at 'group' (group therapy). For the most part these are youths whose alienation from their parents is so complete that it need not even be directly illustrated. The teens are so completely othered to the adults of the community that they are dealt with primarily through abstract authoritative measures such as curfews and random closures of the 'rec' centre, and through the repressive arm of police personnel like Doberman.

Working in a style that confers heavy symbolic weight on structures, and using these structures, well, *structurally*, and in an expressive manner, *Rebel Without a Cause* uses the home without rendering it, as Benjamin would say, comprehensibly. That is, in that film we are given not an experience of the world within which the teens live but an experience of their minds, an experience that is incomprehensible both to them and to us. What is radical about *Rebel Without a Cause* is that it uses a dominant mode of image production to explore teenage alienation from the *inside*. Just as Jim's world is sideways, so too our view of his world becomes canted. Yet because these characters cannot trace why they are so frustrated, or what their 'cause' is (this will come later, in the 1960s), neither is the cause able to be shown. *Rebel Without a Cause* was shot only at the very beginning of 'white flight'. Thus the full effect of suburbanisation is only beginning to be felt. While the film clearly seems to be located in a suburban area, it cannot yet readily comment on suburbanisation as the primary setting of teenage alienation.

Over the Edge, on the other hand, can. What is remarkable about this film is that even while it levels a savage critique against the suburban order, its impressionist visual style presents the suburban landscape in an equivocal, even poetic, way. In one sequence Carl and Cory stroll through a field on a sunny day discussing where they'd like to live and why their families have moved to New Granada. The camera tracks along, catching only the upper parts of their bodies above the dry grass, a highway in the distance in view but out of focus. Cory and Carl are given cinematic space that is mediate between being away from the suburbs and being fully in them. Interesting about this and many other shots in *Over the Edge* is the way they mirror late nineteenth-century French paintings of the *banlieue*, another landscape affected by massive development.[6] The *banlieue* was the name given by Parisians to the 'curious ground between town and country' created by Haussmannisation (Clark 1984: 25). Paintings such as Vincent van Gogh's 'The Outskirts of Paris', Luigi Loir's 'La Fin de l'automne' and Jean-Francois Rafaelli's 'La Butte des chiffonniers' depict, as T. J. Clark writes in *The Painting of Modern Life*, 'the place where autumn was always ending on an empty boulevard, and the last traces of Haussmann's city – a kiosk, a lamppost, a cast-iron *pissotière* – petered out in the snow (1984: 26). The paintings of the *banlieue*, like the images in *Over the Edge*, work to remember landscapes forgotten or ignored, even to grant them a degree of sublimity.[7] Both the *banlieue* and the fields of New Granada, with its solitary lampposts and paved roads leading to nowhere, subvert the dreamed 'tomorrow' evoked by their builders to present a comprehensible and fragmented 'now'.

The ruins we take adventures through in *Rebel Without a Cause* are the ruins of the dreams of the enclosed family, separated and standing against the world. Once held as a universal concept, this dream is shown, like the mansion, to be in decay. As a performance, it breaks at the seams. In *Over the Edge*, family is already a mass-produced concept that has collapsed under its own weight. Unlike the billboard glimpsed by Marty McFly in *Back to the Future*, New Granada's promise of tomorrow consists of the iconographic symbols of leisure and lifestyle: sun, sailboats (despite there being no body of water in sight), roller skating and wilderness. Here the initial ideal of suburbia, the isolation and protection of individual families, is all but dispensed with. Family is incidental to the pursuit of naked self-interest (property values), leisure and individual development ('group' therapy).

Rebel Without a Cause performs the service of legitimising teenage extroversion by offering it as a contemporary cinematic experience like any other. In *Over the Edge* a similar kind of experience is offered, but instead of ending in a reversion to family, it ends in an awakening to collective conditions of existence. Affective bonds are formed on the basis of shared experiences; kids stick together, not families. The film, in turn, is offered as a mass-produced form back to an audience many of whom would see, in 1979 and even through the 1980s, a poetic vision of their own houses, their streets, their fields and their hideouts.

Thanks are owed to Scott Preston and Erika Balsom for their helpful suggestions and encouragement.

Notes

1   An informal survey of some acquaintances, most of whom were pre-teens in 1985, shows that over half saw their parents separate or divorce.

2   Suburban malaise was also registered in the sphere of popular music, in songs such as the Monkees' 'Pleasant Valley Sunday' (1967) and Dionne Warwick's 'Paper Maché' (1970).

3   A 1975 documentary by Ray Connolly names James Dean as 'America's first teenager'.

4   Edward Dimendberg defines America's most 'representative spatial constructions' of the postwar period as 'the freeway, the suburban house, the glass office tower, the public housing project, the superblock, and the shopping centre' (2004: 9).

5   The resemblance to the text and syntax of *Back to the Future*'s billboard is a bit uncanny, but it is unclear if the producers of that film had ever watched *Over the Edge*.

6   In France, the term *banlieue* now denotes the suburbs surrounding major cities.

7   As T. J. Clark points out, Van Gogh's 'The Mowers, Arles in the Background' is a more sympathetic and upbeat *banlieue* painting than his earlier 'Outskirts of Paris' (1984: 30).

1735-72

18

Big Daddies and the Hollywood Myth of Family Capitalism

JERRY MOSHER

> Big Daddy! Now what makes him so big? His big heart? His big belly?
> Or his big money?
> – Brick Pollitt (Paul Newman) in *Cat on a Hot Tin Roof*

When the NBC-TV Christmas special *Rudolph, the Red-Nosed Reindeer* aired to a huge national audience on 6 December 1964, Burl Ives probably had a hunch that his greatest screen acting roles were behind him. The imposing 300-pound actor who just a few years earlier lit up stage and screen as volcanic Southern patriarch Big Daddy Pollitt, hollering about 'mendacity' in Tennessee Williams' *Cat on a Hot Tin Roof* (1958), was now the gentle voice of Sam the Snowman, singing 'A Holly Jolly Christmas'. Ives, of course, had always been first and foremost a folksinger. He had gotten his big break in movies playing a singing blacksmith in the Disney film *So Dear to My Heart* (1948) but his industry blacklisting and subsequent voluntary testimony before the Senate Internal Security Committee in 1952 derailed his acting career for several years. When Ives finally returned to movie screens in March 1955 as the sheriff in *East of Eden* (hired by director and fellow friendly witness Elia Kazan), he began to display a fury not suitable for children. That same month Ives started performing the role of Big Daddy in Kazan's original Broadway production of Williams' play. For the remainder of the decade, in films such as *The Power and the Prize* (1956), *Desire Under the Elms* (1958), *The Big Country* (1958) and *Cat on a Hot Tin Roof*, Ives personified the vengeful, tyrannical patriarch who used the institutions of property and marriage to control his family, his wealth and his legacy in an increasingly corporate – and mendacious – world. After Ives won the Best Supporting Actor Academy Award in 1959 for *The Big Country*, good film roles became harder to find, paradoxically, and he drifted back to his avuncular 'amiable hayseed' persona. The studio system was disintegrating, the acting opportunities were moving to television and audiences possibly had grown weary of his gruff 'Big Daddy' routine. Ives' corpulent patriarchs, after all, were hardly beloved characters; they were bitter, isolated, manipulative old men who could no longer tell the difference between discipline and oppression.

One could not help but compare Ives' 'Big Daddy' figures to the Hollywood studio moguls themselves: fat cats who stubbornly clung to prewar models of entertainment while postwar profits, and their own livelihoods, quickly disappeared in the 1950s. When former MGM head of production Louis B. Mayer died in October 1957, obituaries proclaimed it was the end of an era; within nine months, during the height of Ives' fame, Paramount founder Jesse L. Lasky, longtime Columbia production chief Harry Cohn, and Warner Bros. patriarch Harry M. Warner had died as well. Their deaths marked the end of the original moguls' reign in Hollywood, when flamboyant patriarchs flaunted their autonomy and nepotism, ruling their production companies like extended families. The studios' family capitalism was being supplanted by the faceless multinational corporation, personified by the lean, college-educated 'Organisation Man' – the professional manager who remained loyal only to his stockholders. Ives, an itinerant folksinger condemned as a Communist by a government witch-hunt that Mayer wholeheartedly endorsed, was an unlikely candidate to represent the studio moguls' traditional values onscreen. His distinctive 'Big Daddy' persona, which burned briefly but brightly in the cultural imaginary of the late 1950s, actually was the collaborative product of an Irish American folksinger, a Southern writer and a Greek American director, all of whom were extraordinarily sensitive to American popular myths. But in this essay I want to examine the fat-cat patriarchal figure within the larger context of Hollywood itself – an elite group of men and institutions whose values and system of production were on the verge of extinction – and trace the history that culminated, at the end of the studio system, in Ives' baroque and desperate portrayal of a dying family capitalist.

Empire

'The story of the rise and fall of social classes in Western society', wrote sociologist Daniel Bell, 'is that of the rise and fall of families' (1962: 39). Before corporations and professional managers dominated twentieth-century US business practices, the family had been the primary means by which to maintain and transfer power in American society. The social organisation of the family, Bell asserted, depended on two institutions: property and the dynastic marriage. Through the fusion of the institutions of property and family, Bell noted, 'a class system was maintained: people met at the same social levels, were educated in common schools appropriate to their wealth, shared the same manners and morals, read the same books and held similar prejudices, mingled in the same milieus – in short, created and shared a distinctive style of life' (1962: 40). The patriarch controlled the family's wealth and power and also was expected to embody it, acting as the symbolic figurehead of the family's reputation and renown. Before the modern mass media transformed public figures into small, easily exchangeable images, the appearance of power still largely depended on the aura of physical presence – the ability to convey strength, command respect and appear 'larger than life'. Substantial physical size – often in the form of ample girth – thus contributed to the patriarch's status as figurehead of the family in an era when a fat man was associated with a fat bank account.

A fat paunch, however, did not automatically convey social status; the quality and method of its accumulation – in the form of what Thorstein Veblen in 1899 termed 'conspicuous consumption' – was what truly mattered. Although Veblen did not specifically discuss body size, he extensively catalogued the ritual practice of dietary 'over-indulgence' – especially the consumption of expensive liquors and narcotics – and concluded that, 'since the consumption of these more excellent goods is an evidence of wealth, it becomes honorific; and conversely, the failure to consume in due quantity and quality becomes a mark of inferiority and demerit' (1979: 74). Popular dieting fads had already begun by the time Veblen's work appeared, but he noted that the status one gained for ceremonial displays of dietary over-indulgence far outweighed the negatives: 'the reputability that attaches to certain expensive vices long retains so much of its force as to appreciably lessen the disapprobation visited upon the men of the wealthy or noble class for any excessive indulgence' (1979: 71).

The culture of the burgeoning Hollywood movie industry was based upon these Gilded Age principles of family enterprise and conspicuous consumption. The nouveau-riche studio moguls, most of whom were Jewish immigrants from Eastern Europe, attempted to emulate the European dynasties they witnessed in their youth, while seeking to impress the gentile American power brokers whose sanction they craved. The superficial opulence of the European aristocracy was evident in their lifestyles, their business practices and the narratives they approved for production. Familial connections abounded at the executive level of studios and production companies; film historian Philip French notes that 'at one time it was calculated that there were 29 members of the Cohn family at Columbia, a dozen Schencks at Loew's, half-a-dozen relatives of Louis B. Mayer at MGM, and Paramount could almost have staged a football game between the Zukors and Balabans in its employ' (1969: 50). Each studio tended to have a patriarch – a powerful, distinctive personality such as the avuncular 'Uncle Carl' Laemmle (Universal), the pious Mayer (MGM) or the tyrannical Harry 'King' Cohn (Columbia) – who served as a father figure for the thousands of displaced employees who had migrated to Hollywood. Mayer was known for treating his actors like his own daughters, using a stern but loving manner to tell them what to eat, whom to marry and when it was time to have a baby (or abort one if it conflicted with a production schedule) (see Higham 1993: 2). Actor Robert Taylor, who would play Ives' heir apparent in the MGM corporate melodrama *The Power and the Prize*, once asked Mayer for a raise and told a friend afterwards, 'I didn't get the raise, but I gained a father' (in ibid.). Actress Lucille Ball, who had a similar experience under the tutelage of Samuel Goldwyn, noted that 'from the very beginning, the studios gave us papas' (in Berg 1989: 65). For moguls like Mayer, the conception of family (and, by extension, MGM's organisational structure and screen image) 'was nineteenth-century aristocratic, where the father was the absolute monarch, the mother his deferential help-mate, and the daughters demure, chaste, and obedient' (Gabler 1988: 107). Sons and sons-in-law were groomed for production jobs, while wives and daughters generally were sequestered in family mansions in the Hollywood hills, prohibited from fraternising with employees or entering the tawdry world of screen acting. Primogeniture was such an important concept for some studio heads that Cohn, perhaps the most despotic of the moguls, was compared to Henry VIII after divorcing his first wife 'because she couldn't have children, and he desperately wanted a son' (Gabler 1988: 247).

Maintaining family control of the business had become an obsession for the moguls as a trend towards consolidation in the 1920s led to mega-studio hyphenates such as Metro-Goldwyn-Mayer (1924) and Paramount-Famous-Lasky (1925). With each merger the number of fiefdoms was reduced, creating struggles for power within the studios and with East Coast corporate managers who gained more influence over studio production budgets. After the stock market crash in 1929, when several studios teetered on the edge of bankruptcy or fell into receivership, large-scale loans from East Coast investment banks saved several moguls' jobs but left them even more beholden to corporate overseers such as Amadeo Giannini's Bank of America. By the end of the 1920s, 200 companies controlled one-half of the nation's corporate wealth. Family enterprises were being subsumed within the modern corporation, ruled by professional managers who often had little emotional investment in their products and could not automatically pass their power to their heirs (Bell 1962: 43). In response, ensconced studio moguls espoused the principles of family enterprise not only in their studio offices and back lots but in the screen images themselves.

The importance of image and the aura of power it conveyed was not lost on these executives, some of whom had previously worked in the garment industry (Adolph Zukor had been a furrier, Goldwyn a glove manufacturer). Some executives, such as Goldwyn and Mayer, were fanatical about diet and fitness, and few were fat, even though MGM's hard-working head of production, Irving Thalberg, reportedly complained, 'Why the hell am I killing myself so Mayer and Schenck can get rich and fat?' (in Thomas 1969: 236). But almost anyone would appear fat next to the gaunt, chronically ill Thalberg, who stood five feet six inches tall and weighed only 125 pounds. Mayer, in fact, went horseback riding every morning and 'was robust and powerfully built, with a barrel chest so well muscled that he gave a mistaken impression of fat when he was anything but' (Gabler 1988: 222). Thalberg's complaint, perhaps apocryphal, nevertheless rang true; unlike the bookish boy wonder, most of the moguls cultivated fat-cat personas even as they maintained a hardened physique. This was not necessarily a contradiction; like many Americans, they had grown up poor in an era when a fat belly still signified wealth, authority and privilege. America's 'turn against fat', though a very real phenomenon, did not occur overnight; it was a gradual discursive process of cultural contestation and conflicting ideals. The conflict was evident in two advice books published by the same author in 1917: one titled *Eat and Grow Fat* and the other titled *Eat and Grow Slender*. And in 1919, a fitness programme promising a 'good figure' boasted of reducing the weight of 40,000 women and increasing the weight of 40,000 others (see Levenstein 1988: 166). Popular opinion took a decided turn towards growing slender in the 1920s, but even during the depths of the Depression when breadlines formed across the nation, charismatic fat actors like Charles Laughton, Edward Arnold and Eugene Pallette were still able to rise to stardom playing gluttonous yet sympathetic aristocrats and robber barons.

Within the executive culture of Hollywood, the fat Gilded-Age robber baron, like the European monarch, was considered a quaint anachronism, to be nostalgically resurrected and celebrated on the big screen, where he was played most notably by Edward Arnold in half a dozen pictures in the 1930s. Arnold came to prominence in 1934 as the alcoholic millionaire who marries and then loses Joan Crawford to a younger man (Gene Raymond) in MGM's *Sadie McKee*. Arnold's sympathetic but physically unattractive millionaire would establish the template for most of his characters through to the end of the decade: the ruthless fat cat who is successful in business but unlucky in love. Arnold was 44 years old by the time of *Sadie McKee* and he looked older; for the young women he pursued onscreen, however, it was not so much his age but his wide girth and gluttonous displays of conspicuous consumption that took the lustre off his wealth and authority. Courting younger leading ladies such as Joan Crawford, Frances Farmer, Jean Arthur and Binnie Barnes, Arnold could only stand back and watch in dismay as younger, thinner and better looking co-stars like Cesar Romero (*Diamond Jim* (1935)), Joel McCrea (*Come and Get It* (1936)) and Cary Grant (*The Toast of New York* (1937)), stole away with his women.

Arnold's first headlining role, as Gilded Age financier and gourmand 'Diamond Jim' Brady in Universal's biopic *Diamond Jim*, would secure his status as Hollywood's most recognisable player of business tycoons. Declaring that 'to make money you've got to look like money', the young Brady rents a suit and diamonds and bluffs his way into the railroad business, quickly becoming a captain of industry who wears pounds of jewellry and enjoys legendary feasts with singer Lillian Russell. It was the kind of rags-to-riches story – with chutzpah – that a mogul like Carl Laemmle Sr, Universal's president, could appreciate. The film, scripted by Preston Sturges, mirrored Parker Morell's fawning biography which portrayed Brady as the last of the pre-corporate tycoons and ended with this eulogy: 'The simple days of simple spending were over. The machine-age millionaire was coming into his own. There would never be another Diamond Jim' (1934: 273). The film completely evaded the disastrous consequences of its hero's Gilded Age business monopolies. Although the real Brady liquidated his stocks and sat on his money after the 1893 crash, in the film he declares, 'This ain't the time to sell; this is the time to buy ... There ain't nothin' the matter with this country except you fellas. It was built up with guts.' Even Morell was outraged by the film's factual distortions and Sturges's fanciful tragic ending (borrowed from the George Arliss stage vehicle *Old English* (1930)) in which an ill and broken-hearted Brady, thwarted in romance, sits down to a huge meal and gorges himself to death. *Diamond Jim*'s narrative trajectory would be repeated in several Arnold star vehicles during the 1930s: the fat, flamboyant industrialist cannot consummate his love and thus dies a painful, lonely death, knowing he has not produced any heirs to his enormous fortune. This – not the monopolist's destructive business practices – was the real tragedy in the eyes of the studio moguls. At the time of *Diamond Jim*'s production, Laemmle himself was losing control of the studio he had founded: in 1933 he had put Universal's theatres in receivership, and by 1935 he was forced to borrow money from the Standard Capital Company, which was threatening to exercise its option of purchasing majority control of the studio. It eventually did in March 1936, prompting Laemmle's retirement (see Balio 1993: 17).

Only Frank Capra had the power and resolve to use Arnold's fat-cat persona, *sans* romance, to critique American corruption, which he undercut with his trademark corny populism in *Mr Smith Goes to Washington* (1939) and *Meet John Doe* (1941). A far more devastating critique appeared in another 1941 film, Orson Welles' *Citizen Kane*, which portrayed a corpulent American industrialist's tragic love life *and* condemned his corrupt business practices. In this RKO production, Charles Foster Kane (Welles) inherits his wealth and produces heirs, but he is no model of family capitalism: he does not cultivate his newspaper chain as a family business, is divorced by two wives and dies a lonely man. The story offended the studio moguls, but its resemblance to the life of another media mogul – William Randolph Hearst, whose powerful news syndicate could harm the studios with negative publicity – truly disturbed them. Mayer's reaction is legendary: using Loew's, Inc. chief Nicholas Schenck as an intermediary, he offered RKO president George Schaefer $800,000 (substantially more than the film's $686,000 production costs) to destroy *Citizen Kane*'s negative and prints before its release, but Schaefer declined (see Eyman 2005: 333). The episode offered another example of the studio moguls' diminishing ability to control their own image, their own industry and their own destiny. Corporate takeover and government regulation of their family capitalism would be delayed by World War Two, but their patriarchal reign was in jeopardy.

Decline and Fall

Stunned by postwar anti-trust decisions, the impact of television and a precipitous drop in ticket sales, in the late 1940s the studios' corporate overseers clamped down on the moguls' autonomy regarding production decisions. Typical was the scenario at MGM: its head of production, Louis B. Mayer, had worked in that capacity since 1924; his corporate boss, Nicholas Schenck, had been president of Loew's, Inc. since 1927. As profits dwindled, in 1948 Schenck asked Mayer to appoint a creative executive to oversee and revitalise all MGM productions. That executive, 43-year-old Dore Schary, was never able to usurp Mayer's control over his longtime minions, and in the ensuing power struggle Schenck was forced to oust Mayer in June 1951. Mayer, the figurehead of Hollywood's most prestigious film studio, had earned the highest annual income in the United States for several years in the late 1930s and early 1940s; a decade later, he was out of work.

The decline of the moguls' fortunes coincided with the retreat of America's upper classes from the public eye. By so baldly exposing the gap between the 'haves' and 'have nots' in the American economy, the Great Depression had transformed the public behaviour of the nation's richest citizens, who 'learned to be discreet, almost reticent, in exhibiting their wealth' (Packard 1959: 24). In New York City, the Gilded Age mansions that lined upper Fifth Avenue were abandoned for hideaways in Long Island and Connecticut or high-rise penthouses. In Los Angeles, the movie colonies retreated even farther out of sight into the Hollywood Hills and the secluded beach enclave of Malibu. The kind of conspicuous consumption documented by Veblen at the turn of the century did not diminish but moved largely out of public view, to be glimpsed only through the protective mediation of press agents. Fear of public resentment was not the only motivation; the increasing voracity of exposé journalism, the advent of television news and the proliferation of charitable organisations seeking donations also drove the rich and famous into seclusion. 'Showing off used to be the main satisfaction of being very rich in America', noted historian Paul Fussell; 'Now the rich must skulk and hide. It's a pity' (1983: 30).

Corporeal signifiers of wealth also were transformed. The pot belly (highlighted by the ubiquitous waistcoat chain) that had distinguished the wealthy American industrialist for more than a century was in full retreat. Diet consciousness among Americans of all ages exploded after World War Two, facilitated by an expanding postwar economy and television advertising that promoted the use of dieting aids. Fat had lost any vestiges of its leisure-class signification; it now indicated a failure to 'measure up' in an increasingly corporate society. The image of the fat-cat monopolist celebrated by Arnold was now considered vulgar and bad for business. Like the flamboyant movie mogul, he would be supplanted by the lean, clean-cut, bland corporate manager who in 1956 was the subject of sociologist William H. Whyte's bestseller *The Organization Man* and was personified by Gregory Peck in *The Man in the Gray Flannel Suit* (1956). Writing about 'the executive look', pop sociologist Vance Packard observed: 'The fat executive on the J. P. Morgan model is disappearing completely in the large companies ... I've seen a good many IBM men within the past five years and my recollections do not encourage me to hope that I will ever find a plump one' (1962: 99–100). Indeed, the most popular representations of fat men in the 1950s depicted them as working-class and undereducated: Ralph Kramden (Jackie Gleason), the loudmouthed bus driver in *The Honeymooners* television series (1955–56); and Marty Piletti (Ernest Borgnine), the lonely butcher from the Bronx in the Academy Award-winning *Marty* (1955). The fat actors who had played patriarchs and industrialists disappeared from Hollywood cinema, like the moguls themselves, by the mid-1950s: Sydney Greenstreet and Eugene Pallette died in 1954, Edward Arnold and Guy Kibbee died in 1956, and among them only Arnold had worked in films after 1949. Charles Laughton, in declining health throughout the 1950s, worked only sporadically and died in 1962. The fat cat did not entirely disappear from Hollywood cinema, however. Played by gargantuan actors like Burl Ives and Orson Welles, in the late 1950s the figure of the fat-cat entered a baroque phase in which his exaggerated size and vulgarity frequently bordered on parody. The cantankerous Big Daddy made famous by Ives on stage and screen was a caricature of Southern patriarchy, and Welles' over-the-top portrayal of a Southern family patriarch in *The Long Hot Summer* (1958) was a caricature of Ives. But Ives' 'Big Daddy' figures also reflected Hollywood's nostalgic yearning for rugged individualism and a lost past: the wild West, the antebellum South and the unregulated family capitalism of the early motion picture industry.

Ives' folksy screen persona was aimed initially at children: with his gentle singing voice, rosy face and humongous pot belly, he was the big-screen, Technicolor personification of Santa Claus. Offscreen, however, Ives possessed a violent temper. Kazan, who had directed him in the stage musical *Sing Out, Sweet Land!* in New York City in 1944–45, recalled seeing Ives 'drunk one night, macho and rampant, aroused to a point where he was looking for a fight, anywhere with anybody. He was a formidable man, with a frightening temper; he evoked respect for his violence' (1988: 543). The rugged Ives, who called himself 'the wayfaring stranger' (the title of his early 1940s radio show and 1948 autobiography), had spent most of the 1930s singing, drinking, brawling and riding the rails from town to town; while appearing in stage musicals in New York he preferred to sleep in Central Park. After being blacklisted by the film industry in 1950, he voluntarily named names to save his career and became a pariah in the folk community as well (see Cohen 2002: 80–1). But in 1955, when Kazan was casting the role of Big Daddy Pollitt in Tennessee Williams' new play, the director remembered Ives' violence and 'intolerance of parlor-bred manners' and hired him for the role (Kazan 1988: 543). The Pulitzer Prize-winning melodrama, which depicted the power struggles between family members vying to inherit the dying Big Daddy's estate, was a commercial success and revived the actor's film career. Ives' reprisal of his stage role in Richard Brooks's 1958 screen adaptation of the play remains his best-known film performance.

Cat on a Hot Tin Roof encompasses many issues – family, marriage, homosexuality and the South – but it is ultimately about the decline of a traditional culture and the feelings of sadness and fear it inspires. The Pollitt family has gathered to celebrate Big Daddy's birthday, but their pretence of happiness and solidarity is built upon a shaky foundation of falsehoods: that Big Daddy isn't dying of stomach cancer, for example; that his marriage to Big Mama (Judith Anderson) has been a happy one; that Gooper and Mae (Jack Carson; Madeleine Sherwood) aren't competing with Brick and Maggie (Paul Newman; Elizabeth Taylor) for Big Daddy's inheritance; that Brick doesn't have homosexual desires; and, finally, that Maggie the Cat is pregnant with Brick's child. The imminent death of Big Daddy, and the disappearance of the Old South he represents, is both a blessing and a curse for the next generation and the New South: it will be a relief to bury his overbearing, intolerant view of the world, but it will also be a scary prospect to carry on without the familial rule he imposed, for some may lose their standing in the new social order. Gooper and Mae's prodigious production of grandchildren for Big Daddy can thus be seen as an attempt to maintain the tradition of family capitalism and bolster their own economic standing; Mae exclaims, 'I know that Big Daddy's just as proud as we are knowin' there's a whole dynasty of his flesh and blood waitin' to take over.' Big Daddy's excessive girth is invested with the weight of wealth and power; upon his demise, his flesh and blood must be redistributed but kept symbolically intact within the family. In Mae's scenario, her children – the chubby 'no-neck mon-sters' whose flesh and blood most resemble that of Big Daddy – are naturally his rightful heirs. But her husband, the bland, sycophantic Gooper, lacks the imagina-tion and creativity to inspire Big Daddy's love and inheritance. Brick, a handsome ex-athlete who once had fire in his belly, has that capability, but the fire has been extinguished by self-loathing and alcohol. Neither son appears capable of filling Big Daddy's shoes when he's gone.

Cat on a Hot Tin Roof depicts the ideal of American masculinity making an un-easy transition in the postwar years from a rural, working-class tradition based on brute physical strength to an urban, white-collar culture based on appearances. Big Daddy's fat body still signifies wealth and manliness because, like the Old South itself, he possesses the gravitas of history. His earthy, hyperbolic masculinity may be vulgar, but it enabled him to survive hard times, work his way up to a position of power, and endure all the 'mendacity' that comes with it. Like the nouveau-riche Hollywood moguls, Big Daddy did not inherit his wealth; he earned it, along with the right to be a fat cat. Williams insisted on making this distinction between work and inheritance for a 1982 Royal Shakespeare Company production of the play, when he instructed the players to 'please avoid the mistake' made in a 1976 televi-sion production by Laurence Olivier, 'who conceived the part of Big Daddy as that of the Southern planter gentleman. Big Daddy is a former overseer who struck it rich through hard work' (Devlin 1997: 102). Big Daddy may be flabby and crude, and his potency and imposing girth are being undermined by stomach cancer, but Wil-liams highlights the positive aspects of his work ethic and decisiveness by contrast-ing them with the confused, ambivalent masculinity of the next generation, whose greater social tolerance makes it more vulnerable to the mendacity of adult life.

After his success on Broadway, Ives played variations of Big Daddy Pollitt, es-pousing the values of family capitalism and patriarchal rule, in a series of late 1950s melodramas: an ageing industrialist in *The Power and the Prize*; an elderly New England farmer who marries a young immigrant woman in an adaptation of Eugene O'Neill's 1924 play *Desire Under the Elms*; and the patriarch of a violent ranching family fighting for control of valuable water rights in William Wyler's epic western-melodrama *The Big Country*. In each film, the fat, seemingly elderly Ives (he was actually in his late forties at the time) schemes to pass control of his property to a beautiful younger person, who ultimately betrays him: in *The Power and the Prize* he grooms his company's vice chairman (Robert Taylor) for the top spot and marriage to his niece, but his protégé topples Ives from power and marries another woman; in *Desire Under the Elms* Ives promises his farm to his new wife (Sophia Loren) if she will bear him a child, but eventually he discovers that she has slept with his youngest son (Anthony Perkins), who is the child's real father; and in *The Big Country* Ives' violent son (Chuck Connors) botches schemes to gain control of water rights and then misbehaves during a duel, forcing Ives to kill him. Neither of the film's warring family patriarchs (Ives and Charles Bickford) is able to secure control of the water rights; instead, the rights are snapped up by a handsome former Naval officer from the east coast (Gregory Peck), who uses gentlemanly, nonviolent tactics of logic and diplomacy to gain control. In the film's conclusion, the two ageing patriarchs finally kill each other in a gun battle, signalling the end of a violent, uncivilised era of rampant individualism and the supremacy of negotiation and collective problem-solving.

The moral of *The Big Country* might have espoused the clear-headed, corporate logic of American business practices in the mid-twentieth century, but like many films of the era it also suggested that reasoned negotiation was neither manly nor much fun to watch. The film's warring families (including Peck's fiancée) consider his 'eastern' business tactics to be cowardly, so Peck is repeatedly forced to fight for his principles of nonviolence. Challenges to the corporate take-over of America, guised in the macho code of self-reliance and protection of the family, were promoted by the moguls themselves in the postwar years as studio profits plummeted and corporate restructuring stripped them of power. 'If 75 per cent of the American people didn't feel as I do about the American family, we wouldn't be here', Louis B. Mayer said in a 1947 interview for *Reader's Digest* (see Heggen 1947: 20). The interview, steeped in the mythology of the self-made man, was titled 'The Unchallenged King of Hollywood' and subtitled 'Saga of Louis B. Mayer, the poor man's son who made himself the highest-paid executive in America'. That Mayer sold off his large stable of racehorses the same year indicates that he might have seen the writing on the wall; it was four years later that he was forced to resign from MGM. Mayer's successor Schary, keenly aware of his own precarious status with Loew's, Inc., approved MGM's acquisition and production of *Executive Suite* (1954), a corporate melodrama portraying executives' cut-throat power struggles after an elderly company president dies without a clear successor in place. The film's critical and commercial success spawned a series of business dramas including *Patterns* (Rod Serling's 1955 teleplay and United Artists' 1956 film adaptation) and MGM's *The Power and the Prize*, based on Howard Swiggett's 1954 bestselling novel. In the latter film, the vice-chairman of Amalgamated World Metals (Robert Taylor) thwarts company president Ives' scheme to promote him and marry him to his niece; Taylor believes that Ives' business practices are greedy and criminal, and Taylor and the niece agree that they do not love each other and have no plans to marry. Ives' quest to create a legacy through family capitalism and the dynastic marriage is revealed to be unrealistic and unethical in the world of modern business and modern love. The film uncannily mirrors the last gasps of family capitalism at Loew's/MGM: after Mayer's ouster in 1951, Schenck himself would be forced out in 1955. (Ironically, one of Schenck's own nieces has a small part in the film and appears under a false name to hide the family connection.) Schary, too, would be ousted from MGM in 1956, just after *The Power and the Prize* premiered.

Some of the subsequent corporate managers who oversaw Loew's/MGM would be more charismatic than others, but none would be able to rule with the autonomy and nepotism enjoyed by the moguls between the world wars. After Mayer's death, David O. Selznick, his former son-in-law, wrote to ex-wife Irene Mayer Selznick: 'How strange, this vacuum he has left. It is not love that has been lost, nor tenderness, nor even paternal protection. Rather it is as though we had all lived fearfully in the shadow of a magnificent, forbidding Vesuvius, which is now suddenly removed: no more the little arbors huddled on its slopes, no more the threatening lava ... You, above all others, know that I never ate of the grapes nor feared the eruptions. Yet I could stand in awe' (Selznick 1983: 365–6). The volcanic, larger-than-life studio patriarchs had been replaced by corporate CEOs who lived by Vance Packard's maxim – 'In modern America you can exert power only by denying you have it' (1959: 24) – and kept their names out of the newspapers. Mayer, however, made headlines one more time. In his last will and testament, made public just weeks after his death, he dictated that his oldest daughter, from whom he had been estranged for years, would not receive an inheritance: 'I make no bequest to my daughter Edith Goetz nor to her children nor to any other member of the Goetz family, as I have given them extremely substantial assistance during my lifetime, through gifts and financial assistance to my daughter's husband, William Goetz, and through advancement of his career (as distinguished from that of my former son-in-law, David Selznick, who never requested nor accepted assistance from me) in the motion picture industry' (Selznick 1983: 359–60). The classical Hollywood system of production that Mayer helped to found was no longer in familiar hands, but he continued to espouse his principles of family capitalism from beyond the grave. Tennessee Williams couldn't have scripted it better himself.

Ten Commandments
for a SON
(TO BE READ WHEN MY SON IS 18)

*This is a letter Chuck has written to
his son— A letter that contains some
good advice for most any teen-ager.*

by CHARLTON HESTON

(*Editor's note: Every parent has the urge to advise his
children on what is important in life, to guide them over
the pitfalls and try to help them toward achievement.
That is true of a thoughtful young man named Charlton
Heston. His son, Fraser Clark Heston, was born on Lincoln's birthday, 1955, and is still too young to heed
advice. But on the possibility that he might let the chance
lapse in later years, Charlton has penned what he would
like the lad to know when he is 18. Here is the letter.*)

Dear Fras,

■ When you read this, you will be a grown-up young
man with long years and a challenging attitude
toward the world. But as I write it, your pants are
still three-cornered and your world is limited
to a few inches feet beyond your nose. Somehow
I think it might be easier to advise than
words in you now. If I waited until later, I might
get cold feet. In fact, I'm sure I'd lose my nerve.
I can remember another young fellow who got some
advice from his father. When I was a baby, my
father wrote a letter telling me what he hoped I
would learn in later years. He sent it to me
when I was 15. I read it carefully then, and I've
studied it many times since. Mainly, your grandfather
said he hoped I wouldn't make some of the
same mistakes he had. (*Please turn to page 79*)

*Proud Charlton Heston, with
renowned Lydia and Chuck
Jr., reclining after closing some
of their very happy married
life, smiling down together.*

19

Wedding Bells Ring, Storks Are Expected, the Rumours Aren't True, Divorce is the Only Answer: Stardom and Fan-Magazine Family Life in 1950s Hollywood

ADRIENNE L. McLEAN

In its November 1957 issue, *Photoplay* introduced a section called 'Baby Talk', which the editors trumpet as something of a novelty: 'Time was when babies weren't mentioned in Hollywood – but all's changed!' Among the items on offer in 'Baby Talk' are a 'nine-month beauty course' with 'maternity camouflage' featuring Vera Miles, a photo spread of a baby shower for Pier Angeli's sister, and an article on the '[Shirley] MacLaine method of childcare'. In addition, babies and children appear or are mentioned throughout the issue – Jane Powell's three children, princess Grace Kelly's new daughter and 'Baby Carrie', daughter of Debbie Reynolds and Eddie Fisher. 'Baby Carrie', or rather her first birthday, is the subject of a colour photo spread, the photos of baby and 'Mama Debbie' ostensibly the 'favorites' of 'Daddy Fisher'. (There is a six-stanza poem to accompany the photos, which ends, 'And one year, when you're grown and free,/You'll meet *your* one and, too, be three!/So, coo to you, now, birthday baby,/*We* love *you* and don't mean maybe!!')[1]

But despite so much adoring attention paid to stars and their actual or impending infant offspring in this issue of *Photoplay*, other aspects of star family life are not represented as blissful or even particularly happy. Along with the paean to Baby Carrie and Mama and Daddy Fisher, for example, is a gossip column that details the 'whispers' circulating around the couple, who are rumoured to be 'on-the-verge' of divorce. The title of the Grace Kelly article, in which it is claimed that Kelly sees herself not as a princess but as 'the wife of a wonderful husband [Prince Rainier of Monaco], and a mother' is 'Is Grace Getting Bored?' Even Jane Powell, who had once had a 'perfect' marriage (it lasted from 1949 to 1953), was now 'kicking over the traces' and 'flabbergasting her friends' with her new image as a 'woman of 28, mother of three and a divorcée on her second marriage'. And there is no trace of opprobrium against Powell for leaving behind that 'sticky-sweet' image, the 'sweet, demure little Janie' of the past. Rather, the new Janie is, 'in a word – Wow!'

The 1950s are of course already well known as an era of 'young marriage, high birthrate, and low divorce', as Elaine Tyler May puts it (2000: 492), a time in which the nuclear family and conservative gender roles were idealised and the American home mobilised to function as a haven from a dangerous and anxiety-provoking world. The call word of the decade was supposedly 'togetherness', coined by *McCall's* in 1954, with working father, stay-at-home mother and, ideally, four children all supposed to find their 'deepest satisfaction' in domestic life and recreation with each other, in their own suburban ranch house (Mintz & Kellogg 1988: 178). In their social history of American family life, Steven Mintz and Susan Kellogg actually call the chapter on the 1950s 'The Golden Age', but in this case irony is intended. For as any number of other revisionist histories of the decade have also shown (for example, Margolis 1984; Matthews 1987; May 1988, 2000; Spigel 1992, 2001; Meyerowitz 1994; Foreman 1997; Weiss 2000; and see also Friedan 1963), the ideal family of the 1950s was something of an illusion, disseminated primarily in certain films, television shows, magazines and other forms of popular mass culture. Indeed, what Jessica Weiss calls 'the baby boom family pattern' was in reality extraordinary mainly for its 'uniqueness and brevity', and even those 'whose lives on the surface' conformed to the gender stereotypes of television sitcoms like *The Adventures of Ozzie & Harriet* (1952–66) or *Leave It to Beaver* (1957–63) were in all sorts of subterranean ways actually 'at the forefront of significant gender change in the postwar years' (2000: 5, 7). As Weiss notes, Harriet Nelson of *Ozzie & Harriet* may have played a domesticated homemaker and mother on the show, but 'Harriet Nelson, the actress, was a working mother with an accomplished career' (2000: 7). Hollywood films of the 1950s, especially film noirs and what film scholars usually refer to as 'domestic' or 'family' melodramas, have also received a lot of attention precisely for the ways in which they both reify and register unease with or ambivalence about conventional gender roles and family life (see, for example, Gledhill 1987). Yet while 1950s films ranging from *Rebel Without a Cause* (1955) to *Peyton Place* (1957) to *Cat on a Hot Tin Roof* (1958) represented marriage and family life as 'a kind of hell', Mintz and Kellogg maintain that 'the underlying message was hopeful. Even the most severe family problems could be resolved by love. All it took was understanding, perseverance, and love' (1988: 193–4).

In some sense, then, my *Photoplay* examples seem to support all of the views of the 1950s presented thus far. On one hand, there is an apparent allegiance to the 'perfect' family of father, mother and many babies or children. And women having babies, and babies and children themselves, are presented in an idealised fashion ('I think a little girl's best preparation for life is to be around her mother when she's carrying a baby', Vera Miles reports, and Grace Kelly 'intends to have many children'). On the other, Baby Carrie's parents are 'spatting' and on the verge of splitting up, and Kelly seems to be suffering 'secret pangs' about giving up acting and success and 'freedom' for the 'boring' life of a European princess. Jane Powell is a mother of three and not only on her second husband but 'going wild on the set' as she makes films, television shows, Vegas appearances and cuts an album, but as it turns out, 'marriage is the answer' to her newfound 'maturity': 'Why? Because a wife – or a husband – who is truly in love will try to improve faults and shortcomings, will try to develop to the utmost, just to make the marriage work … And the deep satisfaction that comes with that knowledge of inner growth is one of the greatest rewards marriage can give. It is something, Jane knows, that a career cannot give – and something that every married woman can achieve.' (The marriage in question would be over within five years.) And finally, what of *Photoplay's* claim that 'baby talking' is something new, because stars do not like to 'mention' their children? In fact, as any perusal of fan magazines of the 1950s and at least the two previous decades makes clear, stars were talking about their babies well before 1957. Despite Richard Dyer's claim that Hollywood fan magazines focus primarily on 'love' and (or as) 'heterosexual emotional/erotic' relationships rather than 'relationships of, surprisingly enough, parents and children' (1998: 45), stars and their children and family life are a regular feature of many of the several hundred fan magazines of the 1930s, 1940s and 1950s that I have examined. Dyer does note that births are featured, but 'seldom the developing relationship of a star and her/his child' (ibid.); yet one of the more curious of the rhetorical flourishes that mark fan magazine discourse generally is that, again and again in stories about stars and their children, they claim to be 'smashing Hollywood's pet taboo' (that those with children 'don't like to talk about them to the press') (Levin 1970: 89). Since stars, their matrimony *and* their children are scarcely peripheral to the fan magazine as a locus of fan interest (nor have they ever been), is there at least a difference in the way that such things are represented in the 1950s that corresponds to or accommodates the discursive hegemony of domestic ideology and 'togetherness'? How do fan magazines of the 1950s participate in the promulgation of an idealised version of family life – particularly in relation to female subordination within marriage – as well as in the well-known 'transformation' of marriage and family life in subsequent decades and the 'burgeoning social acceptance', in Weiss's words, of married women's increasing participation in the labour force? (2000: 79)

With so many myths about the 1950s as a 'golden age' already demolished by film and social historians alike, to claim that the record I trace is marked by an attitude of ambivalence and confusion would hardly be original. But what does remain surprising is the sheer dogged determination with which fan magazines worked to make stars appear to reconcile the competing demands of their careers and those of a married and family life centred on devotion to home and children. That over time such a project could not help but result in a discursive stalemate, and that stalemate in turn lead to new ways of thinking about and evaluating the validity of ideologies of domesticity and 'togetherness', is the primary reason I find these fan magazines useful as an object of study (see also Higashi 2005). This essay will follow the contradictions and frequently bizarre situations that arise as everyone in Hollywood – male or female, big star or featured player, young or 'old'

– tries, hectored or lauded by gossip columnists and journalists who have their own allegiances to power and the maintenance of Hollywood's alternately scandalous and wholesome image, to conform to his or her socially prescribed role as wife or husband and mother or father, without compromising or destroying the glamorous careers or physical attributes that are always already the de facto basis of film stardom itself. Ultimately, I find that the family life represented in fan magazines of the 1950s cannot help but have contributed to the return of the nation to its *true* normality: 'lower birthrates and higher divorce rates' (May 2000: 492). I have tried to organise the material according to the rubrics implied by the essay's title, although there is frequent overlap among them: romance and matrimony, motherhood and fatherhood, and marital trouble and divorce.

Naturally Hollywood Loves Romance

Virginia Wright Wexman has studied the ways in which Hollywood films, which traditionally were 'addressed primarily to young people', functioned as an 'institution' that aided in the modelling of 'appropriate courtship behaviour' in its audiences (1993: 5). Lest anyone doubt that 'romantic love is a major concern' of the average Hollywood film, she cites the research of David Bordwell, Janet Staiger and Kristin Thompson that calculates that '85 per cent of all Hollywood films made before 1960 have romance as their main plot, and 95 per cent have romance as either the main plot or a secondary plot' (1985: 3). As is well known, 'classical' fan magazines – *Photoplay*, *Modern Screen*, *Silver Screen*, *Motion Picture*, *Screenland*, among many others – and their writers were considered allied to and part of Hollywood's discursive machinery, rarely operating in serious opposition to studio demands or desires, and it is not too much to say that the stories and gossip columns of most fan magazines are as concerned as Hollywood films with male/female courtship and romance. Although the studio's control over such organs of gossip, promotion, publicity and occasionally scandal began to weaken in the 1950s, romance remained the staple of both established and newer fan periodicals. The enormous success of tabloid-style magazines like *Confidential*, which began publication in 1952, did increase the proportion of what seem to be exposés of non-normative relationships, but none of the material I examined took the kind of liberty with what Wexman calls 'Hollywood's romantic ideology of the idealized heterosexual couple' (1993: 16) that *Confidential* specialised in taking (see also Desjardins 2001).

If there is little variation in the basic construction of courtship and marriage in the fan magazine from the 1930s through to the 1950s (as Wexman notes, the 'model of the companionate couple' predominated throughout most of the twentieth century (1993: 142)), this does not mean that courtship and marriage are always equally or consistently emphasised. Fan magazines of the 1930s contain many articles not only on extra-romantic issues such as how to get a break in Hollywood, how much money stars make (and how they spend it), what 'voice-dubbing' is, stars and their hobbies (or cars, or pets, or vacations or favourite recipes), or even how the Hays Office affects film content, but also on quite spirited challenges to marriage as an ideal for both men and women. Besides articles about what is 'wrong' with Hollywood love, one finds any number of stars who proclaim, as Loretta Young did in *Motion Picture*, that 'career comes first' (she 'isn't sure yet whether she will mix career and marriage again') (Levin 1970: 85). When ten Hollywood bachelors tell 'Why They Don't Marry' in *Movie Classic* (February 1933), their cynicism about marriage, and their determination to 'cling to their freedom', is treated as quite normal, even logical. In the same issue, Young scornfully dismisses discussion of Hollywood romances altogether: 'I don't see how anybody can take Hollywood love-affair gossip seriously … not even the people involved. But the fact that they do is what makes all these grand, sobby stories we continually read in print … We have a name for them – we call them "Box-Office Romances".' Thus, while heterosexual romance and marriage are still treated as the eventual normative state of every adult, with even *Movie Classic*'s recalcitrant bachelors predicted to marry 'sometime', there also seems to be a wider interest in other aspects of movie-star life, consumer culture and even the mechanisms of film production. The private lives of stars remain of critical interest (indeed, the location of fan interest in the offscreen as well as onscreen image of the star is one of the defining features of film stardom itself), but these private lives are not always bound up in courtship and marriage.

It is more difficult to generalise about fan magazines of the 1940s across the decade because of the disruptions caused by World War Two and its ending. While stars' romances and marriages remained staples, there were, naturally enough, many more articles during the war that criticised any star or would-be star who seemed excessively interested in personal issues like love affairs or even marriage, or who, especially if they were female, behaved in ways that might undermine the morale of fighting men or that were seen as inappropriate to the maintenance of Hollywood's moral credibility. If a female star, like Rita Hayworth, was in love with a fighting man, like Victor Mature, the romance was usually discussed in positive terms. When, as it frequently did, the romance went sour, the treatment of the breakup was managed in relation to the relative marquee value and other patriotic activities of the stars in question. Thus, when in 1943 she dumped Mature to marry Orson Welles (not well-liked in Hollywood generally, and not a fighting man), Hayworth was criticised for hurting Mature while he was overseas, but mildly because she was otherwise known as working hard for the war effort and, equally important, was very popular (both as a pin-up and a musical star) and hence more valuable than Mature. Moreover, prior to becoming a Marine, Mature had not been seen as a particularly suitable mate for Hayworth anyway (see McLean 2004). Young women's behaviour, the problem of 'loyalty', and the viability of wartime romance and the often hasty marriages that resulted from it were written about from time to time in general terms, or dealt with through the stars' advice columns that are one of the most interesting features of the classic fan magazine ('What Should I Do? Your Problems Answered by Bette Davis' (*Photoplay*); 'Joan [Crawford] may help you solve your problem. Write her c/o *Movieland*').

In the first few years after the war, however, the fan magazine depicted the romance, courtship and family life of stars in as utopian a fashion as arguably has ever been the case before or since. While the ubiquitous gossip columns continue to speculate about who is seeing whom, whether wedding bells are about to ring, or whether this or that marriage is working out, the apparently happy and enduring union (which, measured in Hollywood time, means the stars have been married for at least a couple of years), especially if there are children involved, is granted a considerable amount of ideological capital. It is not that there are happier families to feature, but that the happy families that do *appear* to exist – Ingrid Bergman and her husband and young daughter, George Montgomery and Dinah Shore and their baby, John Farrow and Maureen O'Sullivan and their five children, the Bing Crosbys and their four, Eleanor Powell and Glenn Ford and their son, June Allyson and Dick Powell, Jeanne Crain and Paul Brinkman, and, especially, Shirley Temple and John Agar and their new baby – are featured over and over again, in cover stories, in articles, in photo spreads. If all stars are always both unusual in their abilities or physical attributes and at the same time supposedly quite ordinary, similar rather than different from the bulk of their fans in their goals and dreams of personal fulfilment, then in the immediate postwar period the ordinary clearly comes to trump the extraordinary, the domestic to prevail over the glamorous. 'Bravo, Miss Bergman!' writes *Movieland*, applauding Bergman for being a good wife and mother and not sacrificing 'one whit of her integrity' (November 1947). In 'an open letter to Barbara Stanwyck', *Modern Screen* employs the eleven-year marriage of Stanwyck and Robert Taylor to sneer at 'a number of other Hollywood husbands and wives' who use 'that "career-trouble" excuse for not staying wed' and whose prior statements about their own marital happiness 'sound embarrassing today when those who piously uttered them have spent the past decade changing partners as if matrimony were some sort of a hilarious party game' (November 1949).

But as the 'first ever' *Hollywood Yearbook* (1950) had to note, 1949 turned out to be a 'disastrous year' for stars and matrimony generally, with 27 divorces and an equal number of 'rifts', leading the editors to 'a sad reflection: "Why do they bother getting married at all?"' Most significant were the failures of some of the same marriages pointed to so admiringly a few years before, among the most spectacular casualties being Bergman's 'integrity' thanks to her scandalous extramarital liaison with Roberto Rossellini, and the divorce of America's favourite child star, Shirley Temple, from her husband ('Every time I think of raising my baby without her father, I cry'). The title of one article about a divorcing couple – '[Joan] Fontaine vs. [William] Dozier: "How Can You Be Wife, Mother, Friend, Baby Sitter, Career Girl?"' – poses what is among the most basic rhetorical challenges of all fan-magazine discourse, to satisfy both the demand of Hollywood that its women *all* be 'career girls' in some sense and the growing call of American patriarchy that women should be wives and mothers first, if not solely. The advice for Fontaine was not only feeble but feebly put: 'She'll have to learn to keep an even balance.' Even 'fairy-tale' weddings and marriages, like that of Rita Hayworth to Prince Aly Khan in May 1949, were by 1950 no longer discussed with much hope as to their ongoing viability; after the failures of so many of the 'perfect' marriages of the 1940s and before, the editors are gloomy: 'Now we doubt that others will last.'

This dialectic of hope and gloom or cynicism forms a permanent cycle of the fan magazine and its representation of romance and marriage during the 1950s. 'Naturally Hollywood loves romance', claims *Motion Picture* (actually *Motion Picture and Television*) in 1952, although there are still some 'romances Hollywood frowns upon' – between older women and younger men (especially if a man is identified only as a star's husband, for 'Such slights hurt a man's vanity. He hates to be less successful than his wife. Such a set-up is essentially antagonistic to the male ego' (*Modern Screen*, March 1953)), or between any American girl and an older European playboy. The problem is that even the types of marriages on which Hollywood 'smiles its sunniest' (like that of 'sweet Janie Powell and young Geary Steffen') also were ending, and quite quickly, in divorce. (Even Stanwyck and Taylor divorced in 1951.) Sheilah Graham could write syrupy words about the picture-book 'Honeymoon Story' of Elizabeth Taylor and Nicky Hilton in *Modern Screen* ('Of all the days of their years – they'll remember these – the secret golden days of their honeymoon' (August 1950)), but the marriage was over the following year and Taylor would be on her fourth husband by decade's end. Other 'ideal' romantic couples, like 'cutie-pie' Debbie Reynolds and crooner Eddie Fisher, had some rocky moments before reaching the altar (and even rockier moments after the wedding in this case, namely the divorce of Reynolds and Fisher in 1959 so that Fisher could marry Elizabeth Taylor, the same year (see Higashi 2005: 75–6)). There are always stories about certain stars who are not getting married ('Why are they afraid to marry?' asks Sheilah Graham in *Photoplay* (October 1952) of Peter Lawford, Marlon Brando, Rock Hudson, Vera-Ellen, Dorothy Malone, Ann Blyth and Dan Dailey, among others), and always 'constant rumors of trouble' in marriage after marriage. And *Movie Play*, in 'Don't Believe Them! (They say one thing and do another, these unpredictable stars)', seems angry that 'Jeff Chandler said he and Marge [Hoshelle] would work it out – later after separation both of them had an entirely different story'; and in reference to Glenn Ford and Eleanor Powell's marriage, still supposedly one of the secure ones (it would end in 1959), the writer casts doubt on Ford's statement that he 'didn't object to Eleanor's career' ('or did he?') (March 1954).

But if in the 1940s 'that "career-trouble" excuse for not staying wed' was itself denigrated, by the mid-1950s the fan magazines are again bent on having it both ways, reporting on the hard work that stars did to make their films as well as on their glamorous offscreen carousings at premières and parties, and then criticising them for not being 'normal'. In 1953, *Screen Stars*, for example, offered a 'devastating analysis of the world's most desirable divorcees' – Anne Baxter, Joan Crawford, Lana Turner, Rita Hayworth among them – but the 'analysis' turned out to be that the women were too 'possessive and domineering', used to 'playing the star at home as well as on the set' and maybe 'just too tired after a long day of play-acting to participate fully in the pleasures and responsibilities of married life' (August 1953). In the same issue, however, Tony Curtis is the putative author of a story called 'I Married a Working Girl' ('"How does she do it?" Janet Leigh's friends marvel when they see her efficiently run household … We asked her husband how she manages to combine housekeeping and moviemaking so smoothly'). Curtis admits that 'combining her two careers – that of actress and hausfrau – can only be done by careful, efficient planning'. But he claims that whenever he tries to 'help', Janet stops him: '[H]ousework is not for a man. It's a woman's job.' Ultimately, the answer to Janet's ability to 'so efficiently, so capably, combine her housework with her career [is] simple: she loves one as much as the other'. So Curtis can 'truthfully say, I'm glad I married a working girl – my Janet'.

Younger stars, then, are sometimes represented as being able to have it all, to make a 'career' of both their marriages and their jobs as stars; several seemed to be doing it. Considering the record, it was really too early to tell; but one of the most interesting aspects of fan-magazine discourse of this time is precisely the crazy play of competing interpretations and versions of domestic ideology, especially 'togetherness' and its relationship to men and women's careers. *Modern Screen* portrays Charlton Heston and his wife Lydia as being happy even though the 'Hectic Hestons' have a 'long-distance' relationship and 'have had only one joint vacation in ten years of marriage – and even then, they read scripts' (November 1953). But the article that immediately follows is about the marriage of Marge and Gower Champion, who are 'together every hour': 'No two people have ever been so together around the clock – how can they stay so in love?' After 'six solid years, they're still happy with each other', apparently, in spite of what is implied to be a surfeit of togetherness and companionate marriage. Lana Turner and Lex Barker, her fifth husband, 'believe that even a temporary separation is unhealthy', so they not only 'accompany each other everywhere, but take Cherry [Turner's daughter, Cheryl Crane] along too – even on [their] second honeymoon' (*Modern Screen*, October 1954). Since Turner and Barker divorced in 1957, such stories more than suggest that togetherness is *not* the secret of a happy marriage. Of course some older stars, such as Lana Turner or Joan Crawford or Rita Hayworth, had been married so many times by the end of the 1950s that, while perfunctory attention is paid to the lovebirds' courtships and weddings, often in gossip columns rather than articles, the quick ends to the unions are dismissed with barely disguised contempt ('[Lana] said, 'This is forever' when she married Bob Topping. Forever lasted about four years. She asked husband Lex Barker to move' (*Photoplay*, July 1958)).

The more traumatic ruptures were those of marriages around which there had circulated no hint of a problem, or in which both halves of the couple seemed to be doing exactly what *Movie Play* recommended as the 'only' way to make a Hollywood marriage work: 'Happy marriages can only be achieved when both parties choose marriage as their prime consideration and relegate fame and career to a secondary position' (March 1954). The problem, again, is that no one became a Hollywood star by relegating 'fame and career to a secondary position', although some stars lived quiet enough lives that it could be made to seem that way, or were married to people either who had their own established non-film careers (Irene Dunne was married to a dentist for almost four decades) or who seemed not to mind ceding the spotlight to their spouses ('Mrs David Wayne' penned an article for *Screenland* claiming 'every single second of my marriage to David Wayne has been gay, exciting, rich with fulfilment' (September 1952)). When Jack Lemmon, 'one of the nicest guys in town', separated from his wife Cynthia Stone (a television actress) in 1956, 'everyone was floored. What went wrong?' (*Silver Screen*, August 1956). 'When Jeanne Crain's nuptial alliance with Paul Brinkman, the movie colony's shining example of wedded bliss', *Silver Screen* continues, 'exploded into divorce headlines, the reaction of the shocked municipality was that, on the heels of that jolter, nothing could possibly be more surprising'. But the Lemmons were 'that nice couple next door', seemed to be happy together, and they had a young child. So 'If Cupid is sitting on the curb on Sunset Strip, burying his head in his hands, you can't hardly blame him. It's evidently open season on Hollywood's ideal marriages.' When Paul Newman and Joanne Woodward wed in 1958, *Photoplay* entitled its photo spread about them 'The Honeymoon Is Over', as if to imply that the marriage, too, would be soon (July 1958).[2]

Papa, Won't You Play With Me?

Not all stars had children, but in the 1940s and 1950s, all stars wanted, or were depicted as wanting, to be 'infanticipating'. In the 1930s many stars also had babies and children who were featured in articles from time to time, and again, one of the most noticeable tropes marking references to Hollywood's children is that of the smashed taboo. For a November 1948 *Photoplay* story on 'Hollywood's Nurseries', the writer claims that at 'Hollywood parties today, there is so much chatter about babies. I sometimes feel that nobody talks anything but Pablum. It is very interesting, thinking back to the days when no star mentioned matrimony – let alone motherhood – to realise that today a Hollywood house not blessed with at least two children is pretty hard to find.' Indeed, the number of children that was 'getting to be par' for cinema households (as it was for middle-class baby-boom families across the country) was four, 'whether the youngsters came as bundles from heaven or from adoption centres'. In a single 1949 issue of *Modern Screen* (November), there is an epistolary piece (also called 'Baby Talk') about Tyrone and Linda Powers' 'plans for their first-born', a tribute by Hedda Hopper to 'Hollywood's forgotten wives' ('behind every top actor you'll find a woman – living in the shadows … and giving freely of courage, love and devotion'), an article by Glenn Ford detailing 'the tender little things' that he and wife Eleanor Powell treasure, among them their son Peter and the way that 'Wise Ellie understands that a boy and his Dad need man-to-man hours together to get acquainted', another on Linda Darnell's adoption of her baby Lola, and one about how Jeanne Crain's 'prayer was answered' (the prayer was that she give birth to sons, which she did, twice). And this, I have found, is about standard for any single issue of a regular fan magazine from the late 1940s throughout the 1950s.

Although the most truly sanctified Hollywood fan-magazine families are always those composed of father, mother and several children, in the 1930s and 1940s there was no particular stigma attached to either working mothers or the single-parent household. Indeed, during the war years it was the mothers who wanted to leave public life to stay home with their children who were sometimes criticised. In 'Listen to Me, Alice Faye' (*Photoplay/Movie Mirror*, August 1943), Adela Rogers St. Johns lambastes Faye for wanting to 'be there with your baby, when she wakes up, to put her to sleep at night, to have a good dinner waiting for Phil [Harris], to have your home peaceful and – oh, a real American home, such as you've dreamed of always'. For Alice Faye 'is *not* just a mother and a wife and a housekeeper', she is also an entertainer 'who has sung herself into the love of the American people, who are now going out to fight. You can't, you see, go back on that.' In the late 1940s and 1950s, the single-parent families remain, and in some cases, like that of Joan Crawford, there is even an acknowledgement of the impossible situation that a woman star's fame presents to that fragile 'male ego': 'A man whom I could respect and love would have his own profession, his own responsibilities. Could he understand my dedication to my job? Could he share my devotion to my children? Too much to ask, I think, of the kind of man I would marry' (*Movieland*, April 1955). In the 1950s, then, the matrimonial vies with the parental as the locus of moral capital, with some stars, such as Rita Hayworth, being criticised for displaying excessive devotion to yet another husband (in this case Dick Haymes) at the expense of her children. If Hayworth paid more attention to 'making her daughter's life happier' rather than continuing to seek romantic fulfilment, 'she may find more contentment in her own life. Rita will learn that the sparkle in her child's eyes can outshine Aly's diamonds, her own name in lights, and the fleeting glow of romance' (*Modern Screen*, November 1953). How Hayworth was supposed to support herself and her children after she forsook seeing 'her own name in lights' and in the absence of a male breadwinner goes unaddressed (see McLean 2004).

Motherhood and its declared primacy in all women's lives makes the plight of the woman star especially clear, and especially affecting. On the one hand, Hedda Hopper praises couples who have 'stayed happily married – and saved – for their kids, for their futures' (*Modern Screen*, August 1950); and June Allyson is supposed to have suddenly realised, right before her baby was born, 'how much she enjoyed just sitting around the house and being Mrs Powell' (*Movie Life*, April 1951). But

Rita Hayworth is criticised for trying to find a husband and live-in male parent for her children, and Jane Powell is scolded for *not* leaving her child at home on a publicity tour (it was 'commendable' from a 'sentimental standpoint' that Janie 'took her baby along', but even though Powell had both her mother and her 'devoted housekeeper, Gladys', with her to help care for the baby, it gave her 'that much less time to rest' and almost caused a 'collapse' (*Motion Picture*, March 1952)). It is suggested that Powell might not be able to 'stand the strain of her career, plus her jobs as wife and mother'. Louella Parsons' *Modern Screen* cover story on the 'shocking failure of Susan Hayward's marriage' details the fact that Hayward was beaten 'unmercifully' by her husband (Jess Barker, the father of her twin sons), 'blacking both eyes and bruising her body', but then blithely makes the violence just an aberrant 'defense mechanism against living in a set of circumstances intolerable to a man's pride', namely, Hayward's 'zooming' career (November 1953; see also Higashi 2005). When Lana Turner's marital mistakes are listed and analysed in *Screenland*, the blame for Turner's lack of judgement is even laid at the feet of her mother! (August 1953)

It is not surprising that the 1950 *Hollywood Yearbook* had a lot of 'new parents' to congratulate; but of the seven births whose results are pictured, the father appears in five. If it was understood, albeit incorrectly, that female stars had heretofore been loath to talk about their children, presumably male stars were even more so. But this is not the case in the 1940s and 1950s, when fatherhood becomes one of the primary identifying features of a star's moral value, integrity and even sex appeal. The 'star at home' photo spread became a basic feature of the fan magazine in the 1920s, but in the postwar era a star cavorting with his or her children, narrativised into a sort of play in which the stars and their children perform, makes the movie star into what Simon Dixon calls an 'odd and liminal figure … condemned to live in a strange luxurious space somewhere between art and life. As the role extended into the star's domestic décor, artifice contaminates the actor's offscreen existence, so that the magazine photo shoot of the star "at home" always suggests the star's ambiguous placement between privacy and exhibition' (2003: 81). Dixon claims the domestic realm is also 'radically gendered', and he is interested therefore in considering how the 'domestic setting' of *male* movie stars is constructed – or how it is 'staged' – primarily with such things as 'gun and knife collections' (2003: 84, 89). Although it would seem to make sense that a male star be shown in the context of 'a "masculine" life *actually lived* – the star fixing a car, working in a shop, barbecuing steaks, hacking away at the garden, and so forth' – Dixon finds that these are 'passed over in favor of decoration pure and simple' (2003: 92), the challenge being to show that at the same time that they are fetishised and feminised by static posing amid props the men have no interest in interior decorating (indeed, 'It is this feminisation that must be disavowed with the domestic placement of weaponry' (2003: 100 n.33)). Stars who could or would *not* 'buy into the domestic staging of stars', like Marlon Brando or Marilyn Monroe, therefore have 'no stable screen ecology because they had no stable offscreen environment – and vice versa' (2003: 94–5). I agree with Dixon that a 'star's residence has in general been less a home than a temporary theatre for the display of living' (2003: 96), but the representation of masculinity in 'stars-at-home' spreads of the late 1940s and the 1950s can hardly be limited to guns and knives (of which I found very few, although there were a couple of hunting trips featured). Rather, the most common 'sign' of the married male star is his children – children become visually the new props of the domestic credentials of men, especially, to interesting and ambivalent effect – and the work he does (or is supposed to do, or at least offers to do) around the house. Thus George Montgomery, we are told, made virtually all of the furniture in his and wife Dinah Shore's 'beautiful ranch-type house', where they live with eight-month-old Missy, 'pride and joy of Montgomery household' (*Movie Stars Parade*, November 1948). The fan magazine's representation of fatherhood did not make the male star an exemplar of Dixon's 'unalloyed masculinity' (2003: 89) but it did help to direct attention to and set the stage for what Jessica Weiss calls 'the reformulation and elaboration of prewar trends in fatherhood' (2000: 84). By the early 1950s, parenting experts were re-emphasising 'the importance of father-child relationships – for the good of children, family, and American society' (2000: 85–6).

In the 1950 *Hollywood Yearbook*, Gregory Peck is shown holding his new baby son – and the birth of Carey Paul Peck supposedly has 'helped kill once and for always those unpleasant rumors of marital discord' (until 1955, anyway). A single edition of *Movie Life* (April 1951) has several spreads and stories about parents and children. 'Van, the Freckled Snow Man' shows all of the children of Van and Evie Johnson on a skiing trip – 'Tracy and Ned Wynn (Evie's sons by her previous marriage to Keenan Wynn), Evie, Van and their three-year-old, Schuyler' – employing them all as evidence that 'Van's crazy about the kids, is happiest when he can vacation with the whole family'. Larry Parks and son Garry are shown having a 'high old time baching it' while Betty Garrett is 'off at the hospital keeping her second date with the stork', and Larry is not just 'a' but 'the model pop' who has 'learned to dress his firstborn as fast as Betty can'. Maybe a few of the 'little feminine touches are missing, but these two Parkses are doing pretty well for a pair of mere males'. But while 'Baching it was a lark', it is 'better with Mom home'. Kirk Douglas, divorced father of two, is shown with his sons ('three weary bachelors') after a full day of play at the beach at Santa Monica (*Photoplay*, October 1952). Van Johnson is once more the subject of '"Papa, Won't You Play with Me?" (Hot dogs, ice cream checkerboards and story books ... children splashed with paint. This is Van Johnson's home before the clock strikes bedtime)', a whole fairy-tale story of an evening, complete with dialogue, in which Van does most of the work (*Motion Picture*, August 1955). Even Charlton Heston is photographed with wife and baby (and himself playing Moses) rather than guns in another epistolary essay, 'Ten Commandments for a Son', which Heston writes 'now' because of his fears that the son will not be receptive to such advice when he is grown (*Movie Secrets*, August 1956).

Immediately after the war, the representation of star babies and children signals what feels not just like hope but confidence about the future and its manageability, by both genders. But by the 1950s all of the representations even of happy fatherhood seem to speak to what is perhaps both a fear of the loss of the mother to careers and a corresponding ambivalence about the viability of manly men when what might be needed is a nurturing father. The male and female parent/star is always, despite a few nods to stress, pressure or hard work, shown emphasising only the fun parts of parenthood, the close, happy bonds between parent and child(ren) at play. At least until Cheryl Crane, Lana Turner's daughter, apparently stabbed her mother's boyfriend, Johnny Stompanato, in the stomach in 1958, there are no monster mothers or juvenile delinquents here.[3] And, as Louella Parsons so helpfully imparted to a battered and bruised Susan Hayward, even an abusive husband was 'not really' displaying violence against her but 'against *himself*' (*Modern Screen*, November 1953).

It Just Didn't Work

By late 1953, Jeff Chandler and his wife had been 'married twice – to each other, and now they've come to their second separation. After seven years of trying (and two children), it just didn't work' (*Modern Screen*, November 1953). Regardless of how family-affirming Hollywood fan-magazine discourse attempted to be during the 1950s, the truth was that most of the nuclear families pointed to with such hope during the late 1940s and such wonder in the following decade did not last. The prevalence of divorce as a part of the average Hollywood marriage was sometimes laid at wider cultural 'trends' (is Hollywood life 'so different from life anywhere else? What are the statistics on divorce for the various age groups?' demands *Screenland/TV Land* (August 1953)), but generally the image of 'Cupid sitting on the curb on Sunset Strip' with his head in his hands resonates throughout the 1950s and provides probably the most obvious affront to the hegemony of domestic ideology. Love and romance are clearly not enough to sustain a marriage, although some lip service was usually paid to the notion that they *should* be: 'Caught in the tempest of Vic's inner torment, is love enough to protect the Damone's [sic] from perils that threaten their marriage?' (*Photoplay*, July 1958). Although Damone 'said wistfully, "A wife's place is in the home. I would like it if Anna could always be there"', he was already 'thinking as he spoke that his words were futile, because "Anna" is Anna Maria Pierangeli (Pier Angeli), his beautiful and talented actress wife' (the 'Damone's' had one child). The problem then is irresolvable – if you are beautiful and talented and an actress, is your 'place' in fact the home, or the home *only*? According to Jessica Weiss, 'Postwar women integrated paid employment into middle-class marriage without overturning the sexual division of labour. Yet through their behavioural change, mothers of the baby boom were ultimately able to begin a shift in ideological norms' (2000: 79; see also Higashi 2005). The star mothers of the fan magazine led the way. Stars always had domestic help, of course, but it was relatively rarely mentioned as such (when it was, it was usually to criticise a wayward star, such as showing Rita Hayworth's 'neglected' daughter with her nanny). But at the same time, obscuring this fact may have helped ordinary people to think that they could manage career and family, as long as husbands were as nurturing as so many male stars appeared to be. If stars could have it all – or divorce if things were not working out, with relatively little permanent or even short-lived stigma – why not, on a reduced scale, any ordinary person?

Thus did the fan-magazine family, both in doing its best to maintain fealty to notions like 'togetherness' and in so clearly depicting the inability of Hollywood's denizens – whatever their age or 'maturity', whether with children or without – to achieve it, help to create (not merely to chronicle or depict) the return of the post-baby-boom American family to its normative status. In a 1955 book entitled *The American Family in the Twentieth Century*, John Sirjamaki concludes that one of the biggest changes in the American family to that time was that its members 'are likely to view the family as existing for them and not they for it … Thus, while they have great dependence upon the family, at the same time they want freedom from it so that as individuals they can engage in enterprises outside the home' (1955: 194). If rewritten by Hedda Hopper or Louella Parsons, this might easily serve as the subtitle to any number of fan magazine stories about why this or that marriage 'just didn't work'. There was no way for the hierarchised, traditional nuclear family to be both the exemplar of the hegemony of domestic ideology and of men's and, especially, women's professional non-domestic fulfilment and achievement. No matter how much 'baby talking' the Hollywood fan magazine did, or how many photos of and stories about children at play with their doting parents it spread across its pages, in the end the baby-boom honeymoon, for them as for us, was already over.

Notes

1   Throughout this essay, unless otherwise noted, I will document fan magazine citations in the text only, by magazine title and date.
2   Newman and Woodward remain married to this day.
3   The flip side, if not the source, of the emphasis on the bonds of fatherhood in the 1950s was the criticism of the mother in some areas of popular culture, with Ferdinand Lundberg and Marynia Farnham's *Modern Woman: The Lost Sex* (1947) and Philip Wylie's *A Generation of Vipers* (1955) being perhaps the most famous diatribes against what was seen as the increasing presence of and influence of powerful women and mothers in Cold War society (see Matthews 1987: 207–9).

20

The Look of Love:
Cinema and the Dramaturgy of Kinship

MURRAY POMERANCE

'This age must have more fools than the last, for certainly fools only are most taken with shews and outsides.'
– Daniel Defoe, *The Complete English Tradesman*

Robin Wood asserts that an obsessive emphasis on the family is a 'component of fascism building all over the world' (1998: 22), and like many readers I am fascinated to read his analysis of Leo McCarey's *Make Way for Tomorrow* (1937) as, in large part, a film in which the family is trumped by the couple (1998: 145). The film says, according to Wood – whose perspective, I think, is framed from a position somewhere between contemporary non-parentism and Engels' classic *The Origin of the Family, Private Property and the State* – 'that family unity in the modern world is an illusion and the "ties that bind" a pointless and empty social convention' (1998: 154). Yet while in this view he may be upliftingly anarchic I am surely too bourgeois and too attached to the convention of the family, having been raised on *There's No Business Like Show Business* (1954) and *The Man Who Knew Too Much* (1956), to find it quite so 'empty' and 'pointless' and dispensable as he does. Virginia Wright Wexman also focuses on Hollywood marriage, noting that 'traditional mainstream filmmaking practice has heavily promoted the ideal of monogamous marriage to a "suitable" partner'; and that 'subtle restrictions on accepted exogamic and endogamic practices decisively shaped the ways in which Hollywood moviemakers conceived of plots and characterisations' so as to reflect social practices that could conserve 'resources around which the social fabric is constructed' (1993: 13, 11). This social fabric, or civilisation, is for Stanley Cavell a protagonist in the 'comedy of remarriage', a genre that 'is in possession of the knowledge that the split or doubling is between civilisation and eros' (1981: 64). We might see Wood echoing Cavell when he writes: 'It is the traditional family, of course, that defines and reproduces the patriarchal gender roles and functions; its absence or negation is essential to the equalisation of the couple' (1998: 145). To summarise: freedom, fun and the essentials of pleasure are to be found where the family is not. And what the family is about, more or less exclusively, is perpetuating the hegemony of contemporary (read capitalist) civilisation to the peril of love's body.

Each of these three scholars is far more interested in the romantic couple than the family – the couple, perhaps it need hardly be said, formed and shaped in virtually any way at all (Lou Jacobi with his sheep in *Everything You Always Wanted to Know About Sex * But Were Afraid to Ask* (1972); Candy Clark with her extra-terrestrial in *The Man Who Fell to Earth* (1976); Mia Farrow with her diabolical lover in *Rosemary's Baby* (1968) quite as much as Katharine Hepburn with Cary Grant in *The Philadelphia Story* (1940)); and each scholar detects the importance in forming the solidary couple of what Wexman calls 'suitability': political harmony and aesthetic compatibility are the two components Paul Goodman emphasised once, in conversation with me. The scholars I am citing also – Cavell perhaps least – have a penchant for focusing intensively on the family as, specifically, a narrational construct, not more broadly a performative one, and a knack of doing so, along with most cinema scholars, by writing about exactly those aspects of the family situation that are easiest to find *words* to describe. Here, they buttress and extend a vast preexisting body of criticism that sees films for the stories they tell us through illustration, what I might call a literary history of the cinema. Thus, typically what it is that conventional scholarship wants to see in the screen family is what can be discerned, ironically, *without* seeing, what can be read about or heard about in a narrative account (or by closing one's eyes and listening to dialogue, another way of collecting a narrative account): the events that transpire to link or alienate people; behaviour and aspiration; feeling and motive. If Wood's analysis of *Make Way for Tomorrow* is a discourse about a set of dramatic happenings, its focus is the fact that these happenings are arranged syntactically in a particular way: that particles of eventfulness unfold one after another like the words in a pretty sentence. And Wexman – like virtually all of its critics – gives a similarly 'dialogic' analysis of *Rear Window* (1954). In 'literary analysis' the central problem is what happens in the story, not what happens on the screen. The focus is on something that is altogether invisible, a 'narrative line', and what we see and hear is taken to enchain and lock it; far outside our vision, the 'line' already happens.

While screen stories of the family are certainly galvanising and shiny bright, I am interested here in something else, namely the 'suitability' that is described as the basis and *sine qua non* of proper screen coupling, and this in an extended form that applies to children as well. I want to explore problems and difficulties of staging the family, and therefore wish to consider the family film as a pretext for this staging. Thus, the screen family is essentially a dramaturgical construct, in some ways like other constructs reflecting social groupings that must take their place and make their sense in the same venue: criminal work gangs, outlaw pairings, cowboy and Indian bands, baseball teams, and so on. When in Vincente Minnelli's classic *Meet Me in St. Louis* (1944) we see Margaret O'Brien as Judy Garland's younger sister, and Leon Ames as their father, I want to know through what system and by what opportunities and advantages our eyes can assemble these 'kin relations' in readings that make consistent sense. Garland, Ames and O'Brien were not, after all, related by blood at all. Comic effect is obviously possible, for instance, and intentionally so, when a screen family seems horrifically miscomposed: Sean Connery as Harrison Ford's father in *Indiana Jones and the Last Crusade* (1989), Angelica Huston and Raúl Julia as a couple in *The Addams Family* (1991), or the idea that (offscreen) Sidney Poitier is the father of the character played by Will Smith in *Six Degrees of Separation* (1993). And there is such a thing as impossible casting, a paramount example of which would have been Laurence Olivier and Vivien Leigh (at the time a happily married couple) as a happily married couple in Hitchcock's *Rebecca* (1940); for evidence, one need but espy the screen tests that were made of Leigh, with Olivier's slightly hammy assistance, for the role of the unnamed 'new Mrs DeWinter' (see *Rebecca* DVD and Behlmer 2000: 298–300).

One aspect of the problematisation of family performance is provided by the uncanny experience of freakishness that is discussed at length by Leslie Fiedler (especially 1978: 291–8). In Tod Browning's *Freaks* (1932), a 'normal' woman (Olga Baclanova) becomes engaged to a dwarf (Harry Earles) for his money, and at a startling moment in a wedding celebration rejects him and his deformed 'family' as hideous Others. She is experiencing – Fiedler leads us to see – in anticipation an alienating distance which surely lies at the heart of the audience's fascination for the coupling and deep fear of its possibilities. Similarly intense presentational problems confront later screen couples, who are faced with the need to dramatise bonds of tight intimacy in the face of unforgiving public scrutiny: Glenn Langan and Cathy Downs thwarted by his immensity in *The Amazing Colossal Man* and Grant Williams and Randy Stuart terrified by his inexorable diminution in *The Incredible Shrinking Man* (both 1957). In the latter film, the trouble with staging is explicitly central as a feature of the screen tale: when he is living inside a doll house, it is increasingly strange for her to think that he is a husband in every meaningful way.

Thus, one characteristic that movie families share with families in the real world is a tendency to be read through appearances of 'suitability', since family membership must be demonstrated in order to be in play. A moment of such demonstration, raised to high symbolism, brings *Greystoke: The Legend of Tarzan, Lord of the Apes* (1984) to a crashing conclusion: in Hyde Park, John Clayton (Christopher Lambert), returned from the jungles of Africa to his inheritance in London, is present at the moment when a great ape who has escaped from the Natural History Museum and climbed – as I remember it – into a tree, shot by police, has plummeted to the ground and is dying. It is suddenly palpably evident that this is John's father, if not biologically at least socially, since the creature took him as an infant and brought him fully into the world. As Clayton weeps over the ape, bystanders treat him as an agent of pure entertainment. Consider further that the monogamous patriarchally-structured marriage described by Engels as a 'means of shepherding resources' (see Wexman 1993: 10) is hardly a fact of nature. As a primary social construct, it is formed and reformed in every generation through ideology, worldview, normative constraint and ceremonial observation, this last manifesting itself in the kind of routine everyday performance that can be dramatically corrupted – in *Greystoke* but also in, say, Todd Haynes' *Far from Heaven* (2002) through an 'improper' fascination – or nobly upheld, in such films as *Adam's Rib* (1949) and *Father of the Bride* (1950), and also in children's games (like 'playing parent', which is a substantial basis of the story of *Peter Pan*). Our own bouts of 'playing house' in childhood, after all, were prelude to such horrifying adult investments of our imagination as *The Birds* (1963), *The Money Pit* (1986), *Home Alone* (1990) and *Legends of the Fall* (1994). However serious family is in our culture as a support and productive system, then, it is also a play, a systematic dramatisation; and therefore it must matter to us a great deal what people look like when they presume to take on family roles. The royal family of Great Britain, for one case, apparently found it difficult to conceive of Dodi al-Fayed as even a distant member. We need take only the most cursory look at Roman Polanski's *Rosemary's Baby* or Ivan Reitman's *Twins* (1988) in order to see purported screen kinship that does not lead viewers to immediately accept it warmly as such; and Christopher Walken's cameo as Leonardo DiCaprio's Dad in *Catch Me If You Can* (2002), certainly full of charm, is as incredible as Rosemary's baby's.

Whether the relationships in question are between the central couple, or between siblings, or between parents and children, screened family relations will seem sensible enough to viewers not to disrupt their engagement in a film whenever the casting provides sufficient reason for a belief in special, typically long-term, typically emotional connections among characters, all this despite the almost universal fact that the people onscreen who seem to be related are actually not (every screen familialisation thus being a reflection of the processes of cinema and the social processes whereby we make ascertainments of family). Given that 'family members' onscreen can both (a) look related, and (b) make claims of relationship, we can imagine four possible circumstances, depending on whether either of these conditions is or is not met. Although occasionally actual family members work together to portray familial relationships – Martin and Charlie Sheen as father and son in *Wall Street* (1987) – what follows here makes the assumption that the actors creating the screen families we see are almost always in fact disconnected individuals putting on the proximities and histories with which we credit them.

The screen family that looks related and in which relationship claims are routinely made I call the 'perfect family'. Mary Tyler Moore, Donald Sutherland and Timothy Hutton in *Ordinary People* (1980) – the desperate events which unfold them notwithstanding – are 'perfect', as are Ray Liotta and Lorraine Bracco in *GoodFellas* (1990) (especially when they are courting, the scene at Club 54 being a cinematic apotheosis of the 'perfect' date). The father/son tag-team of Draco and Lucius Malfoy (Tom Felton and Jason Isaacs) in *Harry Potter and the Chamber of Secrets* (2002) embody familial 'perfection', this accomplished through their stunning sneers and bleached-blond hair, as do – uncomfortably, since child theft is implicit in this union – H.I. and Ed (Nicolas Cage and Holly Hunter) in *Raising Arizona* (1987), thanks to considerable work by these two actors in matching their vocalisation. The 'perfection' of a screen family is a matter of viewer response, at least as much as of actors' construction. When a 'perfect family' has been made and sustained we imagine the possibility of a 'family portrait' or tableau. Joe Don Baker, Susan Norfleet and Winona Ryder do not quite manage to make such a group in *Reality Bites* (1994); Harrison Ford and Sean Connery in *Indiana Jones and the Last Crusade*, finally do. And the game we play, going to the movies and accepting the actors who play these roles as successful replicators of family relationships, is the same game we play – 'Who Do You Look Like?' – when we study a newborn baby and determine infallibly that he is an authentic product of the romantic couple, with eyes like his mother's and a chin like his father's, etc. Note that nothing about reality need intrude here except its look. In *The Banger Sisters* (2002), Susan Sarandon's real daughter, Eva Amurri, plays her daughter onscreen, as does Erika Cristensen, who, not related to Sarandon, gives an equally credible performance. Nor does it take more than a moment to articulate a 'perfect family' onscreen: note Jerome K. Jerome's (Jerry Lewis) confrontation with his mother (Jerry Lewis) in *The Ladies Man* (1962). Nor must 'perfect families' avoid exploding, as happens between John Cassavetes, Gena Rowlands and Molly Ringwald in Paul Mazursky's *Tempest* (1982). And I would include here screen 'families' established not only through makeup and costuming, gesture, inflection or stage business but through reliance upon ethnic or racial stereotypes. The families of *The Godfather* (1972, 1974, 1990), for example, including the 'closely related' Marlon Brando, James Caan, John Cazale and Al Pacino but also the 'not-so-closely related' Robert Duvall; or families in Woody Allen movies – I am thinking in particular of Jonathan Munk and Woody as ultimate family members (Alvy Singer at two different points in time) or else Christopher Walken and Diane Keaton as brother and sister in *Annie Hall* (1977); or the extensive family structure depicted in *Roots* (1977) in which LeVar Burton grows into John Amos, or Leslie Uggams gives birth to Ben Vereen. Unquestionably the limiting case of family 'perfection' in contemporary film is achieved through 'cloning': Doctor Evil and Mini-Me (Mike Myers and Verne Troyer) in *Austin Powers in Goldmember* (2002), although the awkward near match of Tom Hardy and Patrick Stewart in *Star Trek: Nemesis* (2002) shows that the cloning trick will not always work.

Hardy as Praetor Shinzon in *Star Trek: Nemesis* and Scott Evil (Seth Green) in *Goldmember*, with his red hair and freckles and his loser hipness, nicely illustrate the second case – what I would call the 'implicit family'. Here we see claims of relationship in the absence of a 'suitable' appearance. In Anatole Litvak's *Anastasia* (1956), the 'implicit family', in this case the conundrum of an unverified royal family link, is the motive of the story. Resolution is easy enough for the actors but rather difficult for viewers, who don't have an opportunity to see more than a diligent and heartfelt set of matched claims by Ingrid Bergman as to her connection with Helen Hayes. A similar difficulty permeates Hugh Hudson's *Greystoke* regarding the grandpaternity of Ralph Richardson over Christopher Lambert; here, a swelling performance of Elgar's First Symphony is drafted to aid our belief as the two men first embrace. Families perfect and implicit need not be flesh and blood of course. Lady and the Tramp, with their many children, are 'perfect'; Roger and Jessica Rabbit are 'implicit', and we have to use a considerable imagination – that I'll not speak about here – to figure out what these two could possibly have in common to back up their claim. There is a subgenre of 'odd-family' films highlighting ensembles in which everyone is supposed to be related and nobody seems to be: *The Addams Family* (where Anjelica Huston and Raúl Julia ostensibly produced Christina Ricci, Dana Ivey and Jimmy Workman); *The Seven-Per-Cent Solution* (1976) (where the Celtic and mercurial Nicol Williamson is sibling to the monumentally Classical Charles Gray); *Parenthood* (1989) (where cardboardish Steve Martin is phlegmatic Jason Robards' son) or *Magnolia* (1999) (where giddy Tom Cruise is); *East of Eden* (1955) (where James Dean keeps behaving like Raymond Massey's son but seems to have sprung out of the cabbage field); Charles Durning as Jessica Lange's father in *Tootsie* (1982), Danny DeVito and Arnold Schwarzenegger as identical twins; Evan Richards as the neurotic child of Richard Dreyfuss and Bette Midler in *Down and Out in Beverly Hills* (1986); and two films to which I'll return, *What's Eating Gilbert Grape* (1993) and *The Royal Tenenbaums* (2001). In all of these cases, the behaviour and the claim embedded in it lead us to imagine family connections our eyes alone do not establish.

The situation is reversed when characters look related and don't claim to be. This is the case of the 'false family', stated onscreen in its most refined expression in *Vertigo* (1958), and also in *Batman & Robin* (1997). In *The Sixth Sense* (1999), Haley Joel Osment looks disturbingly like Bruce Willis's young son, a resemblance that underpins the action throughout. Much is made of family 'falseness' by Hitchcock in *The Man Who Knew Too Much* in the scene at the embassy where we see the nefarious Ambassador speaking on the telephone beneath a portrait of the Prime Minister he has just failed in assassinating; that the two men could be son and father, respectively, is a point telling in the structure of the film but one Hitchcock never explicitly makes. On the surface of the film, this is a 'false' family. Beneath the surface, I suspect it is a 'perfect' one. In *The Wrong Man* (1956), Hitchcock made an ultimate statement about the perils of looking very much like someone else, in this case the unlikely 'familial' resemblance being shared by Henry Fonda's Manny Balestrero and a stranger who comes to take his place in the justice system.

The fourth possibility involves a group of characters who do not claim to be a family, and who do not look like a family either, who are therefore, all effective evidence to their linkage being suppressed or non-existent, only a 'social group'. It will suffice here to give as example the quartet comprised of Billy Crystal, Bruno

Kirby, Meg Ryan and Carrie Fisher on a double date in *When Harry Met Sally* (1989); or Fred Astaire, Oscar Levant and Nanette Fabray (the last two in a marriage that is obviously only a 'marriage') at the cast party in *The Band Wagon* (1953).

Involved in the performance of family bonds onscreen is a complex of arrangements and actions: with makeup, skin tones must be brought into alignment; heights must be adjusted through the use of shoe wedges, platforms and camera mounts; attitudes must be corrected with dialogue; postures must be choreographed and emotions broadcast. An examination of any filmic depiction of officially sanctioned family ritual, such as is to be found in the original version of *The Philadelphia Story*, will give a textbook about postures, body alignments, facial expressions, feelingful states, and so on. Also involved in the construction of the screen family is an 'envelope of liberty', a dramaturgic space bounded by event and rationale within which persons are thought free to make presumptions about, and upon, one another. If we look at the opening of William Cameron Menzies' *Invaders From Mars* (1953), we see a father barging into his son's bedroom when the boy is up watching stars in the middle of the night; then, the mother barges in to catch both of her boys sharing the telescope. With similar affectionate forwardness – the kind of behaviour for which punishment would be available in mere social groups – Roger O. Thornhill (Cary Grant) hires his mother (Jessie Royce Landis, only eight years Grant's senior) to make a call on the house phone at the Plaza in *North by Northwest* (1959).

While mainstream film operates in general to reinscribe hegemonic assumptions and conventions – in the case of the family, the ideal of patriarchy or, as Wood puts it, the assumption that 'under capitalism one must be useful, and one's usefulness is defined by one's ability to make money (if one is a man) or by one's ability to bear and raise children (if one is a woman)' (1998: 154) – I suspect 'perfect family films' and 'implicit family films' operate quite differently to do this, invoking different kinds of audience engagement in the process of producing their educational value. The 'perfect' family on film is an ideal to be recognised, affirmed, desired, aimed for with a continuing devotion to course correction and self-examination. It is a vision of the world as it 'should' be, and therefore a finished product waiting to be capitalised through our recognition. But the 'implicit family' requires of the audience not recognition and affirmation but an investment of faith, intelligence and belief. This is because the 'implicit family' fails in some spectacular way to be recognisable, yet offers the unrelenting promise of being recuperated into vision. The viewer's job is to nurse through witnessing, to assist in the eventual creation of a 'perfect family' from an 'implicit' one by sustaining a vision of perfection to which the characters in the film cannot yet conform but to which they may be approximated as the plot turns and the conclusion approaches. In 'implicit family' films we root for the bonding of those whose claims to relationship are distinctly, troublingly insupportable but whose narrative development we wish to enthusiastically watch, since their claims are the claims legitimate people make. 'Implicit family' films engage us, in other words, in a more subterranean and covert act of identification with prevailing norms than do 'perfect family' films, which need only a superficial glance of assent.

Lasse Hallström's *What's Eating Gilbert Grape*, for example, posits that tanned, innocent and generous Gilbert (Johnny Depp) is the son of obese, depressive dominating Bonnie Grape (Darlene Cates), a woman so large, and also so recalcitrant, she barely ever leaves the sofa in front of her television. Gilbert's father, deceased as of the beginning of the film and therefore the quintessence of extradiegesis, was apparently something of a Jack Sprat, if we are to believe in the affiliation of a slender youth like Johnny, absent any narrative rhetoric about adoption. Gilbert's brother Arnie (Leonardo DiCaprio) is sprattier still, an 18-year-old with the mind and impulse control of a child of ten, who drools and likes to climb the town radio tower. Two sisters, Amy (Laura Harrington) and Ellen (Mary Kate Schellhardt), seem like alien visitors in the home, appearing only to fry eggs, practise the trumpet on the veranda, change their mother's bedding or give Gilbert the finger in what we are to take as a competitive flash of sibling rivalry. The major emotional lines of force are constituted by Gilbert and Bonnie's devotions to Arnie, and by Gilbert's loyal fiefdom to his needy and helpless mother. But because the three principal actors bear no resemblance to one another at all, there being also no attempt on Hallström's part to use visual techniques to assimilate them, it falls to the depiction of behaviour to establish the intimate bonds we will require if we are to invest ourselves in this 'family'.

Three events in particular facilitate the materialisation of the three principle emotional lines of force – Gilbert to his mother, Gilbert to Arnie, the mother to Arnie – and each of these is a cinematic set piece reliant on *mise-en-scène* and performance. Bonnie Grape's attachment to Arnie is shown after he is arrested and jailed for climbing the radio tower one time too many. She brings herself to the point of demanding to be driven into town, a movement utterly unprecedented, the Grape car literally almost rubbing along the road on the side where she is sitting; she storms into the police station; and, blushing, sweating, virtually swelling into a monster out of a Godzilla film, she barks the deputy's first name in the voice of a drill sergeant and demands her child *now*! 'Jer-ry!!!!! I want my son!!!!!!!' That she is brought to the brink of mortification and shame by her exertion is the telltale sign for us of her adoration of this child; and it is less what she says than what she looks like saying it – red, trembling, swaying, locked in a fixation of gaze – that sells her commitment to us. As she leaves the station with Arnie in tow, the townspeople gather to stare in silence, some of them popping snapshots of her, some simply gaping. Soon the family, huddled in the car, is retreating to the security of their farm.

Gilbert's fraternal bond to Arnie calls for him to give Arnie routine baths. One evening he arranges Arnie in the tub and then dashes out for a few moments to visit furtively with Becky (Juliette Lewis), a girl passing through town who has caught his fancy. But Becky and Gilbert are caught up together and spend the entire night. When he returns home, Gilbert finds Arnie shivering uncontrollably, still in the now frigid bath. Overcome by remorse, he seizes a towel and embraces Arnie in it, rubbing him for all his life. The speed and desperation of Depp's moves is suffused with what reads as a genuine responsiveness, not least, I suspect, because Di-Caprio manages so deeply authentic a rendition of shivering to death in a bathtub all night. While through the rest of the film Arnie is something of an albatross for Gilbert, in this scene he is the object of overwhelming love and guilt. The disappointment of Bonnie in him seems a chilling prospect for Gilbert at this moment, and seems to fill the tiny bathroom even though she is nowhere to be seen.

Gilbert's bond to his mother is the most profound of all, and the most profoundly dramatised. By story's end Bonnie Grape has become too worn out to handle her responsibilities any longer. Arnie, it seems, will never change, never quite grow up; Gilbert will fall in love soon and need her no more; the girls will go off and get married. Knowing the strain will probably kill her, she insists on climbing the stairs into the bedroom she shared with her lost husband. Surrounded by her children, she does die, but now Gilbert realises there will be no effective way of getting her body out of the house without Bonnie becoming, in death, yet again a hideous spectacle to entertain the smug population of Endora. The only option that will allow him filial honour is to make a pyre of the entire place, with his mother on her deathbed, which he does. The furniture arrayed on the vast lawns, Gilbert and his siblings watch as his bonfire consumes the house, the body of the mother, his past. He and Arnie travel off with Becky to find their future.

If in the 'implicit family' film the impression of the familial bond is conveyed onscreen principally through performance, not biology, and if the central pillar of familial performance is the knowing, affectionate, intimate regard, surely no actor has been more successful in achieving this, simply through the warmth he can convey with his eyes alone, than Gene Hackman. One of the problems in casting Hackman in bad-guy roles, indeed – Lex Luthor in *Superman* (1978), Little Bill Daggett in *Unforgiven* (1992), John Herod in *The Quick and the Dead* (1995) – is that his eyes twinkle so much, express such merry pleasure at being in the company of the person they are focusing on, that he seems to make even his mortal enemies members of his immediate family. We see, for example, in the conclusion to *Heist* (2001), where he shoots Danny DeVito, and also in *Unforgiven*, a technique he uses of twisting his mouth before doing something morally questionable; through his eyes he does not express unfriendliness. In *The Royal Tenenbaums* he plays the patriarch of a bizarre and dysfunctional family – I mean by this, because surely every family has its problems, a family noteworthy for its dysfunctionality – modelled in many ways after the Glass family in J. D. Salinger's *Franny and Zooey* (1961) and the central mechanism of his performance involves quite an unanticipated use of those eyes.

In this film, the script – by Wes Anderson and Owen Wilson – circumnavigates a family bonded by vituperative jealousy, deceit and secrecy, conniving intelligence, distrust, bitter resentment and suppressed rage, not to mention aphasic face work that never shows a flicker of emotional connection. All of the Tenenbaums, for starters, are geniuses, as the matriarch Etheline (Angelica Huston) – she sounds like a chemical compound – once noted in a bestseller, *Family of Geniuses*. Chas (Ben Stiller) is fabulously wealthy (having started his money-making in earnest at the age of thirteen) and also paranoid; Richie (Luke Wilson) is famous yet uncontrollably anxious, largely because he is in love with his stepsister Margot (Gwyneth Paltrow), who is in deep depression because she was adopted. What makes *The Royal Tenenbaums* so hilarious, and also so illuminating about family structure, is its matter-of-factness about the dysfunctional relations and petty jealousies that characterise family relations here. 'You sued me twice, got me disbarred', says Royal to his son Chas, 'I don't hold it against *you*, do I?' The reason his children hold things against poor, dying Royal (given in a meticulous performance by Hackman in which he interestingly does *not* make use of his eyes for emotional connection) lies in their childhoods. 'This is my *adopted daughter*, Margot Tenenbaum', he says over and over, whenever introducing Margot to anyone – thus crafting the adult alienation that will lead to her spending six hours a day locked in the bathroom. Richie he shepherds all around town, establishing the warm fatherly bond he has made no attempt to build with Chas, so that Chas will come to resent Richie when he grows up. Chas, indeed, Royal shoots in the hand with a b-b gun. 'You're on my team!' squeals the boy; 'There are no teams', says Royal, deadpan. What allows us to see the betrayal and sneakiness between members of this family as funny rather than metaphorical or indexical of real life is the startlingly cerebral quality of the interaction, quite as though no bond of blood existed to warm the feelings of the participants. In this sense, the film gives a delicious postmodern twist to the romantic, yet purely performative, family of typical cinematic representation, reflecting through its deadpan interactions and outrageous juxtapositions of personal motive and design that the parents and children we are watching are not really related at all, not really parents and children, but only strangers caught in a social trap which makes them pretend to family relations. Family life here, then, is something of an elaborate game.

What makes *The Royal Tenenbaums* especially interesting as a film about family relations is precisely the express avowal of dysfunctionality in the narrative. The characters do not – for the most part – look like one another, largely because they have grown up in bubbles of individuality and have in fact been nourished by their separation from one another. And the implicitness of the family that would normally be conveyed through a diegesis of relationship is here brought into question precisely because these people work hard at *not* relating to one another. Both *The Royal Tenenbaums* and *What's Eating Gilbert Grape*, therefore, depict 'implicit' families, but the former simultaneously posits and disavows the familial bonds that in the latter are dramatised so emphatically. Given that in all these films about family it is likely the case that *no family appears onscreen at all*, our belief in the relatively bonded or unbonded relations between characters is resident only in the facts of the story as suggested and performed. I omit from discussion here the much rarer, and surely interesting, obverse situation, where what we see onscreen *is* a family relationship in fact but may appear so only because the narrative stipulates, or, indeed, not at all. Very good examples are the brothers Lionel and John Barrymore as the ailing tycoon and the dissolute brother at the end of his rope in *Dinner at Eight* (1933); the various apparent family connections in *The Long Riders* (1980) between David, Keith and Robert Carradine; James and Stacy Keach; Dennis and Randy Quaid; and Christopher and Nicholas Guest; and Rachel Kempson and Vanessa Redgrave working together (as mother and daughter) in *Déjà Vu* (1997). Thus, real families we are watching are either converted to distorted 'families' or else invisible altogether.

To conclude, a few words about one of the most interesting family films I've seen, Mark Romanek's *One Hour Photo* (2002). Here, a 'perfect' family, the Yorkins (Connie Nielsen, Michael Vartan, Dylan Smith), turns out to be only a simulacrum of one – smiling, together and happy only in the family photographs. (In microcosm, these photographs function much as movies about 'perfect' families do, so rather than being a 'perfect family' movie itself, *One Hour Photo* is, like this essay, a comment upon such things.) But like everyone else in a society that is devoted to appearances and therefore, as Defoe would have it, full of fools, the local one-hour photograph processor, Sy Parrish (Robin Williams) believes what he sees in the pictures he has been making for the Yorkins ever since their kid was born; makes copies of these wafers of reality that he can worship in a secret sanctuary; and holds the people who are posing for the pictures – the 'actual' family, as it were – to the sorts of moral standards befitting the people they so consistently appear to be. Indeed, he takes an additional step and begins to think himself an unacknowledged member of this family. If the coherence of a family, insofar as it presents itself through appearances, is largely a matter of a viewer's belief, why cannot this viewer be the processor of the official family images, and why cannot such a viewer even include himself in the image of the family which has caught his gaze, through an act of will and imagination, if he is despairing enough? In a bizarre scene, Sy, having scoped out the Yorkin pad, sneaks inside through the patio doors. He checks out the kitchen – on the fridge he finds his own photograph among other family snaps – then the child's messy bedroom; sits on the toilet; notes the socks and sneakers dropped casually on the floor in the master bedroom; and sits with the family dog to watch the NFL on the big plasma screen. Suddenly Mom, Dad, and Junior come in. 'Oh there you are, Sy!' they exclaim with perfect familiarity, embracing their missing link. Just as the child comes up to welcome Uncle Sy, we cut swiftly back to the car across the street, where Sy has been daydreaming all this. Screen family life is all a daydream.

Bibliography

Agamben, Giorgio (2000) *Means Without Ends*. Trans. Vincenzo Binetti and Cesare Casarino. Minneapolis: University of Minnesota Press.

Altman, Rick (1981) 'The Lonely Villa and Griffith's Paradigmatic Style', *Quarterly Review of Film Studies*, 6, 2 (Spring), 123–34.

____ (1987) *The American Film Musical*. Bloomington: Indiana University Press.

____ (1992) 'Dickens, Griffith and Film Theory Today', in Jane Gaines (ed.) *Classical Hollywood Narrative: The Paradigm Wars*. Durham: Duke University Press, 9–48.

Andrew, Dudley (1984) *Concepts in Film Theory*. Oxford: Oxford University Press.

Andrew, Geoff (1999) *Stranger than Paradise: Maverick Film-makers in Recent American Cinema*. London: Limelight Editions.

Anon. (1912) 'A Blot in the Scutcheon-Biograph', *New York Dramatic Mirror* (31 January), 56.

____ (1953a) 'All I Desire', *Variety* (24 June), 30.

____ (1953b) 'All I Desire Bows at the Palace', *New York Times* (29 August), 10.

____ (2000) 'AFI's 100 Years . . . 100 Laughs', 14 June, www.afi.com. Accessed 11 August 2006.

Arlen, Michael J. (1977) 'Eros in the Emerald City', *Rolling Stone*, 249, 43–4.

Attali, Jacques (1985) *Noise: The Political Economy of Music*. Trans. Brian Massumi. Minneapolis: University of Minnesota Press.

Aumont, Jacques (1990) 'Griffith: The Frame, The Figure', in Thomas Elsaesser (ed.) *Early Cinema: Space, Frame, Narrative*. London: British Film Institute, 348–59.

Balio, Tino (1993) *Grand Design: Hollywood as a Modern Business Enterprise, 1930–1939*. Berkeley: University of California Press.

Bansak, Edmund G. (1995) *Fearing the Dark: The Val Lewton Career*. Jefferson: McFarland.

Barthes, Roland (1975 [1970]) *S/Z*. Trans. Richard Miller. New York: Hill and Wang.

____ (1977) *Image, Music, Text*. Trans. Stephen Heath. New York: Hill and Wang.

Behlmer, Rudy (1985) *Inside Warner Brothers: 1935–1951*. New York: Viking.

____ (2000) *Memo From David O. Selznick*. New York: Modern Library.

Bell, Daniel (1962) *The End of Ideology: On the Exhaustion of Political Ideas in the Fifties*. New York: Free Press.

Bellour, Raymond (1975) 'Le blocage symbolique', *Communications*, 23, 235–50.

___ (1990) 'To Alternate/To Narrate', in Thomas Elsaesser (ed.) *Early Cinema: Space, Frame, Narrative*. London: British Film Institute, 360–74.

Benjamin, Walter (1985 [1936]) 'The Work of Art in the Age of Mechanical Reproduction', *Film Theory and Criticism: Introductory Readings*. New York: Oxford University Press, 675–94.

___ (1999a [1927]) 'Reply to Oscar A.H. Schmitz', in Michael W. Jennings, Howard Eiland and Gary Smith (eds) *Walter Benjamin Selected Writings, Vol. 2, 1927–1934*. Trans. Rodney Livingstone and others. Cambridge, MA: The Belknap Press of Harvard University Press, 16–19.

___ (1999b [1939]) 'Paris, Capital of the Nineteenth Century (Expose of 1939)', in Rolf Tiedemann (ed.) *The Arcades Project*. Trans. Howard Eiland and Kevin McLaughlin. Cambridge, MA: The Belknap Press of Harvard University Press, 14–26.

Bennett, Tony and Janet Woollacott (1987) *Bond and Beyond: The Political Career of a Popular Hero*. New York: Routledge.

Berg, A. Scott (1989) *Goldwyn: A Biography*. New York: Knopf.

Bergan, Ronald (1992) *Jean Renoir: Projections of Paradise*. Woodstock: Overlook Press.

Bergstrom, Janet (1979) 'Alternation, Segmentation, Hypnosis: Interview with Raymond Bellour', *Camera Obscura*, 3–4 (Summer), 71–103.

Bernstein, Mary and Renate Reimann (eds) (2001) *Queer Families, Queer Politics Challenging Culture and the State*. New York: Columbia University Press.

Bigner, Jerry J. (1999) 'Raising Our Sons: Gay Men as Fathers', in T. Richard Sullivan (ed.) *Queer Families, Common Agendas: Gay People, Lesbians, and Family Values*. New York: Harrington Park Press, 61–77.

Biskind, Peter (1983) *Seeing is Believing: How Hollywood Taught Us to Stop Worrying and Love the Fifties*. New York: Pantheon.

Bordwell, David (1982) 'Happily Ever After, Part Two', *Velvet Light Trap*, 29, 2–7.

Bordwell, David, Janet Staiger and Kristin Thompson (1985) *The Classical Hollywood Cinema: Film Style and Mode of Production to 1960*. New York: Columbia University Press.

Bottomore, T. B. (1966) *Classes in Modern Society*. New York: Pantheon.

Breen, Joseph (1944) 'Letter to Jack L. Warner', Warner Bros. Archives, Special Collections: University of Southern California (17 August).

Bridger, Davis and Samuel Wolk (1976) *The New Jewish Encyclopedia*. New Jersey: Behrman House.

Brink, Carol (1951) *Stopover*. New York: Macmillan.

Brooks, Peter (1985) *The Melodramatic Imagination: Balzac, Henry James, Melodrama, and the Mode of Excess*. New York: Columbia University Press.

___ (1994) 'Melodrama, Body, Revolution', in Jacky Bratton, Jim Cook and Christine Gledhill (eds) *Melodrama: Stage, Picture, Screen*. London: British Film Institute, 11–24.

Browne, Nick (1981) 'Griffith's Family Discourse: Griffith and Freud', *Quarterly Review of Film Studies*, 6, 1 (Winter), 67–80.

Bunting, Madeleine (2004) *Willing Slaves: How the Overwork Culture is Ruling Our Lives*. London: HarperCollins.

Burdette, K. (1998) 'Queer Readings/Queer Cinema: An Examination of the Early Work of Todd Haynes', *Velvet Light Trap*, 41, 68–80.

Buscombe, Edward (1988) 'Johnson County War', in Edward Buscombe (ed.) *The BFI Companion to the Western*. London: British Film Institute, 163.

Butler, Judith (2002) 'Is Kinship Always Already Heterosexual?', *Differences: A Journal of Feminist Cultural Studies*, 13, 1, 14–44.

Cain, James M. (1941) *Mildred Pierce*. New York: Alfred A. Knopf.

Carver, Raymond (1995) *Short Cuts*. London: The Harvill Press.

Cavell, Stanley (1981) *Pursuits of Happiness: The Hollywood Comedy of Remarriage*. Cambridge, MA: Harvard University Press.

_____ (2005) '*North by Northwest*', in William Rothman (ed.) *Cavell on Film*. Albany: State University of New York Press, 41–58.

Chandler, Charlotte (2002) *Nobody's Perfect: Billy Wilder, A Personal Biography*. New York: Simon & Schuster.

Chapman, Tom (1949a) 'Memos to Roy Obringer', *Mildred Pierce* Production Files. Warner Bros. Archives, Special Collections: University of Southern California (4 March).

_____ (1949b) 'Memos to Roy Obringer', *Mildred Pierce* Production Files. Warner Bros. Archives, Special Collections: University of Southern California (8 November).

_____ (1950) 'Memos to Roy Orbringer', *Mildred Pierce* Production Files. Warner Bros. Archives, Special Collections: University of Southern California (12 February).

Clark, T. J. (1984) *The Painting of Modern Life: Paris in the Art of Manet and His Followers*. Princeton: Princeton University Press.

Clendinen, Dudley (1984) 'Ads Try to Tie Reagan with the Best of Times', *New York Times* (17 June), A18.

Cohen, Ronald D. (2002) *Rainbow Quest: The Folk Music Revival and American Society, 1940–1970*. Amherst: University of Massachusetts Press.

Collins, Jim (1993) 'Genericity in the Nineties', in Jim Collins, Hilary Radner and Ava Preacher Collins (eds) *Film Theory Goes to the Movies*. New York and London: Routledge, 242–63.

Cook, Pam (1978) 'Duplicity in *Mildred Pierce*', in E. Ann Kaplan (ed.) *Women in Film Noir*. London: British Film Institute, 68–82.

Corber, Robert (1995) *In the Name of National Security*. Durham: Duke University Press.

Dalton, Stephen (n.d.) 'Scary Monsters, Super Freaks', http://www.toddhaynes.net/text/uncut.shtml. Accessed 18 August 2006.

Dargis, Manohla (2005) 'Wedding Crashers', *New York Times* (5 August), B19.

Darwin, Charles (1996 [1859]) *The Origin of the Species*. Oxford: Oxford University Press.

Dawidoff, Robert (1999) 'Foreword', in T. Richard Sullivan (ed.) *Queer Families, Common Agendas: Gay People, Lesbians, and Family Values*. New York: Harrington Park Press, xi–xii.

DeAngelis, Michael (2005) '1954: Movies and the Walls of Privacy', in Murray Pomerance (ed.) *American Cinema of the 1950s: Themes and Variations*. New Brunswick: Rutgers University Press, 111–33.

De Graaf, John (ed.) (2003) *Take Back Your Time: Fighting Overwork and Time Poverty in America*. San Francisco: Berret-Koehler.

Deleuze, Gilles (1989) *Cinema 2: The Time Image*. Trans. Hugh Tomlinson and Robert Galeta. Minneapolis: University of Minnesota Press.

Deleuze, Gilles and Félix Guattari (1983) *Anti-Oedipus: Capitalism and Schizophrenia*. Trans. Robert Hurley, Mark Seem and Helen R. Lane. Minneapolis: University of Minnesota Press.

Denby, David (2002) 'Classville', *New Yorker* (14 January), 92–3.

____ (2005) 'Royalty', *New Yorker* (16 May), 95.

Desjardins, Mary (2001) 'Systematizing Scandal: *Confidential* Magazine, Stardom and the State of California', in Adrienne L. McLean and David A. Cook (eds) *Headline Hollywood: A Century of Film Scandal*. Piscataway: Rutgers University Press, 206–31.

Devlin, Albert J. (1997) 'Writing in "A Place of Stone": *Cat on a Hot Tin Roof*', in Matthew C. Roudane (ed.) *The Cambridge Companion to Tennessee Williams*. Cambridge: Cambridge University Press, 95–113.

Dimendberg, Edward (2004) *Film Noir and the Spaces of Modernity*. Cambridge MA: Harvard University Press.

Dirks, Tim (2003a) 'Guest in the House', *The Internet Movie Data Base* (9 November), http://www.imdb.com/title/tt0036886. Accessed 11 August 2006.

____ (2003b) 'King's Row', *The Greatest Films* (November 8 2003), http://www.filmsite.org/kingsr.html. Accessed 11 August 2006.

Dixon, Simon (2003) 'Ambiguous Ecologies: Stardom's Domestic Mise-en-Scène', *Cinema Journal*, 42, 2 (Winter), 81–100.

Doane, Mary Ann (1987) *The Desire to Desire: The Woman's Film of the 1940s*. Bloomington & Indianapolis: Indiana University Press.

____ (2002) *The Emergence of Cinematic Time: Modernity, Contingency, The Archive*. Cambridge, MA: Harvard University Press.

Doherty, Thomas (2002) *Teenagers and Teenpics: The Juvenilisation of American Movies in the 1950s* (revised and expanded edition). Philadelphia: Temple University Press.

Dreisinger, Baz (2000) 'The Queen in Shining Armor: Safe Eroticism and the Gay Friend', *Journal of Popular Film and Television*, 28, 1, 2–11.

Dyer, Richard (1998) *Stars*, second edition. London: British Film Institute.

Ebert, Roger (1999) *'Cookie's Fortune'*, *The Chicago Sun-Times* (9 April), http://rogerebert.sunties.com/apps/pbcs.dll/article?AID=19990409/RE-VIEWS/904090303/1023. Accessed 22 May 2006.

____ (2000) *'Meet the Parents'*, *The Chicago Tribune* (6 October), http://rogerebert.sunties.com/apps/pbcs.dll/article?AID=19990409/REVIEWS/904090303/1023. Accessed 14 September 2006.

____ (2001) *'The Royal Tenenbaums'*, *The Chicago Tribune* (21 December), http://rogerebert.sunties.com/apps/pbcs.dll/article?AID=19990409/RE-VIEWS/904090303/1023. Accessed 4 September 2006.

____ (n.d.) http://rogerebert.sunties.com/apps/pbcs.dll/article?AID=19990409/RE-VIEWS/904090303/1023. Accessed 24 May 2006.

Eisenstein, Sergei (1949) *Film Form*. Ed. & Trans. Jay Leyda. New York: Harcourt Brace Jovanovich.

Elsaesser, Thomas (1987) 'Tales of Sound and Fury: Observations on the Family Melodrama', in Christine Gledhill (ed.) *Home is Where the Heart Is: Studies in Melodrama and the Woman's Film*. London: British Film Institute, 43–69.

Elsaesser, Thomas and Adam Barker (1990) 'Introduction – The Continuity System: Griffith and Beyond', in Thomas Elsaesser (ed.) *Early Cinema: Space, Frame, Narrative*. London: British Film Institute, 293–317.

Eyman, Scott (2005) *Lion of Hollywood: The Life and Legend of Louis B. Mayer*. New York: Simon & Schuster.

Fellowes, Julian (2002) 'Afterword', *Gosford Park, The Shooting Script*. New York: Newmarket Press, 164–75.

Fiedler, Leslie A. (1978) *Freaks: Myths and Images of the Secret Self*. New York: Simon and Schuster.

Fischer, Lucy (ed.) (1991) *Imitation of Life*. New Brunswick: Rutgers University Press.

Fishman, Robert (1987) *Bourgeois Utopias: The Rise and Fall of Suburbia*. New York: Basic Books.

Fiske, John (1993) *Television Culture*. London and New York: Routledge.

____ (1996) *Media Matters: Everyday Culture and Political Change*. Minneapolis: University of Minnesota Press.

Foreman, Joel (ed.) (1997) *The Other Fifties: Interrogating Midcentury American Icons*. Urbana: University of Illinois Press.

Foucault, Michel (1978) *The History of Sexuality, Volume 1: An Introduction*. Trans. Robert Hurley. New York: Vintage Books.

____ (1980) *Language, Counter-Memory, Practice*. Ed. Donald F. Bouchard. Ithaca: Cornell University Press.

Frank, Thomas (1997) *The Conquest of Cool: Business Culture, Counterculture, and the Rise of Hip Consumerism*. Chicago: University of Chicago Press.

French, Philip (1969) *The Movie Moguls: An Informal History of the Hollywood Tycoons*. Chicago: Henry Regnery Company.

Freud, Sigmund (1955) 'A Child Is Being Beaten', in James Strachey (ed. and trans.) *The Standard Edition of the Works of Sigmund Freud, Vol. XVII (1917–1919)*, London: The Hogarth Press and the Institute of Psychoanalysis, 177–204.

Friedan, Betty (1963) *The Feminine Mystique*. New York: Deli.

Fussell, Paul (1983) *Class: A Guide Through the American Status System*. New York: Simon & Schuster.

Gabler, Neal (1988) *An Empire of Their Own: How the Jews Invented Hollywood*. New York: Crown.

Gavanas, Anna (2004) *Fatherhood Politics in the United States: Masculinity, Sexuality, Race, and Marriage*. Chicago: University of Illinois Press.

Gelbart, Larry (1998) *Laughing Matters: On Writing M*A*S*H, Tootsie, Oh, God! And A Few Other Funny Things*. New York: Random House.

Gilman, Sander L. (1986) *Jewish Self-Hatred: Anti-Semitism and the Hidden Language of the Jews*. Baltimore MD: John Hopkins University Press.

Gledhill, Christine (ed.) (1987) *Home is Where the Heart Is: Studies in Melodrama and the Woman's Film*. London: British Film Institute.

Gorbman, Claudia (1982) 'The Drama's Melos: Max Steiner and *Mildred Pierce*', *Velvet Light Trap*, 19, 35–9.

Goss, Robert E. (1997) 'Queering Procreative Privilege: Coming Out as Families', in Robert E. Goss and Amy Adams Squire Strongheart (eds) *Our Families, Our Values: Snapshots of Queer Kinship*. New York: The Haworth Press, 3–20.

Grant, Barry Keith (ed.) (2003) *Stagecoach*. Cambridge: Cambridge University Press.

Gunning, Tom (1990) 'Weaving a Narrative: Style and Economic Background in Griffith's Biograph Films', in Thomas Elsaesser (ed.) *Early Cinema: Space, Frame, Narrative*. London: British Film Institute, 336–47.

_____ (1991) *D. W. Griffith and the Origins of American Narrative Cinema: The Early Years at Biograph*. Urbana and Chicago: University of Illinois Press.

_____ (1993) 'Now You See It, Now You Don't: The Temporality of the Cinema of Attractions', *The Velvet Light Trap*, 32, 3–11.

_____ (1994) 'The Whole Town's Gawking: Early Cinema and the Visual Experience of Modernity', *The Yale Journal of Criticism*, 7, 2, 189–201.

_____ (1998) 'Heard Over the Phone: *The Lonely Villa* and the de Lorde Tradition of the Terrors of Technology', in Annette Kuhn and Jackie Stacey (eds) *Screen Histories: A Screen Reader*. Oxford: Clarendon Press, 216–27.

Halliday, John (1972) *Sirk on Sirk*. New York: Viking.

Haralovich, Mary Beth (1988) 'Feminist Film Theory: Mildred Pierce and the Second World War', in E. Deirdre Pribram (ed.) *Female Spectators: Looking at Film and Television*. London: Verso, 12–30.

_____ (1990) 'Proletarian Woman's Film: Contending with Censorship and Entertainment', *Screen*, 31, 2, 172–87.

_____ (1992) 'Too Much Guilt is Never Enough for Working Mothers: Joan Crawford, *Mildred Pierce*, and *Mommie Dearest*', *Velvet Light Trap*, 29, 43–52.

Haralovich, Mary Beth (1997) 'Selling *Mildred Pierce*: A Case Study in Movie Promotion', in Thomas Schatz (ed.) *Boom or Bust: Hollywood in the 1940s*. New York: Charles Scribner's Sons, 196–202.

Haskell, Molly (1974) *From Reverence to Rape: The Treatment of Women in the Movies*. Middlesex: Penguin.

Hayden, Dolores (2003) *Building Suburbia: Green Fields and Urban Growth, 1820–2000*. New York: Pantheon Books.

Heath, Stephen (1981) *Questions of Cinema*. Bloomington: Indiana University Press.

Heggen, Thomas (1947) 'The Unchallenged King of Hollywood', *Reader's Digest*, 50 (June), 29–40.

Henderson, Brian (1991) 'Cartoon and Narrative in the Films of Frank Tashlin and Preston Sturges', in Andrew Horton (ed.) *Comedy/Cinema/Theory*. Berkeley: University of California Press, 153–73.

Higashi, Sumiko (2005) 'Movies and the Paradox of Female Stardom', in Murray Pomerance (ed.) *American Cinema of the 1950s: Themes and Variations*. Piscataway: Rutgers University Press, 65–88.

Higham, Charles (1993) *Merchant of Dreams: Louis B. Mayer, M.G.M., and the Secret Hollywood*. New York: Donald I. Fine.

Hill, Donald R. (1993) *Calypso Calaloo: Early Carnival Music in Trinidad*. Gainesville: University of Florida Press.

Hirsch, Marianne (1997) Family Frames: Photography, Narrative and Postmemory. Cambridge MA: Harvard University Press.

Hoberman, J. (1999) 'Spring Fever', *Village Voice* (31 March–6 April), http://www.villagevoice.com/film/9913,hoberman,4699,20.html. Accessed 24 May 2006.

____ (2001) 'Look Homeward, Angel: *The Royal Tennenbaums*', *The Village Voice* (12 December), 128.

Hohenadal, Kristin (2001) 'Altman on the Loose in Merchant Ivory Territory', *New York Times* (9 September), 2, 52.

Holden, Stephen (2005) 'A Nightmare of a Mom Vs. Her Son's Dreamboat', *New York Times* (13 May), A1, A4

hooks, bell (2000) *Feminism is for Everybody: Passionate Politics*. London: Pluto Press.

Horton, Andrew (1984) *The Films of George Roy Hill*. New York: Columbia University Press.

____ (1991) 'Introduction', in Andrew Horton (ed.) *Comedy/Cinema/Theory*. Berkeley: University of California Press, 1–21.

Howe, Desson (1992) 'Mississippi Masala', *Washington Post* (14 February), http://www.washingtonpost.com. Accessed 23 September 2006.

Ibsen, Henrik (1966 [1879/1881/1882/1886]) *A Doll's House, Ghosts, An Enemy of the People, Rosmersholm*. Trans. Michael Meyer. Garden City: Doubleday.

Jackson, Kenneth T. (1985) *Crabgrass Frontier: The Suburbanization of the United States*. New York and Oxford: Oxford University Press.

Jacobs, Lea (1991) *The Wages of Sin: Censorship and the Fallen Woman Cycle, 1928–1942*. Madison: University of Wisconsin Press.

Jacobs, Lewis (1968) *The Rise of the American Film: A Critical History, with an Essay, Experimental Cinema in America 1921–1947*. New York: Teachers College Press.

Jameson, Fredric (1991) *Postmodernism, or the Cultural Logic of Late Capitalism*. Durham: Duke University Press.

Jeffords, Susan (1993) 'The Big Switch: Hollywood Masculinity in the Nineties', in Jim Collins, Hilary Radner and Ava Preacher Collins (eds) *Film Theory Goes to the Movies*. New York: Routledge, 196–208.

Johnson, Sharon (1983) 'For Kinsey Institute, New Research Efforts', *New York Times* (14 September), C1, C4.

Kazan, Elia (1988) *A Life*. New York: Alfred A. Knopf.

Kinsey, Alfred, Wardell B. Pomery, Clyde E. Martin and Paul H. Gebhard (1953) *Sexual Behavior in the Human Female*. Philadelphia and London: W.B. Saunders.

Kirby, Lynn (1993) *Parallel Tracks: The Railway and Silent Cinema*. Durham: Duke University Press.

Kozloff, Sarah (1988) *Invisible Storytellers: Voice-Over Narration in American Film Fiction*. Berkeley: University of California Press.

Krach, Aaron (1998) 'Stardust Memories: Todd Haynes Recreates the Velvet Revolution', *Independent Film and Video Monthly* (December), 32–9.

Kuhn, Annette (1988) *Cinema, Censorship and Sexuality, 1909–1925*. New York: Routledge.

Kuralt, Charles (n.d.) *Appearing in When Television Was Young*. Museum of Television and Radio: New York City.

Laing, R. D. (1970) *The Politics of the Family*. Toronto: Canadian Broadcasting Corporation.

LaValley, Albert J. (1980) 'Introduction: A Troublesome Property to Script', *Mildred Pierce*. Madison: University of Wisconsin Press, 9–53.

Lawrence, Amy (1991) *Echo and Narcissus: Women's Voices in Classical Hollywood Cinema*. Berkeley: University of California Press.

Lax, Eric (1975) *On Being Funny: Woody Allen and Comedy*. New York: Charterhouse Press.

Leibman, Nina (1995) *Living Room Lectures: The Fifties Family in Film and Television*. Austin: University of Texas Press.

Levenstein, Harvey (1988) *Revolution at the Table: The Transformation of the American Diet*. New York: Oxford University Press.

Levin, Martin (ed.) (1970) *Hollywood and the Great Fan Magazines*. New York: Arbor House.

Lim, Dennis (2002) 'Heaven Sent', *Village Voice* (30 October–5 November), 2.

Limerick, Patricia Nelson, Clyde A. Milner II and Charles E. Rankin (eds) (1991) *Trails: Toward a New Western History*. Lawrence: University Press of Kansas.

Lindsey, Shelley Stamp (1994) 'Screening Spaces: Women and Motion Pictures in America 1908–1917', Unpublished Dissertation, New York University, 27–102.

Lyons, Arthur (2000) *Death on the Cheap: The Lost B Movies of Film Noir*. New York: De Capo Press.

Magee, Patrick (2006) *From Shane to Kill Bill: Rethinking the Western*. Oxford: Blackwell.

Maltby, Richard (1995) 'The Production Code and the Hays Office', in Tino Balio (ed.) *Grand Design: Hollywood as Modern Business Enterprise, 1930–1939*. Berkeley: University of California Press, 32–72.

Maltin, Leonard (2003) *Leonard Maltin's 2004 Movie & Video Guide*. New York: Plume.

Margolis, Maxine L. (1984) *Mothers and Such: Views of American Women and Why They Changed*. Berkeley: University of California Press.

Mast, Gerald (1979) *The Comic Mind: Comedy and the Movies*, second edition. Chicago: University of Chicago Press.

Matthews, Glenna (1987) *'Just a Housewife'*: *The Rise and Fall of Domesticity in America*. New York: Oxford University Press.

May, Elaine Tyler (1988) *Homeward Bound: American Families in the Cold War Era*. New York: Basic Books.

____ (2000) 'Pushing the Limits: 1940–1961', in Nancy F. Cott (ed.) *No Small Courage: A History of Women in the United States*. New York: Oxford University Press, 473–528.

McLean, Adrienne L. (2004) *Being Rita Hayworth: Labor, Identity, and Hollywood Stardom*. Piscataway: Rutgers University Press.

Metz, Christian (2004 [1974]) 'Some Points in the Semiotics of Cinema', in Leo Braudry and Marshall Cohen (eds) *Film Theory and Criticism*, sixth edition. Oxford: Oxford University Press, 65–72.

Metz, Walter (2007) "From Plato's Cave to bin Laden's: The 'Worst Sincerity' of Ron Howard's *The Missing* (2003)," in Ralf Adelmann, Andreas Fahr, Ines Katenhusen, Nic Leonhardt, Dimitri Liebsch, and Stefanie Schneider, eds., *Visual Culture Revisited: German and American Perspectives on Visual Culture*, Köln: Herebert von Halem, 2007, 1-19.

Meyerowitz, Joanne (ed.) (1994) *Not June Cleaver: Women and Gender in Postwar America, 1945–1960*. Philadelphia: Temple University Press.

Mills, C. Wright (1995a) 'The New Middle Class, I', in Arthur Vidich (ed.) *The New Middle Classes: Lifestyles, Status, Claims, and Political Orientations*. New York: New York University Press, 189–202.

____ (1995b) 'The New Middle Class, II', in Arthur Vidich (ed.) *The New Middle Classes: Lifestyles, Status, Claims, and Political Orientations*. New York: New York University Press, 203–14.

Mintz, Steven and Susan Kellogg (1988) *Domestic Revolutions: A Social History of American Family Life*. New York: Free Press.

Mitry, Jean (1985) *Griffith: Anthologie du Cinéma*. Paris: Editions de l'Avant-Scêne.

_____ (1997 [1963]) *Esthètique et Psychologie du Cinéma, Vol. 1: Les Structures*. Trans. Christopher King. Paris: Editions Universitaires.

Modleski, Tania (1991) *Feminism Without Women: Culture and Criticism in a 'Post-feminist' Age*. New York: Routledge.

Morell, Parker (1934) *Diamond Jim: The Life and Times of James Buchanan Brady*. Garden City: Garden City Publishing Company.

Muller, Eddie (1998) *Dark City: The Lost World of Film Noir*. New York: St. Martin's Griffin.

Mulvey, Laura (2003) '*Far from Heaven*', *Sight and Sound*, 30, 3 (March), 40–1.

Neale, Steve and Frank Krutnik (1990) *Popular Film and Television Comedy*. New York: Routledge.

Nelson, Joyce (1977) '*Mildred Pierce* Reconsidered', *Film Reader* (2 January), 65–70.

Nowell-Smith, Geoffrey (1987) 'Minelli and Melodrama', in Christine Gledhill (ed.) *Home is Where the Heart Is: Studies in Melodrama and the Woman's Film*. London: British Film Institute, 70–4.

Ouellette, Laurie (n.d.) 'Nanny TV', *Flow* 1, 11, http://jot.communication.utexas.edu/flow/?jot=view&id=624. Accessed 11 August 2006.

Packard, Vance (1959) *The Status Seekers*. New York: David McKay Company.

_____ (1962) *The Pyramid Climbers*. New York: McGraw-Hill.

Perkins, V. F. (1976) 'The Cinema of Nicholas Ray', in Bill Nichols (ed.) *Movies and Methods*. Berkeley: University of California Press, 251–62.

Pfeil, Fred (1995) *White Guys: Studies in Postmodern Domination and Difference*. London: Verso.

Phipps, Keith (n.d.) 'Interview with Director Todd Haynes', *The Onion*, http://people.we.mediaone.net/rogerdeforest/Haynes. Accessed 11 August 2006.

Pomerance, Murray (2005a) *Johnny Depp Starts Here*. New Brunswick, NJ: Rutgers University Press.

_____ (2005b) 'Stark Performance', in J. David Slocum (ed.) *Rebel Without a Cause: Approaches to a Maverick Masterwork*. Albany: State University of New York Press, 35–52.

Popenoe, David (2005) *War Over the Family*. London: Transaction.

Puig, Claudia (2004) '*Shrek 2*: A Fairy Tale Come True for Audiences', *USA Today* (17 May).

Quimby, Karen (2005) '*Will & Grace*: Negotiating (Gay) Marriage on Prime-Time Television', *Journal of Popular Culture*, 38, 4, 713–31.

Rabinowitz, Paula (2002) *Black & White & Noir: America's Pulp Modernism*. New York: Columbia University Press.

Ramsaye, Terry (1926) *A Million and One Nights: A History of the Motion Picture Through 1925*. New York: Simon & Schuster.

Renov, Michael (1991) 'Leave Her to Heaven: The Double Bind of the Post-War Woman', in Marcia Landry (ed.) *Imitations of Life: A Reader on Film and Television Melodrama*. Detroit: Wayne State University Press, 227–36.

Richie, Donald (1970) *George Stevens: An American Romantic*. New York: Museum of Modern Art.

Richmond, Ray (ed.) (1997) *The Simpsons: A Complete Guide to Our Favourite Family*. New York: Harper Perennial.

Robertson, James C. (1993) *The Casablanca Man: The Cinema of Michael Curtiz*. London: Routledge.

Robertson, Pamela (1990) 'Structural Irony in *Mildred Pierce*, or How Mildred Lost Her Tongue', *Cinema Journal*, 30, 1 (Fall), 42–54.

Rodowick, David N. (1987) 'Madness, Authority and Ideology: The Domestic Melodrama of the 1950s', in Christine Gledhill (ed.) *Home is Where the Heart Is: Studies in Melodrama and the Woman's Film*. London: British Film Institute, 268–80.

____ (2001) *Reading the Figural, Or, Philosophy After the New Media*. Durham: Duke University Press.

Roof, Judith (2002) *All About Thelma and Eve: Sidekicks and Third Wheels*. Champaign: University of Illinois Press.

Rothman, William (1982) *Hitchcock – The Murderous Gaze*. Cambridge: Harvard University Press.

____ (2004) '*North by Northwest*: Hitchcock's Monument to the Hitchcock Film', in William Rothman (ed.) *The 'I' of the Camera*, second edition. Cambridge: Cambridge University Press, 241–53.

Rousseau, Jean Jacques (1966) *Essay on the Origin of Language*. Trans. John H. Morgan and Alexander Godes. Chicago: University of Chicago Press.

Rowe, Kathleen (1995) *The Unruly Woman: Gender and the Genres of Laughter*. Austin: University of Texas Press.

Rushdie, Salman (1992) *The Wizard of Oz*. London: British Film Institute.

Sadoul, Georges (1951) *Histoire général du cinéma, Vol. 2: Les pionniers du cinema, 1897–1909*. Paris: Denoel.

Schatz, Thomas (1981) *Hollywood Genres: Formulas, Filmmaking, and the Studio System*. Philadelphia: Temple University Press.

____ (1989) *The Genius of the System: Hollywood Filmmaking in the Studio Era*. New York: Pantheon Books.

Schivelbusch, Wolfgang (1977) *The Railway Journey: The Industrialization of Time and Space in the 19th Century*. Berkeley: University of California Press.

Schuessler, Alexander A. (2000) *A Logic of Expressive Choice*. Princeton: Princeton University Press.

Seigel, Joel E. (1973) *Val Lewton: The Reality of Terror*. New York: Viking.

Self, Robert T. (2002) *Robert Altman's Subliminal Reality*. Minneapolis: University of Minnesota Press.

Selznick, Irene Mayer (1983) *A Private View*. New York: Alfred A. Knopf.

Sikov, Ed (1994) *Laughing Hysterically: American Screen Comedy of the 1950s*. New York: Columbia University Press.

Silver, Alain and Elizabeth Ward (1992) *Film Noir: An Encyclopedic Reference to the American Style* (revised and expanded edition). Woodstock: Overlook Press.

Silverman, Kaja (1988) *The Acoustic Mirror: The Female Voice in Psychoanalysis and Cinema*. Bloomington and Indianapolis: Indiana University Press.

Siodmark, Curt and Ardel Wray (2003) *Screenplay for I Walked With a Zombie* (10 June).

Sirjamaki, John (1955) *The American Family in the Twentieth Century*. Cambridge, MA: Harvard University Press.

Sklar, Robert (1988) 'Empire to the West: *Red River* (1948)', in John O'Connor and Martin A. Jackson (eds) *American History/American Film: Interpreting the Hollywood Image*. New York: Continuum, 167–81.

Slocum, J. David (ed.) (2005) *Rebel Without a Cause: Approaches to a Maverick Masterwork*. Albany: State University of New York Press.

Slotkin, Richard (1992) *Gunfighter Nation: The Myth of the Frontier in Twentieth-Century America*. New York: Atheneum.

Smith, Ella (1974) *Starring Miss Barbara Stanwyck*. New York: Crown.

Smith, Henry Nash (1950) *Virgin Land: The American West as Symbol and Myth*. Cambridge, MA: Harvard University Press.

Smoodin, Eric (1994) 'Introduction: How to Read Walt Disney', in Eric Smoodin (ed.) *Disney Discourse: Producing the Magic Kingdom*. New York: Routledge, 1–20.

Sobchack, Vivian (1998) 'Lounge Time: Postwar Crises and the Chronotope of Film Noir', in Nick Browne (ed.) *Refiguring American Film Genres: History and Theory*. Berkeley: University of California Press, 129–70.

Sochen, June (1978) '*Mildred Pierce* and Women in Film', *American Quarterly*, 30, 1 (Spring), 3–20.

Spector-Person, Ethel (1997) *On Freud's 'A Child is Being Beaten'*. New Haven: Yale University Press.

Spengler, Oswald (1979) *The Decline of the West*. New York: Alfred A. Knopf.

Spicer, Andrew (2002) *Film Noir*. Harlow: Pearson.

Spigel, Lynn (1992) *Make Room for TV: Television and the Family Ideal in Postwar America*. Chicago: University of Chicago Press.

____ (2001) *Welcome to the Dreamhouse: Popular Media and Postwar Suburbs*. Durham: Duke University Press.

Stacey, Judith (1996) *In the Name of the Family: Rethinking Family Values in the Postmodern Age*. Boston: Beacon Press.

Staiger, Janet (1995) 'The Slasher, the Final Girl, and the Anti-Dénouement: Appreciatively Revising Carol Clover', paper read at Society for Film Studies, New York (2 March).

Stern, Michael (1979) *Douglas Sirk*. Boston: Twayne.

Stevens, Chuck (1995) 'Gentlemen Prefer Haynes', *Film Comment*, 31, 4 (July/ August), 77–9.

Stewart, Robert (1993) 'Reimagining Raymond Carver on Film: A Talk with Robert Altman and Tess Gallagher', *New York Times* (12 September), 1–10, http:// www.nytimes.com/books/01/01/21/specials/carver-altman2.html?oref=login. Accessed 27 December 2005.

Straayer, Chris and Tom Waugh (eds) (2005) 'Queer TV Style', *GLQ: A Journal of Lesbian and Gay Studies*, 11, 1, 95–117.

Sturges, Preston (1990) *Preston Sturges by Preston Sturges*. Ed. Sandy Sturges. New York: Touchstone Books.

Telotte, J. P. (1985) *Dreams of Darkness: Fantasy and the Films of Val Lewton*. Urbana: University of Illinois Press.

Thomas, Bob (1969) *Thalberg: Life and Legend*. Garden City: Doubleday.

Tolstoy, Leo N. (1999 [1873–77]) *Anna Karenina*. Trans. Louise and Aylmer Maude. Oxford: Oxford University Press.

Trohler, Margrit (2000) 'Films with Multiple Protagonists and the Logic of Possibilities', *Iris*, 29, 85–102.

Tueth, Michael V. (2005) *Laughter in the Living Room: Television Comedy and the American Home Audience*. New York: Peter Lang.

Vasquez, Diego (2006) 'Research for Gays: The Media is the Messenger', *Media Life*, http://www.medialifemagazine.com. (Accessed 26 April 2006).

Veblen, Thorstein (1979 [1899]) *The Theory of the Leisure Class*. New York: Penguin.

Vineberg, Steve (2005) *High Comedy in American Movies: Class and Humor from the 1920s to Present*. Lanham: Rowman and Littlefield.

Viviani, Christian (1976) 'Mildred et les autres', *Cahiers cinémathèque*, 20, 25–31.

Wald, Jerry (1945) 'Letter to James M. Cain', *Mildred Pierce* Production Files. Warner Bros. Archives, Special Collections: University of Southern California.

Waldron, Vince (1997) *Classic Sitcoms: A Celebration of the Best in Prime Time Comedy*. Los Angeles: Silman-James Press.

Walker, Michael (1990) 'All I Desire (1952)', *Movie*, 33, 4, 31–47.

Wallace, Inez (n.d.) 'I Walked With a Zombie', *American Weekly*, http://whiskey-loosetongue.com/articles/amweekly.html. Accessed 11 August 2006.

Walsh, Andrea (1984) '"Dark Mirror": *Mildred Pierce* – Obsessed Mother – Evil Daughter', *Women's Film and Female Experience, 1940–1950*. New York: Praeger, 121–31.

Walters, Suzanna Danuta (2001) *All the Rage: The Story of Gay Visibility in America*. Chicago: University of Chicago Press.

Weaver, Tom (1993) 'The Phantom Speaks', in *Poverty Row Horrors!: Monogram, PRC, and Republic Horror Films of the Forties*. Jefferson NC: McFarland, 204–11.

Weems, Erik (2003) *I Walked with a Zombie* webpage, http://www.geocities.com/Hollywood/Set/7321/zomwalked.html. Accessed 11 August 2006.

Weiss, Jessica (2000) *To Have and to Hold: Marriage, the Baby Boom and Social Change.* Chicago: University of Chicago Press.

West, Elliott (1991) 'A Longer, Grimmer, but More Interesting Story', in Patricia Nelson Limerick, Clyde A. Milner II and Charles E. Rankin (eds) *Trails: Toward a New Western History.* Lawrence: University Press of Kansas, 103–11.

Wexman, Virginia Wright (1993) 'Star and Genre: John Wayne, the Western, and the American Dream of the Family on the Land', in *Creating the Couple: Love, Marriage, and Hollywood Performance.* Princeton: Princeton University Press, 67–129.

Williams, Linda (1988) 'Feminist Film Theory: *Mildred Pierce* and the Second World War', in E. Deirdre Pribram (ed.) *Female Spectators: Looking at Film and Television*, 12–30.

____ (2001) *Playing the Race Card: Melodramas of Black and White From Uncle Tom to O.J. Simpson.* Princeton: Princeton University Press.

Williams, Raymond (2001) 'Film and the Dramatic Tradition', in John Higgins (ed.) *The Raymond Williams Reader.* Oxford: Blackwell, 25–41.

Wood, Robin (1986) *Hollywood From Vietnam to Reagan.* New York: Columbia University Press.

____ (1992) '*Duel in the Sun*', in Ian Cameron and Douglas Pye (eds) *The Book of Westerns.* New York: Continuum, 189–95.

____ (1998a) *Sexual Politics and Narrative Film: Hollywood and Beyond.* New York: Columbia University Press.

____ (1998b) 'Man(n) of the West(ern)', *Cineaction* 46, 26–33.

Worster, Donald (1991) 'Beyond the Agrarian Myth', in Patricia Nelson Limerick, Clyde A. Milner II and Charles E. Rankin (eds) *Trails: Toward a New Western History.* Lawrence: University Press of Kansas, 3–25.

Wyatt, Justin (1992) 'Cinematic/Sexual Transgression: An Interview with Todd Haynes', *Film Quarterly*, 46, 3, 2–8.

Yousten, Kenneth (n.d.) *The Val Lewton Home Page.* http://www.acm.vt.edu/~yousten/lewton/. Accessed 10 June 2003.

Index